Media Spectacle and the Crisis of Democracy:
Terrorism, War, and Election Battles

Douglas Kellner

Paradigm Publishers
Boulder • London

Copyright © 2005 by Douglas Kellner

Published in the United States by Paradigm Publishers, 3360 Mitchell Lane Suite C, Boulder, Colorado 80301 USA.

Paradigm Publishers is the trade name of Birkenkamp & Company, LLC, Dean Birkenkamp, President and Publisher.
ISBN 1-59451-118-7 (hardcover)
ISBN 1-59451-119-5 (pbk.)

Cataloging-in-Publication Data for this book is available from the Library of Congress.

Printed and bound in the United States of America on acid-free paper that meets the standards of the American National Standard for Permanence of Paper for Printed Library Materials.

Designed and Typeset by Straight Creek Bookmakers.

09 08 07 06 05 04
5 4 3 2 1

Media Spectacle and the Crisis of Democracy

ALSO BY DOUGLAS KELLNER

Herbert Marcuse and the New Left, edited with introduction (2004)

Fredric Jameson: A Critical Reader, coedited with Sean Homer (2004)

From 9/11 to Terror War: The Dangers of the Bush Legacy (2003)

Media Spectacle (2003)

Grand Theft 2000: Media Spectacle and a Stolen Election (2001)

The Postmodern Adventure, coauthored with Steven Best (2001)

Media and Cultural Studies: Key Works, coedited with Gigi Durham (2001)

Herbert Marcuse: Toward a Critical Theory of Society, edited (2001)

Film, Art, and Politics: An Emile de Antonio Reader, coedited with Dan Streible (2000)

Herbert Marcuse: Technology, War, and Fascism, edited (1998)

The Postmodern Turn, coauthored with Steven Best (1997)

Articulating the Global and the Local: Globalization and Cultural Studies, coedited with Ann Cvetkovich (1996)

Media Culture: Cultural Studies, Identity, and Politics between the Modern and the Postmodern (1995)

The Persian Gulf TV War (1992)

Postmodern Theory: Critical Interrogations, coauthored with Steven Best (1991)

Television and the Crisis of Democracy (1990)

Critical Theory, Marxism, and Modernity (1989)

Jean Baudrillard: From Marxism to Postmodernism and Beyond (1989)

Camera Politica: The Politics and Ideology of Contemporary Hollywood Film, coauthored with Michael Ryan (1988)

Herbert Marcuse and the Crisis of Marxism (1984)

Something is rotten in the state of Denmark.

—*Shakespeare,* Hamlet

American fascism will not be really dangerous until there is a purposeful coalition among the cartelists, the deliberate poisoners of public information, and those who stand for the K.K.K. type of demagoguery.

—*Henry Wallace, "The Dangers of American Fascism,"* New York Times, *Sunday, April 9, 1944*

If this were a dictatorship, it'd be a heck of a lot easier, just so long as I'm the dictator.

—*George W. Bush, December 18, 2000*

They took from us everything they could steal.

—*Bob Dylan*

Contents

Introduction

Media Spectacle and Politics in the Contemporary Era

T HE BUSH-CHENEY YEARS have been among the most contentious in modern U.S. history. The Bush-Cheney administration, seen as illegitimate by many who believe the 2000 election was stolen, veered hard to the right from the beginning, pursuing an agenda of massive tax breaks for the rich, deregulation in favor of the corporations that funded its campaign, and a right-wing social agenda in the interests of the conservative groups that make up its base. Before the September 11, 2001, terrorist attacks, the administration's extremism was being contested and Bush's approval ratings were rapidly declining. After 9/11, the Republicans rallied Americans to their "war on terror," their curtailment of civil liberties and democracy in the USA Patriot Act, and their invasion of Iraq, which they claimed was part of the war on terror.

Once upon a time, Republicans stood for corporate fiscal responsibility and economic rationality. Yet the Bush-Cheney clique robs as much national treasure for its contributors as possible, eliminating regulations and rules that increase fairness and efficiency, and undoing social programs that benefit poor and working people. When Bush ran for president, he campaigned as a "compassionate conservative" and "a uniter, not a divider." Yet George W. Bush has proven to be one of the most divisive presidents in U.S. history, and has pursued extremist and hard-right policies that are neither compassionate nor conservative. Although conservatives at one time cherished the values of truth and accountability, Bushspeak involves systematic deceit, using the tactic of repeating a lie over and over again until the public believes it; despite manifestly failed policies and criminal fiscal irresponsibility, there have neither been apologies nor accountability, as I will demonstrate in the following chapters.

Following the September 11, 2001, terrorist attacks, the aggression and militarism of the Bush-Cheney regime was brazen on the global scale. After military intelligence discerned that the Taliban in Afghanistan was harboring Al Qaeda, the Pentagon unleashed its military machine to destroy that fundamentalist Islamic regime. But since the Bush administration and Pentagon deployed a unilateralist, largely air-war strategy, which relied on the purchase of local warlords to fight on the ground, the leaders of the Taliban and Al Qaeda, including Osama bin Laden and Mullah Omar, got away. No matter. The Pentagon militarists and their White House allies had bigger targets in mind: Saddam Hussein and Iraq, which holds the second-largest reserve of oil in the world. Bush administration Treasury Secretary Paul O'Neill told Ron Suskind (2004) how George W. Bush was intent on invading Iraq from the beginning of his administration, and antiterrorism czar Richard Clarke (2004) documented how the pre–9/11 Bush administration paid little attention to the dangers of terrorism and was obsessed with attacking Iraq. The invasion of Iraq produced a vast bounty of contracts for the military-industrial sector, among which was the Carlyle Group, with whom George H. W. Bush and Bush family consigliore James Baker were involved. Contracts were also given to Halliburton, the corporation of which Dick Cheney was formerly CEO. Cheney pushed fiercely for the war on Iraq, and his corporate allies were well rewarded for his efforts, receiving multibillion-dollar no-bid contracts.

To get away with this banditry, Bush and Cheney needed a compliant populace. In the hysteria following the 9/11 terrorist attacks, they passed with the support of a compliant Congress the USA Patriot Act, through which they could suspend constitutional rights, imprisoning people without legal representation or trial, tapping phones, breaking into houses, and even summoning lists of books checked out in libraries. The administration devised a category of "enemy combatant" to allow them to arrest and throw in prison without due process anyone they deemed a threat to national security (Cole 2003). In their wars in Afghanistan and Iraq, the Bush administration and Pentagon put aside decades of military law, proclaimed the Geneva Conventions irrelevant, and allowed harsh interrogation procedures that created one of the biggest scandals in U.S. military history when the Abu Ghraib prison abuse pictures from Iraq circulated globally and other examples of U.S. abuse and torture of prisoners surfaced (Hersh 2004).

Many believe the United States is devolving into fascism under Bush and Cheney, but it is not the sort of "friendly fascism" that Bertram Gross described in 1982, for never has a more vicious bunch occupied the higher levels of government. Like Hitler and German fascists, the Bush-Cheney clique use the Big

Lie to promote its policies, promote aggressive militarism in the quest for world hegemony, and relentlessly promote the economic interests of the corporations and groups that finance it.[1] To sell their program, Bush and Cheney have a media attack apparatus ready to smear anyone who dared to criticize their hard-right and militarist tactics. An ever-growing right-wing Republican media machine, ranging from the *Wall Street Journal* and the conservative press to the Rupert Murdoch–owned Fox TV, talk radio, and the extreme right sector on the Internet, all disseminate propaganda of a scope and virulence never before seen in U.S. history.[2] Expanding significantly since the 1980s, the Republican propaganda machine has cultivated a group of ideological storm troopers who loudly support Bush-Cheney policies and attack those who criticize them. These extremists are impervious to argument, ignore facts and analysis, and demonize as unpatriotic anyone who challenges Bush-Cheney policies. Groomed on Fox TV and right-wing talk radio, they verbally assault anyone who does not march in lockstep with the administration and wage ideological war against the heathens, liberals, feminists, gays and lesbians, and other dissenters. These ideological warriors allow no disparagement of Bush and Cheney and refuse civil dialogue, preferring denunciation and invective.

Although the mainstream corporate media are vilified as "liberal" by the right-wing attack machine, in fact, mainstream journalists are easily intimidated when the right-wing army e-mails, calls, writes, and harasses any corporate media source that goes too far in criticizing the Bush-Cheney regime. The mainstream corporate media are largely subservient to corporate interests, follow the sensation of the moment, and rarely engage in the sort of investigative journalism that was once the ideal and that now takes place largely in the alternative sphere.[3] Corporate media increasingly promote entertainment over news and information, like the tabloids framed by codes of media spectacle (Kellner 2003c). In general, the mainstream corporate media stand in the middle between hard-right conservative and liberal-progressive discourse and media, although during the Bush-Cheney era, as I show in this book, they have leaned toward support of conservatives and the Bush administration. Traditionally, during presidential elections, the mainstream media produce "fact checks" on political television advertisements.

During Election 2004, conservative campaign strategists obtained a memo by Mark Halperin, ABC's political director, which was leaked to the Drudge Report. Halperin wrote that "Kerry distorts, takes out of context, and [makes] mistakes all the time, but these are not central to his efforts to win. While both sides should be held accountable, that doesn't mean we reflexively and artificially hold both sides 'equally' accountable when the facts don't warrant that."

In other words, Halperin implied that distortion was central to the Bush-Cheney campaign, but what little fact-checking the television networks did equally cited Bush and Kerry misstatements, and the corporate media failed to investigate the deliberate lies of the Bush-Cheney campaign, their appalling record in office, or the dire consequences of four more years of hard-right Republican misrule. As I shall demonstrate in this book, Halperin was right to suggest that while all political candidates spin and misspeak, it was important to grasp the extremity of Bush-Cheney lies.

The right-wing attack apparatus, of course, interpreted Halperin's words as documenting "liberal bias" among the mainstream television networks, and fiercely attacked Halperin and anyone in the mainstream media deemed critical of the Bush-Cheney campaign or positively disposed toward the Kerry candidacy. The right-wing claim of a "liberal media" is absurd, for the mainstream media in the United States have tended to be largely uncritical of Reagan and the two Bush administrations, but were fiercely critical of Clinton and his administration. In particular, 24/7 cable news networks like Fox and the NBC cable networks over the past decade have strongly favored the Republicans and sharply criticized Democrats and "liberals" (Alterman 2003; Brock 2004). As the following chapters will show, during the Bush-Cheney administration, the corporate media tended to be lap dogs, failing to investigate in any depth the scandals of Bush and Cheney, their bogus claims about weapons of mass destruction in Iraq, and the destructive consequences of their domestic and foreign politics. Hence, although the media were *attacks dogs* during the Clinton era, they became *lap dogs* during the Bush-Cheney era and have largely abandoned their role as *watch dogs* investigating economic and political scandal and corruption in the public interest, thus aggravating a crisis of democracy in the United States.

In their coverage of Election 2004, as with previous elections, corporate media inordinately focused on polls and the election process itself, and inadequately focused on issues, the records of the candidates, and the potential consequences of their policies. "Debate" was often reduced to shouting matches, as on CNN's *Crossfire*, MSNBC's *Hardball*, or countless Fox TV programs. The highly charged clash of opposing party spin lines of the day helped to polarize the country and failed to illuminate the issues and differences between the candidates. And, as we will see in the following chapters, the few efforts of investigative journalists on the corporate television networks were highly flawed and grossly inadequate, pointing to a crisis of investigative journalism in the United States.

In reflecting on the concepts necessary to describe the 2004 election, I am reminded of some key tenets of the Frankfurt School. When this group of emigrants escaped from Hitler's Germany to the United States in the 1930s, they characterized fascism as, in part, a gangster clique (see Kellner 1989). In a similar critical spirit, I will frequently use the term "the Bush-Cheney Gang" to describe the dynamics of the Bush administration. While Mark Miller's "Bush and Co." (2004) captures the quasi-fascist corporate nature of the clique, I choose to use the gang metaphor since the Bush administration has systematically robbed the federal treasury to benefit the super-rich, to provide favors for his big corporate contributors, and to dismantle programs that largely benefit working people. In addition, the Bush administration has systematically violated international law and is generally seen in the world as a rogue regime regularly subverting diplomacy, global treaties and organizations, and the national security policies of the post–World War II period in favor of "preemptive war," aggressive unilateralism, and unrestrained militarism (see Chapters 2–4).

To help make sense of the 2004 election, I also make use of Frankfurt School categories of the culture industry, the authoritarian personality, one-dimensional thought, and the "dialectic of enlightenment." Throughout this book, I will focus on the role of the media and culture industry during the Bush-Cheney regime and how the Bush-Cheney campaign used and manipulated the media to advance their interests. Many of their supporters exhibit classic symptoms of authoritarian personalities, who think in binary categories of good and evil, project evil onto an Other, and believe only they are good or right. Such one-dimensional men and women are incapable of critical thought, reject critics of their object of faith and devotion (Bush!), and exhibit herd conformity as they mindlessly reproduce the political slogans of their group. Such empty sloganeering is symptomatic of a decline of individual thought, rationality, and critical reflection. Members of the right wing seem to revel in their conformist behavior, as when listeners of talk radio entertainer Rush Limbaugh call themselves "dittoheads" and repeat his lines of the day, however ill-documented and partisan. Exemplifying what Herbert Marcuse (1964) condemned as one-dimensional thought and behavior, Bush conservatives reproduce the slogans of their master and deify a president who has rarely had a thought of his own and reads and performs the scripts of his handlers.

As the Frankfurt School noted in the 1940s (Horkheimer and Adorno 1972 [1948]), a "dialectic of enlightenment" has been evident in the United States in recent years where culture has turned into its opposite for many, serving to manipulate and not nurture individuals. Critical thought has been replaced by faith in the lexicon of religious political extremists, and science and reason are defamed as secular, in a Talibanesque fundamentalism that refuses to question the authority of its leaders and scorns critical thought. Thus, an enlightenment culture that attempted to unify reason, thought, morality, politics, and art is fragmented and its critical components lost. As in Orwell's prescient novel *1984*, language is used by the Bush-Cheney regime to signify its opposite, as when the concept of the "liberation" of Iraq is used to describe an invasion and occupation, or the "Clear Skies Act" describes environmental deregulation leading to an increase of pollution. "Democracy" in Iraq signifies submission to rulers chosen by the Bush-Cheney Gang, and in the United States it is undercut by brazen violations of constitutional rights, not the least of which is rigging elections with unreliable voting machines purchased from Republican partisan corporations like Diebold, thus, in effect, privatizing and outsourcing voting (see Chapter 6 and the Conclusion).

It is clear that the right-wing forces that have operated during the past four years will continue to challenge the hope of U.S. democracy in the future. The Bush-Cheney Gang controls all of the higher institutions of the U.S. government, perpetuating a state apparatus dedicated to class warfare against the poor and dispossessed, and attempting to transfer as much wealth and power to the rich and the corporate classes as possible. They are dedicated to destroying the institutions of the New Deal and the War on Poverty developed from the 1930s through the 1990s and to undermining civil liberties and democratic institutions (once Bush joked that it would be easier if he were a dictator, as one of the opening epigraphs indicates). On the level of foreign policy, the Bush-Cheney Gang envisages using military power to create a new U.S. empire, which in the short term controls the world's oil and energy resources, and in the long term expands toward control of outer space (see Kellner 2003b). This cartel of hard-right conservatives is supported by a right-wing Republican attack apparatus that conveys Republican ideology and attacks Democrats, liberals, and progressives and that has helped construct a mass base for Bush-Cheney extremism, with support from religious right institutions such as churches and political organizations. Bush has managed to create almost a cult following, a surprising phenomenon during the 2004 election campaign that often had the look and feel of religious revivalism. Thus, part of the tragedy of the Bush years is that many individuals have been indoctrinated by right-wing media into believing the extremist ideology and the outright lies of the Bush-Cheney Gang.

This is not a pretty picture and on the liberal side, many were extremely dispirited and depressed after the 2004 election when an obviously unqualified presidential candidate with the worst political record in recent history was re-elected. However, legions of groups and individuals organized around diverse progressive issues and informed by a variety of alternative media produced record turnouts at the polls, unity against the Bush-Cheney Gang, and a remarkable set of cultural initiatives. Although the liberal and progressive side does not have the financial resources, institutions, or media that the Republican right has at its disposal, the battle is not yet over. An impressive number of people participated in the political struggle and have learned that they have to work harder and do better next time, yet meanwhile preserve their righteous anger at Bush-Cheney policies and corruption.

This text is engaged and partisan, and I readily admit to being partial toward democracy, social justice, accurate information, and good journalism. I am not a partisan for the Democratic Party, although the text is sharply critical of Bush, Cheney, and the Republicans, and sympathetic to Kerry and the Democrats. My deepest sympathies, however, lie with the protest movements against the Bush administration's disastrous Iraq policy and against the Bush-Cheney campaign in Election 2004. I am a partisan for radical democracy and progressive social movements. Thus the focus in the Conclusion is how to promote more reliable and participatory democracy in the United States.

This book continues my efforts to develop a critical theory of contemporary media and society and their influence on U.S. politics. Like Antonio Gramsci, I see contemporary culture and society as a terrain of struggle, and accordingly interpret the media as one of the fields in which political and social struggle takes place in a contest of representations. *Media Spectacle and the Crisis of Democracy* draws upon my work of past years, such as *Television and the Crisis of Democracy* (1990a), which demonstrated how the rise of corporate conglomerate media provided powerful tools for conservative forces and how during the Reagan years the mainstream corporate media were skewed toward his agenda because they wanted deregulation to accomplish their mergers, tax breaks to increase their wealth, and maximum freedom to promote their agendas. I argued that this corporate consolidation undermined a democratic public sphere, and called for increased public broadcasting and alternative media to further U.S. democracy. The text also demonstrated how in the 1988 election, the television networks favored Bush over Dukakis and how the supposedly "liberal bias" of the mainstream corporate media was a myth (see also Alterman 2003). *Television and the Crisis of Democracy* was just published when the first Bush administration went to war against Iraq in 1991, allegedly to drive Saddam Hussein out of Kuwait. Another book published shortly thereafter, *The Persian Gulf TV War* (1992), showed how the mainstream corporate media provided a propaganda apparatus for the Pentagon and the first Bush administration military action against Iraq.

In 2001, my book *Grand Theft 2000* documented the stolen election and how, during the first months of his reign, Bush immediately paid back the corporations and groups who had supported him. His administration deregu-lated environmental and other restrictions on the oil, gas, timber, mining, and other industries; defunded women's rape crisis centers, family planning orga-nizations, and other institutions opposed by the right because they promote feminism and pushed a social agenda pleasing to the religious right (see Flanders 2004; Hammer 2002). Bush continued this form of "cash and carry" gover-nance, providing U.S. cabinet posts, ambassadorships, contracts, and other fa-vors to his contributors, who in turn contributed more money to Bush and Cheney to fund more election cycles, in which victory would serve to produce more corporate giveaways. In addition, the Bush administration provided two trillion-dollar-plus tax cuts that significantly benefited the wealthiest Ameri-cans and simultaneously forced cutbacks in social welfare programs, at the same time producing the largest deficit in modern history, one that may take genera-tions to repay.

After the stolen election of 2000, my work focused most intensely during the Bush-Cheney era on news and information media and in particular, the intersection between media and politics. In *Grand Theft 2000*, I demonstrated how the mainstream media were biased against Al Gore and in favor of George W. Bush (Kellner 2001). After 9/11 and the Afghanistan war, I published a book called *From 9/11 to Terror War: The Dangers of the Bush Legacy* (2003a), which showed once again how mainstream corporate media promoted the Bush agenda after 9/11 and into the Afghanistan war. The text discusses how the hysteria following the 9/11 terrorist attacks allowed the mainstream media to promote the unilateral military solutions advanced by the Bush administration and pro-vided propaganda for Bush's rush to war against Iraq.

In 2003, I followed up these studies with a book called *Media Spectacle*, which demonstrated how the media continue to produce modes of entertainment, sports, news, and political information ever more beholden to spectacle. In-deed, in the past few years global politics have been shaped by spectacles of terror, war, and political conflict and upheaval, topics I address in this book by focusing on media spectacle and the crisis of democracy in the United States during the first years of a new millennium. Part of the problem with contem-porary U.S., and indeed global, society is the overwhelming power of media spectacle disseminated from an ever-proliferating culture industry. Lost in the diversions of entertainment, individuals are becoming less informed and more misinformed by the increasingly tabloidized corporate media. Moreover, poli-tics itself is falling prey to media spectacle, as the dominant parties run cam-paigns and govern through daily media events and major spectacles like party conventions or televised wars.

I focus in this text on the role of media spectacle in the Bush-Cheney era and the intensification of the crisis of democracy in the United States. Yet this text is not merely a polemic against the Bush administration and media, but depicts a highly conflicted country and media system and contrasts to the antidemocratic forces alternative media, honorable mainstream journalists, and progressive groups struggling for genuine democracy. Since the Bush-Cheney administration has been so divisive, there is an unparalleled amount of critical material conveniently collected in websites, databases, and blogs, made accessible through the Internet and Google and other search engines. Despite the large right-wing propaganda and attack apparatus, there are also decent journalists and commentators working in the mainstream media, along with an expanding print media and Internet cadre of investigative reporters and critical analysts voicing a broad range of political interpretation and opinion. Drawing on contemporary journalism easily available on the Internet and on reliable sources of alternative media, I use a variety of materials to analyze and critique the corporate media and the Bush administration. My findings point to a growing contradiction in the news and information system in the United States today and indeed globally between ever-restricted news, information, and opinion in the corporate media contrasted to expanding sources of news and opinion on the Internet. Never before has so much solid information, criticism, analysis, and interpretation been available, but despite this cornucopia, the mainstream media have been increasingly incompetent, easily intimidated, and mediocre in their performance.

Leading up to the election, there were a number of books and documentary films criticizing the lies of George W. Bush (Corn 2003) and every aspect of the Bush administration, from its foreign policy to its impact on the environment (Alterman, et al. 2004; Dean 2004; Ivins and Dubose 2004; Miller 2004; Moore 2003; Waldman 2004). In particular, David Corn (2003) published an excellent book, *The Lies of George W. Bush,* which copiously documented a lifetime of lies by Bush and his handlers about his life during his 2000 election campaign and its aftermath, and every aspect of his administration from tax policy to Iraq. I update the history of Bush-Cheney mendacity by laying bare the Big, Bold, and Brazen Lies of the group in Election 2004 (see Chapters 5 and 6). In a hard-hitting exposé generally overlooked by the mainstream media, *Fraud: The Strategy Behind the Bush Lies and Why the Media Didn't Tell You (2004),* Paul Waldman demonstrates the construction of a myth about the "Good Old Boy" Dubya, his strategy of spin and lies, and how the media let Bush get away with an abundance of fraud and deception.

In addition, Ron Suskind's memoir of former Bush administration Treasury Secretary Paul O'Neill recounted how George W. Bush had no interest in economics and was obsessed by Iraq from the beginning of his administration, a point also made by former antiterrorism czar Richard Clarke (2004). Michael Moore's *Fahrenheit 9/11* and the Media Education Foundation's *Hijacking Catastrophe* (2004) sharply denounced George W. Bush and his economic and foreign policies, and a whole series of documentaries coproduced and distributed by Robert Greenwald took on the stolen election of 2000 (*Unprecedented*), the Iraq war (*Uncovered*), Fox TV (*Outfoxed*), and the USA Patriot Act (*Unconstitutional*). In this book, I draw upon these works and my own daily research from a variety of Internet, print, broadcast, and documentary sources that I cite in the extensive references to the text.

Chapter 1 recounts the theft of the election in 2000 and the bias of the corporate media for George W. Bush and against Al Gore. Chapter 2 focuses on Bush administration discourse and media strategies after 9/11 and how the U.S. corporate media promoted his "war on terror." Chapters 3 and 4 trace the road to Iraq, the key stages of the Iraq war, and the catastrophic aftermath. As I conclude the book in late 2004, the United States has invaded Fallujah and, reminiscent of its actions in Vietnam, is "destroying the city to save it," as insurgency erupts and appears to expand throughout Iraq. So although Iraq is still a Bush-produced disaster in the making, it should be instructive to see how it emerged to produce a daily spectacle of horror, undercutting the triumphant U.S. militarism the Bush-Cheney clique has been promoting.

Chapters 5 and 6 document the key events of Election 2004. I wrote my analysis of the election while it was unfolding, posted daily analyses and links in blogleft, gave a number of talks on the media and the election, wrote several articles, and continued to revise my analysis.[4] The Internet provides the possibility of participatory democracy, a wide range of news and opinion, and a lively public sphere, and thus is an important check against our increasingly arrogant, incompetent, and cowardly mainstream corporate media (see Kahn and Kellner 2003). Of course, sectors of the Internet also provide right-wing ideology and disinformation; one must always be careful in using Internet sources, dramatizing the need for media and information literacy (see Kellner 2000; 2004). Some news and information sites and commentators have proven their reliability over time, and I make use of these sources. My studies are "reality based" and use what I consider to be reliable media sources to criticize the bias and distortions of the corporate broadcasting networks and some mainstream journalists.

In late 2004, as I prepare my work for publication, a controversy whirls concerning whether once again there was election fraud and whether the new computerized voting machines are or are not reliable. I discuss the controversy in the Conclusion, point to the best sources for information about voting and the election, and argue that voting machines are just part of the crisis of democracy in the United States.[5] In addition to computerized voting causing election fraud, I argue that the entire Electoral College system is fatally flawed, that the system of winner-take-all state electoral tallying subverts popular sovereignty, and that the corporate media are strongly biased toward candidates who will pursue a conservative agenda. I suggest the need for reliable paper-trail voting technology and abolition of the Electoral College in favor of direct election of the president. I also advocate reforming the current vote-tallying system to divide electoral votes proportionately among the candidates as is done in Maine and Nebraska, rather than giving all of them to the candidate who supposedly has the most votes according to highly unreliable and suspicious methods of tabulation, as is now the case in most states.

In the past four years since the stolen 2000 election, U.S. democracy has been in its greatest crisis and in need of radical reform to strengthen and even preserve it. Thus the book concludes with some comments on the need to develop alternative media and a progressive vision to direct the struggles of the future, which will only intensify, if U.S. democracy is to be revitalized and even survive. On the domestic level, patriotism, moral values, and democracy need to be reclaimed from conservatives and a new democratic vision, similar to that of John Dewey and other progressives, should be grounded in strengthening citizen participation and civil rights as well as radically reforming voting procedures and the electoral system. It must be multicultural and rights-based, incorporating all of the minority groups, including gays and lesbians.

On a global level, a revitalization of democracy must strongly defend human rights and institutions like the United Nations. It must advocate the strengthening of global treaties like the Kyoto Accords on the environment, the International Criminal Court, and the various treaties to monitor and eliminate weapons of mass destruction and other dangerous weapons like land mines and depleted uranium munitions. In the Conclusion, I argue for a robust cosmopolitan multilateralism that seeks global solutions to problems ranging from terrorism to the environment and that is grounded in local, national, and global social movements for human rights, labor rights, and social justice.

Without an expanded and improved alternative media and an informed citizenry, democracy in the United States will continue to atrophy. Election 2004 saw a highly divided electorate and the emergence of powerful organizations, cultural initiatives, and voting efforts by both sides of the battle. But for democracy to work, there must be intelligent dialogue and debate and an informed and active citizenry, and, as this book will show, these preconditions for democracy are not evident in the United States today. Whether democracy will or will not survive depends on sustained attempts to develop alternative media and a participatory citizenry. If these studies contribute to these goals, they will be worth the time and trouble it took to produce them.

Douglas Kellner
West Hollywood, California

Notes

1. There is an entire website that collects articles that document similarities between the Bush-Cheney administration and fascism; see http://semiskimmed.net/bushhitler.html.

2. The rise and growing influence of a right-wing Republican media propaganda and attack apparatus has been well documented in Alterman (2003); Brock (2004); Conason (2003); Miller (2004); and Waldman (2004). In this book, I update and expand my critique of right-wing and corporate media and show how they have relentlessly promoted the agenda of the Bush administration.

3. By corporate media," I mean print, broadcasting, and digital media owned by big corporations like NBC/RCA/General Electric, Murdoch's News Corporation, ABC/Disney, Viacom/CBS, and AOL/Time Warner. "Corporate media" advance the agendas of the organizations that own them and the politicians they support, who in turn pursue the interests of the media conglomerates in governmental institutions such as the Federal Communications Commission. The studies in this book will demonstrate a frightening decline in the standards of journalism within the corporate media during the past years. On the corporate media and how growing consolidation has produced a crisis of democracy see Herman and Chomsky (1988); Kellner (1990, 1992); and McChesny (1997, 2000, 2004).

4. See blogleft for my daily commentary at http://www.gseis.ucla.edu/courses/ed253a/blogger.php and my home page, especially the Interventions file that contains many of my talks of the past years: http://www.gseis.ucla.edu/faculty/kellner/kellnerhtml.html.

5. See the Conclusion and the following sources, which are tracing problems with computerized and other methods of voting in Election 2004 and possibilities of election fraud: http://www.ejfi.org/Voting/Voting-1.htm; http://www.openvotingconsortium.org; http://www.demos-usa.org; http://www.verifiedvoting.org; and http://www.blackboxvoting.org.

Chapter 1

Grand Theft 2000: Media Spectacle and a Stolen Election

> When the real world changes into simple images, simple images be-
> come real beings and effective motivations of a hypnotic behavior. The
> spectacle has a tendency to make one see the world *by means of various*
> *specialized mediations (it can no longer be grasped directly).*[1]
>
> —*Guy Debord*

T HE 2000 U.S. PRESIDENTIAL ELECTION, one of the closest and most hotly
contested ever, was from start to finish a media spectacle.[2] Despite predictions
that the Internet was on its way to replacing television as the center of the
information system, television in the 2000 U.S. election was perhaps more influential than ever. The proliferation of channels on cable and satellite systems
multiplied political discourse and images, with several presenting round-the-
clock political news and discussion. These cable news programs were organized as forms of media spectacle, with highly partisan representatives of both
sides engaging opponents in dramatic competition. The fight for ratings intensified the entertainment factor in politics, fueling the need to generate compelling political spectacle to attract audiences.

The result was unending television discussion programs with commentators lined up for the Republicans or Democrats, as hosts pretended to be neutral, but often sided with one candidate or another. Of the 24-hour cable news
channels, it was clear that the Rupert Murdoch–owned Fox network was un-
abashedly pro-Republican, and it appeared that the NBC-owned cable networks MSNBC and CNBC were also partial toward Bush.[3] CNN and the three
major networks claimed to maintain neutrality, although major empirical

1

studies of television and press coverage of the election indicated that the media on the whole tended to favor Bush (see below).

By all initial accounts, it would be a close election, and both sides furiously tried to spin the media, getting their "message of the day" and a positive image of their candidate on screen or into the press. Both sides provided the usual press releases and sent out e-mail messages to the major media and their supporters, which their opponents would then attempt to counter. The competing campaigns also constructed elaborate websites that contained their latest "messages," video clips of the candidates, and other information on the campaigns.[4] Both sides staged frequent photo opportunities, saturated the airwaves with ads, and attempted to sell their candidate to the voters. In an era of spectacle politics, presidential candidates were a brand name to be sold to voters and campaigns were dominated by marketing and public relations techniques.

Media Spectacle in Election 2000

We mortals hear only the news and know nothing at all.

—*Homer*

Throughout the summer, there was not much intense focus on the campaigns among the public at large until the political conventions took place, where both parties traditionally produce spectacles to provide positive images of their candidate and party. The Republicans met first, in Philadelphia from July 31 to August 3, filling their stage with a multicultural display of supporters, leading pundits to remark that more people of color appeared on stage than were in the audience of the lily-white conservative party that had not been friendly to minorities. The Democrats met in Los Angeles in mid-August and created carefully planned media events to show off their stars, the Clintons and the Gores, with Al and Tipper's long kiss the most circulated image of the event. For the first time, however, major television networks declared that the political party conventions were not important news stories, but were merely partisan events, and they severely cut back on prime-time coverage allotted the spectacles. In particular, NBC and the Fox network broadcast baseball and entertainment shows rather than convention speeches during the early days of both conventions. CBS's Dan Rather dismissed the conventions as "four-day infomercials" (*CBS News*, August 15).

Nonetheless, millions of people watched the conventions, and both presidential candidates got their biggest polling boosts after their respective events, thus suggesting that the carefully contrived media displays were able to capture an audience and perhaps shape viewer perceptions of the candidates. After the conventions, no major stories emerged and not much media attention was given to the campaigns during the rest of August and September in the period leading up to the presidential debates. The Gore campaign seemed to be steadily rising in the polls as the Bush candidacy appeared to be floundering.[5]

The relatively inexperienced Republican candidate was caught on open mike referring to a *New York Times* reporter as a "major-league asshole," with Bush's vice presidential choice, Dick Cheney, chiming in "big time." Although the Bush team publicly proclaimed that it would not indulge in negative campaigning, a television ad appeared attacking Gore and the Democrats that highlighted the word "RATS." Critics accused the Bush campaign of attempting to associate the vermin with DemocRATS/bureaucRATS. Bush denied that his campaign had produced this "subliminable" message (in his creative mispronunciation) at the same time that an ad producer working for him was bragging about it.

As the camps haggled about debate sites and dates, it appeared that Bush was petulantly refusing the forums suggested by the neutral debate committee and was perhaps afraid to get into the ring with the formidable Gore. Since the 1960s the presidential debates have become popular media spectacles that are often deemed crucial to the election. Hence, as the debates began in October, genuine suspense arose and significant sectors of the populace tuned in to the three events between the presidential candidates and the single debate between the competing vice presidential candidates. On the whole, the debates were dull, in part because host Jim Lehrer asked unimaginative questions that simply allowed the candidates to feed back their standard positions on Social Security, education, Medicare, and other issues about which they had already spoken day after day. Neither Lehrer nor others involved in the debates probed the candidates' positions or asked challenging questions on a wide range of issues from globalization and the digital divide to poverty and corporate crime that had not been addressed in the campaign. Frank Rich described the first debate in the *New York Times* as a "flop show," and Dan Rather on CBS called it "pedantic, dull, unimaginative, lackluster, humdrum, you pick the word."[6]

In Election 2000, commentators on the debates tended to grade the candidates more on their performance and style than on substance, and many believe that this strongly aided Bush. In the postmodern image politics of the 2000 election, style became substance as both candidates endeavored to appear likable, friendly, and attractive to voters. In the presidential debates when the candidates appeared *mano a mano* to the public for the first time, not only did the media commentators focus on the form and appearance of the candidates rather than the specific positions they took, but the networks frequently cut to "focus groups" of "undecided" voters who presented their stylistic evaluations. After the first debate, for instance, commentators noted that Gore looked "stiff" or "arrogant" and Bush appeared "likable." After the second debate, Gore was criticized by commentators as too "passive," and then after the third debate too "aggressive," whereas Bush, as we'll see below, was not strongly criticized for style or substance.[7]

Bush's appeal was predicated on his being "just folks," a "good guy," like "you and me." Thus, his anti-intellectualism and lack of gravity, exhibited every time he opened his mouth and mangled the English language, helped promote voter identification. As sometime Republican speechwriter Doug Gamble once mused, "Bush's shallow intellect perfectly reflects an increasingly dumbed-down America. To many Americans Bush is 'just like us,' a Fox-TV President for a Fox-TV society."[8]

It was, however, the spectacle of the three presidential debates and the media framing of these events that arguably provided the crucial edge for Bush. At the conclusion of the first Bush-Gore debate, the initial viewer polls conducted by CBS and ABC declared Gore the winner. But the television pundits seemed to score a victory for Bush. Bob Schieffer of CBS declared, "Clearly tonight, if anyone gained from this debate, it was George Bush. He seemed to have as much of a grasp of the issues" as Gore. His colleague Gloria Borger agreed, "I think Bush did gain." CNN's Candy Crowley concluded, "They held their own, they both did.... In the end, that has to favor Bush, at least with those who felt ... he's not ready for prime time."[9]

Even more helpful to Bush was the focus on Gore's debate performance. Gore was criticized for his sighs and style (a "bully," declared ABC's Sam Donaldson) and was excoriated for alleged misstatements. The Republicans immediately claimed that Gore had "lied" when he told a story of a young Florida girl forced to stand in class because of a shortage of desks. The school principal of the locale in question denied this, and the media had a field day, with a Murdoch-owned *New York Post* boldface headline trumpeting "Liar! Liar!" Subsequent interviews indicated that the girl *did* have to stand and that there *was* a desk shortage, and testimony from her father and a picture confirmed this, but the damage to Gore was already done. Moreover, Gore had misspoken during the first debate in a story illustrating his work in making the Federal Emergency Management Agency (FEMA) more efficient, claiming that he had visited Texas with its director after a recent hurricane. As it turns out, although Gore had played a major role in improving FEMA and had frequently traveled with its director to crisis sites, and although he had been to Texas after the hurricane, the fact that he had not accompanied the director in the case cited accelerated claims that Gore was a "serial exaggerator" or even a liar who could not be trusted.

Republican pundits obsessively pursued the theme that Gore was a liar. In the *Wall Street Journal* (October 11, 2000), ideologue William Bennett wrote: "Albert Arnold Gore Jr. is a habitual liar. ... The vice president lies reflexively, promiscuously, even pathologically." In fact, the alleged lies were largely Republican propaganda. This Republican mantra was repeated throughout the rest of the campaign, and although the press piled on Gore every time he made a minor misstatement, Bush was able to get away with whoppers in the debate and on the campaign trail on substantial issues.[10] For example, whereas he claimed in a debate with Gore that he was for a "patients' bill of rights" that would allow patients to sue their HMOs for malpractice, in fact, Bush had blocked such policies in Texas and opposed a bill in Congress that would allow patients the right to sue. Few critics skewered Bush over the misstatement in the second debate, delivered with a highly inappropriate smirk, that the three racists who had brutally killed a black man in Texas were going to be executed. In fact, one had testified against the others and had been given a life sentence in exchange; moreover, because all three cases were on appeal it was simply wrong for the governor to claim that the men were going to be executed, since this undercut their right of appeal. The media also had given Bush a pass on the record number of executions performed under his reign in Texas, the lax review procedures, and the large number of contested executions where there were questions of mental competence, proper legal procedures, and even evidence that raised doubts about Bush's execution of specific prisoners.

Although a fierce argument over prescription drugs in the first debate led to allegations by Gore that Bush was misrepresenting his own drug plan, driving Bush to assault Gore verbally, the media did not bother to look and see that Bush *had* misrepresented his plan and that Gore was correct, despite Bush's impassioned denials, that seniors earning more than $25,000 a year would get no help from Bush's plan for four or five years. Moreover, after the third and arguably decisive presidential debate, commentators and pundits were heavily pro-Bush. On MSNBC, for example, in questioning Republican vice presidential candidate Dick Cheney about the third debate, Chris Matthews lobbed an easy question to him attacking Al Gore; moments later when Democratic House Majority Leader Dick Gephardt came on, once again Matthews assailed Gore in his question! Pollster Frank Luntz presented a focus group of "undecided" voters, the majority of which had switched to Bush during the debate and who uttered primarily anti-Gore sentiments when interviewed (MSNBC forgot to mention that Luntz is a Republican pollster). Former Republican Senator Alan Simpson was allowed to throw barbs at Gore, to the assent of host Brian Williams, and no Democrat was allowed to counter the Republican in this segment. The pundits, including Matthews, former Reagan-Bush speechwriter and professional Republican ideologue Peggy Noonan, and accused plagiarist Mike Barnacle, all uttered pro-Bush messages, while the two more liberal pundits provided more balanced analysis of the pros and cons of both sides in the debate, rather than just spin it for Bush.

Gore was on the defensive for several weeks after the debates, and Bush's polls steadily rose. Moreover, the tremendous amount of coverage of the polls no doubt helped Bush. Although Gore had been rising in the polls from his convention up until the debates, occasionally experiencing a healthy lead, the polls were favorable to Bush from the conclusion of the first debate until the election. Almost every night, the television news opened with the polls, which usually showed Bush ahead, sometimes by 10 points or more. As the election night results would show, these polls were off the mark, but they became *the* story of the election as the November 7 vote approached. The majority of the mainstream media polls on the eve of the election put Bush in the lead (although the Zogby/Reuters and CBS News polls put Gore slightly ahead in the popular vote). Media critic David Corn noted that commentators such as John McLaughlin, Mary Matalin, Peggy Noonan, and many of the Sunday network talk-show hosts prophesied a sizable Bush victory and tended to favor the Texas governor.[11] Joan Didion reports, by contrast, that seven major academic pollsters presenting their data at the September 2000 American Political Science Association convention all predicted a big Gore victory, ranging from 60.3 percent to 52 percent of the vote.[12]

Academic pollsters tend to use rational-choice models and base their results on economic indicators and in-depth interviews; they seem, however, to downplay moral values, issues of character, the role of media spectacle, and the fluctuating events of the election campaigns. Indeed, academic pollsters argue that the electorate is basically fixed one or two months before the election. Arguably, however, U.S. politics is more volatile and unpredictable and swayed by the contingencies of media spectacle, as Election 2000 and its aftermath vividly demonstrated. Robert G. Kaiser, in "Experts Offer Mea Culpas for Predicting Gore Win" (*Washington Post,* February 9, 2001), presents interviews with major political scientists who had predicted a strong win for Gore based on their mathematical models and data collected months before election day. One professor admitted that the "election outcome left a bit of egg on the faces of the academic forecasters," whereas others blamed a poor Gore campaign,

"Clinton fatigue," and an unexpectedly strong showing by Ralph Nader. One defiant forecaster said that the election was simply weird, "on the fringe of our known world, a stochastic [random] shock."

The polls were one of the scandals of what would turn out to be shameful media coverage of the campaign. Arianna Huffington mentions in a November 2, 2000, syndicated column that on a CNN/USA Today/Gallup poll released at 6:23 P.M. on Friday, October 27, George W. Bush was proclaimed to hold a 13-point lead over Al Gore; in a CNN/Time poll released later that night at 8:36 P.M., Bush's lead was calculated to be 6 points. When Huffington called the CNN polling director, he declared that the wildly divergent polls were "statistically in agreement ... given the polls' margin of sampling error." The polling director explained that with a margin of error of 3.5 percent, either candidate's support could be 3.5 percent higher or lower, indicating that a spread of as much as 20 points could qualify as "statistically in agreement," thus admitting that the polls do not really signify much of anything, as in fact election night results showed.

In retrospect, the polls were notoriously flawed during the 2000 campaign. Poll fatigue had set in with the public, and the major polling organizations admitted that they were getting a less than 50 percent response rate. Moreover, the national polls were irrelevant, because in an Electoral College system, it is the number of states won that is the key to victory, and not the popular vote. In fact, the Electoral College system, in which the candidate who gets the most votes in a state wins the state and the candidate who wins the most states wins the election, would come under attack during the intense battle for the White House in the Florida recount wars. Gore won one half million more votes than Bush, but many states that were very close were won by Bush, so a more proportional voting system would reflect better the will of the people, as many reformers argued.[13]

Despite the polls' flaws, network news coverage focused on them or the strategies, mechanics, and ups and downs of the campaigns, rather than the key issues or the candidates' actual records as politicians, their policies, and who and what they represented. With a shrinking amount of news coverage on the major network news, and sound bytes in which news and information were condensed into even smaller fragments, media focus on the horse race and strategic dimension of the presidential campaigns meant that less and less time would be devoted to discussion of the issues, the candidates, and the stakes of the election.

In this environment, the campaigns sought to create positive images of their candidates through daily photo opportunities and television ads, thus contributing to intensification of a superficial image politics. The television ads presented positive spectacles of the candidates' virtues and negative spectacles of their opponents' flaws. Contested states such as Florida were saturated with advertising, and consequently in Election 2000, in which a record $3 billion was dispersed, campaign costs were the highest in history. The ads were closely scrutinized for distortions, exaggerations, and lies, with Internet Webzines such as *Slate* providing regular analysis of the ads, and television networks replaying and closely analyzing the more controversial ones.[14]

Both candidates ran intense phone campaigns. Republican voters could be thrilled to get a prerecorded call from George W. Bush himself, telling them that he wanted their votes. On the Democratic side, there was a late-campaign barrage of telephone calls to black voters from Bill Clinton. Ed Asner recorded a call to seniors in Florida warning them about Bush's Social Security program. Of course, Hollywood celebrities and rock stars also campaigned for the candidates. Gore used his Harvard roommate Tommy Lee Jones, *West Wing* President Martin Sheen, and an array of young Hollywood stars to campaign for him, and Bush used members of the Hollywood right such as Bo Derek and Bruce Willis.

Furthermore, Bush, more so than the serious, policy-oriented Gore (demeaned as a "wonk" by many), was entertaining; he was amusing and affable in the debates, even if not commanding in argumentation and substantive position. Like Ronald Reagan, Bush looked good on the run, with a friendly smile and wave, and in general seemed able to banter and connect with his audiences better than Gore. Bush's misstatements and errors were amusing, and on late-night talk shows he poked fun at himself for his mispronunciations and gaffes; *Slate* compiled a list of "Bushisms," and they were as entertaining as David Letterman's Top Ten list and Jay Leno's nightly NBC monologue, which often made jokes about Gore and Bush.

Yet it was perhaps late-night comics and *Saturday Night Live,* the longtime satirical NBC show, that most exemplified the continued importance of television entertainment to electoral politics and made clear that contemporary U.S. politics *is* media spectacle. The comics had a field day satirizing the know-nothing smiling papa's boy "Dubya" (aka "W," Shrub, or the little Bush) and the stiff and pompous senator from Tennessee, Al Gore. Likewise, *Saturday Night Live* ridiculed the candidates after the debates in segments that were widely circulated and repeated frequently on nightly news as well as on a preelection special, giving rise to the claim that the *Saturday Night Live* piece was the "most important political writing of the year" (MSNBC News, November 5 and November 15).[15]

The *Saturday Night Live* satire made Bush and Gore appear equally ludicrous. The presentations of Gore in particular were arguably inaccurate and defamatory, depicting the intelligent and articulate vice president and author as slow-talking, clichéd, and bumbling. It is true that Gore tended to dumb down his discourse for the debates and repeated certain phrases to make key points, but the satire arguably distorted his speech patterns and mannerisms, which were nowhere near as slow as depicted. These often-repeated satires probably went further than Republican attack ads to create a negative public image of Gore. Their constant reiteration on the NBC news channels provided not only advertisements for the popular Saturday night television show, but unpaid attack ads for the Republicans.

Bush's turnaround in the polls in October after his numbers had been steadily dipping for weeks was seemingly boosted by what was perceived as his successful appearance on the debates and on popular talk shows, such as *Oprah*, where an image of the much-beloved African American talk hostess giving him a smooch was widely circulated. Some claimed that the talk shows were a natural for the more relaxed Bush, although there were debates over whether his appearance on the *David Letterman Show* hurt or helped his efforts, as he appeared giddy and was unable to effectively answer the tough questions Letterman posed.

In any case, both candidates made appearances on the major late-night talk shows as well as other popular television venues previously off-limits to presidential candidates. In general, television spectacle helps to boost the chances of the most telegenic candidate, and according to media commentary, Bush repeatedly scored high in ratings in "the likability factor." Polls continued to present Bush as more popular than Al Gore, and many media commentators predicted that he would win the election handily. As David Brock recounts: "A week before the 2000 elections, *Editor and Publisher* asked newspaper executives about their personal political views. 'The nation's newspaper editors and publishers strongly believe the Texas governor will beat Al Gore in Tuesday's election for president,' the magazine found. 'By a wide margin, they plan to vote for him themselves. And, to complete this Republican trifecta, newspapers endorsed Bush by about 2–1 nationally'" (2004, 90).

The U.S. public seems to like entertaining politicians and to sometimes resent media critiques of politicians they like. Hence, when stories broke a few days before the election that Bush had been arrested 20 years before for driving under the influence of alcohol and had since lied to cover this up, the populace and polls did not punish him. When asked about highs and lows of the campaign on election night, Bush said with his trademark smirk that even the lows "turned out to be good for us," alluding to polls that indicated that Bush got a rise in popularity after revelations of his drunk driving charge. As with Clinton's survival of his sex scandals and the Republican impeachment campaign, it seems as if the public empathizes with the politicians' foibles and resents moral indictments at least of those with whom voters sympathize. Obviously, Clinton was a highly sympathetic personality, and many resented the Republican moral crusade against him. Similarly, voters liked Bush and seemed not to be affected by the embarrassing disclosure of his arrest record and its longtime cover-up.[16]

Media Bias in the Representations of Bush and Gore

> You've heard Al Gore say he invented the Internet. Well, if he was so smart, why do all the addresses begin with "W"?
>
> —*George W. Bush*

In the postmodern politics of promotion, candidates are packaged as commodities, marketed as a brand name, and sold as a bill of goods. In a presidential race, campaigns are dominated by image consultants, advertising mavens, spin doctors, and political operatives who concoct daily photo opportunities that make the candidates look virtuous, "messages" that sound appealing, and "events" that present the campaigns in an attractive format. Such campaigns are, of course, expensive and require tremendous budgets that make competing impossible for candidates without access to the megafortunes needed to run a media campaign. In turn, such megaspectacles render politicians beholden to those who cough up the millions of dollars to pay for the extravaganzas and for the vast apparatus of producers, spinners, and operatives to create and distribute them.

Bush's brand name was his family trademark as the son of the former president and Bush dynasty heir apparent, with his own distinctive "compassionate conservatism." The latter phrase shows the spurious nature of Bush's packaging, as there is little "compassion" in the record of the Texas governor who executed a record number of prison inmates, who cut welfare lists and social programs, and who promised more of the same on the national level.[17] In the politics of presidential marketing, however, creation of image takes precedence over ideas, style replaces substance, and presentation trumps policy. With politics becoming a branch of marketing, the more marketable candidate is easier to sell. Thus, it is not surprising that Bush's image, style, and presentation trumped, for poorly informed voters, Gore's ideas, experience, and policies with large segments of the public.

Bush had another major asset in the competition for votes and marketing of the candidates. Cultural historians make distinctions between "character," based on one's moral fiber and history of behavior, and "personality," which has to do with how one presents oneself to others.[18] The new culture of personality emphasizes charm, likability, attractiveness, and the ability to present oneself positively. Bush was clearly Mr. Personality, instantly likable, a hail-fellow-well-met and friendly glad-hander who was able to charm audiences. He was becoming a media celebrity whose achievements and accomplishments were few, but he was able to play effectively the "presidential contender" and provide a resonant personality with whom viewers could identify. Moreover, Bush was able to transmit his likable qualities via television, whereas Gore frequently had more difficulty in coming across as personable and translating his considerable intelligence and experience into easily consumable sound bytes and images.[19]

The Texas governor, who was to many more a figure of personality than character, was also able to turn the "character issue"—with the complicity of the press—against Gore and convince audiences that he, George W. Bush, was a man of "character" as well as personality. The Bush camp used the term "character" as a code word to remind audiences of the moral lapses of Bill Clinton and of Gore's association with the president in a sustained collapse of one into the other. The Bush campaign also systematically attacked Gore's character and credibility, and the media bought into this (see Alterman 2003; Kellner 2001).

The media rarely challenged Bush, who seemed to have not only charmed large sectors of the American public, but was effective in schmoozing the media. The Center for Media and Public Affairs (CMPA) study of television election news coverage before, during, and after the conventions (released on August 14) concluded, "Network evening news coverage of the GOP convention was more favorable toward George W. Bush, while Al Gore received mostly unfavorable TV references, according to a new study released by the CMPA." The study also found that "Bush has received more favorable coverage than Gore throughout the 2000 campaign, reversing a trend that favored Bill Clinton over his GOP opponents in 1992 and 1996."[20] The CMPA is run by Robert Lichter, who has generally been perceived as a conservative critic of the media's liberal bias (although he claims to be a neutral social scientist), so it is interesting that his organization found a bias in favor of Bush.[21] Later CMPA findings indicate that Gore's positive network news coverage went up sharply after the Democratic convention, as did Gore's ratings (September 5, 2000). But a study released by CMPA on October 18 indicated that "network news coverage of Al Gore turned sharply negative after the first presidential debate." It appears that CMPA's positive/negative network news codings of the candidates correlate remarkably with the candidates' rise and fall in the polls, although since polls themselves came under dramatic attack in the election, it is obviously not clear what impact positive and negative presentations of candidates on television news and in print have on voters.

Surprisingly perhaps, Bush fared as well with the print media and establishment press as with television. Supporting the studies of pro-Bush bias, Charlie Peters reported in the *Washington Monthly* that according to the Project for Excellence in Journalism (PEJ) studies, the *New York Times* front page "carried nine anti-Gore articles and six anti-Bush; 12 pro-Gore and 21 pro-Bush" (November 2000). Howard Kurtz, media critic for the *Washington Post,* reported: "Those who believe the media were easier on Bush will find some support in a new Project for Excellence in Journalism study. Examining television, newspaper, and Internet coverage from the last week in September through the third week in October, the report says Bush got nearly twice as many stories as Gore" (November 6, 2000). Moreover, only one in ten of the media reports on the election analyzed the candidates' policy differences, with two-thirds focusing on the candidates' performance, strategy, or tactics. Twenty-four percent of the Bush stories were positive, compared to 13 percent for Gore, and the Bush stories focused more on issues than character or campaign strategy. The PEJ study examined 2,400 newspaper, television, and Internet stories in five different weeks between February and June 2000, and indicated that 76 percent of the coverage included one of two themes: that Gore lies and exaggerates or is marred by scandal. The most common theme about Bush, the study found, is that he is a "different kind of Republican." A follow-up PEJ report concluded:

> In the culminating weeks of the 2000 presidential race, the press coverage was strikingly negative, and Vice President Al Gore has gotten the worst of it, according to a new study released today by the Committee of Concerned Journalists.
>
> Gore's coverage was decidedly more negative, more focused on the internal politics of campaigning and had less to do with citizens than did his Republican rival.
>
> In contrast, George W. Bush was twice as likely as Gore to get coverage that was positive in tone. Coverage of the governor was also more issue-oriented and more likely to be directly connected to citizens.
>
> These are some of the key findings of a major new study of press coverage in newspapers, television and on the Internet during key weeks in September and October.[22]

A German group, Media Tenor, also documented a persistent anti-Gore and pro-Bush bias in mainstream media presentation of the candidates.[23] Thus three different research projects found strong media bias in the election coverage. To be sure, such "positive" and "negative" scoring of images and discourses is difficult, debatable, and not completely accurate, but demonstrated strong pro-Bush and anti-Gore bias in representations in the mainstream corporate media. Indeed, many reporters and commentators despised Gore, as Eric Alterman notes:

> The intensity of the media's anti-Gore obsession is a bit bizarre, but even more so, given the strictures of journalistic objectivity, is the lack of compunction they feel about openly demonstrating it. At an early New Hampshire debate between Gore and Bill Bradley, reporters openly booed him, "objectivity" be damned. "The 300 media types watching in the press room at Dartmouth were, to use the appropriate technical term, totally grossed out," *Time* reported. "Whenever Gore came on too strong, the room erupted in a collective jeer, like a gang of fifteen-year-old Heathers cutting down some hapless nerd."
>
> *Washington Post* White House reporter Dana Milbank offers this reasoned, mature explanation: "Gore is sanctimonious, and that's sort of the worst thing you can be in the eyes of the press. And he has been disliked all along, and it was because he gives a sense that he's better than us—he's better than everybody, for that matter, but the sense that he's better than us as reporters. Whereas President Bush probably is sure that he's better than us—he's probably right, but he does not convey that sense. He does not seem to be dripping with contempt when he looks at us, and I think that has something to do with the coverage."
>
> Bill Keller, who almost became executive editor of the *New York Times,* was no less scholarly than Milbank, but like any good pundit, multiplied his own resentments by 50 million. "One big reason 50 million voters went instead for an apparent lightweight they didn't entirely trust was that they didn't want to have Al Gore in their living rooms for four years," Keller wrote on the paper's op-ed page. Included in his argument was the behavior of his 3-year-old, who, during the 2000 campaign, "went around chanting the refrain: 'Al Gore is a snore.'" Imagine where she might have learned to do that!
>
> During the 2000 election, both the *Times* and the *Post* assigned reporters to Gore who hated his guts and so repeatedly misled their readers. Katharine Seelye's and Ceci Connolly's coverage turned out to be so egregious that the two were singled out by the conservative *Financial Times* of London as "hostile to the [Gore] campaign," unable to hide their "contempt for the candidate." (And don't get me started on the topic of "Panchito" Bruni's daily valentines to George W. during this period, carried on page one of the Paper of Record [i.e., the *New York Times*]).[24]

One of the most utilized examples of Gore the liar and "serial exaggerator" was the alleged claim that he had invented the Internet. In fact, Gore had made no such claim, although the media, the Republican spinners, and Bush himself constantly referred to this urban myth. Bush burst out in one of the debates that "his opponent" claimed to "have invented the Internet" and then smirked in contempt. This lie about Gore, and Bush's systematic exploitation of the myth, speaks volumes about the quality of the Bush campaign and media complicity in its spin. First, it is simply untrue that Gore claimed he "invented" the Internet. A story in *Wired* falsely reported that Gore asserted that he "invented" the Internet, whereas in fact he had simply stated that "During my service in the United States Congress, I took the initiative in creating the Internet," a completely accurate statement that key members of the high-tech community involved in producing the Internet confirmed.[25] The Republicans continued to spread the false smear about Gore, including George W. Bush, who baited Gore in a debate with the lie and repeated it constantly in his stump speeches. This is an example of Republican use of the "big lie" technique, where a falsehood is stated over and over as if it were a truth, which would come to characterize "Bushspeak" during the battle for the White House and Bush presidency (see Kellner 2001, Chapter 9; and Chapters 5 and 6 of this book).

However, even more significant than alleged bias for Bush and against Gore is the preponderance of conservative punditry and the exclusion of widespread discussion of key aspects of George W. Bush's life and record in business and government. Clearly, media pundits tended to favor Bush over Gore. As Eric Alterman demonstrated in *Sound and Fury: The Making of the Punditocracy* (2000), conservatives had trained a cadre of media commentators well versed in the art of sound byte and staying on message, and there were many, many more conservatives than liberals on the airwaves (see also Brock 2004). Talk radio was an important medium during the campaign, just as it had been over the last decade in U.S. politics. It was the relatively new form of unrestrained talk radio that first mobilized conservatives against Bill Clinton after his election in 1992, fueling indignation and anger and circulating the details of the Clinton sex scandal, generating support for his impeachment. The very excesses of right-wing talk radio provided a backlash, and some stations chose liberals to counter the conservative hosts, but most liberal programs were soon cancelled and by 2000 right-wing hosts completely dominated talk radio.

Indeed, during Election 2000 and the ensuing struggle for the presidency, right-wing talk radio made a comeback, energizing its old audience and finding new ones, all the while projecting the hatred of Clinton onto Gore. The narcissistic Rush Limbaugh, who had been taken off television because of declining ratings and who had seemed to disappear from the front stage of national mainstream media, reappeared in all his virulence, frequently appearing on NBC channels, which restored the discredited demagogue to celebrity and credibility.[26] Limbaugh and other right-wing blowhards grew louder and more aggressive than ever, demonizing Gore and mobilizing conservative constituents to vote for Bush, helping as well to organize against the Democrat candidate once the postelection struggle for the presidency erupted. The conservative punditocracy trashed Gore daily, while Bush escaped critical scrutiny of his record in Texas, his limited experience, his problematic proposals, and his almost daily misstatements. Promoting the Republican "message of the day" throughout the media, conservative media served as ubiquitous shock troops for the Bush machine.

It is interesting how Bush and his handlers utilized the "W" as a trademark to distinguish Bush from his father and how Bush became popularly identified as "W," or the Texas-inflected "Dubya." Whereas JFK's initials were an apt summary of his style and achievements, and LBJ earned the gravity of his initials through many years in the Senate, culminating in his becoming Senate majority leader and then gaining the vice presidency and presidency, "W" is an empty signifier, although had the media probed the infamous initial, they would have discovered a truly spectacular story. In fact, the "W" in Bush Junior's name refers to Herbert Walker, the father of Dorothy Walker, who married George W. Bush's grandfather, Prescott Bush (the H. W. in Bush Senior's name also refers to Herbert Walker). Prescott Bush managed the bank that represented German business interests who helped fund Hitler and the Nazis, and Herbert Walker, Prescott Bush's close business associate, helped run businesses for Stalin's Russia and Mussolini's Italy as well as Hitler's Germany.[27]

The mainstream media favoritism toward Bush not only came through in how the media presented and framed the two opposing candidates, but in how they failed to pursue George W. Bush's family history, scandalous business career, dubious record as governor, lack of qualifications for the presidency, and serious character flaws. None of the many newspaper, magazine, and television reports on the Bush family history, for instance, mentioned the reports on the origins of the Bush dynasty fortune in a bank that financed German fascism or pursued the Bush family financial scandals that continued through Jeb, Neil, and George W. Bush. However, during the battle for the White House, a story appeared in the Saragosa *Herald-Tribune Coast News* entitled "Author Links Bush Family to Nazis" (December 4, 2000), which claimed that Prescott Bush (George Senior's father and George Junior's grandfather) was a principal figure in the Union Banking Corporation in the late 1930s and 1940s. The article cited a lecture by John Loftus, a former prosecutor in the Justice Department's Nazi War Crimes Unit and author of a book with Mark Aarons entitled *The Secret War against the Jews* (1994). Loftus noted that Prescott Bush was a director of the Union Banking Corporation, which was secretly owned by leading Nazi industrialists and helped finance the Third Reich; when the bank was liquidated in 1951, the Bushes made $1.5 million from their investment. A Lexis-Nexis search indicated that there were no references to the origins of the Bush family fortune until an article by Michael Kranish, "Triumphs, Troubles Shape Generations" (*Boston Globe*, April 23, 2001), including the following:

> Prescott Bush was surely aghast at a sensational article the *New York Herald Tribune* splashed on its front page in July 1942. "Hitler's Angel Has 3 Million in US Bank" read the headline above a story reporting that Adolf Hitler's financier had stowed the fortune in Union Banking Corp, possibly to be held for "Nazi bigwigs."
>
> Bush knew all about the New York bank: He was one of its seven directors. If the Nazi tie became known, it would be a potential "embarrassment," Bush and his partners at Brown Brothers Harriman worried, explaining to government regulators that their position was merely an unpaid courtesy for a client. The situation grew more serious when the government seized Union's assets under the Trading with the Enemy Act, the sort of action that could have ruined Bush's political dreams.
>
> As it turned out, his involvement wasn't pursued by the press or political opponents during his Senate campaigns a decade later.

Although the Loftus and Aarons study (1994) provided a well-documented exploration of connections between a major Nazi bank and the Bush dynasty, this episode was never explored by the U.S. corporate media. Neglect of the unsavory origins of the Bush family fortune and later financial scandals is one of the major journalistic and academic outrages in U.S. history. Indeed, most books and articles on the Bushes are white-washes, and there has been little investigative study of the family by the U.S. media, political, and academic establishment.[28]

There was also no probing during Election 2000 of the Bush family involvement in the savings and loan (S&L) scandal, arguably one of the biggest financial debacles in U.S. history, costing American taxpayers over one half trillion dollars to bail out the failed S&L institutions that had gone on a spending orgy after deregulation in the early 1980s. George H. W. Bush and James Baker were instrumental in the deregulation of the industry during the Reagan administration, and their families and friends had bought up and looted S&Ls, including the Silverado S&L involving Neil Bush (see Brewton 1992).

The political scandals in which Bush Senior had been involved were also ignored in 2000 election coverage, such as the Iran-Contra scandal, the U.S.

arming of Saddam Hussein, or the misdeeds of the Central Intelligence Agency under Bush's directorship (see Kellner 1990, 1992; Parry 1992). In addition, there was almost no reporting on George W. Bush's personal or financial history, including his use of favoritism to get out of military service, his absence without leave, and his failure to complete his military reserve service. There was little discussion of his checkered business career, including allegations that his father's friends bailed out his failing oil company and that he then unloaded his own stock in the Harken Energy Company (which had bailed him out), sold it before revelations of a bad financial report, and failed to report the sale to the Securities and Exchange Commission, giving rise to charges of "insider trading."

Books, articles, and easily accessible Internet sites document the entire scandalous history of George W. Bush and his dubious dynasty, but cowardly and incompetent functionaries of the mainstream media failed to probe this rich mine of material—whereas there were few embarrassments or negative aspects of Al Gore's past that were not endlessly discussed on talk radio and among conservative television pundits. Likewise, there were few in-depth discussions of the record of Bush's vice-presidential choice Dick Cheney, the major role he would play in a Bush White House, and his precarious health. Cheney had one of the most hard-right voting records in Congress and was heavily involved in the oil industry as CEO of Halliburton industries, one of the worst polluters and most ruthless corporations in an industry known for its hardball robber barons.[29]

In his 1992 book *Fooling America,* Robert Parry documents the pack journalism of the mainstream media in the 1980s and 1990s, arguing that the horde follows "conventional wisdom," recycling the dominant and predictable opinions, and fails to pursue stories or develop positions outside of or against the prevailing views of the day. During Election 2000, journalists on the whole tended to accept the line of the Bush campaign concerning Gore's purported negatives; at the same time they promoted the view the Bush camp advanced that Bush was a "uniter, not a divider," a "compassionate conservative," and someone who pursued "bipartisan" politics in order "to get things done." When the election would heat up in the fall, the Bush campaign would exploit these motifs, and the mainstream media would generally go along with this line, without serious investigation of Bush's record or his own exaggerations and misstatements.[30] Moreover, and importantly, major research studies of the nexus between media and politics revealed that this bias perhaps won the Republicans enough votes ultimately to wrest the election victory from Gore and the Democrats (although, of course, many maintain that the election was stolen and that Gore had won the plurality of Electoral College votes as well as the popular vote).

A Stolen Election

Election 2000 was the closest in history, and election night and the aftermath comprised one of the most gripping media spectacles in recent history. During the subsequent 36 days, a gripping drama unfolded in the Florida recount wars, halted by a Supreme Court decision that handed George W. Bush the presidency. In *Grand Theft 2000* (2001), I argue that the theft of Election 2000 took place on three levels. First of all, before the election, Florida Governor Jeb Bush, brother of the Republican presidential candidate; his secretary of state, Katherine Harris; and the state Republican Party did everything possible to augment Republican votes and block Democratic votes, displaying partisanship bordering on illegality. The Florida Republicans hired a Republican-based company, DataBase Technologies, to "cleanse" the voting lists of felons, which also eliminated thousands of legitimate voters, mostly poor and African American. Jeb Bush allowed Republican political operatives to illegally fill in absentee ballot applications in Seminole and Martin Counties, breaking the law and denying Democrats equal privileges. Jeb Bush vetoed a $100,000 voter literacy bill, depriving first-time voters of obviously necessary education on how to vote. Jeb Bush sent out from his office absentee ballots, instructions, and a letter to Republican voters urging recipients to vote. Katherine Harris employed Gulf War hero General Norman Schwartzkopf, a Bush supporter who frequently campaigned for George W. Bush and a close friend of his father, to participate in a get-out-and-vote television ad campaign that was, in effect, using state funds to tell people to vote for Bush.[31]

Secondly, on the day of the election, the Florida Republican Party did everything possible to facilitate Republican votes and block Democratic ones. African American voters were harassed by police as they drove in vans to vote; largely first-time African American voters and many other longtime voters found that their names were purged from the voting lists and were denied their votes. There were not enough poll workers at many lower-income and predominantly Democratic Party precincts, inadequate computer lists of eligible voters, and insufficient language help for Spanish-speaking and Haitian voters. Moreover, there were a record number of undervotes that did not register because of faulty voting machines, primarily in low-income and/or heavily Democratic Party districts. In addition, there were a record number of overvotes due to faulty ballots, including the infamous butterfly ballot in Palm Beach County and a two-page ballot of presidential candidates in Duval County that contained instructions to vote for candidates on each page. Finally, there were many other voting irregularities and the manufacturing of many votes for George W. Bush and erasure of votes for Al Gore that I documented throughout *Grand Theft 2000*. Hence, whereas there was not one "smoking gun" that dramatized the stolen election, there was a preponderance of disturbing examples, which, shamefully, were never investigated by the U.S. government or local law authorities or the media due to the influence of the Bush family. There were many Internet sites documenting details of the theft, studies of statistical anomalies of peculiar voting patterns, and differences between the preelection and even election day polls and the actual tabulated vote (see Kellner 2001).[32] As we shall see in the Conclusion to this book, some of these same problems turned up in Election 2004.

Third, after the deadlocked election on November 7, the Bush machine and Florida Republican Party did everything possible to block the manual recount of selective counties called for by the Gore campaign. The Republicans pushed to certify Bush as president as quickly as possible, even though many thousands of votes had not been counted. In addition, the Bush camp was prepared to use the Florida legislature to name its electors, an act never before carried out that risked constitutional crisis and chaos. Finally, the Republicans ultimately called upon the U.S. Supreme Court to block the tallying of undervotes mandated by the Florida Supreme Court and in effect to give the presidency to Bush, in one of the most brazen examples of judicial activism and most controversial Supreme Court decisions in U.S. history (see Bugliosi 2001; Derschowitz 2001).

In *Grand Theft 2000*, I recount the heist of the presidency as it proceeded during the Florida recount wars, provide documentation of the step-by-step and multifaceted theft of an election, show how the mainstream media aided and abetted the Bush camp, and call attention to the crisis of democracy the theft of that election revealed. It was an audacious theft, taking place on television in front of an audience of millions. But despite the drama of the election, there was little self-criticism of the role of the mainstream media in Election 2000, and after the September 11 terrorist attacks, discussion of electoral problems was off the agenda. Although there were efforts to reform election finances and voting technology, there were no significant reforms of the U.S. electoral system, which appeared to be dysfunctional in Election 2000, with arguable malfunctioning of the media, voter technology, and the democratic system itself. Discussion of Electoral College reform disappeared and no commissions studied the flaws in the U.S. voting system that made possible the scandals of Election 2000. Many states still chose in 2004 to deploy computer voting machines that did not leave a paper trail and that were subject to mischief, as we shall see in the Conclusion. Thus U.S. democracy remains in crisis and there will probably be no significant reform until a critical mass of people see the flaws of the U.S. system and demand democratic reform, a topic I take up in the Conclusion.

Notes

1. The concept of spectacle I am using derives from Guy Debord and the French situationists; for previous articulations of this concept, see Best and Kellner (1997, 2001); and Kellner (2003c).

2. This study draws upon and expands arguments set out in *Grand Theft 2000* (Kellner 2001). It also draws upon major books on Election 2000 including Brunei (2002); Bugliosi (2001); Ceaser and Busch (2001); Derschowitz (2001); Milbank (2001); Miller (2001); the *New York Times* (2001); Sabato (2002); Sammon (2001); Schechter (2001); Tapper (2001); and the *Washington Post* (2001). Oddly, no definitive book has been written on Election 2000, surely a watershed in recent U.S. history and one of the most momentous and scandalous events in U.S. presidential election history.

3. Systemic Fox TV bias was documented in the 2004 film by Robert Greenwald, *Outfoxed*. On Fox and the NBC cable network bias, see Brock (2004) and Miller (2004); I will provide examples of pro-Republican/conservative and anti-Democratic/liberal media bias throughout this book.

4. For an excellent overview of the role of Internet sites in Election 2000 and issues involved in online politics, see Stephen Coleman, "What Was New? Online Innovation in the 2000 Elections," in Schechter (2001), pp. 120–133.

5. See the daily commentary on the campaign in Howard Kurtz's media columns archived at www.washingtonpost.com; Brunei (2002), pp. 163ff.; and Milbank (2001), pp. 307ff.

6. Pundit quotes and analysis of the debate are found in Kurtz, "Media Notes," *Washington Post,* October 4, 2000.

7. See the columns on the debates in Kurtz, "Media Notes," *Washington Post,* October 4, 2000.

8. Doug Gamble, cited in Martin A. Lee, www.sfbg.com/reality/12.html. See also Jake Tapper's discussion of Bush's "Dumb Chic," *Salon,* November 2, 2000, and Miller's probing analysis (2001). *New York Times* correspondent Frank Brunei's history of Bush and the 2000 election (2002), by contrast, puts on display how Bush seduced the press. Although Brunei complains about Bush's superficiality and the shallowness of political campaigns in the media age, his book exhibits the shallowness of the press and political correspon-

dents. Alexandra Pelosi's HBO documentary *Journeys with George* (2001) puts on display both the superficiality of George W. Bush and those journalists who covered him.

9. See the detailed selection and analysis of pundit quotes on the debate in Kurtz, "Media Notes."

10. See the analysis of "Twenty-Five Bush Flubs in the Second Debate" and "Fifteen [Bush] Flubs in the Third Debate" at http://www.tompaine.com/news/2000/10/20/index.html.

11. See David Corn at www.tompaine.com/news/2000/11/24. As Jamieson and Waldman (2003) note: "One study comparing network news coverage of the last four presidential elections found that 71 percent of stories in 2000 were primarily concerned with the 'horse race' as opposed to issues, compared to 48 percent in 1996 and 58 percent in both 1992 and 1988. Our own content analysis of television news in 2000 showed that fewer than a third of the statements in election stories mentioned any issue at all, no matter how briefly" (p. 168).

12. See Didion, "In God's Country," *New York Review of Books,* November 2, 2000.

13. See the discussion in Kellner 2001, pp. 159ff., and the Conclusion to this book, pp. 213–250.

14. On political ads, see Milbank (2001), pp. 359ff., and the study of television advertising by the Alliance for Better Campaigns in Schechter (2001), pp. 77–92. In an illuminating study of ads in Election 2000, Lynda Lee Kaid argues that Bush's television ads established eye contact with viewers in 26 percent of his spots compared to only 6 percent for Gore. Bush was three times as likely to be shown with a smiling expression than Gore; and Bush was shown in close-up or tight shots in 41 percent of his ads compared to 24 percent for Gore, thus using video imagery to sell Bush's "personality" to voters. See "Videostyle and Technological Distortions in the 2000 Political Spots," International Communications Association Convention, Washington, D.C., May 2001.

15. For discussion of the *Saturday Night Live* effect, see *Suck,* November 16, 2000. On comedy and the media, see Marshall Sella, "The Stiff Guy vs. the Dumb Guy," *New York Times,* September 24, 2000.

16. On Bush's DUI incident and how his campaign and the Gore camp dealt with it, see Timothy J. Burger, "In the Driver's Seat: The Bush DUI," in Sabato (2002), pp. 69–93. Karl Rove, by contrast, had claimed that the DUI revelation near the end of the campaign helped Gore close the gap against Bush and cost conservative votes; see Nicholas Lemann, "The Controller: Karl Rove Is Working To Get George Bush Reelected, but He Has Bigger Plans," *New Yorker,* May 12, 2003.

17. See the following books on Bush's record by Begala (2000), Hatfield (2000), Ivins and Dubose (2000), Miller (2001), and Mitchell (2000). Corn (2003) provides an excellent account of how Bush systematically lied during the 2000 election about his past life and poor record as governor of Texas; Waldman (2004) has a chapter on "Putting the Con in Compassionate Conservative" (pp. 157ff.).

18. See Gabler (1999), p. 197; Sussman (1984).

19. For an excellent analysis of the qualifications of Gore to be president and lack of substantial achievements and qualifications of Bush, see Alterman (2003), pp. 148ff.

20. Cited in www.cmpa.com/pressrel/electpr2.htm. See also the discussion of positive/negative coding and the work of the German group Media Tenor in Markus Rettich, "Into the White House through the Television Screen," in Schechter (2001), pp. 100–102.

21. On the Lichters' conservatism, see Brock (2004), pp. 85ff.

22. For the Project for Excellence in Journalism report, see http://www.journalism.org/publ.research/campaign1.html. For a good overview of the PEJ findings and critique of mainstream media news coverage of the election, see Bill Kovach and Tom Rosenstiel, "Campaign Lite: Why Reporters Won't Tell Us What We Need to Know," *Washington Monthly*, January–February 2001.

23. See the summary in Schechter (2001), pp. 100ff., and the website www.medientenor.de/english.

24. Eric Alterman, "Al Gore, Democrat," *Nation*, October 21, 2002. Alterman repeats this analysis in his 2003 book, which systematically devastates the myth of the "liberal media," with a whole chapter documenting mainstream media hatred toward Gore and complicity with Bush (pp. 148–174). Waldman (2004, pp. 99ff.) also has a discussion detailing how members of the press corps hated Gore and how Bush charmed them.

25. For convincing demolitions of the allegation that Gore claimed to "invent" the Internet, see "The Red Herring Interview: E-Gore," *Red Herring*, October 30, 2000.

26. Right-wing ideologue Rush Limbaugh emerged as "the highest paid info-broadcaster in history," clocking in with $30 million this year, more than the network anchors combined (http://www.drudgereport.com/rr.htm). On Limbaugh, see Seib (1993) and Brock (2004), pp. 261ff.

27. On how Herbert Walker and Prescott Bush managed Nazi financial interests in the United States, see Loftus and Aarons (1994) and Phillips (2004). Prescott Bush and Herbert Walker's involvement in the Union Banking Corporation and other businesses connected with National Socialism had earlier been documented in a biography of George H. W. Bush by Tarpley and Chaitkin (1992), pp. 26–44.

28. Exceptions are Phillips (2004), Kelley (2004) and Parry (2004), who provide sharply critical and detailed portrayals of Bush family history. Kevin Phillips is a former Republican strategist who was appalled by the Bush family and wrote a hard-hitting exposé of their political history. Kitty Kelley, by contrast, specializes in celebrity scandal books and focuses on the sordid personal lives and business affairs of three generations of Bushes while investigative reporter Robert Parry broke many important stories during the Bush I era.

29. For books on George W. Bush's history, ignored in the 2000 election, see the sources listed in Note 17. Websites that document the history of Bush family scandals and George W. Bush's life include: www.moldea.com; www.bushwatch.com; http://prorev.com/bush3.htm; and www.gwbush.com. For a useful overview of Cheney's health, history, voting record, and hard-right credentials, see Begala (2001), pp. 126–136. More

recently, Nichols (2004) has provided an in-depth look at Cheney's scandalous economic and political history.

30. For a wealth of studies of the media and politics of Election 2000 that document these claims, see the Project for Excellence in Journalism, http://www.journalism. org, and the studies in Schechter (2001). In a *Columbia Journalism Review* article, "Gore Media Coverage—Playing Hardball," Jane Hall systematically analyzes negative and often misleading coverage of Gore, contrasted to soft and generally uncritical coverage of Bush (September–October 2000). For analyses of distortion of Gore's record and refutations of Republican mantras about his "lying," see Robert Parry's "Al Gore v. the Media," February 1, 2000, www.consortium.com, his article in the April 2000 *Washington Monthly* and Parry 2004. See also the compilation of Bob Somerby's critiques of false Bush campaign claims and the media buying into these at www.dailyhowler.com; Sean Wilentz, "Will Pseudo-Scandals Decide the Election?" *American Prospect* 11(21), September 24, 2000; Eric Boehlert, "Gore's Too-Willing Executioners," *Salon*, October 27, 2000; Mollie Dickenson, "Who's Lying? Gore or the Media?" at www.tompaine.com, October 18, 2000; and Susan Douglas, "Bush's Fifth Column," *In These Times*, December 25, 2000. The prize for most inept media criticism goes to Camille Paglia, who declared "the only thing worse than the candidates this year is the shockingly biased liberal press" (*Salon*, December 6, 2000), a judgment rendered without one example of liberal bias and in the face of stacks of studies documenting conservative and pro-Bush bias.

31. Joan Sekler and Ray Perez's documentary *Unprecedented* (2003) interviews journalists who investigated the voting purges and people who describe how it was done. See also Danny Schecter's documentary on the 2000 election, *Counting on Democracy* (2002; updated 2004 DVD version) and Greg Palast's 2003 book *The Best Money Democracy Can Buy* (updated in his 2004 video of the same title).

32. The U.S. Commission on Civil Rights documented many of the irregularities, especially regarding African American voters, and released the *Probe of Election Practices in Florida during the 2000 Presidential Election*, www.usccr.gov/vote2000/flmain.htm. See also other sources listed in Kellner (2001), pp. 181–182. Shortly after the September 11, 2001, terrorist attacks, a consortium of major news organizations released results of a detailed examination of all of the Florida ballots which indicated that if all of the Florida undervotes and overvotes were counted Al Gore would have become the President. In the post–9/11 environment, findings of the examination were suppressed and some media reports even suggested that under some recount scenarios Bush would have won. But, in fact, the actual recount ordered by the Florida Supreme Court and the plan envisaged by Judge Terry Lewis in charge of overseeing the vote would have resulted in a clear Gore victory (see Parry 2004, pp. 316ff).

Chapter 2

Spectacles of Terror and Perpetual War

The greatest generation was used to storming beachheads. Baby boomers such as myself was used to getting caught in a quagmire of Vietnam where politics made decisions more than the military sometimes. Generation X was able to watch technology right in front of their TV screen, you know, burrow into concrete bunkers in Iraq and blow them up.

—*George W. Bush, first press conference after 9/11*

THE SEPTEMBER 11, 2001, ATTACKS ON THE WORLD TRADE CENTER (WTC) in New York and on the Pentagon near Washington, D.C., were shocking global media events that dominated public attention and provoked reams of discourse, reflection, and writing. These spectacles of terror were intended to intimidate the United States, to attack symbolic targets, and to provoke a Jihad, or holy war, against the West that would undermine the U.S. and global economies. The WTC is an apt symbol of global capitalism in the heart of the New York financial district, and the Pentagon stands as an icon of U.S. military power. In striking these targets, terrorists were attacking key symbols of U.S. global power and demonstrating the vulnerability of the superpower to attack. In this chapter, I show how Osama bin Laden and various cells of Al Qaeda have used spectacles of terror to promote their agenda in a media-saturated era and how two Bush administrations have also deployed terror spectacle to promote their geopolitical ends.[1]

Weapons of Mass Hysteria

The term "terrorism" is one of the most loaded and contested terms in contemporary political vocabulary.[2] First used to describe the "reign of terror" following the radical phase of the French Revolution, the term was also used in the nineteenth century to describe the violent activities of Russian revolutionaries. By the late 1960s, the Nixon administration was using the term to describe a wide range of activities and groups. It established the Cabinet Committee to Combat Terrorism in 1972, and subsequent U.S. administrations continued to develop agencies and task forces to fight "terrorism," which became a widespread designation to label groups the U.S. government and its allies were fighting. But during this era, the United States was also widely accused of crimes against civilians in Vietnam and elsewhere and of using violence to intervene in other countries' politics. Thus, the term "state terrorism" began to emerge, a term also frequently applied to Israel (see Herman 1998).

Hence, terrorism is highly constructed and contested; one group's "terrorists" are another group's "freedom fighters." Various political groups labeled terrorists have long created media spectacles of terror to promote their causes, attack their adversaries, and gain worldwide publicity and attention. There had been many major terror spectacles before, both in the United States and elsewhere. Hijacking of airplanes had been a standard form of constructing spectacles of terror, but in 1970, the Popular Front for the Liberation of Palestine upped the ante when it hijacked three western jetliners, forced them to land in the Jordanian desert, and then blew them up. The incident, known as "Black September," became the topic of a Hollywood film. In 1972, Palestinian gunmen from the same movement stunned the world when they took Israeli athletes hostage at the Munich Olympic Games, producing another media spectacle that was depicted in an Academy Award–winning documentary film.

In 1975, an Organization of Petroleum Exporting Countries (OPEC) meeting was disrupted in Vienna, Austria, when a terrorist group led by the notorious Carlos the Jackal entered, killing three people and wounding several in a chaotic shootout. Americans were targeted in a 1983 terror campaign in Beirut, Lebanon, orchestrated by a Shiite Muslim suicide bomber. The deaths of 243 U.S. servicemen led the United States to withdraw its troops from Lebanon. U.S. tourists were victims of another media spectacle in 1985 when Palestinians seized the cruise ship *Achilles Lauro* and killed Leon Klinghoffer, 69, a crippled Jewish American, throwing his body and wheelchair overboard.

In 1993, the WTC was assaulted in New York by Islamist radicals linked to Osama bin Laden, providing a preview of the more spectacular September 11, 2001, attack. An American-born terrorist, Timothy McVeigh, bombed the Alfred P. Murrah Federal Building in Oklahoma City in 1995, killing 168 people and wounding more than 500. Osama bin Laden's group assaulted U.S. embassies in Africa in 1998 and a U.S. destroyer harbored in Yemen in 2000. Consequently, terror spectacle is a crucial part of the deadly game of contemporary politics. But the 9/11 terror spectacle was the most extravagant strike on U.S. targets in its history and the first foreign attack on the United States since Pearl Harbor in 1941.

In a global media world, sensationalist terror spectacles have been orchestrated in part to gain worldwide attention, dramatize the issues of the groups involved, and achieve specific political objectives. Previous Al Qaeda strikes against the United States hit a range of targets to demonstrate that the United States was vulnerable to terrorist attacks. The earlier 1993 WTC bombing in New York, the embassy assaults in Kenya and Tanzania in 1998, and the strike on the *USS Cole* in 2000 combined surprise with detailed planning in highly orchestrated terror spectacles.[3]

Spectacles of terror thus use dramatic images and montage to catch attention, hoping thereby to catalyze unanticipated events that will spread further terror through domestic populations. The September 11 terror spectacle looked like a disaster film, leading Hollywood director Robert Altman to chide his industry for producing extravaganzas of terror that could serve as models for more terror campaigns. Was *Independence Day* (1996), in which Los Angeles and New York were attacked by aliens and the White House was destroyed, the template for 9/11? The collapse of the WTC indeed was reminiscent of *The Towering Inferno* (1975), which depicted a high-rise building catching on fire, burning, and collapsing, or even *Earthquake* (1975), which dramatized the collapse of entire urban environments. For these two Hollywood disaster films, however, the calamity emerged from within the system in the case of the first, and from nature itself in the second. In the September 11 terror spectacle, by contrast, the villains were foreign terrorists obviously committed to wreaking maximum destruction on the United States, and it was not certain how the drama would end or if order would be restored in a "happy ending."

The novelty of the September 11 terror spectacle was the use of hijacked airplanes to crash into buildings and destabilize urban and economic life. The attacks were symbolic, yet had material effects, disrupting the airline industry, the businesses centered in downtown New York, and the global economy itself through the closure of the U.S. and other stock markets and subsequent downturns of the world's markets. Indeed, as a response to terror, an unparalleled shutdown occurred in New York, Washington, D.C., and other major cities throughout the United States, with government and businesses closing up for the day and the airline system canceling all flights. Wall Street and the stock market were shut down for days, baseball and entertainment events were postponed, Disneyland and Disneyworld were closed, McDonald's locked up its regional offices, and most major U.S. cities became eerily quiet.

The 9/11 terror spectacle unfolded in a city that was one of the most media-saturated in the world and thus played out the deadly drama live on television. The images of the planes hitting the WTC towers and their collapse were broadcast repeatedly, as if repetition were necessary to master a highly traumatic event. The spectacle conveyed the message that the United States was vulnerable, that terrorists could create great harm, and that anyone at any time could be subject to a deadly terrorist attack, even in Fortress America. Suddenly, the suffering, fear, and death of loved ones that many people endure on a daily basis in violent and insecure situations in other parts of the world were also deeply experienced by U.S. citizens, in some cases for the first time. The terrorist attacks thus had the material effect of harming the U.S. and global economies, and the psychological effect of traumatizing a nation. The spectacle of terror was broadcast throughout the global village, with the whole world watching the assault on the United States and New York's attempts to cope with the attacks.[4]

The media became "weapons of mass hysteria" by playing the 9/11 Twin Tower attacks over and over, focusing on the devastation at "Ground Zero," a term first used to describe the epicenter of the Hiroshima atomic bomb that was appropriated to signify the devastation and enormity of the 9/11 attacks. Day after day, terrorist "experts" described bin Laden and Al Qaeda and repeatedly disseminated everything that was known about the terrorists, creating a culture of hysteria, as the Bush administration trotted out John Ashcroft and Dick Cheney to frighten the public with further warnings of impending terror attacks. The media thus served in a perverse way as instruments of Al Qaeda and terrorism, since one of the goals of terror attacks is to spread fear and anxiety.

The U.S. media and the Bush administration thus created a legend of bin Laden and Al Qaeda, projecting into the figure of bin Laden enormous evil and power, which in turn elevated his status in the Arab and Muslim world to a quasi-demigod able to inflict harm on the American superpower. In the following section, I note the similarities in discourses and mindset of Bush and bin Laden and show how the Bush administration exploited the terror spectacle to push through their right-wing and militarist agendas with the complicity of the U.S. corporate media.

The 9/11 Spectacle

The live television broadcasting brought a "you are there" drama to the September 11 spectacle. The images of the planes striking the WTC, the buildings bursting into flames, individuals jumping out of the windows in a desperate attempt to survive the inferno, the collapse of the towers, and the subsequent chaos provided unforgettable images viewers would not soon forget. The drama continued for days with the poignant search for survivors being pulled from the rubble, and their attempts to deal with the attack. Many people who witnessed the event suffered nightmares and psychological trauma. For those who viewed it intensely, the spectacle resonated in much the same way as the footage of the Kennedy assassination, photographs of Vietnam, the 1986 explosion of the space shuttle *Challenger,* or the death of Princess Diana in a fiery automobile accident.

For several days, U.S. television suspended broadcasting of advertising and entertainment programs and focused solely on the terrorist attacks in New York, leading to the claim in a May 2002 HBO film, *In Memoriam,* that 9/11 was "the most documented event in history." The Bush administration and the images and discourses of the corporate media failed to provide a coherent account of what happened, why it happened, and what would count as intelligent and responsible responses. The Bush administration and corporate media privileged the "clash of civilizations" model, established a binary dualism between Islamic terrorism and civilization, and largely circulated retaliatory discourses that whipped up war fever and called for military intervention. Such one-dimensional militarism, however, has the potential to generate a cycle of violence and perpetual war that makes the current situation even worse. Thus, although the media in a democracy should critically debate urgent questions facing the nation, such as whether to declare war, in this crisis the mainstream U.S. corporate media, especially the television networks, promoted only military solutions to the problem of global terrorism and provided a propaganda machine for Bush administration militarism.

The network anchors as well as political commentators framed the event as a military attack. The constant invocation of analogies to Pearl Harbor inevitably elicited a need to strike back and prepare for war. For example, Peter Jennings of ABC stated, "The response is going to have to be massive if it is to be effective." News programs featured logos such as "War on America," "America's New War," and other inflammatory slogans that assumed that the United States was already at war. On the day of the strikes on the WTC and Pentagon, the networks brought out an array of national security consultants, usually ranging from the right to the far right, to explain the horrific events of September 11. These "experts" had close connections to the Pentagon and usually would express the Pentagon viewpoint and message of the day, making them propaganda conduits for the U.S. military rather than independent analysts.

The Fox Network presented former UN Ambassador and Reagan administration apologist Jeane Kirkpatrick, who rolled out a simplified version of Huntington's clash of civilizations (1996), arguing that we were at war with Islam and should defend the West.[5] Kirkpatrick was the most discredited intellectual of her generation, legitimating Reagan administration alliances with unsavory fascists and terrorists as necessary to beat Soviet totalitarianism. In the 1980s, she made a false distinction between fascism and communist totalitarianism and argued that alliances with authoritarian or right-wing terrorist organizations or states were defensible since these regimes were open to reform efforts or historically undermined themselves and collapsed. According to Kirkpatrick, Soviet totalitarianism, by contrast, should be resolutely opposed since a communist regime had never collapsed or been overthrown; communism was an intractable and dangerous foe that must be fought to the death by any means necessary. Of course, the Soviet Union disintegrated in the early 1990s, along with its empire, and although Kirkpatrick was totally discredited, she was awarded a professorship at Georgetown and continued to circulate her views through Fox TV and other right-wing venues.

Commentators like Senator John McCain, former U.S. Secretaries of State Henry Kissinger and James Baker, and other longtime advocates of the military-industrial complex described the 9/11 attack as an "act of war" immediately that day and in the days following. For these pundits, the terrorist attacks required an immediate military response and dramatic expansion of the U.S. armed forces. Many of these hawks were former government officials currently tied into the defense industries; their warmongering would be rewarded in large personal profits. The Bush family, James Baker, and other advocates of large-scale military retribution were connected with the Carlyle Fund, the largest investor in military industries in the world. Dick Cheney's Halliburton Corporation would benefit from military and reconstruction contracts, as would the Bechtel Corporation and other military-industrial corporations with which Donald Rumsfeld and other major figures in the Republican Party and prowar community were connected.[6] These advocates of war would profit immensely from sustained military activity, a fact rarely mentioned on television or in the mainstream press, but widely discussed in alternative media and on the Internet.

Although many critics cautioned against calling the terrorist attacks "war" and called for multilateral legal, police, and military coalitions to go after the Al Qaeda network, such debates did not take place in the U.S. broadcasting media. Instead, after September 11, the networks kept their cameras aimed at "Ground Zero" to dramatize the destruction, the harm done to victims, and the discovery of dead bodies, and constantly speculated on the whereabouts of bin Laden and the Al Qaeda terrorists who had committed the atrocities, helping to generate and sustain widespread public desire for a military response.

On the afternoon of September 11, Prime Minister Ariel Sharon of Israel, himself implicated in war crimes in Saba and Shatila in Lebanon in 1982, came on television to convey his regret, condolences, and assurances of Israel's support in the war on terror. Sharon called for a military coalition against terrorist cells. He contrasted the civilized world with terrorism, representing Israel and the United States as the "good versus evil," "humanity versus the blood-thirsty," "the free world against the forces of darkness" that are trying to destroy "freedom" and "our way of life."

Bush took up the same tropes, using the word "evil" five times in his first public statement on the September 11 terrorist assaults and repeatedly portraying the conflict as a war in which the United States was going to "eradicate evil from the world" and "to smoke out and pursue ... evil-doers, those barbaric people." The semantically insensitive and dyslexic Bush also used cowboy metaphors, calling for bin Laden "dead or alive" and describing the campaign as a "crusade," until he was advised that this term carried offensive historical baggage of earlier wars of Christians upon Muslims. At the same time Bush was declaring a "crusade" against terrorism, Bush administration Deputy Defense Secretary Paul Wolfowitz said the administration's retaliation would be "sustained and broad and effective" and that the United States "will use all our resources. It's not just simply a matter of capturing people and holding them accountable, but removing the sanctuaries, removing the support systems, ending states who sponsor terrorism." The Pentagon at first named the war against terror "Operation Infinite Justice," until they were advised that only God could dispense "infinite justice," and that Americans and others might be troubled about a war expanding to infinity. Such hyperbolic rhetoric is a salient example of Bushspeak, which communicates through codes to specific listeners; in this case the domestic Christian right-wing groups that are Bush's preferred audience.[7]

Disturbingly, in outlining the goals of the war, Bush never mentioned "democracy," and the new name for the "war on terror" became "Operation Enduring Freedom." The Bush administration repeated constantly that the war against terrorism was being fought for "freedom," but the history of political theory suggests that freedom must be paired with equality, justice, civil rights, and democracy to provide adequate legitimation for political action. It is precisely the contempt for national self-determination that has characterized U.S. foreign policy in the Middle East for several decades that is a prime reason groups and individuals in the area passionately hate the United States.

In a historical analysis of "calls to arms" discourse that compares orations by Bush after September 11 with Pope Urban II, Queen Elizabeth I, and Adolf Hitler, Graham, Keenan, and Dowd (2004) identify generic features in such speeches, including an appeal to a legitimate power source external to the speaker, an appeal to the importance of the national culture under attack, the construction of an evil enemy, and an appeal for unification. Illustrating Bush's appeal to support his war on terror, the authors cite a speech the president made five days after the 9/11 attacks:

> We're a great nation. We're a nation of resolve. We're a nation that can't be cowed by evil-doers. I've got great faith in the American people. If the American people had seen what I had seen in New York City, you'd have great faith, too. You'd have faith in the hard work of the rescuers; you'd have great faith because of the desire for people to do what's right for America; you'd have great faith because of the compassion and love that our fellow Americans are showing each other in times of need.

Graham, Keenan, and Dowd note how Bush merges the concepts of "a great nation," "resolve," faith, compassion, and love in his talk to appeal to common values and to unite the nation. His use of "we," "I," and "you" serve as rhetorical devices to bind himself with the country. It should also be noted that Bush uses the fact that the images of the destruction of the WTC and the Pentagon were an iconic part of the mediascape at the time to make his case ("If the American people had seen what I had seen in New York City"). Indeed, Bush and his administration continued to exploit these images throughout Election 2004 (see Chapters 5 and 6).

Bush also notoriously uses Manichean, or binary, discourse to construct the "evil Other" who attacked the United States and to highlight the goodness of the United States against the malevolence of terrorism. In his September 20 speech to Congress, Bush drew a line between those who supported terrorism and those who were ready to fight it. Stating, "you're either with us, or against us," Bush declared war on any states supporting terrorism and laid down a series of nonnegotiable demands to the Taliban who ruled Afghanistan, as Congress wildly applauded. Bush's popularity soared with a country craving blood revenge and the head of Osama bin Laden. Moreover, Bush also asserted that his administration held accountable those nations who supported terrorism— a position that could nurture and legitimate military interventions for years to come. In the same speech, Bush described the conflict as a war between "those governed by fear" who "want to destroy our wealth and freedoms," and those on the side of freedom. Yet "freedom" for Bush has come to signify U.S. freedom to strike preemptively anywhere it wishes at any time, ironically projecting onto other countries the same sense of vulnerability the terrorist attacks were meant to create in the United States. Furthermore, the Bushspeak dualisms between fear and freedom, barbarism and civilization, and the like can hardly be sustained in empirical and theoretical analysis of the contemporary moment. In fact, there is much fear and poverty in "our" world, and wealth, freedom, and security in the Arab and Islamic worlds—at least for privileged elites. To doubt freedom, fear, and wealth are distributed in both worlds so as to polarize these categories and to make them the legitimating principles of war is highly misleading. Meanwhile, the unilateralist Bush administration considered itself "free" from major global treaties ranging from Kyoto to every conceivable international effort to regulate arms and military activity (see Kellner 2001, 2003c).

Interestingly, Bush's fundamentally Manichean discourses, like those of bin Laden and radical Islamists, posit a binary opposition between good and evil, us and them, civilization and barbarism, and also replicate the friend/enemy opposition upon which Nazi politics were based. Osama bin Laden, Al Qaeda, and "the terrorist" provide the face of an enemy to replace the "evil empire" of Soviet communism, which was the face of the Other in the Cold War. The terrorist Other, however, does not reside in a specific country with particular military targets and forces, but is part of an invisible network supported by a multiplicity of groups and states. This amorphous terrorist enemy, then, allows the crusader for good to attack any country or group supporting terrorism, thus promoting a foundation for a new doctrine of preemptive strikes and perennial war. Theocratic Islamic fundamentalists , of course, engage in similar simplistic binary discourse and projection of evil onto the Other, which they use to legitimate acts of terrorism. For certain Islamic fundamentalists, the United States is "evil," the source of all the world's problems, and deserves to be destroyed. Such one-dimensional thought does not distinguish between U.S. policies, leaders, institutions, or people when it advocates a Jihad against the American monolithic evil. The terrorist crimes of September 11 appeared to be part of this Jihad, and show the horrific consequences of totally dehumanizing an "enemy" as so evil that even innocent members of the group in question deserve to be exterminated.

As Tariq Ali noted (2002), the war on terror became a "clash of fundamentalisms" in which both sides deployed Manichean discourses to whip up hatred of the Other and to incite violence and war. The media were the instruments of both. Conservative commentators on U.S. television, for example, offered one-sided accounts of the cause of the September 11 events, blaming their favorite opponents in the current U.S. political spectrum. For Christian fundamentalist Jerry Falwell, with the verbal agreement of Christian Broadcast Network President Pat Robertson, the culpability for this "horror beyond words" fell on liberals, feminists, gays, and the American Civil Liberties Union (ACLU). Jerry

Falwell said: "The abortionists have got to bear some burden for this because God will not be mocked. And when we destroy 40 million little innocent babies, we make God mad. I really believe that the pagans, and the abortionists, and the feminists, and the gays and the lesbians who are actively trying to make that an alternative lifestyle, the ACLU, People for the American Way—all of them who have tried to secularize America—I point the finger in their face and say, 'You helped this happen.'" But in fact, when Falwell's critics pointed out that this argument is similar to a right-wing Islamic claim that the United States is fundamentally corrupt and evil and thus deserves God's wrath, they forced him to apologize.

For right-wingers like Gary Aldrich, president and founder of the Patrick Henry Center, it was the liberals who were at fault: "Excuse me if I absent myself from the national political group-hug that's going on. You see, I believe the Liberals are largely responsible for much of what happened Tuesday, and may God forgive them. These people exist in a world that lies beyond the normal standards of decency and civility." Rush Limbaugh argued incessantly that it was all Bill Clinton's fault. James Baker blamed the catastrophe on the 1976 Church report, which led to limits on the powers of the Central Intelligence Agency.

On the issue of appropriate response, right-wing columnist Ann Coulter declared: "We know who the homicidal maniacs are. They are the ones cheering and dancing right now. We should invade their countries, kill their leaders, and convert them to Christianity."[8] Shortly after this and other outbursts, Coulter was fired from *National Review* when she reacted negatively to efforts by its editors to tone down her rhetoric, making her a martyr among right-wing sympathizers. Later, Coulter stated in a speech that American Taliban John Walker Lindh should be executed so that liberals and the left can get the message that they can be killed if they get out of line! Ideologue William Bennett came out and urged that the United States declare war on Iraq, Iran, Syria, Libya, and whoever else harbored terrorists. On the Canadian Broadcasting Network, former Reagan administration Deputy Secretary of Defense Frank Gaffney suggested that the United States needed to go after the sponsors of these states as well, such as China and Russia, to the astonishment and derision of the Canadian audience. Right-wing Internet sites buzzed with talk of dropping nuclear bombs on Afghanistan, exterminating all Muslims, and whatever other fantasy popped into their heads.

Radio was even more frightening. Not surprisingly, talk radio oozed hatred, calling for violence against Arabs and Muslims, nuclear retaliation, and global war. As the days went by, even mainstream radio news became hyperdramatic, replete with patriotic music and war propaganda. National Public Radio, Pacifica, and some programs attempted rational discussion and debate, but on the whole talk radio was all propaganda, all the time. Hence, broadcast media allowed dangerous zealots to circulate the most aggressive, fanatic, and sometimes lunatic views, creating a consensus around the need for immediate military action and all-out war. Few cooler heads appeared on any of the major television networks, which repeatedly beat the war drums day after day, driving the country into hysteria and making it certain that there would be a military response and war.

Anthrax, Afghanistan, and Terror Hysteria

Clearly, the media and the Bush administration cultivated post–9/11 panic with their obsessive focus on terrorism, warnings of further threats, and demands for retaliation. But as Michael Moore's 2001 film *Bowling for Columbine* and his 2004 film *Fahrenheit 9/11* demonstrate, the U.S. corporate media have been exploiting fear for decades in their incessant dramatization of murder and violence, along with a wide range of threats from within everyday life ranging from fears of diseases like SARS to growing crimes, as well as hyping threats from terrorism and foreign enemies. After 9/11, the media became weapons of mass hysteria that made Americans look to the government for protection, rendering the population malleable to manipulation.

Indeed, since the September 11 strikes, the Bush administration had arguably used fear tactics to advance its political agenda, including tax breaks for the rich and deregulation for corporate supporters, curtailment of social programs, military buildup, draconian assaults on U.S. constitutional rights in the so-called USA Patriot Act, and a new doctrine of preemptive strikes.[9] Both the corporate media and Democratic Party did not vigorously contest Bush's positions on terrorism and the Democrats voting overwhelmingly for Bush's authority to take whatever steps necessary to attack terrorists, as well as supporting the so-called USA Patriot Act. Most of the rest of the world, and significant sectors within U.S. society (however invisible on television) opposed Bush administration policies and called for more multilateral approaches to problems like terrorism.

The Bush administration was able to push through his extremist agenda because the complicit media helped continually generate fearful citizens ready to accept curtailment of their freedoms to make them secure. Within a short time after the 9/11 terrorist attacks, the mail system was polluted by anthrax, intensifying the hysteria. Since infected letters were sent to politicians and corporate media, there was maximum public attention to the dangers of a lethal anthrax attack, making postal work, mail delivery, and the opening of mail a traumatic event, infused with fear. This is exactly the goal of terrorism, and media hysteria over anthrax attacks went far in promoting the war fever that led the public to unquestionably support whatever military retaliation or domestic politics the Bush administration chose to exert. Although the Bush administration seemed at first to blame the Al Qaeda network and then Iraq for the anthrax attacks, it appears that the high grade of anthrax used had the genetic footprint of U.S. laboratories in Fort Detrick, Maryland. Eventually the FBI and academic experts came to believe the source of the attacks was an individual working for the U.S. defense and biological weapons establishment.[10] In August 2002, the FBI very publicly interviewed a U.S. anthrax scientist suspected in the case, who strongly denied his guilt, raising the question of whether the FBI had collared the culprit or were setting up a patsy. Later reports that the CIA received the Ames anthrax cultures from Fort Detrick create the chilling possibility that groups within the CIA were involved in the anthrax attacks and may have had previous knowledge of the September 11 attacks.[11]

From September 11 to the beginning of the U.S. bombing acts on Afghanistan in October, the U.S. corporate media intensified war fever, and there was an orgy of patriotism such as the country had not seen since World War II. Media frames shifted from "America under Attack" to "America Strikes Back" even before any military action was undertaken, as if the media frames were to conjure the military response that eventually followed. From September 11 to and through the war on Afghanistan, the networks generated escalating fear as the mouthpieces of the military-industrial complex demanded military action with little serious reflection on its consequences visible on the television networks. There was, by contrast, much intelligent discussion on the Internet of the problematical nature of U.S. military intervention in Afghanistan and the need for more multilateral forces.

For example, Sir Michael Howard, the eminent British historian, gave a talk against calling the terror attacks "war" that was widely reproduced and discussed in the print media and on the Internet. Howard argued that it was "a terrible and irrevocable error" to refer to the current campaign against terrorism as a "war," rather than a criminal action, since it bestowed unwarranted legitimacy on the terrorists, mythologized them within the Arab and western world, and created unrealistic expectations for successful military action and victory. Saying the U.S. saturation bombing of Afghanistan was "like trying to eradicate cancer cells with a blowtorch," Howard argued that a "police operation conducted under the auspices of the United Nations" would have been far preferable.[12] In retrospect, using police and military forces from the many U.S. allies who had volunteered their services and were shoved away by Bush, Cheney, and Rumsfeld would have provided a better chance of capturing key Al Qaeda and Taliban forces involved in terrorism and could have arguably produced a more secure Afghanistan (see Kellner 2003a).

Instead, the United States was seized by war fever and there was little criticism of Bush administration or Pentagon policy, despite the many flaws of their Afghan intervention. To keep the public in a constantly heightened state of fear, new Homeland Security Director Tom Ridge and Attorney General John Ashcroft repeatedly made highly publicized and frightening warnings of the dangers of new terrorist attacks, issuing one alert on October 11, another on October 29, and a third on December 3. The media, especially Fox TV and the cable news networks, hyped these reports and helped foment growing mass hysteria that made the public susceptible to political manipulation.

It was, of course, in the corporate media's interest to keep the public in a heightened state of alert with their eyes fixed on media screens, thus increasing corporate profit. Questioning the Bush administration, however, was labeled unpatriotic and even treasonous. Right-wing groups circulated lists of allegedly suspect citizens who refused to go along with the Bush administration war on terrorism and put heavy pressure on any media organization that dared to criticize the Bush administration.[13] During the war on Afghanistan, top executives of CNN circulated a memo telling reporters that if they showed news unfavorable to the United States, such as civilian casualties from U.S. bombing there, they should remind viewers that thousands of Americans died in the 9/11 attacks. In a memo to his international correspondents, Walter Isaacson said: "As we get good reports from Taliban-controlled Afghanistan, we must redouble our efforts to make sure we do not seem to be simply reporting from their vantage or perspective. We must talk about how the Taliban are using civilian shields and how the Taliban have harbored the terrorists responsible for killing close to 5,000 innocent people."[14] Likewise, an editor of the *Panama City News-Herald* in Florida sent a memo telling reporters, "DO NOT USE photos on Page 1A showing civilian casualties from the U.S. war on Afghanistan. Our sister paper in Fort Walton Beach has done so and received hundreds and hundreds of threatening e-mails and the like. DO NOT USE wire stories which lead with civilian casualties from the U.S. war on Afghanistan. They should be mentioned further down in the story. If the story needs rewriting to play down the civilian casualties, DO IT. The only exception is if the U.S. hits an orphanage, school or similar facility and kills scores or hundreds of children."[15]

The Taliban quickly collapsed, but bin Laden, Mullah Omar, and other Al Qaeda and Taliban leaders got away. Stories eventually emerged indicating that the U.S. reliance on airpower and bombing for the Afghanistan intervention had killed hundreds, perhaps thousands, of innocent Afghan civilians.[16] The Pentagon refused to make any estimates concerning civilian casualties from U.S. bombing in Afghanistan. But various human rights organizations estimated between 1,200 to 2,000 civilian casualties, and the interim Afghanistan government estimated them at 1,000 to 2,000. Marc Herod estimated "that between 3,125 and 3,620 Afghan civilians were killed between October 7 [2001] and July 31 [2002]."[17] Jonathan Steele wrote:

> The direct victims of American bombs and missiles have commanded most political and media attention, though no one is certain how many even of these there were.
>
> A *Guardian* report in February estimated these casualties at between 1,300 and 8,000 deaths. A *Guardian* investigation into the "indirect victims" now confirms the belief of many aid agencies that they exceeded the number who died of direct hits.
>
> As many as 20,000 Afghans may have lost their lives as an indirect consequence of the U.S. intervention. They too belong in any tally of the dead.
>
> The bombing had three main effects on the humanitarian situation. It caused massive dislocation by prompting hundreds of thousands of Afghans to flee from their homes. It stopped aid supplies to drought victims who depended on emergency relief. It provoked an upsurge in fighting and turned a military stalemate into one of chaotic fluidity, leading yet more people to flee.[18]

Yet there was little corporate media criticism of the Afghanistan intervention and the Bush administration fiercely resisted any attempts to investigate how 9/11 had happened. When the Democrats suggested that a bipartisan inquiry of the sort that had taken place after Pearl Harbor or the Kennedy assassination look into how so many U.S. agencies failed to prevent the 9/11 terrorist attacks, Vice President Dick Cheney told Tom Daschle that no investigation into 9/11 was possible while the United States was at war. The Bush administration continued to strongly resist any 9/11 hearings until public pressure finally forced them to appoint an official 9/11 Commission, which eventually published a report indicating structural problems with U.S. intelligence but not pointing fingers of responsibility at specific members of the Bush administration.[19]

The lack of debate in the U.S. corporate media over the proper response to the 9/11 terrorist attacks and the Bush administration's largely unilateral military response points to an intensifying crisis of democracy in the United States.[20]

The media in a democracy are supposed to provide facts and a wide range of opinions for an informed citizenry, debate issues of national importance, reject spin and lies, and hold leaders accountable for mistakes and wrong policies. The Bush administration was not held accountable by the corporate media for allowing 9/11 to happen on its watch by ignoring clear warnings of coming attacks, for their flawed response in attacking Afghanistan, or for their disastrous invasion of Iraq, upon which I will focus in the next two chapters of this book.

In a way, the Bush administration and corporate media intensified bin Laden and Al Qaeda's success. Bin Laden had become a "revolutionary myth," looked upon with awe by millions throughout the world, and Bush had helped Jihad recruitment with an excessively focused air war on Afghanistan, but failed to put U.S. or other allied troops on the ground to shut down Al Qaeda. Yet the 9/11 attacks had magically transformed the bumbling Bush into a wartime leader, he was able to push through his right-wing agenda, and he was soon to create another major war and media spectacle to promote a complex set of interests. As we shall see in the following pages, using war and media spectacle to promote covert agendas is a Bush family strategy.

Bush Family War Spectacles

War itself has become a media spectacle in which successive U.S. regimes have used military extravaganzas to promote their agendas. The Reagan administration repeatedly used military spectacle to deflect attention from its foreign policy failures and economic problems. Two Bush administrations and the Clinton administration famously "wagged the dog," using military spectacle to deflect attention from embarrassing domestic or foreign policy blunders, or in Clinton's case, a sex scandal that led to his impeachment (Kellner 2003c).

The Gulf War of 1990–1991 was the global media spectacle of its era, captivating worldwide audiences as the first live television war, and was intended in part to save the first Bush presidency, before the war's ambiguous outcome and a declining economy helped defeat the Bush presidential campaign of 1992. In the summer of 1990, the elder Bush's popularity was declining, he had promised "no new taxes" and then raised taxes, and it appeared that he would not be reelected. Bush Senior's salvation seemed to appear in the figure of Saddam Hussein and his August 1990 invasion of Kuwait, which allowed Bush to organize a military intervention to displace him.

Bush and the Reagan administration had supported Iraq during the Iran-Iraq war of 1980–1988, and during his presidency, Bush Senior continued to provide loans and programs that enabled Hussein to build up his military (Kellner 1992; Friedman 1993). In a series of articles in the *Los Angeles Times*, Murray Waas documented how George H. W. Bush actively promoted U.S. trade with Iraq in the 1980s and helped block attempts to criticize Iraq or impose sanctions on it until weeks before the Iraqi invasion of Kuwait. Classified documents show that Bush, first as vice president and then as president, intervened repeatedly over a period of almost a decade to obtain special assistance for Saddam Hussein—financial aid as well as access to hi-tech equipment critical to Iraq's quest for nuclear and chemical arms. In Waas's summary:

In June 1984 Vice President Bush telephoned the president of the Export-Import Bank to urge approval of a $500 million loan guarantee for Iraq to build an oil pipeline. Ex-Im, which had been reluctant, approved.

In February 1987 Vice President Bush telephoned the Ex-Im president to press for $200 million in loan guarantees. Economists warned the bank that Iraq could not repay the loans, but the bank approved the guarantees.

In March 1987 the Commerce Department approved export licenses for shipment to Iraq of dual-use technology, useful for scientific or military purposes. Over the next few years exports of this kind totaled $600 million, and much of the equipment may have gone into aerial spying and other military uses.

In August 1988 a cease-fire ended the Iran-Iraq war. But the American tilt toward Iraq continued. Some intelligence was being provided as late as May 1990.

In 1989 Bush, now president, signed a national security order directing government agencies to improve ties with Iraq.

In October 1989 Secretary of State James A. Baker telephoned Secretary of Agriculture Clayton Yeutter and urged him to approve $1 billion in new loan guarantees to Iraq despite fears that the credits were being misused. In November Yeutter approved the guarantees.

In January 1990 President Bush signed an executive order finding that it would not be "in the national interest" for the Ex-Im Bank to stop loan guarantees to Iraq.

In April and again in June 1990 the Commerce Department proposed restrictions on hi-technology exports to Iraq. An interagency group chaired by Robert M. Gates, then deputy national security adviser to Bush, rejected the proposals.

In July 1990 the Senate voted overwhelmingly to cut off loan guarantees to Iraq because of Saddam's human rights violations, including the gassing of a Kurdish village. The administration condemned the vote.

On July 31, 1990, with 100,000 Iraqi troops massed at the Kuwait border, Assistant Secretary of State John Kelly went to Capitol Hill and testified against ending loan guarantees to Iraq.

On Aug. 2, 1990, Iraq invaded Kuwait.[21]

Bush Senior's friend Saddam Hussein was not grateful for all of the favors received and used the impressive military machine that the Reagan and Bush Senior administrations had helped finance to invade oil-rich Kuwait, which Iraq claimed was stealing its oil and was historically part of its empire (see Kellner 1992). When Iraq marched into Kuwait, Bush Senior mobilized an international coalition to wage war to oust the Iraqis from their neighboring oil emirate, demonizing Hussein as "another Hitler" and major threat to world peace and the global economy. Bush refused serious diplomatic efforts to induce Iraq to leave Kuwait. Instead, Bush the elder appeared to want a war to promote U.S. military clout as the dominant global police force, to save his own failing political fortunes, and to exert more U.S. influence over oil supplies and policies (Kellner 1992). The televised drama of the 1991 Gulf War provided exciting media spectacles that engrossed a global audience and that seemed to ensure Bush's reelection (he enjoyed 90 percent popularity at the end of the war).

After the war, Bush Senior and his National Security Advisor Brent Scowcroft enthusiastically proclaimed a "New World Order" in which U.S. military power would be used to settle conflicts and solve problems, and make the United States the hegemonic force in the world. Such a dream was not (yet) to be, however, as the Gulf War peace negotiations allowed Saddam Hussein to remain in power and the United States failed to aide Shiite forces in the south and Kurds in the north of Iraq to overthrow him. Images of the slaughter of Kurds and Shiites throughout the global media proved negative and helped code the 1991 Gulf War as a failure, or extremely limited success. Hence, the spectacle of a messy endgame to the war in Iraq and the continued reign of Saddam Hussein, combined with a poor economy, helped defeat Bush Senior in 1992.

At the time of the September 11 terrorist attacks, Bush Junior faced the same prospects of a failed presidency that his father confronted in the summer of 1990. The economy was suffering one of the worst declines in U.S. history, and after ramming through a right-wing agenda on behalf of the corporations that had supported his 2000 election (Kellner 2001), Bush lost control of the political agenda in May 2001 when a Republican senator, James Jeffords, became an independent who mostly voted with the Democrats. But the September 11 terrorist attacks provided an opportunity for George W. Bush to reseize political initiative and to boost his popularity.

The brief war against the Taliban—which hosted Osama bin Laden and Al Qaeda—in Afghanistan from early October through December 2001 appeared to be a military victory for the United States. After a month of stalemate following ruthless U.S. bombing, the Taliban collapsed in the north of the country, abandoned the capital Kabul, and surrendered its southern strongholds (Kellner 2003a). Yet the war in Afghanistan, like the elder Bush's Gulf War, was ambiguous in its outcome. Although the Taliban regime collapsed under U.S. military pressure, the top leaders and many Al Qaeda militants escaped. Violent warlords the United States used to fight Al Qaeda kept the country in a state of disarray, record amounts of opium poured out of the country, and Taliban sympathizers and Islamicists continue to wield power. Because the United States did not use ground troops or multilateral military forces, Osama bin Laden escaped, Pakistan was allowed to send in planes that took out hundreds of rebel Pakistanis and numerous top Al Qaeda militants, and Afghanistan remains a dangerous and unstable country (Kellner 2003a).

Unlike the 1991 Gulf War, which produced media images of precision bombs and missiles destroying Iraqi targets and the brief spectacle of the flight of the Iraqis from Kuwait during the liberation of Kuwait City, the Afghanistan war was more hidden in its unfolding and effects. Many of the images of Afghanistan circulated throughout the global media were of the civilian casualties (labeled "collateral damage" by the Pentagon), the suffering of Afghan people caused by U.S. bombing, and the thousands of refugees from war, which raised questions about the U.S. strategy and intervention. Moreover, just as the survival of Saddam Hussein ultimately coded Gulf War I as problematic, the continued existence of Osama bin Laden and his top Al Qaeda leadership pointed to the limitations of the younger Bush's leadership and policies.

By early 2002, George W. Bush faced a situation similar to that of his father after the Gulf War. Despite victory against the Taliban, the limited success of the war and a failing economy provided a situation that threatened his reelection. Thus Bush Junior needed a dramatic media spectacle that would help produce positive election prospects for 2004, and once again Saddam Hussein provided a viable target. We'll see in the next two chapters how Bush's war on terror policy envisages an era of perpetual war against terrorism and the countries that support it, a situation in which media spectacle is used to promote policies of unilateral aggression.

Notes

1. This study draws upon my books *The Persian Gulf TV War* (1992); *Media Spectacle* (2003c); and *From 9/11 to Terror War: The Dangers of the Bush Legacy* (2003a).
2. See Collins in Collins and Glover 2002, pp. 155–174. Collins and Glover's collection *Collateral Language* interrogates many of the concepts used in post–9/11 politi-

cal discourse, highlighting the importance of language in mobilizing political consensus, legitimizing policies, and constructing political realities.

3. For histories of the Al Qaeda network, see Kepel (2002); and Rashid (2001, 2002).

4. In the winter of 2001, I attended a three-part symposium telecast live in the Beverly Hills Museum of Radio and Television, which included media executives and broadcasters throughout the world who described how they processed the events of September 11. Representatives from Canada, European countries, China, and elsewhere described how they obtained footage to broadcast, how the 9/11 story dominated their respective media sources, and how the story was truly global in reach. An archive of worldwide video and commentary on September 11 is available at http://www.911digitalarchive.org and http://tvnews3.televisionarchive.org/tvarchive/html/index.

5. For critique of Huntington's "civilization" versus "barbarism" discourse, see Achcar (2002); Chomsky (2001); and Kellner (2003a).

6. The connections between Bush, Baker and Carlyle, along with Cheney and Halliburton were documented in many British newspapers, the *New York Times,* and other sources collected on www.bushwatch.com, along with Phil Agre's Red Rock Eater at http://dlis.gseis.ucla.edu/people/pagre/rre.html. See also Melanie Warner, "The Big Guys Work for the Carlyle Group," *Fortune,* March 18, 2002, and Kellner (2003b). On Bechtel, Rumsfeld, and oil, see David Lindorff, "Secret Bechtel Documents Reveal: Yes, It Is about Oil," *Counterpunch Special Report,* April 9, 2003, at http://www.counterpunch.org/lindorff04092003.html. I probe the role of the Cheney-Halliburton connection in Election 2004 in Chapter 3 and in the Conclusion.

7. For systematic analysis of Bushspeak and its Orwellian lineage, see Kellner (2001) and Chapter 5 of this book.

8. For systematic critique of Coulter and other extreme right media pundits, see Alterman (2003); Brock (2004); and Franken (2003).

9. See Kellner (2003a) and Chapters 3 and 4 of this book.

10. See the evidence assembled by scientist Barbara Hatch Rosenberg at http://www.ph.ucla.edu/epi/bioter/compilationofanthraxevidence.html, indicating the likelihood that the anthrax attacks were the work of a U.S. bioweapons establishment insider.

11. See "Anthrax Attack Bug 'Identical' to Army Strain" at www.newscientist.com, May 2, 2002. See also the study by Richard Ochs, "Government by Anthrax," at www.freefromterror.net, and Wayne Madsen's "Anthrax and the Agency—Thinking the Unthinkable," at http://www.counterpunch.org/madsenanthrax.html, April 8–9, 2002, p. 3. Curiously, as I write in the winter of 2004, the anthrax mystery has not yet been officially solved.

12. Howard's speech was published on www.thisislondon.com, on October 31, 2001, and was widely distributed via the Internet.

13. Lynne Cheney, wife of Vice President Dick Cheney and a longtime right-wing activist, distributed one such list; see Defense of Civilization Fund, "Defending Civilization:

How Our Universities Are Failing America and What Can Be Done About It?" at www.goacta.org, November 2001. Another missive widely distributed at the same time had Senator Joseph Lieberman (D-Conn.) as Cheney's cosigner, an ignoble fall for Al Gore's vice-presidential running mate. Lynne Cheney and her right-wing allies had long dreamed of crushing radical voices of dissent in the universities and had long waged a cultural war against their academic enemies. The conservative Jihad was launched during the Reagan era when Ms. Cheney was head of the NEH, which she governed like a Taliban, rooting out all "politically incorrect" policies and personnel. There was some speculation that the U.S. left/right culture wars were suspended in favor of national unity against terrorism, but obviously Cheney and her Taliban were not going to miss a chance to go after their longtime adversaries.

14. Howard Kurtz, "CNN Chief Orders 'Balance' in War News: Reporters Are Told to Remind Viewers Why U.S. Is Bombing," *Washington Post,* October 31, 2001, p. C01.

15. "ACTION ALERT: Fox—Civilian Casualties Not News." FAIR, November 8, 2001, at http://www.fair.org/activism/fox-civilian-casualties.html. The article contains many examples of pundits excoriating anyone who complains about civilian casualties from U.S. bombing of Afghanistan.

16. See Dexter Filkins, "Flaws in U.S. Air War Left Hundreds of Civilians Dead," *New York Times,* July 21, 2002.

17. Marc C. Herod, "Counting the Dead," *Guardian,* August 8, 2002, and http://www.cursor.org/stories/civilian_deaths.htm. See also Carl Conetta, "Operation Enduring Freedom: Why a Higher Rate of Civilian Bombing Casualties," Project on Defense Alternatives Briefing Report #11 at http://www.comw.org/pda/0201oef.html. David Zucchino, in "'The Americans … They Just Drop Their Bombs and Leave'" (*Los Angeles Times,* June 2, 2002), writes that in an investigation of 194 incidents of civilian casualties from U.S. bombing from October 7 to February 28, the *Times* found at least 1,071 to 1,201 civilians could be confirmed as killed by U.S. bombs.

18. Jonathan Steele, "Forgotten Victims," *Guardian,* May 20, 2002.

19. See the *9/11 Commission Report* (2004).

20. For my previous accounts of the media and the crisis of democracy, see Kellner (1990, 1992, 2001, and 2003a).

21. Murray Waas, *Los Angeles Times,* May 7, 1992. A recent book by Chambers Johnson, *The Sorrows of Empire* (2004, pp. 223ff.), documents how the CIA helped install Saddam Hussein, provided military assistance to Iraq during the 1980s war with Iran, and provided loans and material that enabled him to develop his weapons programs, including chemical and biological weapons.

Chapter 3

Preemptive Strikes and the War on Iraq: A Critique of Bush Administration Unilateralism and Militarism

BUSH ADMINISTRATION FOREIGN POLICY has exhibited a marked unilateralism and militarism in which U.S. military power is used to advance U.S. interests and geopolitical hegemony. The policy was first evident in the Afghanistan intervention following the September 11, 2001, terrorist attacks, and informed the 2003 war against Iraq. In *From 9/11 to Terror War* (2003) I sketched out the genesis of Bush administration foreign policy and its application in Afghanistan and the build-up to the Iraq war. In this study, I update my critique of the Bush doctrine of preemptive strikes with its application in the 2003 Iraq invasion, and develop a critique of Bush's unilateralism and militarism. Against the Bush administration, I will defend multilateral and global solutions to problems such as terrorism, so-called "weapons of mass destruction," and "rogue regimes."[1]

The "Axis of Evil," Operation Infinite War, and Bush's Attacks on U.S. Democracy

> There is no worse mistake in public leadership than to hold out false hopes soon to be swept away. The British people can face peril or misfortune with fortitude and buoyancy, but they bitterly resent being deceived or finding that those responsible for their affairs are themselves dwelling in a fool's paradise.
>
> —*Winston Churchill*

45

In his televised State of the Union address on January 29, 2002, George W. Bush promised an epoch of "War on Terror," expanding his doctrine to not only go after terrorists and those who harbor terrorist groups, but to include those countries making weapons of mass destruction. Claiming that Iraq, Iran, and North Korea constituted "an axis of evil, arming to threaten the peace of the world," Bush put the "world's most dangerous regimes" on notice that he was planning to escalate the war on terror. Rattling the saber and making it clear that he was perfectly ready to "wag the dog" if domestic scandals and economic failures threatened his popularity, Bush put "rogue states" and terrorists everywhere on notice that he was prepared to go to war indefinitely against an array of targets.

As was becoming the norm, Bush's team was able to orchestrate an impressive media event for his State of the Union speech, with celebrities like Hamid Karzai, interim president of Afghanistan, in the audience next to Laura Bush, along with members of U.S. military families, New York firefighters, and other icons of September 11. Moreover, Bush was learning to read his teleprompter speeches with proper emphasis and pronunciation, but was not able to rid himself of his telltale smirk, darting eyes, and increasing arrogance and self-satisfaction. He also took the occasion to announce new dangers to the United States via plans found in Afghanistan to blow up U.S. nuclear installations, public monuments, and other targets.

In fact, these documents had been found weeks before and had already been discussed in the media, so Bush was simply using the threats to legitimate his own militarist agenda and to deflect attention from his own failings at economic policy, along with his involvement and that of others in his administration in the Enron and other corporate scandals. Certainly, terrorism remained a threat to the United States, but to exaggerate the dangers, to escalate war, and to engage in hyperbolic rhetoric is arguably not the way to deal with the problem. In a round of television interviews that preceded Bush's address, his adviser Karen Hughes claimed that Americans face dangers from up to 100,000 terrorists trained in Afghanistan and deployed worldwide. Hughes, who has made a career of lying for Bush, made it clear that the war on terror would be a major focus of Bush administration policy. Terrorist experts were dumbfounded at the spinmistress's far-fetched numbers; Stanley Bedlington, a former CIA terrorism analyst, insisted that "Al Qaeda has never had that kind of strength." Bedlington continued: "I just came back from a luncheon with about 15 specialists. If I dropped that like a rock into a stagnant pool, there would be roars of laughter" (Associated Press, January 29, 2002).

Likewise Bush's use of the term "evil" (five times in his State of the Union address alone) was becoming tiresome and worrisome to many. Furthermore, what Bush did not talk about in the State of the Union speech was also significant. He did not mention Osama bin Laden and the Al Qaeda and Taliban leadership that he had failed to apprehend. Bush did not refer to the stunning budget deficit that his fiscal mismanagement had produced, glossing over the reversal in one year from the largest surplus in U.S. history to a stunning $100-billion-plus deficit (with estimates rising by the week).[2] Bush claimed that the "state of the union had never been so good," but in fact during Bush's presidency the U.S. economy was suffering massive unemployment, the Enron scandal was harming investor confidence and pointing to glaring problems that Bushonomics had helped produce, and the national deficit was skyrocketing.

Not only had the Bush administration declared war against open government by refusing to release reports of Dick Cheney's meetings with Enron and other energy corporation executives in formulating Bush administration energy policy, but there were accounts that both Bush and Cheney were pressuring Democratic Senate Majority Leader Tom Daschle against looking too closely into the failures of U.S. intelligence that made September 11 possible. Cheney himself was head of a U.S. counterterrorist group and it would be interesting to know if he had heard any of the warnings of September 11. Several websites have collected a series of prior warnings to foreign and U.S. governments that a major terrorist attack was aimed for the United States in September of 2001, which the Bush administration seemed to neglect. If the public knew of this documentation, it would surely be a major scandal for Bush (see Kellner 2003a).[3]

As the Enron Wars heated up, there were dangers for the Bush administration that the entire web of entanglements with Enron and other shady corporations would become unraveled. If the shocking program of deregulation pushed by Bush and Cheney, favors to corporate contributors, and failure to provide security, making the United States vulnerable to terror attacks and economic collapse, were brought to the light of day, the Bush administration would suffer the consequences. Incredibly, Bush was using the Enron collapse to push his tax give-away-to-the-rich program and discredited pension plan. Although Bush did not mention Enron in his speech, the day after the State of the Union speech, Bush called for pension reform in the light of the Enron collapse, using the tragedy to push Social Security privatization, telling workers that they would be better off with retirement plans in which they could choose to invest their own savings, as if the Enron scandal had not revealed the danger of investment in the stock market![4]

Moreover, in his State of the Union address, George W. Bush out-voodooed Ronald Reagan in his calls for wildly increased military spending, a jump in homeland security spending, large tax cuts for the wealthy, *and* a 9 percent increase in basic government programs. Bush was willing to finance this budget with a more than $100 billion budget deficit for 2002, an $80 billion deficit for 2003, and a projected $5-trillion-plus deficit by 2008! One tries to imagine the uproar this would create if the Democrats had urged such irresponsible deficit-funding of the government. It was startlingly clear that the Bush administration was returning to the giant deficit spending that had doubled the national debt during the Reagan years, and as his father before him in his failed four years of economic mismanagement doubled the national debt once again. Responsible economists believed that it was necessary to keep the deficit and national debt under control to ensure U.S. economic stability, but once again the Bush administration embarked on an extremely dangerous economic policy for the U.S. and global economy.

Looked at more closely, Bush's State of the Union address could be read as a cunning use of terror to push through his indefensible domestic programs like the Star Wars missile program, his tax giveaway to the rich, and his conservative social programs (for example, the idea that people and charities would solve social problems and not government). The "evil axis" countries could be used to legitimate producing the Star Wars missile defense system, which critics claimed had not been proven workable.[5] Although on one hand, the very notion of an "axis of evil" suggests Bush administration geopolitical confusion and misunderstanding, on the other, it opens the way to arbitrary military intervention. By calling attention to countries that produce weapons of mass destruction, it legitimates a missile defense system that will allegedly protect the United States against nuclear missile attack.

The emphasis on patriotism and community service in the State of the Union seemed to give Bush credence as a compassionate conservative, as opposed to a hard-right ideologue and selfish manipulator of crisis and tragedy for his own political ends. But the themes of patriotism, national unity, and moral community function both to identify his party and policies with patriotism, but also to identify anyone who criticized his foreign or domestic policies as "unpatriotic." Lynne Cheney, wife of U.S. Vice President Dick Cheney and a longtime cultural warrior against the left, circulated texts documenting "unpatriotic" statements by university professors. Since September 11, 2001, Mrs. Cheney had led an assault against dissidents to Bush administration policy on the grounds that they were not patriotic when they did not support the president in a time of war and danger.[6] Stressing national unity and patriotism was thus providing a cover for suppressing dissent, which in itself threatened U.S. democracy, revealing the dangerous antidemocracy sentiments of the Bush-Cheney regime. Moreover, appropriating the language of moral community for "homeland defense" redefines that community as those who identify with conservative U.S. government policy. It also subordinates discourse of social justice, civil rights, and democracy in the name of national unity, a move that can easily be used to suppress progressive agendas.

Thus Bush was using the terrorist attacks and national security concerns to push through his right-wing agenda. Although Congress wildly applauded Bush's jingoistic and aggressive speech, the rest of the world was stunned by the irresponsibility of Bush's "axis of evil" doctrine. The *Guardian* labeled Bush's escalation of militarist rhetoric "Hate of the Union," and an editorial in the paper cited "George Bush's delusion" that the September 11 tragedy gave him a free hand to lead the world into infinite war (January 31, 2002). The French paper *Liberation* found Bush's tone "more martial than ever," and *Le Monde* noted that U.S. allies Russia and China were chief suppliers of "military programs" in the countries Bush singled out. The Russians complained that their allies were being included in the axis and that their improving relations with Washington would be subverted if Bush expanded the field of war. Close allies Germany and Japan were put off that Bush used the loaded word "axis," which evoked World War II and the crimes of the Third Reich and Japanese, legacies their countries had tried to overcome.

A number of countries were upset about Bush's threat to act unilaterally against terrorism if "some governments were timid in the face of terror." Bush's jibe was aimed against countries like the Philippines, which insisted that it had been resolute and effective allies in the work against terrorism. And, of course, Iran, Iraq, and North Korea were shocked that Bush had collapsed them into "an axis of evil," which inadvertently strengthened the hands of hard-liners within these regimes to resist accommodation with the West, especially the United States, which was threatening them with extinction.

The State of the Union address showed the dangerous demagoguery overtaking George W. Bush. Bereft of ideas and insight, Bush seemed an empty vessel programmed by right-wing ideologues. The surreal nature of the "axis of evil" discourse shows a desperate willingness to say and do anything to assert U.S. power and to justify U.S. aggression. Yet the Bush doctrine is the logical extreme of his father's "new world order" in which the United States acts as the superpolice of the world, the beacon of civilization able to define "evil" and go after whoever it labels in this category. But such discourse serves as a cloak for a project of U.S. domination and global hegemony, promoting the "full spectrum dominance" certain Pentagon ideologues have long dreamed of achieving.

In the view of European critics Bush's speech showed that "the Bush administration is not now primarily engaged in a war against terrorism at all," but of

U.S. world dominance, thus "abandoning whatever remaining moral high ground the U.S. held onto in the wake of September 11."[7] David Talbot commented in *Salon* (February 14, 2002) that Bush's rhetoric is a "flight of idiocy" that reveals how Bush sees the world in the simplistic "black-and-white terms of the born-again fundamentalist that he is."

Bush's term "axis of evil," a throw-back to the fascist triadic axis of the 1940s, is indeed highly misleading and semantically inaccurate. An "axis" implies a coalition between countries embarking on a common project of domination. Iraq and Iran have long been bitter enemies, fighting a vicious war between 1980 and 1988 (in which the United States covertly supported both sides, leading to the Iran-Contra scandal and helping to produce the Iraqi military machine that invaded Kuwait and prompted the Gulf War; see Kellner 1992). North Korea, of course, has no connection to Iraq and Iran, and its neighbors South Korea, Japan, and bordering countries were extremely distressed by Bush's rhetoric, which reportedly harmed the faction in South Korea trying to moderate North Korea's behavior, and helped the conservative faction promoting a hardline stance against North Korea.

Choosing Iran as part of the tripartite axis is an act of stupendous geopolitical ignorance, which stunned that country and others around the world. Iran had shown great sympathy for the U.S. intervention in Afghanistan, strongly condemned the September 11 attacks and the Al Qaeda network (which had long been a strategic enemy), pledged itself to help extricate U.S. troops in danger in Afghanistan, and supplied humanitarian aid there. Moreover, within Iran there had been pro-American and antigovernment demonstrations in recent months, showing a desire especially on the part of the young to reach out to the West. There have also been recurrent reports of Iran currying favor with Afghan warlords, perhaps undermining the central government in the region. But counter to many western powers' efforts to aid and strengthen serious reform movements in Iran, Bush's hostility against Iran was reinforcing the credibility of conservative and antiwestern factions in the country.

Moreover, how could Iran be deemed part of an "axis of evil" over, say, Saudi Arabia, after 15 of the 19 terrorists came from that kingdom? It was well known that Al Qaeda had its strongest financial and personnel support network in Saudi Arabia, where bin Laden's family had long lived. There were reportedly over 100 Saudis in the Guantanamo Bay camp that had been the focus of controversy, with a Saudi diplomat recently calling for their release. The controversial "dinner with bin Laden" videotape that had been played with such fanfare by the Bush administration near the end of the war on Afghanistan showed strong support within Saudi Arabia for bin Laden, and a recent poll had indicated that 95 percent of the Saudis were sympathetic to bin Laden (see Unger [2004], Hersh [2004]).

Furthermore, after Bush's "axis of evil" speech, the *Guardian* (January 31, 2002), printed articles indicating that there had been at least eight terrorist attacks on westerners in Saudi Arabia over the last year, and that westerners had been tortured to confess to responsibility for the attacks, including one British citizen who was himself a victim of a bombing! Yet applying the label of "evil" even to Saudi Arabia is highly problematic. In a series on the troubled relationship between the Saudi Kingdom and the United States in the aftermath of September 11, the *Washington Post* revealed hitherto undisclosed information that Saudi Arabia had dropped oil prices immediately after the terrorist attacks, instead of raising them as planned, in order to help the U.S. economy recover (February 14, 2002).

Despite the irresponsible tone and dangerous potential consequences of Bush's speech, the U.S. media gushed over Bush's performance, failing to criticize it. Throughout the day of the State of the Union address, the cable television networks outdid each other in building anticipation for Bush's speech and hyping the president's popularity and brilliant accomplishments. After the speech, CBS's Dan Rather celebrated it as "a solid, even eloquent address," and NBC's Andrea Mitchell found it "amazing." On CNN, William Bennett, the country's self-proclaimed morality czar, praised Bush's "speech of moral confidence," and Rudy Giuliani deemed it "philosophical" and "spiritual." Television commentators went on about how President Bush was "transformed." In fact, Bush delivered a preprepared speech that was well-rehearsed, and there was nothing spiritual or transformed about his bellicose rhetoric.

The day after the speech, newspaper commentators almost universally applauded Bush, including *Washington Post* columnist Mary McGory, who lauded his "stunning" speech and "phenomenal" popularity in an article entitled "Triumphal Oratory." Walter Shapiro in a *USA Today* piece gushed over Bush's "awe-inspiring popular support," deeming "Bush more than entitled to enjoy this moment." Bob Herbert in a *New York Times* op-ed piece, "As Bush's Stature Rises," effused over "the bond that is developing between President Bush and the American people," and William Safire in a commentary "To Fight Freedom's Fight" praised Bush's speech and urged him on to attack Iraq, Iran, and North Korea!

Although Bush's arrogant posturing was playing well domestically, it was faring increasingly poorly in the global arena where it is necessary to gain allies to effectively combat terrorism. Responding to global anxieties concerning Bush's militarism and to allies' fears that Bush was going to lead the world into war, Bush administration spokespeople tried to assure the world that Bush would be restrained in choosing military targets and that his rhetoric was simply to "put on notice" countries that supported terrorism that they would be subject to U.S. intervention. Visiting British Foreign Minister Jack Straw told the British press that Bush's "evil axis" speech was "vote-getting rhetoric" for domestic consumption, rather than a serious threat of immediate military action, and that "when the British government speaks about foreign policy, it's not about British politics." At first, Bush administration spokespeople seemed to back away from the implications of Bush's speech. By the end of the week, however, Condoleezza Rice sternly rebuked Jack Straw, Bush himself repeated the "axis of evil" rhetoric in domestic speeches and interviews, and other top administration figures, including Colin Powell, defended the axis of evil doctrine as "a wake up call" to the international community.

The main problem with Bush's rhetoric, however, is that it alienated both Arabs and allies. Whereas a responsible global policy against the international threat of terrorism would imply bringing in as many Arab allies and other countries as possible into a multilateral coalition in the war against Islamic extremism, Arabs have been extremely incensed over Bush's fast and loose use of the word "evil" to apply to their countries, and the "axis of evil" language in particular serves to position many Arabs against the West. Moreover, U.S. allies were expressing distress over Bush's speech, which implied that the United States would go it alone in its "crusade," worrying the rest of the world that U.S. intervention would become increasingly unilateral. Bush's threat of military force was likely to help recruitment of Islamic militants and to make acts of terrorism against the United States more likely. Although a major challenge for U.S. diplomacy was to build a global coalition against terrorism, Bush's aggressive unilateralism was likely to weaken global coalitions and undermine global efforts. Indeed, top European officials at a major NATO security conference over the weekend of February 2–3, 2002, despaired over Bush's unilateralism, fearing that it would destroy NATO and create serious political divisions in the years to come.

Furthermore, the highly respected British Conservative Party leader Chris Patten, former governor of Hong Kong and current European Commissioner for International Relations, deemed Bush's doctrine "absolutist and simplistic." French Prime Minister Lionel Jospin warned the United States not to give in to "the strong temptation of unilateralism." European commentators worried that Bush's bellicose rhetoric would alienate allies and isolate the United States. Others condemned Bush's continual perpetuation of fear of terrorism, leading to a paradoxical syndrome of "arrogance and fear," which Anatole Kaletsky dissected in the London *Times* (February 7, 2002).

Some critics suggested that Bush's "axis of evil" speech was intended to draw attention away from his failure to apprehend major Taliban and Al Qaeda leadership or to make progress on homeland security. In fact, it has rarely been noted in the U.S. media that efforts to arrest terrorists have been much more effective elsewhere in the world than the United States. The Bush administration failed to apprehend the source of the anthrax attacks that followed the September 11 attacks, and despite thousands of arrests, so far had not charged one suspect of terrorist involvement or publicly exposed one plan targeted at the United States.[8]

By contrast, the British newspapers regularly document arrests of terrorist suspects and break up of terrorist groups all over England. Likewise, other countries have also been highly effective in arresting local terrorists, foiling plots, and seriously damaging the terror networks. Thus, although the overthrow of the Taliban and destruction of the Al Qaeda camps in Afghanistan definitely struck at the bin Laden network, the failure to apprehend top leaders rendered the U.S. military intervention a mixed result at best.[9]

Moreover, continued U.S. military blundering in Afghanistan in 2002–2003 and the fierce global controversy over the treatment of prisoners of war undercut U.S. authority to lead the war against terrorism and revealed the stark limitations of Bush administration policies and personnel.[10] During the first week of February 2002, for instance, there was a stream of revelations of U.S. military mistakes in which for the first time the Pentagon acknowledged that they may have killed Afghan civilians in recent raids by mistake. The Pentagon acknowledged, for instance, that the much criticized raid on a village in Uruzgan province, south of Kandahar, on January 24 had killed civilians. Twenty-seven Afghans held in the raid were released and there were reports that U.S. Special Operations Forces were handing out $100 bills to families of survivors, with *ABC News* showing tribesman displaying their bills. Soon after, several of those released claimed that they were beaten and kept in cages by the U.S. troops, suffering serious injury.

Bill Moyers' PBS program *Now* on February 9, 2002, featured an Afghan American woman going back to her native country and interviewing relatives who had lost family members because of U.S. bombing errors. On February 11, the Pentagon conceded that a missile strike the previous week at a suspected Al Qaeda hideout had killed peasants and supporters of the Afghan government. Thus, it appeared that continued U.S. military presence in Afghanistan was taking a serious death toll and creating international scandal and outrage among the Afghans. The Karzai government tried to minimize the uproar, blaming the problems on poor intelligence and local Afghans using the United States to settle ancient hatreds and scores.

President Bush's constant rhetoric of "evil" was wearing thin, as was his administration's failure to come up with rational proposals and policies. Fear was escalating that the Bush administration was becoming a major liability in the global struggle against terror, and that the escalation of its unilateralist military interventions would no doubt make matters worse. There were also criticisms beginning to circulate that the Bush administration was manipulating and exaggerating reports about future terrorist attacks to whip up hysteria in order to deflect attention from its domestic problems, failures, and growing scandals, and to produce a climate of fear in which they could invade Iraq.

The Bush Doctrine and the Road to Iraq

> To initiate a war of aggression is not only an international crime; it is the supreme international crime differing only from other war crimes in that it contains within itself the accumulative evil of the whole.
> —*Judges at the Nuremberg trials of Nazi leadership*

In a speech to West Point cadets on June 1, 2002, George W. Bush proclaimed the new "doctrine" that the United States would strike first against its enemies. It was soon apparent that this was a major shift in U.S. foreign policy, replacing the Cold War doctrine of containment and deterrence with a new policy of preemptive strikes, one that could be tried out in Iraq. U.S. allies were extremely upset with this shift in U.S. policy; a move toward an aggressive U.S. unilateralism. In an article called "Bush to Formalize a Defense Policy of Hitting First," David E. Sanger wrote in the *New York Times* (June 17, 2002), that: "The process of including America's allies has only just begun, and administration officials concede that it will be difficult at best. Leaders in Berlin, Paris, and Beijing, in particular, have often warned against unilateralism. But Mr. Bush's new policy could amount to ultimate unilateralism, because it reserves the right to determine what constitutes a threat to American security and to act even if that threat is not judged imminent."[11]

After a summer of debate on the necessity of the United States going to war against Iraq to destroy its "weapons of mass destruction," on August 26, 2002, U.S. Vice President Dick Cheney applied the new preemptive strike and unilateralist doctrine to Iraq, arguing: "What we must not do in the face of a mortal threat is to give in to wishful thinking or willful blindness.... Deliverable weapons of mass destruction in the hands of a terror network or murderous dictator or the two working together constitutes as grave a threat as can be imagined. The risks of inaction are far greater than the risks of action." Cheney was responding to many former generals and high-level members of the first Bush administration who had reservations against the sort of unilateralist U.S. attack against Iraq that hawks in the Bush administration were urging.

During the late summer and fall of 2002, former U.S. political and military leaders warned about adverse consequences of an Iraq invasion and occupation that could create ongoing havoc in Iraq, destabilize the Middle East, turn significant portions of the world militantly against the United States, disrupt oil supplies, interfere with the war on terrorism, and drive down an unstable U.S. economy. Questions were raised concerning how the Bush administration could pay for a war in Iraq and the "war on terrorism" at the same time, and whether the U.S. military could take on so many challenges. There were worries that a chaotic post-Saddam Iraq might involve the United States in a hazardous and violent period of stabilization and reconstruction that could go badly wrong.

Major figures from Bush's father's administration, including former National Security Advisor Brent Scowcroft, Secretary of State James Baker, and Lawrence Eagleburger made strong arguments that it would be a disaster for the United States to go it alone in Iraq and that the United States would be in an untenable position without significant support from allies and the United Nations. The head of the U.S. NATO force in the Kosovo war, General Wesley Clarke, wrote a long piece on the follies of the Bush administration Iraq plan; Norman Schwarzkopf, head of U.S. forces in the Gulf War, came out against an Iraq invasion; and General Anthony Zinni, who had recently served as Bush's top envoy to the Middle East, warned against war with Iraq, "saying it would stretch U.S. forces too thin and make unwanted enemies in the volatile region." In a pointed statement against hawks like Dick Cheney and Richard Perle, who were lusting for war although they had never served in the military, Zinni remarked: "It's pretty interesting that all the generals see it the same way, and all the others who have never fired a shot and are hot to go to war see it another way."[12]

Dick Cheney, however, continued to make saber-rattling speeches for war against Iraq in late August 2002. Cheney said that UN weapons inspectors "would provide no assurance whatsoever" of Iraqi compliance with UN disarmament resolutions and would instead increase the danger by providing "false comfort." Cheney was, in effect, ruling out any political mediation of the Iraq situation at a time when global forces were furiously attempting to get UN weapons inspectors back in Iraq to get a vigorous weapons inspection process under way again. In a September 1 interview with the BBC, Colin Powell stated that UN weapons inspectors should be sent back to Iraq as a "first step" to deal with the threats posed by the regime of Saddam Hussein. Commentators noted that the White House had not cleared Cheney's speech and that there was evident "disarray" in the Bush administration over Iraq policy.[13]

As Cheney was calling for war against Iraq, reports spread on the Internet about how, as CEO at Halliburton, Cheney did more business with Iraq than any other U.S. company. A *Washington Post* story had reported that Halliburton had signed contracts under Cheney's leadership worth $73 million through two subsidiaries that sold Iraq oil production equipment and spare parts when there were restrictions against U.S. corporations doing business with Iraq.[14] Cheney denied knowledge of these ventures, but an investigation into his Halliburton stewardship could have proven otherwise. Indeed, current Halliburton CEO David Lesar has stated that Cheney "unquestionably" knew about the Iraq dealings, implying that the vice president was lying. Inquiries into Halliburton's history could also reveal how the company set up dummy corporations, much like Enron did, to cover business losses and to provide fake profits, among other questionable activities that transpired during Cheney's years as CEO. Cheney was being sued on behalf of stockholders for the collapse of the company's stock value under his leadership and investigation of this explosive issue could put Cheney in the same category as former Enron CEO Ken Lay.

It was not only Cheney who was desperately promoting a war against Iraq, but an entire cadre of neoconservatives in the Bush administration who had long been seeking the overthrow of Saddam Hussein, U.S. military bases in Iraq, and control of its oil, a project also shared by George W. Bush. When Tony Blair arrived in the United States for a war summit on Iraq the weekend of September 8, 2002, the Bush administration released photos of "new evidence" of an Iraqi nuclear facility, and as Blair stood beside him, Bush waved the pictures and a 1998 report that Iraq was six months away from nuclear bomb capacity at the media, proclaiming "I don't know what more evidence you need" [to demonstrate that Iraq was producing weapons of mass destruction]. But as ABC, NBC, and the *Washington Post* quickly reported,[15] these pictures and reports were fraudulent, suggesting that the Bush-Cheney clique was resorting to deception to legitimate their Iraq venture. Nevertheless, Fox Television and other U.S. cable networks played stories about the threat of Iraqi arms programs to the United States and its allies day after day.

This is not to deny that "weapons of mass destruction" are a serious issue and that eliminating them would be a rational and highly desirable goal. But in fact it is precisely the Bush administration that has refused participation in every major treaty to control or eliminate such weapons (see Kellner 2001). The U.S. is a rogue nation in terms of development of weapons of mass destruction and blocking treaties that could lead to their elimination. A rational plan to eliminate weapons of mass destruction would thus be to criminalize their use, to build a coalition of nations that renounced these weapons, and to work to systematically eliminate them.

On September 8, 2002, Cheney and the other top warmongers of the Bush administration were all over the Sunday talk shows making their case for war against Iraq. Cheney repeated on *Meet the Press* all of the well-known crimes of Saddam Hussein, insinuated long-discredited ties between Iraq and Al Qaeda, and even tried to pin the September 2001 anthrax attacks on Iraq, although all evidence pointed to U.S. weapons-grade facilities. Cheney was going to have a war against Iraq no matter what the price and it appeared that George W. Bush was equally set on war.

Indeed, George W. Bush was focused on invasion, regime change, and occupation of Iraq from the beginning of his administration. Several 2004 books make it clear that Bush Junior was highly interested in the overthrow of Saddam Hussein and that just as Cheney, Rumsfeld, and other neoconservative hawks pushed hard for the Iraq war, Bush was a key part of the militarist forces. Ron Suskind's 2004 memoir of the "education" of Bush's fired Treasury Secretary Paul O'Neill presents Bush as obsessed with Iraq even before 9/11. Antiterrorism "czar" Richard Clarke's memoir (2004) notes that Bush repeatedly told him just after the September 11 attacks to focus on Iraqi complicity. Bob Woodward's 2004 book *Plan of Attack* also affirms Bush's obsession with Saddam Hussein and deep interest in war against Iraq, citing Bush's religious fundamentalism and belief that he was doing God's will in invading Iraq.

Throughout the fall of 2002, the Bush administration continued to multiply claims of dangers from Iraqi "weapons of mass destruction." The Bush administration insinuated constantly that Iraq was allied with terrorist groups and despite no evidence of links between the Saddam regime and Al Qaeda, by October 2002, a Pew Research Center poll indicated that 66 percent of the U.S. population believed Saddam Hussein was involved in the 9/11 attacks and 79 percent believed that Iraq possessed, or was close to possessing, nuclear weapons (cited in Rampton and Stauber 2003, 78ff.). Moreover, Bush and others in his circle regularly described the "war against terrorism" as World War III; Donald Rumsfeld said that it could last as long as the Cold War; and Dick Cheney said it could go on for a "long, long time, perhaps indefinitely." Such an Orwellian nightmare could embroil the U.S. in countless wars, plunge the world into a new millennium of escalating war with unintended consequences, and normalize war as conflict resolution, creating countless new enemies for the would-be American hegemon.[16] Indeed, as Chalmers Johnson writes in *Blowback* (2000), empire has hidden costs. Hegemony breeds resentment and hostility, and when the empire carries out aggression it elicits anger and creates enemies, intensifying the dangers of perpetual war (see also Johnson 2004).

On September 12, 2002, Bush made a speech to the United Nations where he warned once again that Iraq "continues to develop weapons of mass destruction," including nuclear weapons. On September 20, 2002, Bush spoke in New York City, with the Statue of Liberty in the background, requesting that the UN Security Council approve his march to war. The same day, it was apparent that the hawks in the Bush administration had triumphed, at least on the level of official military doctrine, when the Bush administration released a document signaling some of the most important and far-reaching shifts in U.S. foreign and military policy since the end of the Cold War. Titled "The National Security Strategy of the United States," the 33-page report outlined a new doctrine of U.S. military supremacy, providing justifications for the United States to undertake unilateral and preemptive strikes in the name of "counter-proliferation." This Orwellian concept was offered as a replacement for the concept of "nonproliferation" and would legitimate unilateral destruction of a country's presumed "weapons of mass destruction." The document, in effect, renounced the multilateralism and rule by international law that had informed U.S. thinking on global security since World War II and that appeared to be a consensus among western nations during the era of globalization.

The Bush administration presented the Orwellian euphemisms of "preemptive strikes," "regime change," and "anticipatory self-defense" for raw military aggression. Critics assailed the new "strike first, ask questions later" policy, the belligerent unilateralism, and dangerous legitimation of preemptive strikes by other countries.[17] Indeed, Israel, Pakistan, Russia, China, and lesser powers had already used the so-called Bush doctrine and "war against terrorism" to legitimate attacks on domestic and external foes, and the danger that it could proliferate wars and make the world more unstable and violent was rising. As William Galston states:

> A global strategy based on the new Bush doctrine of preemption means the end of the system of international institutions, laws, and norms that we have worked to build for more than half a century. What is at stake is nothing less than a fundamental shift in America's place in the world. Rather than continuing to serve as first among equals in the postwar international system, the United States would act as a law unto itself, creating new rules of international engagement

without the consent of other nations. In my judgment, this new stance would ill
serve the long-term interests of the United States.[18]

To be sure, the United States itself had engaged in countless military aggres-
sions in the post–World War II era and often subverted international law and
global institutions. Nonetheless, the Bush administration doctrine of preemptive strikes was perceived as a sharp break with previous U.S. and regnant global military doctrine and could unleash a series of wars that would plunge the
world into the sort of nightmare militarism and totalitarianism sketched out
in George Orwell's *1984*. The Bush policy is highly repressive, taking the global
community into a Social Darwinist battleground where decades of international law would be put aside and a new era of barbarism could unfold. The
Bush doctrine portends a possible future in which an escalating militarism
could generate a cycle of unending violence and retribution, such as has been
evident in the Israel and Palestine conflict.

On October 10, 2002, the House of Representatives voted 296 to 133 to grant
Bush the authority to attack Iraq, and the Senate approved 77 to 23 the next
day. Later, John Kerry, John Edwards, and others who had voted in the affirmative insisted that they were voting for a resolution that would empower Bush to
mobilize the Union Nations to ensure that arms inspections in Iraq continued
vigorously, and that this did not constitute a declaration of war.[19] On November 8, 2002, the Bush administration pressured the UN Security Council to
adopt Resolution 1441, which gave Iraq "a final opportunity to comply with its
disarmament obligations" and "set up an enhanced inspection regime." Inspections began, the Iraqis submitted a massive report on their arms program, part
of which documented how U.S. and European firms contributed to the program, and the arms inspectors found nothing. After tensions with the Iraqis
the inspections were temporarily halted.[20]

Around the same time that the Bush administration was seeking to apply its
new strategic doctrine in a war against Iraq, a 2000 report circulated, titled
"Rebuilding America's Defenses: Strategies, Forces, and Resources for a New
American Century." Drawn up by the neoconservative think tank Project for a
New American Century (PNAC) for a group including Dick Cheney, Donald
Rumsfeld, and Paul Wolfowitz, the document clearly spelled out a plan for U.S.
world hegemony grounded in military dominance and control of the Persian
Gulf region's oil supplies.[21] Its upfront goals were a "Pax Americana" and U.S.
domination of the world during the new millennium. The document shows
that core members of the Bush administration had longed envisaged taking
military control of the Gulf region, stating: "The United States has for decades

sought to play a more permanent role in Gulf regional security. While the un-resolved conflict with Iraq provides the immediate justification, the need for a substantial American force presence in the Gulf transcends the issue of the regime of Saddam Hussein."

The PNAC document argues for "maintaining global U.S. pre-eminence, precluding the rise of a great power rival, and shaping the international security order in line with American principles and interests." The vision is long-range, urging U.S. domination of the Gulf "as far into the future as possible." It is also highly militaristic, calling for the U.S. to "fight and decisively win multiple, simultaneous major theatre wars" as a "core mission." U.S. armed forces would serve as "the cavalry on the new American frontier," blocking the emergence of rival countries challenging U.S. domination. It would enlist key allies such as Britain as "the most effective and efficient means of exercising American global leadership," and would put the United States, not the United Nations, in charge of military interventions or peacekeeping missions. Moreover, it envisages taking on Iran after Iraq, spotlights China for "regime change," calls for the creation of "U.S. Space Forces" to dominate outer space, and positions the United States to control cyberspace to prevent "enemies" from "using the Internet against the U.S."

The architects of the PNAC document became key members of the Bush administration and in early February 2003, reports circulated that a major U.S. intervention in Iraq leading to regime change was inevitable. Richard Perle, a senior adviser to U.S. Secretary of Defense Donald Rumsfeld, indicated that war with Iraq was likely even if Baghdad backed down and allowed inspectors back in to hunt for weapons of mass destruction, according to an interview in early February at a Munich Security conference:

> "I don't think there's anything (Iraqi leader) Saddam Hussein could do that would convince us there's no longer any danger coming from Iraq," said Richard Perle, head of the Defense Policy Board of the U.S. Department of Defense. . . . Perle, quoted in an interview with the German edition of the *Financial Times* at the Munich Security Conference, said the only thing that would convince the United States regarding Iraq would be a change of regime. U.S. President George W. Bush was now on "a very clear path heading toward war with Iraq," said Perle.[22]

Colin Powell's February 5, 2003, speech to the United Nations clearly indicated that the Bush administration was dead-set on war. Powell opened by declaring: "My colleagues, every statement I make today is backed up by sources, solid sources. These are not assertions. What we are giving you are facts and conclusions based on solid intelligence." Powell thundered repeatedly "we know" that Iraq contained this or that weapons program and actual so-called "weapons of mass destruction." Supported by graphs, satellite pictures of alleged weapons facilities, presentations of intercepted Iraqi messages, statistics concerning Iraqi chemical and biological weapons programs, signs of a dangerous nuclear weapons program, and other "evidence," Powell, with CIA Director George Tenet sitting impassively behind him, made the case for war on Iraq to a global audience.[23]

As the hawks in the Bush administration accelerated their war talk, there was a sustained array of strong criticism of the Bush war plans from throughout the world, gigantic global peace demonstrations, and objections from close U.S. allies like Canada and Germany that usually went along with U.S. military interventions. On February 13, 2003, more than 8 million people on five continents demonstrated against the planned war against Iraq. This demonstration was, according to Tariq Ali, "unprecedented in size, scope, and scale.... The turnout in western Europe broke all records: three million in Rome, two million in Spain, a million and a half in London, half a million in Berlin" (2003, 144). There was a fierce debate in Britain over whether the United Kingdom should support Bush's venture and an indication that Tony Blair might lose support in his own party and possibly the next election if he went along with Bush.

An attempt to produce a compromise resolution in the United Nations collapsed and it was simply a matter of when the war would begin.[24] Whereas the explicit war aims were to shut down Iraq's "weapons of mass destruction," and thus enforce UN resolutions mandating that Iraq eliminate its weapons, there were many hidden agendas in the Bush administration offensive against Iraq. To be reelected, Bush needed a major victory and symbolic triumph over terrorism in order to deflect from the failings of his regime both domestically and in the realm of foreign policy.

Moreover, ideologues within the Bush administration wanted to legitimate a policy of preemptive strikes, and a successful attack on Iraq could inaugurate and normalize this policy. Some of the same unilateralists in the Bush administration envisage U.S. world hegemony, the elder Bush's "New World Order," with the United States as the reigning military power and world police (Kellner 2003b). Increased control of the world's oil supplies provided a tempting prize for the former oil executives who maintain key roles in the Bush administration. Furthermore, key members of the neoconservative clique in the Bush administration were linked to Israel's reactionary Likud party, which wanted to destroy Saddam Hussein's regime because he was seen as a threat to Israel. Finally, one might note the Oedipal Tex drama wherein George W. Bush desired to conclude his father's unfinished business and simultaneously defeat evil to constitute himself as good, motivations that may have helped drive Bush Junior to war against Iraq with the fervor of a religious crusade.[25]

With all these agendas in play, a war on Iraq appears to have been inevitable. Bush's March 6, 2003, press conference made it evident that he was ready to go to war. His handlers told him to speak slowly and keep his Texas machismo out of view, but he constantly threatened Iraq and evoked the rhetoric of "good" and "evil" that he used to justify his crusade against bin Laden and Al Qaeda. Bush repeated the words "Saddam Hussein" and "terrorism" incessantly, mentioning Iraq as a "threat" at least 16 times and attempting to link that country with the September 11 attacks and other terrorism. He used the word "I" as in "I believe" countless times, and talked of "my government" as if he owned it, depicting a man lost in self-importance. Unable to make an intelligent and objective case for a war against Iraq, Bush could only use moralistic rhetoric, attempting to present himself as a strong nationalist leader who could prevent further terrorist attacks with a preemptive war.

Bush's rhetoric, like that of fascism, deploys a mistrust and hatred of language, reducing it to manipulative speechifying, speaking in codes, repeating the same phrases over and over. This is grounded in anti-intellectualism and contempt for democracy and intellectuals. It is clearly evident in Bush's press conferences and snitty responses to questions that Bushspeak plays to anti-intellectual proclivities in the extreme conservative and fundamentalist Christian constituencies who support him.

But Bush's Iraq war discourse failed to convince those who were not already true believers in the need to invade Iraq. Many traditional U.S. allies were deeply angered by Bush's arrogance and were not convinced by his rhetoric. Indeed, it appears that Bush's press conference was orchestrated to shore up his base and prepare his supporters for a major political struggle rather than to convince those opposed to a war with Iraq that it was a good idea.

Bush's discourse also displayed Orwellian features of doublespeak: war against Iraq is for peace, the occupation of Iraq is its liberation, bombing its cities and civilian infrastructure enables "humanitarian" action, and the murder of countless Iraqis and destruction of the country will produce "freedom" and "democracy." In a prewar summit with Tony Blair in the Azores and in his first talk after the bombing began, Bush went on and on about the "coalition of the willing" and how many countries were supporting and participating in the "allied" effort. In fact, however, it was a Coalition of Two, with the United States and United Kingdom doing most of the fighting and with many of the countries that Bush claimed supported his war quickly backtracking and expressing reservations about the highly unpopular assault that was strongly opposed by most people and countries in the world.[26]

Weapons of Mass Deception: The Media and the War on Iraq

> We must make clear to the Germans that the wrong for which their fallen leaders are on trial is not that they lost the war, but that they started it.... No grievances or policies will justify resort to aggressive war. It is utterly renounced and condemned as an instrument of policy.
> —*Robert l. Jackson, U.S. representative to the International Conference on Military Trials at the end of World War II*

The corporate media had done little to critically discuss Bush administration claims that Iraq had deadly weapons of mass destruction, ties to Al Qaeda, and posed an imminent threat to the United States. The Fox network served up daily dishes of Bush administration propaganda and the other television channels followed pack journalism in demonizing Iraq and Saddam Hussein. Even the elite newspapers, the *Washington Post* and *New York Times,* later admitted that they had too readily and uncritically published accounts of alleged Iraqi weapons programs fed to them by the Bush administration and Iraqi dissidents around Ahmed Chalabi and the Iraqi National Congress.[27] During the war itself, U.S. corporate media were "weapons of mass deception" that served as propaganda instruments for the Bush administration and Pentagon.

The 2003 Iraq war was a major global media event constructed very differently by varying broadcasting networks in diverse parts of the world. Whereas the U.S. networks framed the event as "Operation Iraqi Freedom" (the Pentagon concept) or "War in Iraq," the Canadian Broadcasting Corporation (CBC) used the logo "War on Iraq," and various Arab networks presented it as an "invasion" and "occupation." In this section, I provide a critique of the U.S. broadcasting network construction of the war, which I interpret as providing a conduit for Bush administration and Pentagon propaganda, and show how events spinning out of control in Iraq created a spectacle of chaos that undermined Bush administration claims of victory and the liberation of Iraq.[28]

On March 19, 2003, the media spectacle of the war against Iraq unfolded with a dramatic attempt to "decapitate" the Iraqi regime. Large numbers of missiles were aimed at targets in Baghdad, where Saddam Hussein and the Iraqi leadership were believed to be staying, and the tens of thousands of ground troops on the Kuwait-Iraq border poised for invasion entered Iraq in a blitzkrieg toward Baghdad.[29] The media followed the Bush administration and Pentagon slogan of "shock and awe," and presented the war against Iraq as a great military spectacle, as triumphalism marked the opening days of the U.S. bombing and invasion of Iraq.

The al Jazeera network live coverage of the bombing of a palace belonging to the Hussein family was indeed shocking as loud explosions and blasts jolted viewers throughout the world. Whereas some western media presented this bombing positively as a powerful assault on "evil," for Arab audiences it was experienced as an attack on the body of the Arab and Muslim people, just as the September 11 terrorist attacks were experienced by Americans as assaults on the very body and symbols of the United States. Whereas in Gulf War I, CNN was the only network live in Baghdad and throughout the war framed the images, discourses, and spectacle, there were more than 20 networks broadcasting in Baghdad for the 2003 Iraq war, including several Arab networks, and all of the television companies presented the war differently.

Conservative U.S. networks like Fox and the NBC cable networks played patriotic music as the soundtrack to their news reports, and all U.S. networks engaged in extremely patriotic discourses and avoided showing casualties or the destructive elements of the Iraq incursion.[30] But al Jazeera and other Arab networks, as well as some European networks, talked of an "invasion" and an illegal U.S. and British assault on Iraq. As Donald Rumsfeld bragged that the bombings were the most precise in history and were aimed at military and not civilian targets, Arab and various global broadcasting networks focused on civilian casualties and presented painful spectacles of Iraqis suffering. Moreover, to the surprise of many, after a triumphant march across the Kuwaiti border and rush to Baghdad, the U.S. and British forces began to take casualties, and during the weekend of March 22–23, images of their POWs and dead bodies of their soldiers were shown throughout the world. Moreover, the Iraqis began fiercely resisting, rather than cheering on British and U.S. forces.

Soon after, an immense sandstorm slowed down the march on Baghdad, and images of Iraqi civilians maimed or killed by U.S. and British bombing, accounts of mishaps, stalled and overextended supply lines, and unexpected dangers to the invading forces created dramatic stories. The intensity and immediacy of the spectacle was multiplied by "embedded reporters" who were accompanying the U.S. and British forces and who beamed back live pictures, first of the triumphant march through Iraq and then of the invading forces stalling and subject to perilous counterattack.

A great debate emerged about the embedded reporters and about whether journalists who depended on the protection of the U.S. and British military, lived with the troops, and signed papers agreeing to a rigorous set of restrictions on their reporting could be objective and critical of their protectors (see the studies in Miller 2004). From the beginning, it was clear that the embedded reporters were indeed "in bed with" their military escorts, and as the United States and Britain stormed into Iraq, the reporters presented exultant and triumphant accounts that trumped any paid propagandist. The embedded U.S. reporters were largely cheerleaders and spinners for the U.S. and UK military and lost any veneer of objectivity. But as the incursion stalled, a sandstorm hit, and U.S. and British forces came under attack, the embedded TV reporters displayed genuine fear, helped capture the chaos of war, provided some vivid accounts of the fighting, and occasionally, as I note below, deflated propaganda lies of the U.S. or UK military.

Indeed, U.S. and British military discourse was exceptionally mendacious, as happens so often in recent wars that are as much for public opinion and political agendas as for military goals. British and U.S. sources claimed in their first days in Iraq that the border port of Umm Qasar and major southern city of Basra were under coalition control, whereas television images showed quite the opposite. When things went badly for U.S. and British forces on March 23, a story originated from an embedded reporter with the *Jerusalem Post* that a "huge" chemical weapons production facility was found, a story allegedly confirmed by a Pentagon source to the Fox TV military correspondent who quickly spread it through the U.S. media (BBC was skeptical from the beginning).[31]

When U.S. officials denied that they were responsible for major civilian atrocities in two Baghdad bombings the week of March 24, reporters on the scene cited witnesses describing planes flying overhead and in one case found pieces of a missile with U.S. markings and numbers on it, shown repeatedly on BBC.[32] After a suicide bombing killed four U.S. troops at a checkpoint in late March, U.S. soldiers fired on a vehicle that ran a checkpoint and killed seven civilians. The U.S. military claimed that it had fired a warning shot, but a *Washington Post* reporter on the scene noted that a senior U.S. military official had shouted to a younger soldier to fire a warning shot first and then yelled that "you [expletive] killed them" when the soldier fired directly on the civilian vehicle.[33] Embedded newspaper reporters also often provided more vivid accounts of "friendly fire" and other mishaps, getting their information from troops on the ground, instead of from military spinners who tended to be propagandists. Hence, the embedded and other on-site reporters provided documentation of the more raw and brutal aspects of war in telling accounts that often called into question official versions of the events as well as military propaganda. But since their every posting and broadcast was censored by the U.S. military, it was the independent "unilateral" journalists who provided the most accurate account of the horrors of the war and the Coalition of Two military mishaps.

Moreover, the U.S. broadcast networks were on the whole more embedded in the Pentagon and Bush administration than the reporters and print journalists were in the field. The military commentators on the major U.S. television networks constantly provided the Pentagon spin of the moment and often repeated gross lies and propaganda, as in the examples mentioned above concerning the U.S. bombing of civilians or the checkpoint shooting of innocents. Entire networks like Fox and the NBC cable networks provided little but propaganda and one-sided patriotism, as did for the most part CNN. All of the cable networks, as well as the big three U.S. broadcasting networks, tended to provide highly sanitized views of the war, rarely showing Iraqi casualties, thus producing a view of the war significantly different than that shown in other parts of the world.

The dramatic story of "Saving Private Lynch" was one of the more spectacular human interest stories of the war that revealed the constructed nature of the Iraq media spectacle and the ways that the Pentagon produced mythologies replicated by the television networks. Private Jessica Lynch was one of the first American POWs shown on Iraqi television, and since she was young, female, and attractive her fate became a topic of intense interest. Stories circulated that she was shot and stabbed and was tortured by Iraqis holding her in captivity.[34] Eight days after her capture, the U.S. media broadcast footage of her dramatic rescue, obviously staged like a reality TV show. Soldiers stormed the hospital, found Lynch, and claimed to have carried out a dramatic rescue under fire from Iraqis. In fact, several media institutions interviewed the doctors in the hospital who claimed that Iraqi troops had left the hospital two days before, that the hospital staff had tried to take Jessica to the Americans but the troops fired on them, and that in the "rescue" the U.S. troops shot through the doors, terrorized doctors and patients, and created a dangerous scene that could have resulted in deaths, simply to get some dramatic rescue footage for television audiences.[35]

The Fox network was especially militaristic and chauvinistic, yet its own April 5–6 footage of the daring U.S. incursion into Baghdad displayed a road strewn with destroyed Iraqi vehicles, burning buildings, and Iraqi corpses. This live footage, replayed for days, caught something of the carnage of the hi-tech slaughter and destruction of Iraq that the U.S. networks tended to neglect or downplay. An Oliver North commentary to footage of a U.S. warplane blasting away one Iraqi tank or armored vehicle after another put on display the asymmetrical war in which the Iraqi military had no chance whatsoever against the

U.S. war machine. In an April 6 interview on Fox, *Forbes Magazine* publisher and former presidential candidate Steve Forbes stated that the United States intended to get all the contracts on rebuilding Iraq for U.S. firms and that Iraqi debts held by French and Russians should be cancelled. Such discourse put on display the arrogance and greed that drove the U.S. effort and subverted all idealistic rhetoric about democracy and freedom for the Iraqis. This kind of gloating, which accompanied the slaughter of Iraqis and destruction of the country, showed the new barbarism that characterized the Bush era.[36]

U.S. military commanders claimed that in the initial foray into Baghdad, 2,000–3,000 Iraqis were killed, suggesting that the broadcasting networks were not really showing the brutality and carnage of the war. Indeed, most of the bombing of Iraqi military forces was invisible and dead Iraqis were rarely shown. An embedded CNN reporter, Walter Rogers, later recounted that the one time his report showed a dead Iraqi the CNN switchboard "lit up like a Christmas tree" with angry viewers demanding that CNN not show any dead bodies, as if the U.S. audience wanted to be in denial concerning the human costs of the war.[37]

Comparing U.S. broadcasting networks with the British and Canadian Broadcasting Corporations, among other outlets, showed vastly different wars being presented. The U.S. networks tended to ignore Iraqi casualties, Arab outrage about the war, and global antiwar and anti-U.S. protests, but the BBC and CBC often featured these more critical themes.[38] As noted, the war was framed very differently by various countries and networks, and analysts remarked that in most Arab media, the war was presented as an invasion of Iraq, slaughter of its peoples, and destruction of the country. On the whole, U.S. broadcasting networks tended to present a sanitized view of the war and tended toward pro-military patriotism, propaganda, and technological fetishism, celebrating the weapons of war and highlighting the achievements and heroism of the U.S. troops. Other global broadcasting networks, however, were highly critical of the U.S. and UK military and often presented negative features of the assault on Iraq.

The dirty little secret of U.S. corporate broadcasting networks was that they profited greatly from war, tended to promote U.S. military interventions, and then became cheerleaders for the country's war effort. The Fox network was a propaganda machine for Bush administration policy and conservative militarism and significantly boosted its ratings and profits from the war effort. The NBC networks were affiliated with General Electric, one of the major military contractors, and proudly presented oft-repeated advertisements of their company's weapons systems. Dan Rather of CBS had long been a war correspondent and reveled in the superpatriotism and excitement of war. Indeed, all of the networks fetishized U.S. military technology, the power of the U.S. military, and the valor of U.S. troops, thus providing wall-to-wall advertisements for war and militarism.

Thus the logic of ratings and profit dictated that during times of war the broadcasting media, and to a lesser extent the press, would be cheerleaders for the war effort. Embedded reporters tended to present the U.S. military point of view and network television commentators all presented pro-Pentagon and prowar views. If any images and discourses appeared that questioned the war effort, the offending network or paper would be attacked with flack from conservative networks who would question its patriotism, support of the troops, and respect for the president. Antiwar voices and protests were necessarily excluded in the profit-driven and prowar atmosphere of media coverage of U.S. military intervention. Thus to get accurate accounts of what actually happened in Afghanistan or Iraq during the active phase of the U.S. military intervention, one needed to go to the foreign or alternative press on the Internet.[39]

In a sense, the United States and United Kingdom found themselves in a double bind: the more thoroughly they annihilated Iraqi troops and conquered the country, the more aggressive, bullying, and imperialist they would appear to the rest of the world. Yet the dramatic pictures of civilian casualties and harrowing images of U.S. bombing and destruction of Iraq made it imperative to end the war as soon as possible. An apparently failed attempt to kill Saddam Hussein and his top leadership on April 7 destroyed a civilian neighborhood and killed a number of people. Followed by the death of journalists in two separate episodes by the U.S. military on April 8, this produced a negative media spectacle. But the seeming collapse of the Iraqi regime on April 9—where for the first time there were significant images of Iraqis celebrating the demise of Hussein—provided the material for a spectacle of victory.

Indeed, the destruction of a statue of Saddam Hussein on live global television provided precisely the images desired by the Pentagon and Bush administration. Closer analysis of this spectacle revealed, however, that rather than displaying a mass uprising of Iraqis against the Baath regime, there were relatively few people assaulting the Hussein statue. Analysis of the pictures revealed that there was a relatively small crowd around the statue of Saddam Hussein, but most of the square was empty. Those attacking the statue were largely members of the U.S.-supported Iraqi National Congress, including aides of its infamous leader Ahmed Chalabi. Moreover, the few Iraqis in the square were unable to destroy the statue until some U.S. soldiers on the scene used their tank and cable to pull it down. In a semiotic slip, one soldier briefly put a U.S. flag on top of Hussein's head, providing an iconic image for Arab networks and others of a U.S. occupation and takeover of Iraq.[40]

Subsequent images of looting, anarchy, and chaos throughout Iraq, however, including the plundering of the National Museum; the National Archive, which contained rare books and historical documents; and the Ministry for Religious Affairs, which contained rare religious material, created extremely negative impressions.[41] Likewise, growing Iraqi demonstrations over the U.S. occupation and continued violence throughout the country illuminated a highly uncertain situation in which the spectacle of victory and the triumph of Bush administration and Pentagon policy were called into question domestically as well as globally.

Notes

1. This study updates Kellner (2003a, 2003b). Thanks to Rhonda Hammer, Carl Boggs, Richard Kahn, and the anonymous reviewers of *New Political Science* for comments on earlier versions of this text. I am putting "weapons of mass destruction" in quotes at this point because, strictly speaking, many of the weapons programs that the Bush administration alleged Iraq was developing were really not weapons of "mass destruction." The term primarily refers to nuclear weapons or mass delivery of biological and chemical weapons, a capacity the United States continues to develop despite international treaties and global demands for more arms control. Many critics contend that the Bush administration is undermining the kind of global arms control that should be vigorously developed in order to prevent the spread and use of the noxious and lethal weapons that have become known as "weapons of mass destruction."

2. Budget analysts noted that although page 396 of Bush's budget claimed that the 2002 deficit would be $106 billion, page 417 admitted that "the amount of government debt outstanding at the end of this year will rise by fully $367 billion to a new world record of $6.1 trillion," Thomas Oliphant, *Boston Globe,* February 12, 2002. When Senator Fritz Hollings confronted Bush administration budget director Mitch Daniels with this discrepancy, Daniels admitted that "we hid it but you found it." According to Oliphant, the Bush administration planned to help cover the gargantuan deficit by raiding Social Security and Medicare as they proceeded to do.

3. *The 9/11 Commission Report* documented many failures of the Bush administration prior to 9/11 but did not name names; there were reports near the end of the 2004 election campaign that a secret CIA memo named top figures of the Bush administration as negligent in regard to the 9/11 attacks, but so far the report has not been released.

4. Bush would be rebuffed on his radical plan to undermine Social Security during his first term, but the day after John Kerry conceded the 2004 election, Bush claimed

that he now had more "political capital" and was going to "spend" it on his plan to privatize Social Security (see the Conclusion).

5. During the 2004 election campaign, the Pentagon cancelled a test for the missile defense system amid fears that it was still seriously defective; critics continued to argue that the system was flawed in principle and a gigantic waste of resources. A test after the 2004 election did indeed result in failure—see David Stout, "Important Test for Missile-Defense System Ends in Failure," *New York Times,* December 15, 2004.

6. Defense of Civilization Fund, "Defending Civilization: How Our Universities Are Failing America and What Can Be Done about It?" November 2001; accessible at www.goacta.org.

7. See Seamus Milne, "Can the U.S. Be Defeated?" *Guardian,* February 14, 2002.

8. Zacarias Moussaouri was arrested before the September 11 attacks and later charged with involvement with Al Qaeda and the September 11 attacks, but the Ashcroft Justice Department bungled his prosecution (see the account in Hersh [2004]). By the last weeks of the 2004 election, there were reports that the U.S. Justice Department had failed to crack one terrorist cell and despite thousands of arrests and detentions of suspects, not one prosecution was advanced. Thus Attorney General John Ashcroft resigned in disgrace in November 2004.

9. Although the Bush administration's Justice Department has generally failed to produce dramatic domestic results in the war against terror, U.S. Attorney General John Ashcroft struck a blow against the terror of nudity when he demanded that a 12 foot high statue of a nude woman figure of Justice have her breasts covered. Ashcroft was reportedly embarrassed at being photographed with the bare-breasted woman and the puritanical attorney general demanded coverage to protect him and other like-minded puritans from the dangers of female nudity.

10. For detailed dissection of U.S. internment of "enemy combatants" at Guantanamo Bay, Cuba, and elsewhere and the international scandals caused by their mistreatment, see Hersh (2004).

11. See also Thomas E. Ricks and Vernon Loeb, "Bush Developing Military Policy of Striking First," *Washington Post,* June 10, 2002, p. A1. For a sharp critique of Bush's Iraq and preemptive strike policy, see Johnson (2004) and Ritter (2003).

12. See Mike Salinero, "Gen. Zinni Says War with Iraq Is Unwise," *Tampa Tribune,* August 24, 2002. Zinni later published a book with Tom Clancy, *Battle Ready* (2004), which fiercely critiques Bush administration Iraq policy.

13. Julian Borger, "White House in Disarray over Cheney Speech," *Guardian,* September 2, 2002; Andrew Gumbel and Marie Woolf, "U.S. in Disarray over Iraq as Powell Backs Call for Weapons Inspectors," *Independent,* September 2, 2002; and Howard Fineman and Tamara Lipper, "Same as He Ever Was," *Newsweek,* September 9, 2002. The latter contains the claim that Cheney had not cleared all the details of his speech with the Bush administration. In his fly-on-the-wall history of Bush administration Afghanistan and Iraq military policy, *Bush at War,* Bob Woodward writes: "Cheney was beyond hell-bent for action against Saddam. It was as if nothing else existed" (2002,

346). In his 2004 book *Plan of Attack,* Bob Woodward records Cheney's "war fever" and "obsession" with an Iraq invasion, but makes clear that George W. Bush was also strongly behind the Iraq invasion from the beginning of his administration.

14. Colum Lynch, "Firm's Iraq Deals Greater Than Cheney Has Said; Affiliates Had $73 Million in Contracts," *Washington Post,* June 23, 2001. For a critique of Cheney's tenure as CEO of Halliburton, see Robert Bryce, "Halliburton's Boss from Hell," *Salon,* July 21, 2004, at http://www.salon.com/news/feature/2004/07/21/halliburton/index.html.

15. See Karen DeYoung, "Bush, Blair Decry Hussein," *Washington Post,* September 8, 2002.

16. In Kellner (2003a), I suggest how Bush administration policy could lead to an Orwellian nightmare future; see Orwell (1961), the analysis of Orwell's *1984* in Kellner (1990), and the application of Orwell to the Bush administration in Chapter 6.

17. See William Saletan, "Shoot First: Bush's Whitewashed National Security Manifesto," *Slate,* September 20, 2002; Peter Slevin, "Analysts: New Strategy Courts Unseen Dangers—First Strike Could Be Precedent for Other Nations," *Washington Post,* September 22, 2002; and Paul Krugman, "White Man's Burden," *New York Times,* September 24, 2002.

18. William Galston, "Perils of Preemptive War," *American Prospect* 13(17) (September 2002).

19. The vote would come back and haunt John Kerry and John Edwards, who during the 2004 Democratic primary season and then the election had trouble defending their vote to empower Bush to go to war in Iraq. Others like Senator Robert Byrd saw that this resolution could constitute a slippery slope to Bush's rush to war and adamantly opposed the resolution, arguing: "This is the Tonkin Gulf resolution all over again…. Let us stop, look, and listen. Let us not give this president or any president unchecked power. Remember the Constitution." Byrd continued to be an outspoken critic of Bush war policy, and published a book attacking Bush's foreign policy and usurpation of what he saw as illicit presidential power, *Losing America: Confronting a Reckless and Arrogant Presidency* (New York: W. W. Norton, 2004).

20. This led Bush and Cheney in the 2004 election to lie that Saddam Hussein had thrown the inspectors out and would not allow further inspections, thus necessitating war; see Chapter 6. For refutation of the claims that Iraq had weapons of mass destruction and threw out arms inspectors in 2003, see the thorough discussion of arms inspections throughout the 1990s and from 2002 to 2003 in Ritter (2004).

21. An article by Neil Mackay, "Bush Planned Iraq 'Regime Change' before Becoming President," *Sunday Herald,* September 15, 2002, widely circulated via the Internet, called attention to the militarist and unilateralist global strategic vision that informed Bush administration policy. The 2000 PNAC plan is available at http://www.new americancentury.org/RebuildingAmericasDefenses.pdf. The PNAC plan for regime change in Iraq goes back to a 1992 report prepared for then Secretary of Defense Dick Cheney by Paul Wolfowitz, which called for development of a plan to overthrow Saddam Hussein and use U.S. military power to secure Middle East oil supplies; it was redevel-

oped in a 1997 PNAC "Statement of Foreign Policy Principles," which focused on regime change in Iraq and the removal of Saddam Hussein from power; see Ritter (2003), pp. 71ff.

22. See "Attack on Iraq Is Unavoidable: U.S. Official's Warning," *Dawn*, February 5, 2002. For a telling portrait of Perle, known as the "Prince of Darkness," see Chris Suellentrop, "Richard Perle—Washington's Faceful Bureaucrat," at www.slate.com, August 23, 2002. Jude Wanniski once described Perle as "the world's No. 1 hawk ... who has been the chief architect of our policy toward the Arab/Islamic world. There is no single American more responsible for inciting outrage among Muslims globally than Richard, whose maniacal prescriptions led inexorably to last week's cataclysm." See "The Prince of Darkness" at http://polyconomics.com/showarticle.asp?articleid=1634. Eric Boehlert provides a useful overview documenting how many times Perle has been wrong about Iraq and other Middle East issues on which he presents himself as an expert. For Boehlert, Perle can consistently be seen as one of "Israel's strongest, most ardent right-wing allies in Washington." See "The Armchair General," *Salon*, September 5, 2002, at http://archive.salon.com/news/feature/2002/09/05/perle/index.html. Former U.S. ambassador and diplomat Joseph Wilson (2004) described Perle and his neoconservative colleagues as a "cult" who had taken over U.S. foreign policy in the Bush administration. Wilson's wife had been "outed" as a CIA agent by Bush administration officials in retaliation for Wilson's going to the media and contesting Bush administration claims concerning Iraqi nuclear programs, a story that Wilson recounts in his book *The Politics of Truth*. Seymour Hersh (2004) in turn provides a look at Perle's sleazy business practices and using his ultra right-wing politics and connections to personally profit. Yet it would be a mistake to blame the Iraq debacle on a few misguided neocon ideologues, for clearly George W. Bush, Dick Cheney, Donald Rumsfeld, and others in the Bush administration and Pentagon had agendas for supporting the war that often went beyond the neocon agenda.

23. Robert Greenberg, *Uncovered* (2003). This documentary featured Powell's UN speech and other allegations from members of the Bush administration concerning Iraqi "weapons of mass destruction." The documentary presented systematic refutation of Bush administration claims by former U.S. intelligence officers, members of the U.S. government, and academic specialists. Powell's claims were critically dissected and he was judged a particularly poor reader of intelligence and interpreter of satellite pictures. Powell's UN presentation was perhaps the low point of U.S. public diplomacy, and in retrospect completely discredits the Bush administration, CIA, and Colin Powell. Tenet resigned as head of the CIA in June 2004.

24. Information surfaced that alleges that both the United States and United Kingdom were spying on their UN allies, who were attempting to find a compromise resolution that might prevent war, suggesting that the two countries were illegally undermining UN operations. Evidence of the spying may have led to the collapse of final peace measures; see Peter Beaumont, Martin Bright, and Jo Tuckman, "Spying Games on the Road to War" and "British Spy Op Wrecked Peace Move," *Observer*, February 15, 2004.

25. See Clarke (2004); Philips (2004); Suskind (2004); and Woodward (2004).

26. On the phoniness of the Bush administration discourse of the "coalition of the willing," see Rampton and Stauber (2003), pp. 116–118; and Corn (2003).

27. On how mainstream newspapers including the *New York Times* and *Washington Post* fell prey to Bush administration propaganda concerning alleged Iraqi weapons of mass destruction before the war, see Michael Massing, "Now They Tell Us," *New York Review of Books*, February 26, 2004, and "Unfit to Print," June 24, 2004.

28. For my previous studies of war, media, and propaganda, see Kellner (1992, 2003a). For my daily Internet commentary on the media, Bush administration, Iraq, and other topics, see blogleft at http://www.gseis.ucla.edu/courses/ed253a/blogger.php.

29. On May 29, 2003, *CBS News* reported that no bunker, bodies, or evidence that Saddam Hussein or his family was at the site bombed the opening night of the war was found. Woodward's "insider" account (2004) describes the Iraqi agents who presented this (mis)information and how their reports led to the Iraq invasion getting off to a bad start.

30. See the studies in Artz and Kamalipour (2004); Kamalipour and Snow (2004); and Miller (2004).

31. Soon after, British and then U.S. military sources affirmed that the site was not a chemical weapons production or storage facility. For a critique of a series of "smoking gun" discoveries of weapons of mass destruction facilities and their subsequent debunking, see Jake Tapper, "WMD, MIA?" *Salon*, April 16, 2003, and "Angry Allies," *Salon*, May 30, 2003. Corn (2003) provides systematic analysis of Bush administration lies about alleged Iraqi "weapons of mass destruction," although at one point George W. Bush claimed that the United States had found the weapons (277ff.). Corn also makes the point that the U.S. failure to secure known Iraqi weapons sites meant that Iraqi weapons circulated widely and fell into dangerous hands, a point that came out near the end of the U.S. presidential campaign (see Chapter 6).

32. Eyewitness accounts of the U.S. bombing of civilian neighborhoods in Baghdad and descriptions of finding U.S. missile parts can be found in the London *Independent* during the last week of March 2003, including Robert Fisk, "In Baghdad, Blood and Bandages for the Innocent," *Independent*, March 30, 2003, at http://argument.independent.co.uk/commentators/story.jsp?story=392161. For documents confirming that it was indeed a U.S. missile that killed Iraqis in Baghdad in late March, when the U.S. military authorities were denying the claims, see http://www.indymedia.org.uk/en/2003/03/60676.html.

33. For the story that questioned official U.S. military accounts of the checkpoint shootings of a civilian family, see William Branigin, "A Gruesome Scene on Highway 9," *Washington Post*, April 1, 2003, p. A01.

34. An April 3 *Washington Post* story by Susan Schmidt and Vernon Loeb headlined "She Was Fighting to Her Death," based on unnamed military sources, claimed that Lynch "continued firing at the Iraqis even after she sustained multiple gunshot wounds," and that she was also stabbed by Iraqis who captured her. In fact, Lynch's vehicle took a wrong turn, overturned, and she was hurt in the accident, not by fighting Iraqis.

35. See Mitch Potter, "The Real 'Saving Pte. Lynch,'" *Toronto Star,* May 5, 2003. The Associated Press also confirmed this story, as did the BBC on May 15 and *CBS News* on May 29.

36. For systematic analysis of the new barbarism accompanying and in part generated by the Bush administration and their hard-right supporters, see Kellner (2003a). See also Jim Rutenberg, "Cable's War Coverage Suggests a New 'Fox Effect' on Television," *New York Times,* April 16, 2003. Rutenberg provides examples of Fox's aggressively opinionated and biased discourse, as when anchor Neil Cavuto said of those who oppose the war on Iraq: "You were sickening then, you are sickening now." Fox's high ratings during the war influenced CNN and the NBC networks to be more patriotic and dismissive of those who criticized the war and its aftermath.

37. Rogers was interviewed on Howard Kurtz's CNN media review *Reliable Sources* on April 27, 2003. On the UK broadcasting networks' attitude toward showing images of dead or injured civilians and soldiers, see Julian Petley, "'Let the Atrocious Images Haunt Us,'" in Miller (2004) pp. 164–175. The United States and United Kingdom avoided providing Iraqi casualty figures for the war although various websites have attempted to compile figures; see http://www.iraqbodycount.net, which as of December 21, 2004, estimated a minimum 14,880 and possible 17,076 Iraqi dead from the war and its aftermath.

38. On bias and distortion in U.S. networks' presentation of the Iraq war, see Rampton and Strauber (2003) and Norman Solomon, "'Look, I'm an American,'" in Miller (2004), pp. 157–163. On UK broadcasters' presentation of the war, see Justin Lewis and Rod Brooks, "Reporting the War on British Television," in Miller (2004), pp. 132–143.

39. There were, to be sure, reliable war correspondents on the ground in Iraq, especially reporters from the *New York Times, Washington Post,* and *Los Angeles Times,* which had fairly large crews and good reporters in the war zone. British papers like the *Guardian* and *Independent* also had first-rate reporters and critical commentary. Occasionally, the BBC or CBC would have critical reports. On the whole, however, during the Bush era U.S. corporate broadcasting is little more than a war propaganda bureau for the U.S. military, giving the Pentagon "full spectrum dominance," including the sphere of information seen to be crucial to contemporary war.

40. Although mainstream media at the time used headlines like "Iraqis Topple Statue of Saddam and Celebrate the Fall of Baghdad," Associated Press, April 10, 2003, it was later revealed in an internal army study that the statue toppling was a SYYOPS project maneuvered by the military. A Marine colonel had decided to topple the statue and "it was a quick-thinking army psychological operations team that made it appear to be a spontaneous Iraqi undertaking," said David Zucchino in "Army Stage-Managed Fall of Hussein Statue," *Los Angeles Times,* July 3, 2004.

41. Evidently, the museum community thought it had an understanding with the U.S. military of the need to preserve Iraqi national treasures, which were allowed by the U.S. military to be looted and destroyed while they protected the Petroleum Ministry;

see http://www.nytimes.com/2003/04/16/international/worldspecial/16MUSE.html. On the looting of the Ministry for Religious Affairs, see http://www.nytimes.com/2003/04/16/international/worldspecial/16BAGH.html. Later reports indicated that some of the museum artifacts believed destroyed were hidden, but there were also reports of continued looting of Iraqi archaeological sites throughout the country that were not protected by the United States; see Edmund L. Andrews, "Iraqi Looters Tearing Up Archaeological Sites," *New York Times,* May 23, 2003. Joseph Wilson (2004) claims that Rumsfeld associate Douglas Freith was given a list of the important cultural sites to defend, but no action was taken to defend any major Baghdad site except the Oil Ministry.

Chapter 4

Pandora's Box: The Iraq Horror Show

F OR WEEKS AFTER THE FALL OF THE IRAQI REGIME, negative images continued to circulate of clashes between Iraqi and U.S. forces, gigantic Shia demonstrations and celebrations that produced the specter of the growing radical Islamic power in the region, and the continued failure to produce security and stability. The spectacle of the Shia on the march taking over power in many regions of the country created worries that "democracy" in Iraq could produce a religious fundamentalist regime. This disturbing result suggests the limitations of a politics of spectacle that can backfire, spiral out of control, and generate unintended consequences.

Reversal of the Spectacle

> It is the photographs that give one the vivid realization of what actually took place. Words don't do it.... You see the photographs, and you get a sense of it, and you cannot help but be outraged.
> —*Donald Rumsfeld, U.S. Secretary of Defense*

In Gulf War I, Iraq's flight from its occupation of Kuwait and apparent military defeat was followed by the spectacle of Shiite and Kurdish uprisings and their violent suppression by the Hussein regime, ultimately coding the success of the Gulf War as ambiguous and contributing to George H. W. Bush's defeat in 1992. Likewise, although the September 11 terrorist attacks on the United States by the Al Qaeda network appeared to be a triumph by the Islamic radicals, worldwide revulsion against the attacks and the global and multilateral attempts to close down the network appear to have seriously weakened the Al Qaeda forces. Yet the brutal spectacle of the U.S. military unilaterally attacking Afghanistan and then invading Iraq may have helped revive Al Qaeda and inspire recruits to similar Jihadist groups.[1]

Politics of spectacle are thus highly unstable, subject to multiple interpretations, and often generate unanticipated effects, as when the Republican attempts to use Bill Clinton's sexual escapades to promote his impeachment backfired and created sympathy and support for him (Kellner 2003c). Media spectacles are subject to dialectical reversal as positive images give way to negative ones. Spectacles of war are difficult to manage, and can be subject to different framings and interpretations, as when non-U.S. broadcasting networks focus on Iraqi civilian casualties, looting and chaos, and U.S. military crimes against Iraqis rather than the U.S. victory over the "evil" of Saddam Hussein. It is obviously too soon to determine the long-term effects of Bush's 2003 Iraq war, but the consequences are likely to be complex and unforeseen, thus rendering claims that the reckless venture represents a great victory premature and quite possibly erroneous.

Attempting to counter the negative spectacle, the Bush administration on May 1, 2003, organized a dramatic presentation of Bush piloting a naval aircraft onto the *USS Abraham Lincoln.* In this carefully orchestrated media event, Bush emerged in full *Top Gun* regalia from a jet plane with "Navy One" and "George W. Bush, Commander-in-Chief" logos. Strutting out of the aircraft, helmet in hand, Bush crossed the flight deck accompanied by a cheering crowd and with full television crews that had been anticipating the big event for hours. Delivering a "victory" speech from a podium with a giant banner "Mission Accomplished" behind him, Bush declared that the "major combat operations in Iraq have ended. In the battle of Iraq, the United States and our allies have prevailed."[2] Following Bush's attempt at a triumphant spectacle, insurgency against the U.S. occupation intensified, and the spectacle of guerilla warfare and terrorism proliferated. During the summer of 2003, Iraqi attacks on U.S. troops rose from about 15 a day to 35 a day. Starting in August 2003, attacks multiplied against the UN troops, other foreign troops, reconstruction teams, and Iraqi police and military forces being trained to stabilize the chaotic country.[3] The attacks were violent political spectacle aimed at the global media, which quickly broadcast each assault, circulating images of death throughout the global village.

The spectacle of insurgency was temporarily displaced in December 2003 with the capture of Saddam Hussein, who appeared dazed, beaten, with a long flowing beard, uncut hair, and dirty clothes. The sight of an American doctor going through his hair for lice and examining his mouth was played over and

over, producing images of the mighty leader fallen to the depths of degrada-
tion.[4] Yet Saddam's capture did not lead to the end of the Iraqi insurgency, and
throughout the spring and into the summer of 2004, attacks on U.S. troops
increased, and the killing of Iraqis working with the U.S. forces escalated dramatically. By early 2004, reporters questioned whether Iraq ever had the "weapons of mass destruction" attributed to it and debates intensified as to whether
the Iraq venture was a positive or negative event.[5] Indeed, the eruption of violence in April 2004, weeks before the United States had planned to hand over
power to the Iraqis, raised serious issues concerning whether democracy could be
constructed in Iraq and what role the United States would have in Iraq's future.

On March 28, 2004, the U.S. occupation forces closed the newspaper *al-
Hawza* run by supporters of Shiite radical Muqtada al-Sadr, and shortly thereafter arrested Mustafa Yaqubi, his deputy in Najaf. Around the same time, U.S.
forces killed civilians in Fallujah. Insurgents in the town captured four U.S.
contractors, brutally murdered them, dragged their corpses through the streets,
and hung their bodies on a bridge, to the accompaniment of cheering towns-
people and global media coverage. The United States retaliated with fierce fire-
power, bombing a mosque and killing more than 800 Iraqis. As this drama
played out, al-Sadr forces took over police stations in Baghdad and cities in
southern Iraq, and in the fights against insurgent Iraqi forces throughout the
country the death toll of U.S. troops and Iraqis rose dramatically, leading to
comparisons with the Vietnam debacle.[6]

The April 2004 battle in Fallujah was fought to a standstill, and with negative publicity and growing anger of Iraqis over U.S. violence in Iraq, U.S. military forces withdrew from the city rather than engaging in an expected all-out
attack. Moreover, signaling a reversal in policy, the U.S. occupation forces agreed
to let former members of Saddam Hussein's military control Iraqi forces who
would supposedly patrol Fallujah. The Fallujah debacle was accompanied by
the first photos of U.S. coffins, a topic hitherto forbidden. After a Kuwaiti con-
tractor sent pictures to her home newspaper, the website "Memory Hole" released hundreds of pictures of coffins that quickly circulated via the Internet,
broadcasting media, and print press. On the one-year anniversary of George
W. Bush declaring that "major combat operations" had ended, accompanied
by a large poster "Mission Accomplished," ABC's *Nightline* broadcast photos, if
available, of the 721 soldiers who had died in Iraq.

To complicate the U.S. occupation, in late April 2004, pictures were released
of U.S. soldiers torturing and humiliating Iraqi prisoners in Saddam Hussein's
notorious military fortress Abu Ghraib. The entire world was appalled by this
behavior, undermining what little legitimacy the U.S. occupying forces had and

creating immense public relations problems for the Bush administration and Pentagon. Indeed, the repetitive stream of images of Iraqi prisoner abuse by U.S. soldiers and the quest to pin responsibility on the soldiers themselves and/ or higher U.S. military and political authorities produced one of the most intense media spectacles of the contemporary epoch.

Although the photos put on display the ubiquity of media spectacle and the powerful impact of images, their digital origins and circulation also require consideration. Upon obtaining more than 1,000 digital photos shortly after the initial cycle of images was released by CBS and the *New Yorker,* the *Washington Post* commented in a display of photos on May 7, 2004, that although many of the images revealed shocking poses of prisoner abuse and torture, many more were of mundane scenes of daily life in Iraq. Moreover, the digital archive was not the work of professional photojournalists but of young U.S. soldiers. It was as if a generation raised on the media and in possession of digital cameras and camcorders naturally documented its own life, as if it was participating in a reality television show or political documentary. Although there were reports that the images were intended for use to intimidate new Iraqi prisoners to "soften them up" for interrogation,[7] the pictures also emerged from fascination with taking pictures and the digital documentation of everyday life. They revealed as well how quickly such images could leave a foreign country under U.S. military control by way of the Internet and circulate around the world.

Whereas during the 1991 Gulf War, the United States censored every image and word in the media pool system concocted for that intervention, and had strict guidelines and control mechanisms for the embedded reporters in the 2003 Iraq intervention, the digital age has made it ultimately impossible to hide the dark sides of the current Iraq occupation. The widespread use of digital cameras and the ease with which images could be shot and disseminated, including direct transmission through wireless connections, demonstrated how media spectacle could trump U.S. military control. As Donald Rumsfeld exclaimed during the Iraq prisoner abuse hearings on May 7: "people are running around with digital cameras and taking these unbelievable photographs and then passing them off, against the law, to the media, to our surprise, when they had not even arrived in the Pentagon." The Pentagon indicated during these Senate and House hearings that many, many more photos and videos were in play, but in the light of the negative publicity already received, military leaders managed to prevent circulation of more scandalous material.

The role of media images in warfare and the new role of digital spectacle was dramatized further on May 11, 2004, when gruesome imagery of American Nick Berg's beheading was released to the global media. The horrifying shots quickly circulated and made it clear that digital technology was an asymmetric tool of war that any side could use to sway public opinion. Revelations during the same week that photos of alleged Iraqi prisoner abuse by British soldiers were counterfeit also reveals the fragile nature of digital imagery, that it can be altered and faked, and that it is hard to differentiate between real images and digital simulacra. Yet the sheer volume and ugliness of the images of U.S. prisoner abuse focused attention on the catastrophe of the Iraqi war itself and what it was doing to both the Iraqis and U.S. occupation forces.

Deeply rooted racism lies behind the Iraqi prisoner abuse, as soldiers and the U.S. public have widely viewed Iraqis and Arabs as less than human at least since the Gulf War of 1991. Arabs and Iraqis have been villains of countless Hollywood films and television shows, and racism toward Arabs and Muslims intensified after the 9/11 attacks. Near the end of the first Gulf War, U.S. soldiers went on a "turkey shoot," slaughtering hundreds of Iraqis escaping from Kuwait City. During the current Iraq war, U.S. snipers talk of "rats' nests" of Iraqi troops and cheer when they take out the "vermin." U.S. architect for the Iraq invasion Paul Wolfowitz speaks of "snakes" and "draining the swamps" in "uncivilized parts of the world."

Such racist and dehumanizing perceptions facilitate reducing Iraqi prisoners to animals, as when one of the U.S. Abu Ghraib prison guards, Lyndee England, tied a leash around a naked Iraqi prisoner as if he were a dog, or U.S. soldiers perversely constructed stacks of naked Iraqi bodies into sexually humiliating positions. The image of Lyndee England pointing to a masturbating Iraqi male prisoner with one thumb up and another pointing to the Iraqi's genitals, accompanied by a grotesque leer, again points to the pornographic nature of prisoner abuse. Shortly after the initial pictures of Abu Ghraib had been released, Seymour Hersh released another set of photos taken over a twelve-minute period on December 12, 2003, in Abu Ghraib that showed U.S. military authorities using army dogs to terrorize the Iraqi prisoners, including one that showed an Iraqi prisoner "naked. His hands are clasped behind his neck and he is leaning against the door to a cell, contorted with terror, as the dogs bark a few feet away" (2004, 35). In another shocking image, a hooded Iraqi prisoner standing atop a box has his arms stretched out and wires attached to his fingers connected to electrical lines. The hood evokes Ku Klux Klan lynchings, the pose of the Iraqi with his arms spread out evokes Christ on the cross, and the grotesque figure as a whole reminds art-sensitive viewers of Goya's sketches of the horrors of war.

To be sure, the pornographic overtones and participation by men and women, along with the gloating and smirking faces of the U.S. prison guards, made the particular Abu Ghraib prison images especially distressing. Yet any number of other images of dead Iraqi civilians, U.S. bombing errors, brutal treatment by the U.S. forces of Iraqis, and the like could be easily documented and distributed through the world media. Part of the shock and distress of the images resulted from the sanitized view of the Iraq intervention in the U.S. corporate media. Wars are often defined in the public mind by negative images of atrocity, such as the naked young girl fleeing in Vietnam, with her body scarred by napalm, or the image of a young U.S. soldier lighting a peasant hut on fire with his cigarette lighter. Iraq, too, may be remembered by horrific images, in this case taken by the U.S. troops themselves.

The pictures also depict a brutal colonial mentality. The *Washington Post* noted that the cache of more than 1,000 digital pictures revealed that the young troops took pictures of camels, exotic vistas of Iraq, and scenes of ordinary people as well as copious photos of prisoner abuse. Many of the quasi-pornographic images released of the Iraqi male prisoners depicted a feminization of them, naked or in women's undergarments, humiliated and emasculated. There is, of course, a long tradition of taking pictures of exotic places, just as there is a tradition of documenting bloody atrocity scenes in wartime. In a digital age, these genres and impulses merged together, producing a panorama of horror that may end military careers and deflate U.S. imperial ambitions in the Middle East for a generation.

Summer of 2004 reports by the U.S. Army and by the Pentagon inspector general tended to cover over the Abu Ghraib prison scandals, blaming them on the guards and absolving higher-up officers from responsibility, a whitewash that was roundly criticized. Meanwhile, stories circulated, but were rarely highlighted on television, concerning Iraqi "ghost prisons," where inmates were taken from one prison to another, unofficially detained, and interrogated. Other stories hinted at children's prisons and even "rape rooms," with stories of pictures and tapes documenting the sexual abuse of Iraqi children prisoners.[8] A twist occurred in the prison abuse scandal in August 2004 in which U.S. National Guards from Oregon discovered Iraqi soldiers torturing prisoners and intervened to get them to stop, and when they were ordered to ignore the prisoner abuse, they revealed the incident to a hometown newspaper.[9]

Previously, it was largely the Arab media that focused upon the unsavory aspects of the U.S. Iraq invasion and occupation, showing many bloody images of Iraqi civilian victims of U.S. military action and unflattering images of U.S. military forces and politicians. This is documented in *Control Room* (2004), a film about the al Jazeera network watching the horrible destruction of the Iraq war from the Iraqi point of view. The Abu Ghraib spectacle brought home the brutality, horror, and monstrousness of the Iraq war to many U.S. audiences for the first time. Moreover, as Katha Pollitt noted, the Abu Ghraib "pictures and stories have naturally caused a furor around the world. Not only are they grotesque in themselves, they reinforce the preexisting impression of Americans as racist, cruel, and frivolous. They are bound to alienate—further alienate—Iraqis who hoped that the invasion would lead to secular democracy and a normal life and who fear Islamic rule. Abroad, if not here at home, they underscore how stupid and wrong the invasion of Iraq was in the first place, how predictably the 'war of choice' that was going to be a cakewalk has become a brutal and corrupt occupation, justified by a doctrine of American exceptionalism that nobody but Americans believes."[10]

With the Pandora's box of American evils in Iraq opened and the media's tendency toward pack journalism, the Abu Ghraib spectacle was the feeding frenzy of the moment, but within weeks the controversy had died down. The military and media both attempted to cover up the horrific scandal, which was soon replaced by the new media spectacle of the moment. Yet the episode showed that in a media age, images are impossible to control and a media spectacle concocted to be a triumphal display of U.S. military power, like Bush's Iraq adventure, can easily reverse into a spectacle of U.S. arrogance, brutality, and malfeasance. The images displayed the errors of U.S. policy, the dehumanization of both Iraqis and U.S. troops, and the monstrousness of prisoner abuse and torture. They also graphically demonstrated the need for international law to regulate treatment of prisoners of war. The Abu Ghraib images circulated throughout the world and constituted strong anti–United States propaganda spectacles. As trials of those involved in the Iraqi prisoner abuse and torture continue into 2005, so far no official in the Bush administration or Pentagon has taken responsibility, has been charged with crimes, or has been punished.

Iraqi "Sovereignty," the Chalabi Scandals, and the Battle for Najaf

> Rarely has a passage of powers been so furtive. The ceremony—held two days ahead of schedule, deep within Baghdad's fortified Green Zone—lasted just ten minutes, with thirty U.S. and Iraqi officials present. Outside the cement stockade, the military realities remain the same: an occupation force of 160,000 U.S.-led troops, an additional army of commercial security guards, and jumpy police forces.
>
> —*Susan Watkins, "Vichy on the Tigris"*

The big news of the summer of 2004 was the June 28 transfer of sovereignty to Iraq in a secret ceremony a few days before the official hand-over of power was planned. Citing security concerns, the United States passed over "sovereignty" to Iraq in a brief ceremony, followed by the quick exit out of the country by U.S. pro-consul Paul Bremer, seen by Iraqis as a dictator. In the eyes of many critics, Bremer had done a disastrous job, refusing to allow military and professional Baathist party members to participate in the new government, controlling Iraqi politics in a heavy-handed fashion, and privatizing as much of the economy as possible, at the same time handing out contracts to U.S. firms like Halliburton that were paid by Iraqi oil money and not the delegated U.S. reconstruction funds.[11] When Bremer left Baghdad on June 28, the United States had spent less than 2 percent of the billions of dollars allocated by Congress to repair Iraq's shattered infrastructure. Critics joked that Bremer's Coalition Provisional Authority (CPA) stood for "Can't Provide Anything," and indeed after 18 months of de facto U.S. rule, Iraq was still in a state of chaos without adequate security, medical care, electricity, or sewer control. Scandalously, Bremer had signed "100 Orders" before leaving that privatized key Iraqi industries and put U.S. corporations in positions of control as well as allowing 100 percent foreign ownership of Iraqi businesses, unrestricted tax-free remittance of all profits, and 40-year ownership leases. Critics claimed that the Bremer orders were illegal, violating the Hague regulations of 1907, which ruled out fundamental transformation of an occupied country's laws.[12]

To replace Bremer, the United States, with the reluctant assent of UN officials, had chosen an ex-Iraqi intelligence functionary, Ayad Allawi, with alleged ties to the CIA, M16, and other foreign intelligence forces, to serve as interim prime minister and to presumably help lead the way for eventual elections. He and others on the handpicked Iraqi council were seen as U.S. stooges and did not have real popular support. In light of the fact that 160,000 U.S. troops still occupied the country and were the target of a violent anti-U.S. insurgency, and that the United States had set up the structure through which Iraq was governed and handpicked the leaders, Iraqi sovereignty was dubious at best.

The politician who had received the strongest U.S. backing, Ahmed Chalabi, saw his fortunes rapidly decline when he was first accused of having connections with the Iranian government, allegedly revealing, among other things, that the United States had broken Iranian codes. He was then accused in August 2004 of laundering counterfeit money. Chalabi's nephew Salem, in charge of the prosecution of Saddam Hussein and other Baath party officials, was accused of the murder of a judge who had been investigating his finances and business activities.[13]

Meanwhile, following the hand-over of sovereignty in Iraq, the drama of insurgency almost disappeared from U.S. television, especially the cable networks. In his campaign rhetoric, George W. Bush began proclaiming that "we have turned a corner" in Iraq and on the economy, a mantra he intoned in daily speeches, which was obviously being tested as a basis for reelection in November. The two months following the apparent hand-over to Iraqi leaders, however, exhibited sharply increased violence, with an escalation of kidnappings and some dramatic beheadings, continued daily assaults on U.S. troops, bombs killing scores of Iraqis, and daily horrors in the Pandora's box of Iraq that the Bush administration had so unwisely opened. Indeed, in July of 2004 as the U.S. media tended to ignore Iraq, the killing of U.S. troops surpassed the previous month's total. In Eric Boehlert's summary, during the last days of July there were unremitting episodes of daily violence including:

- July 26: Attackers shot and killed Iraq's senior Interior Ministry official and two of his bodyguards in a drive-by shooting.
- July 26: A suicide bomber detonated a car filled with explosives, mortars, and rockets near the gates of a U.S. base in Mosul, killing three.
- July 27: The dead body of a kidnapped Turkish truck driver was found.
- July 27: One Iraqi was killed and 14 coalition soldiers were injured when a mortar hit a Baghdad residential district.
- July 28: A car bomb exploded on a busy boulevard in Baquba, killing 68 people and wounding nearly 100. The attack stood as the deadliest insurgent strike since the U.S. occupation began last year.
- July 28: Seven Iraqi soldiers and 35 insurgents were killed during a firefight in Suwariyah.
- July 29: Reeling from the violence and a wave of kidnappings, Iraqi officials once again postponed a three-day national conference to choose an interim assembly in preparation for the country's first elections.

Experts say that week was typical of the chaos that has transpired in Iraq this summer, with or without the spotlight of the U.S. press shining on the region. "Iraq remains very much in the balance. That's the only fair assessment you can make right now," says Brookings' Singer.

"I've talked to friends who served in the CPA, and I don't know anybody with on-the-ground experience in Iraq who doesn't think the situation there isn't completely screwed up," adds Cook.

"Iraqis are so embittered and [have] completely lost any faith in us, even the most pro-American Iraqis," says the *Philadelphia Inquirer*'s Dilanian, who says he has had a profound change of heart on the topic. Last April, fresh from reporting in Iraq, an optimistic Dilanian wrote that the press was ignoring improvements in Iraq and underplaying the chance for a real turnaround. In late

June he returned to Baghdad to cover the sovereignty hand-over. Summing up his new grim impressions in an Aug. 1 article, Dilanian admitted his earlier prediction was wrong and wrote, "The situation in Iraq right now is not as bad as the news media are portraying it to be. It's worse. Most Iraqis aren't seeing the improvements they had hoped for, and they're not blaming the guerrillas—they're blaming the Americans. Sovereignty seems to have had zero effect on this equation."

That's the key story many American news outlets have missed since June 28. [14]

As Boehlert documents, both the press and television systematically downplayed the Iraq fiasco during this period, even as violence escalated and more and more critics began to see the situation as impossible, at least as long as George W. Bush remained president.[15] A major confrontation in August 2004, however, between the U.S. occupation troops and the militia of radical cleric Muqtada al-Sadr threatened to bring more chaos into Iraq and further destabilize the country and the entire Middle East. A report by U.S. professor Michael Schwartz provides a useful summary of the unfolding of the Battle of Najaf:

[a] truce in May ended the first round of armed confrontation between U.S. Marines and Muqtada al-Sadr's militia, the al-Mahdi Army, but was never fully honored by either side. American troops were supposed to stay out of Najaf, and al-Sadr's militiamen were supposed to disband as an army. In the intervening months of relative peace, neither side made particularly provocative moves, but the U.S. still mounted patrols and the al-Mahdi Army continued to stockpile arms, notably in the city's vast, holy cemetery. Lots of threats were proffered on both sides.

The new confrontation began after the Americans replaced Army troops with Marines in the area outside Najaf and then sent two armed patrols, including local police, to al-Sadr's home. The arrival of the second patrol led to a firefight with casualties on both sides. In the meantime, the Marines and the Iraqi police detained at least a dozen al-Mahdi Army members.

The al-Mahdi soldiers retaliated by attacking a local police station. Previously, there had been a modest pattern of peaceful coexistence between the police and al-Sadr's followers, except when the Sadrists were directly attacked. They also took policemen as hostages, a new tactic that they justified by pointing to the detained Sadrists and calling for an exchange of prisoners.

On Aug. 5, the U.S. counterattacked in force—with the official blessing of Iraqi Prime Minister Allawi—using a remarkably similar military strategy to the one that had created an international crisis in Falluja back in April. After first surrounding the city, they assaulted al-Mahdi positions with long range weapons, notably helicopter gunships armed with rockets, and even jets. They then sent Marines (and Iraqi security forces) into the holy cemetery at the heart of Najaf to root out dug-in al-Mahdi soldiers and capture their weapons caches. This fierce attack produced two days of heavy fighting, heavily reported in the press, and evidently destroyed significant portions of the downtown area. A tank, for instance, was described in one report as firing directly into hotels where al-Mahdi fighters were said to be holed up.

In the three days that followed, the Marines penetrated ever further into the city (at a cost so far of 5 dead, 19 wounded, and one helicopter downed) and for a period, even took the cemetery itself, though in a description which had a Vietnam-era ring to it, "A Marine spokesman said insurgents had fled the cemetery after an assault on Friday. But when U.S. forces withdrew from the area, the insurgents moved back in." By day six, American tanks had moved into the cemetery and helicopters were strafing the area. The Sadrists warned that further attacks would be met by extending the fight to other cities (as had happened in the previous round of fighting in April and May) and al-Sadr himself swore he would never leave the city but would defend it to "the last drop of my blood," calling for a more general uprising. At least some Shia clerics supported this call for general insurrection.[16]

Schwartz concluded that the Najaf intervention "was anything but a small incident that had spun out of control; it was, on the American side, a concerted effort to annihilate the Sadrist forces." He maintained that the events constitute "a deliberate U.S. provocation" and that the incursion could be a desperate attempt by the Bush administration to win a decisive battle that could help it claim that they have "turned the corner" in Iraq. A failure, however, could be catastrophic for the region and for Bush's reelection.

As a three-day meeting took place in Baghdad of Iraq's interim government to begin planning for democratic home rule, al-Sadr and the U.S. forces continued to fight in Najaf; a member of the governing council went to Najaf to try to negotiate with al-Sadr, offering him an invitation to form a party and participate in the new government. Al-Sadr did not show up at a planned meeting, although on August 19 he appeared to consent to the agreement, which called for a cease-fire and abandoning the holy Najaf mosque in which his militia were quartered. On August 20, after days of heavy U.S. bombing of the area around the mosque, there were reports that Iraqi police had stormed the building and arrested al-Sadr militants, but later reports the same day claimed that the al-Sadr forces continue to control the shrine.[17]

For several days the cat-and-mouse tactics continued with the Iraqi government threatening to crack down on al-Sadr's forces and then offering him amnesty, with Sadrist spokespeople telling the government that they would hand over control of the mosque to Shia authorities and abandon the site—and then not doing so. During this interim the U.S. forces continued to pound the al-Sadr militia relentlessly, bombing sites in the old city near the mosque, reducing neighborhoods to rubble, terrorizing those who had remained in the city, and engaging in street fights that killed many on both sides.[18]

Meanwhile, violence continued in many other parts of Iraq, with near assassination of two Iraqi ministers and the usual mayhem throughout the country. In a powerful column, Jimmy Breslin passionately described the deaths of U.S. soldiers killed and the corruption of Bush administration and Pentagon bureaucrats who sent them to these horrible deaths.

> There were four Marines and an Army soldier killed in Iraq in one 24-hour period over the weekend. George Bush, who does not like people who go to war, probably will say that they are not dead. As of Aug. 20, we list 952 of our troops killed in fighting. That is the Defense Department figure. When the figure goes over 1,000, that can be devastating in an election. But the figure of 1,000, so easily remembered, already has been reached. That was on July 7, when a rocket-propelled grenade killed Pfc. Samuel Bowen of Cleveland. The people keeping track at the *Army Times* newspaper, which has given the best, and often the only, coverage of the war, made Bowen the 1,000th. The *Army Times*, with no election to effect, properly includes deaths in Afghanistan.
>
> The names of the dead in Iraq over the weekend have not been released yet, except for Army Pfc. Kevin A. Cuming, 22, of White Plains. And so you sat yesterday with all these Department of Defense death notices for the last weeks covering the desk and you glanced at them, with the ages of the dead reaching up from the paper to grab your throat. Now and then you called one of their homes to get a small idea of what they were like when they lived, and what we have lost in a war that now pleases only the mentally unbalanced. Printing as many names and as often as possible is a gloomy task.
>
> These are the deaths that the president and his people try to sneak past the country. The dead were brave men. The president is craven. He buries the war, and the news reporters, indolent and in fear of authority, follow like cattle going into pens. For so long, the public believed the news it was given. Saddam Hussein was going to blow us up with an atom bomb! The Muslims of Iraq love us![19]

On August 25, Iraq's most revered Shiite cleric, Grand Ayatollah Ali al-Sistani, announced that he was returning to Iraq after medical treatment in London to take control of the mosque in Najaf and end the fighting. The frail and allegedly apolitical cleric arrived in Basra and called upon his followers to march the next day to Najaf to take control of the mosque. The following day, al-Sistani and his entourage arrived in the outskirts of Najaf, but his entrance was accompanied by violence. A mosque in Kufa near Najaf was hit by three mortar shells, leaving dozens dead and wounded. As thousands gathered to march into the city, al-Sistani's followers were fired upon by Iraqi police (who claimed they were attacked by the crowd), setting off a stampede that killed at least 15 and wounded scores.[20] Fierce fighting continued around the mosque and a U.S. Marine was killed in action, the second to die in two days, bringing to 11 the number of U.S. service personnel lost in Najaf since fighting broke out August 5.[21]

The deal between al-Sadr and al-Sistani seemed to hold, however, making the Grand Ayatollah Ali al-Sistani the ruling force in southern Iraq after his bold and courageous move to enter the city and force an accord on al-Sadr. Yet the siege of Najaf can be seen as a defeat for the United States since, like Fallujah, the U.S. forces had backed out leaving their enemy forces quasi-triumphant, and because al-Sadr and all his militia could sneak out of the city to regroup and attack U.S. forces another day.[22] Indeed, many of al-Sadr's troops left the city, and there were reports that many carried guns and others hid their weapons for later use.

Furthermore, al-Sadr seemed to have received amnesty against charges that he had murdered a rival cleric and found his political position enhanced as one who could stand up to the United States. Moreover, much of the old city of Najaf around the mosque was destroyed after weeks of U.S. bombing and heavy fighting, and images of the devastation circulated through Iraqi and global television, thus creating another spectacle of U.S. destruction, showing again that the United States can win fights but lose the battle of hearts and minds.[23] The extent of anti-U.S. feeling after the destruction of much of old Najaf was striking. In *New York Times* reporter Dexter Filkins' account: "The end of the fighting here revealed a city center utterly devastated. Hotels crumbled into the street. Cars lay blackened and twisted where they had been hit. Goats and dogs lay dead on the sidewalks. Pilgrims from out of town and locals coming home walked the streets agape, shaking their heads, stunned by the devastation before them. 'Look at all the damage,' an Iraqi man said to a friend as he walked down a street whose every building had been broken and crushed. 'Let God take revenge on the Americans for this.'"[24] A *Washington Post* report noted:

Anger at the Americans and the interim government was easy to find among civilians who stepped gingerly into the streets Friday to inspect horrendous damage in sections of the city of 600,000. Millions of Muslims worldwide know Najaf from pilgrimages to the Imam Ali shrine and the seminaries that long made the city the world's leading center of study for Shiites.

"We blame Ayad Allawi and the government for this damage," said Jasim Aziz, 31, referring to the Iraqi interim prime minister. Aziz had traveled from Balad, 140 miles to the north, to visit the shrine. "They could have waited until Sistani arrived and solved the problems without destroying the city and killing all the civilians and the Iraqis."

"They asked the Americans to destroy the city," said Hussein Mailu, 55, referring to government leaders. "If they did not ask them, they wouldn't do it. Is this the democracy of Allawi? Saddam was so bad but he didn't do this thing," he said, referring to former president Saddam Hussein. "It was beautiful, but not any more."[25]

Although the Najaf wars seemed to have quieted down, violence continued in the rest of Iraq, as a car bomb apparently aimed at a U.S. military convoy went off in the northern city of Mosul, wounding at least 10 Iraqi civilians. In Baghdad, a U.S. patrol was hit by a grenade attack, wounding 12 soldiers. There was another attack on an oil tanker. In Kufa, an Iraqi police patrol was attacked with a rocket-propelled grenade, killing one officer and wounding five, according to Najaf police.

Animal House, Rumsfeld, and Iraqi Chaos

> There is no flag large enough to cover the shame of killing innocent people for a purpose which is unattainable.
> —*U.S. historian Howard Zinn (1993)*

The same week as the Najaf fighting came to an end, there were two reports released that implicated U.S. officials in Iraqi prisoner abuse ranging from the CIA, "contractors," and medical doctors to commanders and soldiers out of control in an "Animal House" atmosphere. A report commissioned by the Pentagon chaired by former Defense Secretary James Schlesinger and a report for the U.S. Army by Generals George Fay and Anthony Jones described a situation in which mistreatment of Iraqi prisoners was more extensive than previously indicated and in which military leadership was seriously wanting. Generals Fay and Jones confirmed that at least 34 U.S. officers were implicated in at least 44 cases of recorded abuse over a period of at least six months. A *Washington Post* article indicated:

Recent reports on Iraq prison abuse blow away the Bush administration and Pentagon claims that Abu Ghraib scandal was a mere "aberration." What began several months ago with the emergence of shocking photographs showing a handful of U.S. troops abusing detainees in Iraq has led this week to a broad indictment of U.S. military leadership and acknowledgement in two official reports that mistreatment of prisoners was more widespread than previously disclosed.

The reports have served to undercut earlier portrayals of the abuse as largely the result of criminal misconduct by a small group of individuals. As recently as last month, an assessment by the Army's inspector general concluded the incidents could not be ascribed to systemic problems, describing them as "aberrations."[26]

Yet Schlesinger's report made a distinction between "direct responsibility" on the part of the commanders on the scene up to the brigade level and "indirect responsibility at higher levels," thus, in effect, letting Rumsfeld and top officials in the Bush administration and Pentagon off the hook, even though they had established policies indicating that Geneva Conventions did not apply to the Taliban or Al Qaeda and allowed a variety of "stress positions" in interrogation techniques.[27] Although the two reports provided copious examples of interrogation abuse, which were widely reported in the press and broadcast media, in his first comments on the reports,

Defense Secretary Donald H. Rumsfeld on Thursday mischaracterized one of their central findings about the American military's treatment of Iraqi prisoners by saying there was no evidence that prisoners had been abused during interrogations.... The reports, one by a panel Mr. Rumsfeld had appointed and one by three Army generals, made clear that some abuses occurred during interrogations, that others were intended to soften up prisoners who were to be questioned, and that many intelligence personnel involved in the interrogations were implicated in the abuses. The reports were issued Tuesday and Wednesday.

But on Thursday, in an interview with a radio station in Phoenix, Mr. Rumsfeld, who was traveling outside Washington this week, said, "I have not seen anything thus far that says that the people abused were abused in the process of interrogating them or for interrogation purposes." A transcript of the interview was posted on the Pentagon's website on Friday. Mr. Rumsfeld repeated the assertion a few hours later at a news conference in Phoenix, adding that "all of the press, all of the television thus far that tried to link the abuse that took place to interrogation techniques in Iraq has not yet been demonstrated." After an aide slipped him a note during the news conference, however, Mr. Rumsfeld corrected himself, noting that an inquiry by three Army generals had, in fact, found "two or three" cases of abuse during interrogations or the interrogation process. In fact, however, the Army inquiry found that 13 of 44 instances of abuse involved interrogations or the interrogation process, an Army spokeswoman said. The report itself explicitly describes the extent to which each abuse involved interrogations.[28]

This *New York Times* article raised serious questions concerning Rumsfeld's relationship with reality.[29] As a *Washington Post* editorial, "A Failure of

Accountability" (August 29, 2004), pointed out, accountability seems to have disappeared in the Bush administration and Pentagon where policy blunders, failures, and even crimes go unpunished:

> Only a few years ago, it seemed the slightest suggestion of malfeasance by a presidential administration—allegations of tampering with a minor administrative office, say, or indications that a cabinet secretary might have understated the amount of money given to a former girlfriend—could trigger a formidable response from the other two branches of government: grand juries, special prosecutors, endless congressional hearings, even impeachment proceedings. Some of that auditing, especially during the Clinton administration, went too far. Yet now the country faces a frightening inversion of the problem. Though there is strong evidence of faulty and even criminal behavior by senior military commanders and members of President Bush's cabinet in the handling of foreign detainees, neither Congress nor the justice system is taking adequate steps to hold those officials accountable.

In particular, Rumsfeld seems to be beyond accountability, refusing to admit any mistakes and escaping all responsibility:

> What's particularly troubling about this breakdown of checks and balances is that some of the most disturbing behavior by senior officials has yet to be thoroughly investigated. For example, Mr. Rumsfeld is now known to have approved, in December 2002, the use of dogs to frighten detainees under interrogation. That technique, which was immediately adopted in Afghanistan and later in Iraq, was described by Army Maj. Gen. George R. Fay as "a clear violation of applicable laws and regulations." Mr. Rumsfeld has also publicly acknowledged that he ordered that some prisoners in Iraq not be registered with the International Red Cross, an unambiguous violation of Army regulations and the Geneva Conventions. Yet Mr. Rumsfeld has never been called upon to explain these actions to legal investigators or to Congress. (ibid.)

Thus, despite copious documentation of Rumsfeld's responsibility for the prison abuse scandals in Afghanistan, Iraq, and elsewhere, and despite the lack of a coherent plan to govern or even stabilize Iraq after the U.S. and UK invasion, Rumsfeld was not forced to resign. Accountability was not expected of Bush's coconspirators. Like the Mafia, Bush merely demanded personal loyalty, so there were no resignations of those culpable for the corrupt intelligence that supposedly justified the U.S. invasion of Iraq, for those who made mistake after mistake following the invasion, and for those like Rumsfeld who had approved of contravening the Geneva Conventions and international law in the treatment of prisoners that led directly to the Abu Ghraib scandals, one of the most shocking episodes in U.S. military history.

By late August 2004, violence and chaos ruled in Iraq with daily eruptions of bloodshed and fierce battles throughout the country between the U.S. occupying forces and insurgents. (run in "The situation wasn't much better in Afghanistan…")

The situation wasn't much better in Afghanistan where explosions on August 29 killed eight students and an adult at a provincial school, as in Kabul an explosion outside of the DynCorp Inc. offices, which carry out security for President Hamid Karzai, killed a number of people, including two Americans. Twelve election workers trying to get Afghans to register for forthcoming elections had been assassinated, the long-active French medical group Medicines sans Frontiers had left the country because it was deemed too violent, and UN aid workers also considered leaving the country. Taliban and Al Qaeda forces continued to attack westerners and destroy government installations as warlords ruled much of the country and drug exports were at an all-time high. Obviously, the Bush administration had not adequately dealt with the Afghanistan problem and now faced an even worse situation in Iraq.

Although Bush and his allies continued to tout his alleged successes in the "war on terrorism," in fact, his efforts had been a miserable failure, with chaos in Afghanistan and Iraq, growing numbers of Al Qaeda and other terrorist forces, and continuous criticism from the closest U.S. allies who had distanced themselves from U.S. policy under Bush. An article in the *Los Angeles Times* by Patrick J. McDonnell indicated that two months after the United States handed over sovereignty to Iraq, "more than 110 U.S. troops have been killed and much of the country remains hostile territory." Moreover, nationwide "U.S. forces are being attacked 60 times per day on average, up 20 percent from the three-month period before the handover." [31]

Iraqi insurgent strategy seems to oscillate between daily attacks on U.S. forces, engaging them in sustained urban combat occasionally, disrupting oil installations and the economy, and hitting soft targets. On September 1, a video showed 12 Nepalese workers had been kidnapped and executed in Iraq, and there were reports that sabotage of Iraqi oil installations in both the southern and northern parts of the country had brought exports to a halt, helping to drive world oil prices to record highs. There were also reports of how the U.S. occupation forces had destroyed the ancient archaeological site of Babylon as well as allowing other sites and national treasures to be looted. [32]

An article by Dexter Filkins indicated that much of the Sunni Triangle was occupied by forces hostile to the United States and that the U.S. Army rarely visited Fallujah, which was being run by an increasingly Talibanesque Islamic government, Anbar province in the western desert regions, and "Ramadi, where the Sunni insurgents appear to have the run of the city; and the holy Shiite cities of Karbala and Najf to the South."[33] Filkins' article suggests that, in effect, the insurgency seemed to be winning throughout much of Iraq, in which U.S. soldiers are seen as a problem by the majority of Iraqis, who are coming to believe that there will be no solution to their problems until the United States withdraws its troops. Indeed, there was already talk that the upcoming January election scheduled in Iraq might not take place, or could only take place in relatively pacified regions of the country.[34]

On September 7, seven U.S. troops were killed in Fallujah when a suicide car bomb hit a patrol, blowing apart part of a convoy of Humvees, and the U.S. deaths went over 1,000, reaching a macabre milestone. More than 7,000 U.S. troops had been seriously wounded and taken out of action, with a startling record 1,000 seriously injured the previous month. U.S. military spokespeople revealed that there were more than 646 attacks on U.S. troops the previous week and 86 Improvised Explosive Devices (IEDs) in Sadr City, a new and disturbing phenomenon. Moreover, Donald Rumsfeld claimed that 1,500–2,500 Iraqi fighters had been killed in the last month (*ABC News*, September 7, 2004), an incredible figure that suggested the Iraqi opposition was much greater than the Bush administration had indicated.

Rumsfeld claimed that the U.S. casualties in Iraq were "relatively small," which is probably true if you compare casualty rates with the Civil War, World Wars I and II, or Vietnam at its apex, but in general the comment showed the utter insensitivity of a Pentagon boss who has never shown much concern for loss of life on either side. Moreover, Rumsfeld did not comment on how the Iraqi puppet-government chosen by the United States was rapidly losing credibility. During the siege of Najaf, the regional government rounded up the press and tried to tell them what they could and could not cover, and the government in Baghdad raided and permanently closed down the al Jazeera network offices, after claiming that they were temporarily shutting down the network for a month. The government claimed that it had captured one of Saddam's henchman, Izzat Ibrahim, and then was forced to admit that it had made a mistake in identification. On September 7, the Baghdad governor barely survived an assassination attempt as gunfire on his convoy killed and seriously wounded some of his party.

Indeed, in Baghdad itself, there was frequent mortaring of the "Green Zone" where the United States had its embassy, kidnapping of foreign workers and the press, and growing insecurity. A battle in the Shiite ghetto of Sadr City on September 7 left 40 Iraqis and one GI dead, threatening another round of fights between the United States and al-Sadr forces. According to one account, there were no services in Sadr City; the streets were rotten with refuse, food, and raw sewage.[35] On September 8, four humanitarian aide workers were kidnapped by insurgent forces in broad daylight from their offices in Baghdad, leading to predictions that most nongovernmental and aide organizations would vacate an impossibly dangerous country. The same day, the United States pounded rebel strongholds in Fallujah, claiming to kill 100 insurgents. The United States was now facing two well-organized insurgencies, a well-trained Sunni opposition rooted in Saddam Hussein's own government, which had killed about 12 U.S. soldiers in the past week, and a fanatic and well-armed Islamicist resistance, consisting of Iraqi and foreign forces.

Bush had opened a Pandora's box in that his policies were obviously radicalizing Iraqis and creating enemies throughout the world for the United States. As evidence that lawlessness in Iraq was demolishing plans for reconstruction, the Bush administration announced on September 14 that it was diverting more than $3 billion from reconstruction work to beef up security, a sign that its policy in Iraq was in serious trouble. There was increased speculation that the elections coming in January would have to be postponed. Peter Galbraith published an article in the *New York Review of Books* arguing that Bush administration Iraq policy was an utter fiasco and that from the beginning, U.S. reconstruction efforts were hampered by incompetence, nepotism, and corruption. Galbraith suggested that Iraq's Transitional Administrative Law (TAL) had been effectively undermined by the Allawi regime, which had allowed repression of news media; that the country was splitting into different factions at an alarming rate; and "that the breakup of Iraq seemed more likely than a successful transition to centralized democracy.... Iraq can be held together only as a loose federation consisting of Kurdistan, a Sunni entity in the center, and a Shiite entity in the south, with Baghdad as a jointly administered federal capital."

Accounts of the stunning failure of Bush administration Iraq policy proliferated through the media as the U.S. election heated up. A *New York Times* article by Douglas Jehl revealed that U.S. intelligence reports were extremely pessimistic on Iraq's future, presenting a picture of a chaotic situation only getting worse, which counters Bush administration discourse that the situation is improving in Iraq.[36] The publication of the report suggested that anti-Bush factions in the intelligence sector were leaking reports that contradicted Bush administration policy and statements, indicating an internal battle in the Bush establishment. More criticism of Bush's Iraq policy emerged the same day when UN Secretary-General Kofi Annan stated in a BBC interview that the war on Iraq was illegal, a story that got big play in Britain but not the United States. The *Guardian* story indicated:

Mr. Annan said that the invasion was not sanctioned by the UN Security Council or in accordance with the UN's founding charter. In an interview with the BBC World Service broadcast last night, he was asked outright if the war was illegal. He replied: "Yes, if you wish."

He then added unequivocally: "I have indicated it was not in conformity with the UN charter. From our point of view and from the charter point of view it was illegal."

Mr. Annan has until now kept a tactful silence and his intervention at this point undermines the argument pushed by Tony Blair that the war was legitimised by Security Council resolutions. Mr. Annan also questioned whether it will be feasible on security grounds to go ahead with the first planned election in Iraq scheduled for January. "You cannot have credible elections if the security conditions continue as they are now," he said.

His remarks come amid a marked deterioration of the situation on the ground, an upsurge of violence that has claimed 200 lives in four days and raised questions over the ability of the interim Iraqi government and the U.S.-led coalition to maintain control over the country.[37]

"Freedom Is on the March"

> Once you get to Baghdad, it's not clear what you do with it. It's not clear what kind of government you put in place of the one that's currently there now. Is it going to be a Shia regime, a Sunni regime, a Kurdish regime? Or one that tilts toward the Baathists, or one that tilts toward Islamic fundamentalists? How much credibility is that going to have if it's set up by the American military there? How long does the United States military have to stay there to protect the people that sign on for that government, and what happens once we leave?
> —*U.S. Secretary of Defense Dick Cheney (1991)*

As the situation in Iraq was deteriorating dramatically in mid-September, Bush was presenting upbeat assessments, glowing about how "wonderful" it is that "elections are going to be held in Afghanistan and Iraq." Leaning over at his audience, Bush roared: "Freedom is on the march!" Unfortunately for Bush, the freedom on the march was the Iraqi insurgents' march for freedom from U.S. occupation and domination. This freedom involved around 80 daily attacks on U.S. troops, killing of Iraqi police and those who support the U.S. puppet regime, kidnapping and assassinating of foreigners, disruption of oil supplies, and insurgents freeing Iraq from all constraints so it could descend into pure anarchy and chaos. "Freedom is untidy," Donald Rumsfeld famously said as looting broke out after the Saddam Hussein regime collapsed. Freedom in Iraq was indeed very untidy and very ugly, although for George W. Bush the word served as a catchall cover for all his failed policies. Freedom is on the march, indeed.

Freedom marched along on September 16, 2004, as Iraqi insurgents kidnapped one British and two American construction workers in broad daylight in the upscale al-Mansour neighborhood, bringing to more than 100 the number of kidnapped foreigners. Freedom marched forward the next day as a suicide car bomb blew up in central Baghdad in front of a row of parked police cars, wounding and killing scores. Hours later explosions were heard throughout Baghdad, and U.S. troops were caught in gun battles with militants on a main thoroughfare, Haifa Street, where U.S. bombing had killed 16 earlier in the week. As video footage showing kids prancing around a shot-up U.S. fighting vehicle, with a Palestinian reporter filming the incident, and then portraying the U.S. bombs hitting the crowd and the journalist, played and replayed throughout the world, U.S. authorities took pains to deny that they had fired indiscriminately into a crowd. Their first story was that they fired to disperse the crowd and retake their fighting vehicle, then that they had destroyed it to prevent looters taking its equipment, and then, after outrage that the shooting killed at least 47 people and wounded 114, that U.S. troops were fired on from the vehicle and were defending themselves. But the video footage contained no gunshots, and observers insisted that the United States had bombed the crowd full of civilians because they were rejoicing at the U.S. vehicle's destruction.

In one of the deadliest weeks in Iraq in recent months, more than 250 Iraqis had been killed. A project in Chicago was documenting the names of dead Iraqi civilians, and in a ceremony read the 3,000 names they were able to document out of more than 15,000 killed. For the seventh day in a row, U.S. warplanes hammered Fallujah, killing at least 60 insurgents, according to the U.S. military. A spokesman for the Health Ministry, Saad Amili, said 44 people were killed and 27 wounded, including 17 children, 2 women, and 2 elderly men. The Associated Press reported: "Early Friday, police found the corpse of a man they believed to be a westerner about 40 miles north of Baghdad. The body was pulled from the Tigris River near the central Iraqi village of Yethrib, said Capt. Hakim al-Azawi, the head of security at Tikrit's Teaching Hospital."

Fighting and bombings continued in many parts of Baghdad, and the United States once again pounded Fallujah as reports circulated that the United States was planning an all-out invasion of the city that had resisted control and that was a "no go" zone for both U.S. and Iraqi government forces. In a *New York Times* article, Dexter Filkins wrote about "senior military commanders" telling of how they were planning major incursions into areas controlled by insurgents.[38]

The same weekend, Iraqi Prime Minister Ayad Allawi was in Britain and on the way to the United States to insist that the January elections were on track, that the Iraqi government was successfully battling the insurgents, and that with more support they could ensure a democratic transition. Commentators in the United States and United Kingdom were skeptical, and it was striking that on Sunday television talk shows, top Republicans were distancing themselves from Bush's "Freedom is on the march" mantra and the positive assessment of the Iraqi prime minister. According to a Reuters report:

> Leading members of President Bush's Republican Party on Sunday criticized mistakes and "incompetence" in his Iraq policy and called for an urgent ground offensive to retake insurgent sanctuaries.
>
> In appearances on news talk shows, Republican senators also urged Bush to be more open with the American public after the disclosure of a classified CIA report that gave a gloomy outlook for Iraq and raised the possibility of civil war.
>
> "The fact is, we're in deep trouble in Iraq . . . and I think we're going to have to look at some recalibration of policy," Republican Sen. Chuck Hagel of Nebraska said on CBS's *Face the Nation*.
>
> "We made serious mistakes," said Sen. John McCain, an Arizona Republican who has campaigned at Bush's side this year after patching up a bitter rivalry.
>
> McCain, speaking on *Fox News Sunday*, cited as mistakes the toleration of looting after the successful U.S.-led invasion of Iraq in 2003 and failures to secure Iraq's borders or prevent insurgents from establishing strongholds within the country.[39]

On Monday, September 21, there were wire reports that a video was released on a website showing the beheading of three Iraqi Kurds accused of cooperating with U.S. forces, and a separate group claimed to have captured 18 Iraqi National Guardsmen and threatened to kill them unless a detained aide of Muqtada al-Sadr was released. There were also reports that two prominent Sunni clerics were murdered in Baghdad in 24 hours. Hazem Muhammad al-Zeidi was kidnapped from the Sajjad mosque in Sadr City by gunmen after prayers on Sunday night and his body was found near his mosque the next day. The other victim, Sheikh Muhammad Jadoa al-Janabi, was shot dead as he entered a mosque for noon prayers, in a mostly Shiite area, raising the issue of whether tensions were rising between Sunnis and Shiites as some were claiming. The same day, Eugene Armstrong, one of the two American engineers being held hostage, was beheaded by his kidnappers, and after a videotape of the beheading was posted on the Internet, his body was found.

A story by James Glanz indicated "Iraqi officials in charge of rebuilding their country's shattered and decrepit infrastructure are warning that the Bush administration's plan to divert $3.46 billion from water, sewage, electricity, and other reconstruction projects to security could leave many people without the crucial services that generally form the backbone of a stable and functioning democracy."[40] Iraqi officials complained that of the $18.4 billion that Congress approved in 2003 for Iraq's reconstruction, only about $1 billion had been spent so far. Officials in charge of electricity, water plants, sewage, and other infrastructural components were reportedly grievously disappointed that money would be taken from their projects, barely underway, and put into security.

As more hostages faced gruesome deaths, companies, countries, and aid organizations considered withdrawing operations from Iraq. More than 130 foreigners had been kidnapped already in 2004. Edward Wong reported in the *New York Times* that

> an entire industry seems to have sprung up around them. American officials and security advisers here say criminal gangs usually carry out the initial abduction, then try to sell the hostages to other groups. Most of the hostages have been freed, though the number of killings has surpassed two dozen since July.... They also come at a time when insurgents have been pushing forward with a relentless campaign to topple the interim Iraqi government, setting off suicide car bombs and staging ambushes that have killed more than 300 Iraqis in the past 10 days. The growing bloodshed is raising serious doubts about whether legitimate elections can be held in January, though the Bush administration and Prime Minister Ayad Allawi insist that they will remain on schedule.[41]

As U.S. media focused on the growing number of U.S. casualties, global media focused on the alarming growth in Iraqi civilian deaths. Jefferson Morley noted that

> Many news organizations have run stories about civilian deaths in Iraq. But overseas reporters and commentators emphasize the issue more than their American counterparts and play up civilian casualties in ways the U.S. media rarely pursue. After recent U.S. bombing raids on Fallujah, al-Jazeera.net published graphic photos of wounded children that are unlikely to appear in a U.S. news outlet.
>
> While American journalists can say, correctly, that definitive statistics on civilian casualties are hard to come by, the true number is certainly a multiple of U.S. casualties, according to Human Rights Watch. In a 2003 study, the New York–based watchdog group said "thousands" of Iraqi civilians had been killed or wounded in the three weeks between the invasion and the fall of Baghdad.
>
> Human Rights Watch cited two other attempts to quantify the dead. The *Los Angeles Times* did a survey of 27 hospitals in the Baghdad area after the U.S. invasion and found that at least 1,700 civilians died. In June 2003, the Associated Press canvassed 60 of Iraq's 124 hospitals and calculated that at least 3,420 civilians died in the first months of the war. AP described the count as "fragmentary"

and said, "the complete toll—if it is ever tallied—is sure to be significantly higher."

Since then, other figures have been floated. Commentators for the *Jordan Times* and the *Daily Star* in Beirut, Lebanon, have cited an estimate of 30,000 deaths. That is the figure disseminated by the Iraqi Human Rights Organization, an independent group in Baghdad.

A more conservative figure comes from Iraqbodycount.net, a British Web site that compiles media reports on Iraqi civilian deaths. Based on such reporting, the site says there have been a minimum of 12,778 civilian deaths in Iraq and a maximum of 14,820.[42]

In November the respected British medical journal the *Lancet* cited a Johns Hopkins study indicating that more than 100,000 Iraqi civilians had been killed.[43] But the Iraqi elections and their fate were tightly bound up with the U.S. elections, which we shall examine in the next two chapters.

Notes

1. Several studies indicated that Bush's Iraq policy had made the world much more dangerous and unstable, and had strengthened Al Qaeda and other terrorist group recruiting, including a report by Amnesty International. See Ashleigh Collins, "U.S. War on Terror Leads to Violations, Group Says," *Los Angeles Times*, May 27, 2004, p. A12.

2. When Bush was asked at an October 28, 2003, press conference whether the mission in Iraq had indeed been accomplished as the banner proclaimed, Bush snippily remarked, "The 'Mission Accomplished' sign, of course, was put up by the members of the *USS Abraham Lincoln* saying that their mission was accomplished. I know it was attributed somehow to some ingenious advance man from staff." In fact, the Bush administration had orchestrated every detail of the spectacle; see Elisabeth Bumiller, "Keepers of Bush Image Lift Stagecraft to New Heights," *New York Times*, Friday, May 16. When questions were raised in early 2004 concerning whether Bush had fulfilled his National Guard duty in 1972–1973, the *USS Abraham Lincoln* pictures were replayed in a context that reflected negatively on him, providing another example of how media spectacles are difficult to control and may have unintended effects; see Kellner (2003c).

3. See the first-hand account and detailed analysis by Mark Danner, "Delusions in Baghdad," *New York Review of Books*, December 18, 2003, pp. 92–97. On the history of Iraqi resistance against foreign invaders and analysis of reasons why an Iraqi insurgency will continue, see Ali (2003).

4. There were widespread reports that the Kurds had actually captured Saddam Hussein and held him for some time before giving him up to U.S. forces. Although Bush undeniably got a boost in popularity through Hussein's capture, it was not clear what ultimate effects a capture and trial of the Iraqi dictator, long supported by Bush Senior, will have. On how George H. W. Bush was point man for getting the Iraqi re-

gime aide and support in the 1980s, see Friedman (1993); Phillips (2004); and my discussion in Chapter 2 of this book.

5. See the revealing set of reflections by Kenneth Pollack, who was a major defender of the necessity for a war against Iraq, "Spies, Lies, and Weapons: What Went Wrong," *Atlantic*, January–February 2004. Pollack dissects how western intelligence went wrong in appraising reports on Iraqi "weapons of mass destruction," and criticizes the Bush administration for systematically distorting intelligence, not having a postwar plan of reconstruction, and going in largely alone without significant support from allies, NATO, or the United Nations. See also Ritter (2003).

6. For a vivid overview of the events of April 2004, see the first-person reporting by Jon Lee Anderson, "The Uprising," *New Yorker*, May 5, 2004. For sharp analysis of the Fallujah uprising, see Michael Schwartz, "The Causes and Consequences of the April Uprising in Falluja," *Z Magazine*, July–August 2004, pp. 54–62.

7. This was indeed the defense that the soldiers who took the pictures gave, claiming that they were ordered by superiors to take the photos; see, for example, Terence Neilan, "7 Charges Filed against a Central Figure in Iraq Prison Abuse," *New York Times*, May 14, 2004. Subsequent stories revealed, however, that orders that enabled the systematic prisoner abuse in Iraq came from the top of the Pentagon and Bush administration; see Seymour Hersh, "The Grey Zone," *New Yorker*, posted May 15, 2004, at http://www.newyorker.com/fact/content/?040524fa_fact. See also John Barry, Michael Hirsh, and Michael Isikoff, "The Roots of Torture," *Newsweek*, May 24, 2004. In retrospect, it is now clear that the Iraqi/Afghanistan prisoner abuse scandal was a direct result of U.S. policy, beginning with the detainment of supposed Al Qaeda terrorists in Afghanistan, and then the "enemy combatants" at Guantanamo Bay, Cuba; see Hersh (2004). For a systematic depiction of torture in Iraq and how the practices derived from U.S. policy, see Mark Danner, "Torture and Truth," *New York Review of Books* 51(10), June 10, 2004, and "The Logic of Torture," *New York Review of Books* 51(11), June 24, 2004. Further, in June 2004, a UN report claims that U.S. prisoner rights' violations in Iraq could constitute war crimes; see Maggie Farley, "U.N. Report Alleges U.S. Rights Violations in Iraq," *Los Angeles Times*, June 5, 2004, p. A7.

8. See Neil MacKay, "Iraq's Child Prisoners," *Glasgow Morning Herald*, August 1, 2004. *Rolling Stone* received access to 106 "annexes" to the Taguba Report on the Abu Ghraib scandals, documenting sexual abuse of children and adults, and there were reports that Seymour Hersh was investigating the child abuse issue for another *New Yorker* exposé; see the discussion in Tom Engelhardt, *TomDispatch*, August 2, 2004.

9. Mike Francis, "Ordered to Just Walk Away," *Oregonian*, August 16, 2004.

10. Katha Pollitt, "Show and Tell in Abu Ghraib," *Nation*, May 24, 2004, p. 9.

11. On Bremer's attempts to privatize the Iraqi economy and failed attempts at reconstruction, see Naomi Klein, "Baghdad Year Zero," *Harpers*, September 24, 2004. Regular reports came out concerning Halliburton scandals during Cheney's tenure as CEO in which allegations spread that Halliburton had done illegal business with Iran and Iraq, had bribed Nigerian officials for a contract, and were engaged in the same

sort of "creative accounting" (such as opening offshore bank accounts to avoid taxation) associated with Enron; a report surfaced that an internal Pentagon audit found that Halliburton failed to adequately account for as much as $1.8 billion of the $4.2 billion that it received for providing logistical support in Iraq and Kuwait; see Elizabeth Becker, "Halliburton Is Faulted by Pentagon on Accounts," *New York Times,* August 12, 2004.

12. Antonia Juhasz, "The Hand-Over That Wasn't," *Los Angeles Times,* August 5, 2004, p. B15.

13. Chalabi had earlier been accused of corruption and theft of millions in a bank scandal in Jordan. Patrick Cockburn notes some of the scandals involving the Chalabis, but insists that corruption has been endemic in the U.S. occupation of Iraq; see "The Chalabis, Iraq, and American Power," *Independent,* August 11, 2004.

14. See Eric Boehlert, "War? What War?" in *Salon,* August 12, 2004, at http://www.salon.com/news/feature/2004/08/12/iraq_press/index.html. See also Michael Massing, "Iraq, the Press, and the Election," *New York Review of Books,* December 2, 2004.

15. See Robert Fisk, "Iraq to Explode: Can't Blair See That This Country Is about to Explode? Can't Bush?" *Independent,* August 3, 2004. Fisk's website collecting his articles is an important source of information on Iraq; see http://www.robert-fisk.com/index_fisk_articles.htm.

16. See Michael Schwartz, "Iraq, A Battleground State," available August 14, 2004, at http://www.alternet.org/waroniraq/19538.

17. Reports were extremely contradictory concerning whether al-Sadr was or was not willing to negotiate a solution, whether a cease-fire was or was not in place, and what was actually going on in Najaf. An August 19 BBC World report captured the conflicting reports. A *New York Times* reporter who gained access to the mosque claimed that his colleagues were greatly exaggerating the amount of military activity around the mosque, and that there was little fighting. A live BBC reporter refuted the claim, arguing that fighting had been going on for days in the vicinity of the mosque and that a reported cease-fire was not really in place; pictures accompanying her report seemed to suggest that the bombing was going on. For a vivid account of activity in the mosque area, see Mark Follman, "How I Got Out of the Shrine Alive: *Salon*'s Phillip Robertson Talks about His Harrowing Ordeal Inside the Imam Ali Shrine in War-Ravaged Najaf," *Salon,* August 19, 2004.

18. Alex Berenson and Dexter Filkins, "Iraqi Government Gives Rebel Cleric an Ultimatum," *New York Times,* August 24, 2004, available at http://www.nytimes.com/2004/08/24/international/middleeast/24CND-IRAQ.html?hp.

19. Jimmy Breslin, "What We've Really Lost in This Indefensible War," *Newsday,* August 24, 2004.

20. Dexter Filkins, "Violence Flares in Najaf Area as Top Shiite Cleric Returns," *New York Times,* August 26, 2004.

21. Karl Vick, Rajiv Chandrasekaran, and Fred Barbash, "Sistani Arrives in Najaf; Dozens Killed in Kufa," *Washington Post,* August 26, 2004, available at http://www.washingtonpost.com/wp-dyn/articles/A34370–2004Aug26.html.

22. Dexter Filkins and John F. Burns, "Tentative Accord Reached in Najaf to Halt Fighting," *New York Times,* August 27, 2004, available at http://www.nytimes.com/2004/08/27/international/middleeast/27iraq.html.

23. Karl Vick, "Iraqi Holy City Left Broken by Urban Warfare," *Washington Post,* August 27, 2004, available at http://www.washingtonpost.com/ac2/wp-dyn/A37040–2004Aug26?.

24. Dexter Filkins, "Militants Leave Shrine as Cease-Fire Deal Appears to Hold," *New York Times,* August 27, 2004.

25. Karl Vick and Naseer Nouri, "Najaf Militiamen Surrender Shrine: Truce Holds as Pilgrims Enter Holy City," *Washington Post,* August 28, 2004, p. A01.

26. http://www.washingtonpost.com/ac2/wp-dyn/A33789–2004Aug25. On the role of military intelligence and "contractors," see http://www.nytimes.com/2004/08/26/politics/26abuse.html. On the CIA role, see http://www.washingtonpost.com/ac2/wp-dyn/A33805–2004Aug25.

27. James P. Pinkerton, "What a Shock!" *Salon,* August 27, 2004.

28. Eric Schmitt, "Rumsfeld Denies Abuses Occurred at Interrogations," *New York Times,* August 28, 2004.

29. On the issue of U.S. military commanders, it might be worth noting that Lt. Gen. William "Jerry" Boykin, deputy undersecretary for intelligence, created an uproar in 2003 when on a tour of Christian churches he declared that the United States was engaged in a religious war "and the enemy is a guy named Satan." In a summary of Boykin's speeches, James P. Pinkerton, in "What a Shock!" *Salon,* August 27, 2004, reported

A year ago last June, a two-star Army general stood in the pulpit of First Baptist Church of Broken Arrow, Okla., and identified the source of all America's problems.

Pointing to a dark shadow on several photographs he shot of Mogadishu's skyline from a helicopter shortly after 18 Americans were killed in the "Black Hawk Down" debacle, Army Lt. Gen. William "Jerry" Boykin assured the congregation that, indeed, they were witnessing the faint outline of Satan hovering over Somalia.

Gen. Boykin isn't one to resort to metaphors when speaking of the battle between good and evil. "It is a demonic presence in that city that God revealed to me as the enemy," he said, indicting the devil for the murder of 18 American soldiers.

Quoted in a different article, Boykin further describes the dark shadow in the photos: "Whether you understand it or not, it is a demonic spirit over the city of Mogadishu. Ladies and gentlemen, that's not a fake, that's not a farce."

Let's be as blunt as we can. The No. 2 man in the Pentagon's intelligence operation sees Satan in photographs. How different is that from seeing white unicorns? Or pink elephants? Or little green men? If we put hallucinators in charge, is it any wonder that we've had trouble with our intelligence?

Those news reports about Boykin caused a stir, but not enough of one. Last November, the conservative *National Review* opined, "It is hardly good for the morale of the troops to understand that their commander is a wacko who goes around photographing Satan zooming overhead. General Boykin is manifestly insubordinate, and should be sacked. Yesterday." But Boykin had some fans in the right places, too. Writing in the *Washington Times* last fall, Tony Blankley, the editorial page editor, was inspired to write, "I thank God that we have such a man as General Boykin in our midst."

At the insistence of Congress and other forces of enlightenment, the Pentagon launched an investigation of Boykin's crusading. But at the insistence of the Pentagon (when the story broke, Rumsfeld announced, preemptively, that Boykin had an "outstanding record"), the investigation concluded with a wrist slap. Boykin, it said, shouldn't have been wearing his uniform when he encouraged the Christian soldiers onward. But as the *Washington Post* reported, senior defense officials considered the findings to be a "complete exoneration."

So Boykin is still on the job, free to further foment the clash of civilizations.

And the rest of us are left to wonder what comes next. If our intelligence services find room at the top for zealots who create more enemies than they negate—and who hallucinate even more foes than that—then papery reports seem almost useless. Because after the token courts-martial, the light letters of reprimand and the occasional grudging mea culpa, the real problem America confronts is not its painful past but a fiery future.

30. John. F. Burns and Erik Eckholm, "In Western Iraq, Fundamentalists Hold U.S. Forces at Bay," *New York Times*, August 29, 2004. The article indicates that although the United States installed former Baathist commanders in Fallujah after a vicious month-long fight had led to a draw, the U.S.-appointed police chiefs and other U.S.-appointed and supported officials throughout the region had been thrown out of office and replaced by Islamicist fundamentalists. See also Alissa J. Rubin, "All's Quiet in Najf, but Not in the Sunni Triangle," *Los Angeles Times*, August 29, 2004, p. A15.

31. Patrick J. McDonnell, "Sovereign Iraq Just as Deadly to U.S. Forces," *Los Angeles Times*, September 1, 2004.

32. "Video Claims to Show Execution of 12 Nepalese Hostages in Iraq," Associated Press, August 31, 2004. See also Zainab Bahrani, "Days of Plunder: Coalition Forces Are Doing Little to Prevent the Widespread Looting and Destruction of Iraq's World-Famous Historical Sites," *Guardian*, August 31, 2004, available at http://www.guardian.co.uk/Iraq/Story/0,2763,1294027,00.html.

33. Dexter Filkins, "One by One, Iraqi Cities Become No-Go Zones," *New York Times*, September 5, 2004.

34. Eric Schmitt and Steven R. Weisman, "U.S. Conceding Rebels Control Regions of Iraq," *New York Times*, September 8, 2004.

35. Dexter Filkins, "Battles in Baghdad Slum Leave 40 Iraqis and a GI Dead," *New York Times*, September 8, 2004.

36. Douglas Jehl, "U.S. Intelligence Shows Pessimism on Iraq's Future," *New York Times,* September 15, 2004.

37. Ewen MacAskill and Julian Borger, "Iraq War Was Illegal and Breached UN Charter, Says Annan," *Guardian,* September 16, 2004.

38. Dexter Filkins, "U.S. Plans Year-End Drive to Take Iraqi Rebel Areas," *New York Times,* September 19, 2004.

39. "Republicans Criticize Bush 'Mistakes' on Iraq," *Reuters,* September 19, 2004.

40. James Glanz, "Iraqis Oppose New Bush Plan to Cut Back on Reconstruction to Boost Security," *New York Times,* September 21, 2004.

41. Edward Wong, "Iraqi Video Shows Beheading of Man Said to be American," *New York Times,* September 21, 2004, at http://www.nytimes.com/2004/09/21/international/middleeast/21iraq.html.

42. Jefferson Morley, "The War's Toll on Iraqi Civilians," *Washington Post,* September 21, 2004.

43. "Civilian Death Toll in Iraq Exceeds 100,000," *Lancet,* October 29, 2004.

Chapter 5

Media Spectacle and Election 2004

> Our enemies are innovative and resourceful, and so are we. They never
> stop thinking about new ways to harm our country and our people,
> and neither do we.
>
> —*George W. Bush, August 5, 2004*[1]

DURING A MEDIA AGE, image and spectacle are of crucial importance in
presidential campaigns. Media events like party conventions and daily photo
opportunities are concocted to project positive images of the candidates and to
construct messages to sell the candidate to the public. These events are supple-
mented by a full range of media advertising that often attempts both to project
negative images of the opposition candidate and positive images for the presidential aspirant. In an era of media spectacle, competing parties work hard to
produce an attractive presidential "brand" that can be successfully marketed to
the public.

Spectacles of the Primary Season and the Democratic Convention

> That's just the nature of democracy. Sometimes pure politics enters
> into the rhetoric.
>
> —*George W. Bush, Crawford, Texas, August 8, 2003*

The primary season requires that candidates raise a tremendous amount of
money to finance travel through key campaign states, organize support groups,
and purchase television ads.[2] Although the primaries involve numerous debates,
media events, advertising campaigns, and then statewide votes for delegates,

usually a few definitive images emerge of the various candidates, such as the negative image in 1972 of Democratic Party frontrunner Edmund Muskie crying on the New Hampshire state capital steps while responding to a nasty newspaper attack on his wife, or 1984 frontrunner Gary Hart's sex scandal, replete with pictures in the newspaper front pages. Michael Dukakis arguably lost the 1988 election because of images of him riding a tank, looking silly in an oversized helmet, as well as being the subject of negative television ads that made him appear too "soft" on crime and defense. George H. W. Bush was undermined during the 1992 election with repeated images of his convention pledge, "Read my lips. No new taxes" after he had raised taxes and doubled the national deficit.

Positive spectacles or images can make or break campaigns for the presidency. In 1980, Ronald Reagan's decisive seizing of a microphone in the New Hampshire debates and insistence that since he was paying for the debate, he would decide who would participate, produced an oft-repeated image of Reagan as a strong leader; in 1984, Reagan's zinging of Walter Mondale during their presidential debates ("There you go again!") and making light of his age arguably ensured his reelection. By contrast, Al Gore's sighs and swinging from aggressive to passive and back in the 2000 presidential debates probably lost crucial support that might have prevented the Bush-Cheney Gang from stealing the election.[3]

For much of the 2003 Democratic Party preprimary season, Howard Dean was positively portrayed as the surprise insurgent candidate. An energetic Dean was shown nightly on television and received affirmative publicity as the frontrunner in cover stories in the major national newsmagazines. Dean raised a record amount of money from Internet contributions and mobilized an army of young volunteers. As the time approached for the Iowa and New Hampshire primaries, however, media images of an angry Dean increased, and taken out of context, his outspoken remarks and critical positions made Dean look like an irate radical.[4] Although he received significantly more media coverage than any other Democratic Party candidate in 2003, Dean received almost totally negative coverage in 2004 and his campaign came to an abrupt halt the night of the Iowa primary. Coming in a distant third, Dean tried to catch the crowd's attention in order to energize his screaming young supporters by emitting a loud vocal utterance following an energetic recitation of the states in which he would campaign. Dean's "scream" was perhaps the most-played image of the campaign season and effectively ended his campaign.[5]

Howard Dean was the first candidate to excite the Democratic Party base with fierce attacks on George W. Bush and his Iraq intervention, and it was clear that many Democrats fervently wanted Bush out of the White House. Hence, the issue of "electability" became the key issue for Democratic Party voters as the primaries began; John Kerry benefited from this concern and won primary after primary, capturing the nomination well before the convention.

Kerry became the target of a right-wing Internet spectacle, which portended more sleazy attacks to come, when Matt Drudge released a rumor on his website in February 2004 that Kerry had an affair with an intern. Murdoch newspapers spread the story in various parts of the world. Drudge then linked their stories to his website to get a bandwagon going. One of the British tabloids said that the parents of the intern were angry with Kerry, but when U.S. reporters contacted the parents they denied the story, saying that they liked Kerry and were going to vote for him. Meanwhile, when the former intern heard about the scandal while she was working in Africa, she denied the rumor and insisted that Kerry had treated her with respect. The U.S. mainstream media had avoided the story, but the right wing had made it clear that it was going to go all out to destroy Kerry.[6]

At the same time the fraudulent Kerry intern story was circulating, a cropped photo of Kerry next to Jane Fonda at an antiwar rally in the early 1970s circulated widely, framing Kerry as a comrade to "Hanoi Jane." This image was also revealed to be a con, edited so that Kerry and Fonda appeared next to each other.[7] As Kerry won primary after primary and clinched the Democratic Party nomination, it was clear that he was going to be the target of one of the nastiest smear campaigns in recent election history.

Presidential elections always generate convention spectacles to sell candidates to a broader public, to mobilize their respective party faithful, and to provide the rituals of democratic inauguration for the would-be president. The Democratic Party convention in Boston in late July 2004 attempted to present a spectacle of diversity and unity, using speakers from a variety of different ethnicities, genders, ages, social groups, and positions. All of these speakers strongly affirmed the candidacy of John Kerry and his choice for vice president, North Carolina Senator John Edwards, who had fought Kerry for the presidential nomination and was generally seen as one of the best campaigners in the party.

The Democratic Party convention opened with a theme of "the Kerry-Edwards plan for America's future," followed by a second night themed "a lifetime of strength and service" with key individuals testifying to John Kerry's qualifications and admirable record. During the third night of the convention, the theme switched to national security and "making America stronger," as a bevy of former military commanders took center stage to criticize Bush administration military and national security policy and to praise the virtues of John Kerry. In recent elections, it has become increasingly important to sell the personality and biography of a candidate, so much of the final night of the convention leading up to Kerry's acceptance speech featured Kerry's family and friends telling his personal story and affirming his strong leadership qualities and bedrock American values.

Presenting a spectacle of the triumphant warrior, Kerry staged an event in Boston Harbor where he arrived in a boat with his "band of brothers" who had served with him in Vietnam. The 'Nam vets came on stage just before Kerry's speech and he was introduced by former Georgia Senator Max Cleland, a three-limb amputee. In the 2002 Georgia Senate race, the Republican attack apparatus led by political operative Karl Rove had run ads associating the highly decent and admirable Cleland with Osama bin Laden and Saddam Hussein. The mudslinging media barrage insinuated that the war veteran Cleland was "soft" on terrorism, and helped enable Saxby Chambliss to pull off an upset victory against him. Senator Cleland rose to the occasion, making a rousing speech about his personal trust in the abilities of John Kerry and offering arguments that the United States would be safer and stronger with a Kerry presidency. The usually stiff Kerry was limbered up for the occasion, beamed genuine smiles, gave a vigorous, if sometimes too rapid, critique of Bush administration policies, and articulated his own policies on national and domestic security.

I watched the conventions on C-Span, which gave unfiltered presentations of the Democratic Convention spectacle, but when I did turn to the big four networks (ABC, CBS, NBC, and Fox) or cable channels, I was generally appalled by the biased negative framing of the speeches and events. In the words of *Washington Post* media critic Howard Kurtz:

> I was going to talk about *Fox News*'s coverage of Al Gore's speech, but the fair-and-balanced network blew off the former veep's speech in favor of Bill O'Reilly.
>
> O'Reilly interrupted his segment to toss to the Gore address for about 40 seconds, then started to rebut Gore. When Jimmy Carter took the podium, Fox joined it late and got out way early. Instead, viewers were treated to an interview with Republican activist Bill Bennett. While Carter was talking, Sean Hannity told Bennett: "I call this the reinvention convention. One of the things the Democrats want to do is create a false perception of who they are."
>
> How would Fox fans know, since they weren't able to hear Gore (the man who won the popular vote last time) or former president Carter? What happened to "we report, you decide"? While Carter continued, Hannity played the video of Teresa Heinz Kerry telling a reporter to "shove it." This is the kind of thing that makes critics question whether Fox has a Republican agenda.

I've long argued that people should separate Fox's straight reporters from its opinionated talking heads. ... But virtually pulling the plug on live coverage of Gore and Carter? How about letting them speak and then ripping them, or critiquing them, or whatever. The network is supposed to be covering the convention, not just using it as a backdrop.[8]

Obviously, the empty media spectacle of the conventions, which turned them into political campaign ads, has turned off many viewers; a July 28, 2004, Reuters report indicated that "Bare-Bones DNC Coverage Draws Lower Ratings." The four major television networks limited coverage to one hour of prime-time television viewing, and audiences declined from 2000. Although viewing was up for the three cable news networks' coverage, cumulative audience viewing of the entire convention was down. The second night the networks did not even offer an hour to the convention. The third-night network television hour, which presented John Edwards' speech, received 11 percent fewer network viewers than the Monday broadcast. Overall, in comparison to the 2000 Democratic Convention, viewing was down sharply on the networks, up for cable networks, and down slightly as a whole compared to 2000.[9]

The one-hour prime-time limitation meant that viewers of the major television networks did not get to see former Vice President Al Gore's opening night speech or many other Democratic Party luminaries including Ted Kennedy, Wesley Clarke, Howard Dean, and Jessie Jackson. Shockingly, none of the chief television networks ran late-night highlights of the speeches of the day (with the exception of ABC's *Nightline*). Of course, it is ultimately the responsibility of viewers and citizens to choose their own sources of information, and U.S. network television can be one of the poorest sources of news and information. To be sure, there are alternatives: one of the novelties of the 2004 conventions was the presence of bloggers who presented moment-by-moment highly detailed, Internet coverage. Moreover, those seeking to see speeches neglected by television could often go to websites that collected videos or transcripts of the speeches.

Another problem with corporate television coverage of U.S. politics is what Paul Krugman calls "The Triumph of the Trivial" (*New York Times*, July 30, 2004). Krugman points out that study of transcripts of the major cable and broadcast television networks reveals almost no coverage of John Kerry's plan "to roll back high-income tax cuts and use the money to cover most of the uninsured." Yet there was saturation coverage of Teresa Heinz Kerry's telling a newspaper reporter to "shove it." There was little attempt to contextualize even this event, as few noted that the newspaper writer in question was a right-wing hatchet man for Richard Mellon Scaife, who funded the attempts to smear the Clintons, and that the paper in question had repeatedly published personal attacks on Heinz Kerry's previous husband, Senator John Heinz (R-Penn.), and continually attacked her own activities, especially after she married Senator John Kerry.

Krugman also cites the frequent framing of John Edwards and John Kerry as "millionaires," a label rarely applied to Dick Cheney and George W. Bush, although they not only are multimillionaires, but push through economic policies that benefit the economic elite. By contrast, Kerry and Edwards at least claim to represent the interests of the middle class and working people. Also important, Krugman notes, are stories that are not covered at all, such as the Florida Republican Party call to supporters to send in absentee ballots because the new voting machines lack a paper trail and cannot "verify your vote," a position that flew in the face of Jeb Bush's contention that the new Florida voting machines were safe and reliable.

Perhaps the most recurrent scandal of U.S. corporate media coverage concerns the focus on the horse-race and polling dimensions of important elections. In 2000, the polls that showed George W. Bush constantly ahead of Al Gore in the popular vote were wildly off, because Gore received more than one half million more votes than Bush. Indeed, all national polls should be downplayed significantly by media coverage of presidential elections; what matters most are figures for states in the Electoral College, so national polls tell little about where the race is really going. In the summer of 2004, for instance, national polls generally showed a dead heat, with Bush ahead on occasion, although the most in-depth state polls showed Kerry with a lead in the necessary number of states to win the Electoral College. Nonetheless, in a waste of airtime, the television networks and print press presented in detail every new poll, no matter how flimsy the sample interviewed or ultimately unilluminating the results.

Framing Kerry

> The fact that he relies on facts—says things that are not factual—are going to undermine his campaign.
> —*George W. Bush*, New York Times, *March 4, 2000*

While the Democrats were battling it out in the primaries and then nominating Kerry at their convention, the Republicans were using a record amount of money raised to purchase an unprecedented number of negative television advertisements against John Kerry. The Bush ads highlighted Kerry's alleged "flip-flopping" as he took different positions over the years on Iraq, national security, and other issues. In one set of ads, Kerry was associated with Adolph Hitler, an ironic juxtaposition given that the Bush family earned money from selling its shares in Union Banking Corporation, for which Bush's grandfather Prescott Bush and great-uncle Herbert Walker had managed financial interests for major supporters of the Nazi party.[10]

The first set of ads promoting the Bush presidency in early 2004 featured 9/11 imagery and "resolute wartime leader" George W. Bush insisting that the country was "stronger and safer," words obviously chosen to be the mantra of Bush's reelection campaign. There was an immediate outcry against Republican exploitation of 9/11 in a political campaign. Richard Clarke, former anti-terrorism czar in the Clinton and first Bush administrations, released a book, *Against All Enemies: Inside America's War on Terror* (2004), participated in widely publicized television interviews, and made an appearance before the 9/11 Commission arguing that before 9/11 the Bush administration had completely ignored terrorism and that Clarke had not even been able to meet with George W. Bush.[11] Meanwhile, the Iraqi insurgency movement intensified, the deaths of U.S. troops and Iraqis and others working for the U.S.-imposed government escalated, and the Abu Ghraib Iraqi prisoner abuse and torture scandals emerged (see Chapter 4). Reports also came out that the number of terror attacks globally was on the rise, and major studies of the effects of Bush's foreign policy on terrorism indicated that anti-Americanism had significantly increased and terrorists were recruiting large numbers. Hence, far from being safer, Americans were more at risk.

At the same time, the mainstream U.S. corporate media began framing John Kerry in the same sort of negative ways that undermined Al Gore in the 2000 election. Several cable networks, including the Fox and NBC networks, seemed to trumpet daily whatever Republican National Committee talking points and negative Kerry ads were being produced. The right-wing pundits who dominate network news parroted the Republican claim that Kerry had voted "against every major weapons system we now use in our military" (Sean Hannity, *Fox News*, March 1, 2004). The Republicans liked to list 13 to 27 weapons systems against which Kerry allegedly voted. Later, it came out that in one single vote on the Pentagon's 1991 appropriations bill, Kerry voted along with many other Republican and Democratic senators to cut a series of weapons systems deemed obsolete or defective by then Secretary of Defense Dick Cheney.[12]

The Republican attack machine also claimed that Kerry had tried to cut $1.5 billion from the intelligence budget without noting, as documented in a March

12 *Washington Post* story, that Kerry's proposed cut was smaller than the eventual $3.8 billion cut passed by the Republican Congress, which claimed it wanted to eliminate mismanaged intelligence programs that wasted funds. In an ad called "Pessimism," Bush declared "I'm optimistic about America because I believe in the people of America"; meanwhile the ad tried to evoke an image of Kerry and the Democrats as "pessimistic" because of their negative spin on the economy. The Kerry team countered with an ad titled "Optimists," asserting that Kerry was bullish on America, which showed that both sides could engage in empty demagoguery.

But the major Republican spin after the Democratic Convention was that in nominating John Kerry and John Edwards as candidates, the Democrats were putting forth, respectively, the most liberal and fourth most liberal senators of their party. The numbers were plucked from a *National Journal* article on 2003 voting records. Although it was quickly revealed that the reason for the ratings was that Kerry and Edwards had missed a number of votes while out campaigning and thus scored atypically high on the liberal scale for 2003; overall, they did not score in the top ten for lifetime vote ratings put forth by the same group. This intrusive little fact did not stop a bevy of Republican spinners from repeating over and over that the Democrats were advancing candidates more liberal than Hillary Clinton and Ted Kennedy. Although Jon Stewart nailed a hapless congressman from Texas for repeating the Republican spin after it had been clearly refuted by honorable journalists, that didn't stop Newt Gingrich from beginning his closing remarks on the August 1, 2004, *Fox News Sunday*:

> I think what decides this race in the end is, do you think America can go forward better with President Bush continuing to lead, or do you really want *the most liberal member of the Senate and the fourth most liberal member of the Senate*, people to the left of Teddy Kennedy, people to the left of Hillary Clinton? And I think that choice is going to be so wide and so clear by mid-September. [emphasis mine]

Vice President Cheney also repeated the charge on the campaign trail, telling an East Grand Forks, Minnesota, audience on August 6:

> John Kerry is, by *National Journal* ratings, *the most liberal member of the United States Senate*. Ted Kennedy is the more conservative of the two senators from Massachusetts.
> (laughter)
> *It's true. All you got to do is go look at the ratings systems.* And that captures a lot, I think, in terms of somebody's philosophy. *And it's not based on one vote, or*

one year, it's based on 20 years of service in the United States Senate.[emphasis mine]

Although this claim had been refuted for at least a week, Cheney continued to trumpet the Big Lie signaled in italics in the quotes above.[13] Throughout the election, Bush and Cheney told bald-faced lies about Kerry on the campaign trail and the media rarely took them to task for their mendacity. In a revealing article, "The Boys and Girls on the Bus," *Columbia Journalism Review* commentator Zachary Roth describes accompanying Cheney and the campaign press corps on a trip through northeastern Pennsylvania in late August. Roth notes how Associated Press reporter Marc Levy called his wire service with an account of Cheney's speech, parroting Cheney's line that Kerry claimed "America will resort to military force only when attacked," whereas Kerry had repeatedly said he would use preemptive force if necessary. Roth commented: "Indeed, not once all day did I hear a reporter attempt to assess the accuracy of anything Cheney said. They were concerned only with accurately transcribing his words and actions, and with assessing the strategic purpose of the trip. Fact-checking the vice president's assertions didn't appear to be on the agenda."[14] All too often, the mainstream corporate media merely reported what Bush or Cheney said on the campaign trail, allowing them to frame Kerry with lies and distortions of his record and statements.

The Republican campaign strategy was to personally attack and mock Kerry just as they had gone after Al Gore in the previous election, presenting him as a tax-and-spend liberal and defaming him to create a negative image. The Big Lie was a political strategy devised by Adolph Hitler and the Nazi party, who maintained that if you repeated anything enough times, even if it was false, people would come to believe it. Bush had won the 2000 election with big lies (not to mention stolen votes and a partisan Supreme Court) that he was a "compassionate conservative," "a uniter not a divider," and a man who could "bring Democrats and Republicans together to get things done." Bush went hard-right from the beginning of his presidency, belying these slogans (see Corn 2003; Kellner 2001, Chapter 9). Bush had justified his Iraq invasion with the big lies that Iraq had weapons of mass destruction, that Saddam Hussein refused to disarm and was a menace, and that the United States had no other option than to invade the country and overthrow the regime (Corn 2003). His 2004 campaign also depended upon Big Lies, systematically misrepresenting Kerry's record and his campaign.

A major anti-Kerry mantra repeated by the Republicans and their network and print pundits throughout the 2004 campaign was that Kerry would raise taxes and endanger Bush-era tax cuts. As Peter Hart indicated in the August 2004 *Extra!:* "CBS reporter Byron Pitts (3/5/04), for example, announced a Republican claim that the Bush tax cuts would be in jeopardy under a Kerry administration, then turned to Commerce Secretary Don Evans, who stated, 'Senator Kerry has voted for tax increases over 350 times.'" No one questioned Evans' undocumented claim. Moreover, even after Kerry affirmed in his convention speech that he would institute a middle- and working-class tax cut and roll back the tax breaks only for the richest, George W. Bush in his first day of campaigning following the Democratic Convention warned that Kerry would raise taxes on everyone, and few media analysts exposed these false claims. Bush astonishingly claimed that he had not heard Kerry's speech, thus raising the question of how he could go out and refute the Democrat if he had ignored his opponent's speech.

One of Bush's punch lines in his early August postconvention campaigning was that Kerry was a "flip-flopper" on Iraq and that his opposition to an $87 billion spending measure to support the troops in Iraq after voting to support the Iraq war showed his inconsistency. But, Bush blared over and over, day after day, "There is nothing complicated about supporting our troops in combat!" In fact, Kerry had repeatedly made clear that he voted against the Iraq bill because it linked support for the troops with an aid package to Iraq, and Kerry wanted them separated (as did many senators of both parties). Moreover, demonstrating the complexity that he was decrying in Kerry, Bush himself had threatened to veto the $87 billion Iraq bill if the $18 billion earmarked for Iraq aid was deemed a loan rather than an outright grant. Yet Bush was able in his stump speech to attack Kerry for refusing to support U.S. troops in Iraq, an argument he repeated at the Republican Convention.

By mid-August, the punch lines of Bush's reelection campaign were "we've turned the corner in Iraq" and "results matter." But the corners turned by the Bush administration and "results" of its policies had led to disaster in Iraq and dubious economic results based on massive tax cuts for the rich accompanied by a skyrocketing deficit. Indeed, Bush was not really able to campaign on the positive achievements of his administration since there really weren't any, and so focused on attacking Kerry and the Democrats. The one "idea" Bush had promoted of an "ownership society," calling on Americans to go out and "own something" had been scorned by critics, who noted that this was a front for privatizing Medicare, Social Security, and other key social programs. These critics pointed out that Bush's plans would advantage private health insurance, private investment funds, and well-to-do citizens who could afford such programs, whereas they would disadvantage the poor by cutting back welfare programs that Republicans continue to detest, but that because of their popularity cannot be attacked head on.[15]

On August 13, Dick Cheney excoriated Kerry for allegedly promoting a more "sensitive" policy on terrorism: "Those who threaten us and kill innocents around the world do not need to be treated more sensitively. They need to be destroyed!" In fact, Kerry had said: "I believe I can fight a more effective, more thoughtful, more strategic, more proactive, more sensitive war on terror that reaches out to other nations and brings them to our side." Kerry was obviously not saying that he would be more sensitive to terrorists, but rather that he would reach out to allies and promote policies that would gain international support and not alienate potential antiterrorism partners. ABC, CBS, and various pundits countered Cheney's mockery with news clips from Bush calling for more "sensitive" policies, but few mainstream media commentators exposed Cheney's complete misrepresentation of Kerry's quote.

Cheney's use of "sensitive" was an attempt to feminize Kerry, as was Arnold Schwarzenegger's infamous "girlie men" phrase. In fact, gender became a major subtext of the campaign, with both candidates trying to present themselves as the most masculine. Bush was frequently shown chopping wood, swaggering about in a Texas cowboy hat and jeans, working out frequently in the gym, and appearing tough and manly, as in his infamous appearance in a flight suit declaring victory in Iraq.[16] Kerry too was frequently shown participating in hunting, appearing with his Vietnam "band of brothers," and vigorously exercising (also one of Bush's favorite activities). As the campaign evolved, however, there would be fierce battles over who was the true "man" and who was the pretender.

Bush's Media Events and the Swift Boat Battles

> See, one of the interesting things in the Oval Office—I love to bring people into the Oval Office—right around the corner from here—and say, this is where I office, but I want you to know the office is always bigger than the person.
>
> —*George W. Bush, January 29, 2004*

Staging media events is a key part of a presidential campaign, and the Republicans specialized in staged, controlled events at which only Bush-Cheney supporters were allowed. No one carrying an anti-Bush message would be allowed into Republican events and in some cases, the Bush event organizers demanded that individuals sign a support letter for the ticket before they could hear Bush or Cheney speak. *Washington Post* reporter Ann Gerhart describes how before a carefully crafted Bush campaign event "a master of ceremonies drills the crowd in hollering 'U-S-A! U-S-A! U-S-A!' and 'Boooooo!' at mentions of the opposition, [which] ... permits Bush to recite lines respectful of the Massachusetts senator, only to be interrupted by his boisterous supporters." Gerhart notes how these events provide a "warm ego bath" for Bush, concluding: "This is a multimillion-dollar Americana extravaganza, the image-making machinery of the White House working at its precision peak, nothing left to chance, building to the great Wow moment.... This ... is October political theater in May."[17]

On Labor Day in 2002 when Bush visited Pittsburgh, retired steelworker Bill Neel was arrested at a Bush campaign event for carrying a sign that read: "The Bush family must surely love the poor, they made so many of us." When he was told he could not show the sign on the route Bush was to travel and refused to go one-third of a mile to an approved protest site (where no one would see his sign), Neel was arrested. At his trial a police detective testified that prior to Bush's visit, the Secret Service told police to confine "people that were there making a statement pretty much against the president and his views" to a "free-speech area," out of the way of the Bush event.[18]

The judge in Pittsburgh threw out the charges, but when Bush was speaking at the University of South Florida Sundome in 2003, a man holding a sign saying "War is good business, invest your sons" was arrested. In a series of other events protesters were cordoned off in "secure" areas and were carried away by the police if they refused to comply.[19] On the whole, the Bush campaign events were staged with handpicked audiences throwing friendly questions to Bush, who would then offer his simple comforting answers. An article by Hanna Rosin provides a revealing look at Bush's managed media events:

> Hudson, Wis., Aug. 18—The audience gathered at Lakefront Park is small, intimate, the size of a crowd at a high school play. They've been instructed before he arrives not to be shy; this is their one chance to ask the president anything, and the president wants them to; after all, he calls this event "Ask President Bush." As they wait, it's raining one minute, sunny the next. In the background, Lake Croix, the pride of western Wisconsin, looks choppy. Hawks are circling overhead. Anything could happen.
>
> "What do you got?" the president taunts them when the questioning session opens, and then calls on the first hand.
>
> "Mr. President," begins a young man in a baseball hat. "I just want to say I'm praying for you and God bless you."
>
> And then one questioner later:

"I would just like to say that I agree with this gentleman, that we should all pray for you."

Every campaign has its preferred way of cavorting with the common man, and they are always somewhat canned. John Kerry and John Edwards have their "front porch" meetings, highly staged hangouts on a suburban stoop, just the two Johns, an average American family and 200 reporters. Bush prefers the "Ask President Bush" sessions, the campaign equivalent of the infomercial, with an audience designed to look as if it's been plucked randomly off the street, delighted anew at each twist and turn of the master's demonstration, irrepressibly bursting with questions and comments.

Typical of the exchanges at Bush's town hall meetings is this one from last week in Beaverton, Ore.

"Mr. President, you were a fighter pilot and you were with the 147th Fighter Wing?"

"Yes," answers Bush.

"And flew a very dangerous aircraft, the Delta F102?"

"Right, and I'm still standing."

"I want to thank you for serving our country."

"Thank you."

"Thank you for serving."

Last week he held four "Ask President Bush" events in Virginia, New Mexico, Oregon, and a Florida town named Niceville. Wisconsin marks his 12th, one shy of the number of news conferences he has held in the past 3 1/2 years in the White House. The campaign insists that the audience is not heavily screened and the questions are not planted. And if protesters are weeded out, that's only a question of hospitality.[20]

Staging media events coordinated with ads gains attention if they can be synchronized with current events. Hence, the Bush campaign produced an ad to be played during the Olympics that showed Afghani and Iraqi athletes playing in the games. The ad, titled "Victory," opened with pictures of a smiling George W. and Laura Bush, then cut to pictures of the Olympic athletes with a narrator intoning: "And this Olympics, there will be two more free nations [the flags of Iraq and Afghanistan flash on the screen] and two fewer terrorist regimes. With strength, resolve, and courage, democracy will triumph over terror [shot of the American-looking swimmer emerging from the pool, her fist clenched in victory]. And hope will defeat hatred."

The previous week, Bush had noted: "The image of the Iraqi soccer team playing in this Olympics, it's fantastic, isn't it? It wouldn't have been free if the United States had not acted." Iraqi soccer players, however, were outraged and told Bush to stop exploiting them for his campaign purposes. In an article in

Sports Illustrated, Iraqi soccer players and their coach said that they do not agree that their nation is yet "free." One player insisted "Iraq as a team does not want Mr. Bush to use us for the presidential campaign. He can find another way to advertise himself." Another player had an even harsher response, asking: "How will he meet his god having slaughtered so many men and women? ... He has committed so many crimes." [21]

A nastier Republican attack apparatus surfaced, however, when television ads appeared showing several members of the group Swift Boat Veterans for Truth, claiming that Kerry had faked war injuries, exaggerated the dangers he faced, had not deserved his medals, and then had "betrayed" his Vietnam comrades by becoming an antiwar protester. "Swift boats" were lightly armored Vietnam-era vehicles armed with .50 and .30 caliber machine guns and an arsenal of M-16s and grenade launchers. They were designed to patrol contested areas to interdict enemy supplies and troop movements on Vietnam waterways, and service in them was extremely dangerous. John Kerry had commanded one of these boats and received medals for bravery in fighting along with three Purple Hearts, all of which were questioned by the swift boat veterans group in one of the fiercest attacks on a former member of the U.S. military in history. Although the ad at first had a modest market buy, it was quickly circulated through the media; passionately discussed on talk television and radio, the Internet, and mainstream media sources; and helped shape a negative image of Kerry after he had taken pains to promote his military record as grounds for seeing him as a strong leader.

John O'Neil, one of the organizers of the Swift Boat Veterans for Truth group, had long been an adversary of John Kerry, debating him as early as 1971 when Kerry was a member of Vietnam Veterans against the War. The Nixon administration saw young John Kerry as a dangerous and effective antiwar spokesman and chose O'Neil to dig up as much dirt on Kerry as he could find and attempt to destroy him. O'Neil failed to find anything damning against Kerry earlier, but he had stayed in touch with other swift boat veterans, and with funding from Republican groups coauthored a book with Jerry Corsi, *Unfit for Command* (2004), that was heavily promoted by right-wing groups and became a best-seller. The book was the basis for the series of ads that O'Neil and his group ran against Kerry. Corsi soon disappeared from the campaign and media spotlight when it was revealed that he had made anti-Catholic, anti-Semitic, and anti-Muslim comments on a right-wing website. [22]

The ads were condemned by Vietnam veteran Senator John McCain (R-Ariz.) and many former military officers who supported Kerry. It was soon disclosed that the ads were funded by right-wing Republicans who helped organize the veterans' group, some of whom had served on the same type of boat that Kerry had commanded. Although most of their charges were called into question by investigative reporting that demonstrated the claims against Kerry were false, the charges were presented in the media as "one side" of a debate rather than as outright lies, and thus gained a certain credibility and wide-spread circulation that definitely harmed Kerry.[23] Interestingly, Republican campaign manager Karl Rove had long followed such Nixonian policies of smearing political opponents, planting negative stories about them in the media to destroy their reputations. Although O'Neil maintained that his group was independent of the Republicans, it was on record that one of his Texan funders was closely connected with Karl Rove and had long been a supporter of George W. Bush. Many other Republican connections with the swift boat smear campaign would emerge as the days went by.

In an indictment of the fabrications of the Swift Boat Veterans for Truth, William B. Rood, an editor for the *Chicago Tribune* and the only other surviving commander of a swift boat who had witnessed the events in question first-hand, defended Kerry's version of the events. O'Neil and his swift boat veterans group had claimed that Kerry had not really been wounded; that during the episode in which he had saved a comrade (who had appeared with him on the Democratic Convention stage) there was no real enemy fire and little danger; that Kerry's command that day had been erratic; and that he made up the events that had won him commendations and a Purple Heart. To counter these allegations, Rood wrote:

There were three swift boats on the river that day in Vietnam more than 35 years ago—three officers and 15 crew members. Only two of those officers remain to talk about what happened on February 28, 1969. One is John Kerry, the Democratic presidential candidate who won a Silver Star for what happened on that date. I am the other.

For years, no one asked about those events. But now they are the focus of skirmishing in a presidential election with a group of swift boat veterans and others contending that Kerry didn't deserve the Silver Star for what he did on that day, or the Bronze Star and three Purple Hearts he was awarded for other actions.

Many of us wanted to put it all behind us—the rivers, the ambushes, the killing. Ever since that time, I have refused all requests for interviews about Kerry's service—even those from reporters at the *Chicago Tribune*, where I work.

But Kerry's critics, armed with stories I know to be untrue, have charged that the accounts of what happened were overblown. The critics have taken pains to say they're not trying to cast doubts on the merit of what others did, but their version of events has splashed doubt on all of us. It's gotten harder and harder for those of us who were there to listen to accounts we know to be untrue, especially when they come from people who were not there.[24]

Boot went on to describe the dangerous situation and refuted in detail the specific claims made by the swift boat veterans, none of whom had actually been present on the day in question. Gunner's Mate Van O'Dell claimed in the first swift boat ad: "John Kerry lied to get his Bronze Star. I know, I was there, I know what happened." As it turns out O'Dell was lying. Although he was in Vietnam, he was not present during the swift boat episode in which Kerry earned his Bronze Star and could not testify as to what happened. Swift boat accuser Larry Thurlow's records and previous statements "contradicted his version of events and confirmed Kerry's."[25] Although Medical Officer Lewis Letson stated in the ad "I know John Kerry is lying about his first Purple Heart because I treated him for that injury," official Navy records show that it was another doctor who treated him, and Letson was able to marshal no evidence for his claims.

In addition, Rep. Terry M. Musser, a Vietnam veteran and cochair of Wisconsin Veterans for Bush, attacked the Bush-Cheney campaign in the *Milwaukee Journal Sentinel*, stating "I think it's un-American to be attacking someone's service record. Period. The president has an opportunity here to stand up and demand that the attacks be stopped." Another swift boat vet, Jim Russell, penned an angry letter to the editor of the *Telluride Daily Planet* to dispute the claim that Kerry was not under enemy fire when he rescued Jim Rassman from the water, a feat that brought Kerry a Bronze Star and Purple Heart. "I was on No. 43 boat, skippered by Don Droz, who was later that year killed by enemy fire," Russell wrote in the letter. "Forever pictured in my mind since that day over 30 years ago [is] John Kerry bending over his boat picking up one of the rangers that we were ferrying from out of the water. All the time we were taking small arms fire from the beach; although because of our fusillade into the jungle, I don't think it was very accurate, thank God. Anyone who doesn't think that we were being fired upon must have been on a different river."

Eventually, other members of Kerry's crew, many who had never spoken out before, came to defend his version of events against the swift boat vets' Big Lies. The Kerry campaign officially requested that the Federal Elections Commission force the group to withdraw the commercials and called upon the Bush administration to denounce the slander and mendacity. But during the weekend of August 21–22, the swift boat veterans came out and insisted that they had no connection to the Republican Party and continued their assaults on Kerry. However, the Texas group that funded the ads had long connections with the Bush family and Karl Rove; the producers of the commercials had made the infamous Willie Horton ad that helped Bush Senior win the 1988 election, and one of the major organizers of the group, John O'Neil, had long been a Republican operative and Kerry nemesis. The anti-Kerry group's claims to be independent of the Republicans rang as hollow as their claims about Kerry's war activities, which were generally refuted in the print media but continued to circulate through cable television, right-wing talk radio, and right-wing sectors of the Internet.

It was clear that Vietnam was still a festering sore in the U.S. body politic and that the war would be refought once again. Kerry's campaign put out an ad accusing the Bush administration of using the same smear tactics that they'd used in the 2000 Republican presidential campaign against John McCain. In a tough 2000 South Carolina primary campaign against John McCain, Bush's operatives had spread rumors that McCain might be unhinged by his Vietnam captive experience as a prisoner of war and that he might be a "traitor" who cooperated with the communist enemy. (They had also spread rumors that McCain had an illegitimate black child, circulating photos of McCain and his dark-skinned adopted Bangladeshi daughter.) Bush campaign managers were now using the same tactics to impugn Kerry's heroic war record that they had used against McCain (which is one of the reasons why McCain was so quick to denounce the ads).

The Bush Gang had used similar tactics in their upset of Ann Richards in the 1994 Texas gubernatorial race as well. Richards' strength was "inclusiveness," and she had appointed a significant number of women and people of color as well as gays and lesbians to her administration. A Texas state senator began complaining about the number of "homosexuals" in the Richards administration, and then a gossip campaign began that Ann Richards was a lesbian. Bush's Texas cronies had a long record of smearing political opponents and lying about the many embarrassing aspects of George W. Bush's business career, Texas Air National Guard service, and drug and alcohol abuse. Karl Rove was the Machiavellian political operative who specialized in dirty tricks and discrediting opponents, and adviser Karen Hughes specialized in lying about Bush's personal life. (Machiavelli was the Italian writer for whom the "ends justified the means," and who advised politicians to lie if it helped augment their power.) Bush operatives browbeat and intimidated anyone who dared criticize Bush, and Bush-Rove-Hughes unleashed the full arsenal of their mudslinging weapons at Kerry in the swift boat campaign.

Since Kerry's war record and national security credentials were assets far greater than Bush's meager Texas Air National Guard record and failed foreign policy, it was precisely in this area that the Bush campaign continued to work to destroy Kerry's credibility. Former Republican presidential candidate Bob Dole went on television on August 22 to impugn Kerry's Vietnam record and got caught up in false statements. Dole, a World War II veteran who had lost an arm in the war, claimed that Kerry's wounds were minimal and possibly self-inflicted, that he did not deserve a Purple Heart, and that his heroism was exaggerated. In a *Washington Post* summary by Lois Romano and David Naramura, Dole "questioned Kerry's commendations. 'Three Purple Hearts and never bled that I know of,' Dole said of the medal one gets for a combat injury. 'I mean, they're all superficial wounds. And as far as I know, he's never spent one day in the hospital. I don't think he draws any disability pay. He doesn't have any disability. And boasting about three Purple Hearts when you think of some of the people who really got shot up in Vietnam.'"[26] The reporters also pointed out that Dole erroneously stated, "He got two in one day, I think," when, in fact, "Kerry's Purple Hearts were received for different injuries over his four-month tour in Vietnam, during which he also received a Silver Star and a Bronze Star" (ibid.).

Bob Dole's participation in the attacks on Kerry's war record made it clear that the swift boat smear campaign was a key component of the Republican strategy to destroy Kerry. Dole's attack on Kerry backfired on him, however, as a series of rebuttals of Dole's lies about Kerry spread and stories were recirculated, based on Dole's own autobiography, indicating that his own wounds in World War II were induced by a misfired grenade that he himself had thrown. Reports reemerged concerning how Dole had gone to considerable lengths to avoid service in World War II from 1942–1945 and that he'd only served for seven rather uneventful weeks. Yet former President George H. W. Bush endorsed Dole's criticism. Appearing on CNN on August 30, Bush Senior stated that he found the complaints against Kerry by the swift boat veterans "rather compelling." Over the weekend before the Republican Convention both Laura Bush and Karl Rove separately noted that they agreed with criticism in the ads concerning Kerry's statements opposing the Vietnam War. The swift boat ads were thus clearly a major tactic of the Republican offensive against Kerry in a time-tested Bush family strategy to use outside groups to smear opponents and orchestrate coordinated media attacks.

There appeared to be a growing backlash against refighting the Vietnam War, however, when so many other issues faced the country, a position strongly articulated by Ellen Terich: "While an over-the-hill group of men are obsessing about a war that ended nearly 40 years ago, the issues of concern to women, children, and ordinary citizens of all ages are being ignored. While a crazed coterie of old warriors bring up a long buried and once controversial period of time in our nation's history in order to smear John Kerry, we have lost sight of the things that really matter today: health care; jobs; the budget deficit; education; terrorism; and all the issues that concern our children's future." Terich pointed out that the Republicans had long used "an irrelevant issue to try to win an election. They used a longstanding prison furlough policy in Massachusetts to demonize Michael Dukakis with the infamous 'Willie Horton' ads. The dishonest ads worked and the Republicans won the White House."[27]

But the media and the public continued to obsess over the swift boat veteran replay of the Vietnam War. On August 19, Kerry finally spoke out, claiming that the Republican-funded group of veterans was lying about his Vietnam service and was operating as a "front organization" for the Bush campaign. Kerry attacked the Bush administration for smearing his record, and John Edwards challenged Bush to distance himself from the mendacious ads. The Bush-Cheney campaign bluntly stated on a daily basis that they had nothing to do with the particular ads attacking Kerry's patriotism and Vietnam service. But almost every day new connections came forth: Ken Cordier, one of the vets denouncing Kerry in the ad, was a member of the Bush-Cheney campaign veterans' steering committee and was forced to resign; Benjamin Ginzberg, who had been a Bush lawyer during the Florida election theft, admitted that he had advised the swift boat vets and also resigned as legal adviser; others who had done public relations, fundraising, and other activities for the group were connected to the Bushes.[28]

Finally, on August 23 Bush addressed the issue, emerging from his Crawford, Texas, ranch swaggering and bantering with Cheney, Rumsfeld, and Rice at his side. Rather than disavowing the particular swift boat veterans ads, he basically reiterated what his campaign had been saying for weeks; namely that they supported closing down all the independent 527 groups putting out campaign ads. This was easy for Bush to say, since most of the independent groups such as www.moveon.org were supporting the Democrats. But Bush refused to condemn the particular slander of the swift boat campaign against John Kerry, and the Kerry campaign said the president's intervention "fell short of the clear denunciation it had demanded. Democrats said the president's remarks treated the veterans' claims as no worse than other attack ads by supposedly independent groups, questioning the group's source of finance rather than the substance of the ads, which they reject as a smear." Kerry's running mate, John Edwards, added: "The moment of truth came and went, and the president still couldn't bring himself to do the right thing. Instead of hiding behind a front group, George Bush needs to take responsibility and demand that the ad come off the air."[29]

Although the print media had debunked the specific claims of the swift boat veterans, cable networks failed to present the swift boat group as part of the Republican smear campaign.[30] Because the standard format of television news dictates that both sides of a specific issue be presented, many of the television interviewers purport to be objective and neutral when they are not, and other talking heads are not well informed enough to make particular judgments; lies can masquerade as one side in a partisan debate. Media critic Bob Somerby, on his www.dailyhowler. com website, documented how the mainstream corporate media failed to portray the extent to which the swift boat veterans were lying even after the initial charges were largely rebutted. Somerby documented in detail how George Stephanopoulos in an August 22, 2004, ABC *This Week* program failed to confront John O'Neil with articles that had recently circulated containing testimony from Kerry's Vietnam comrades who rebutted O'Neil's group's lies. On August 27–28, Somerby documented how on August 26 three MSNBC shows in a row featuring Chris Matthews, Keith Olbermann, and Deborah Norville allowed one allegation after another concerning Kerry's Vietnam record to pass without questioning them, without bringing up testimony of the past few days that refuted the smears, and without commenting on how right-wing Republicans long tied to Bush had financed and organized the ads.

Continuing a series of "Profiles in Cowardice" on August 30, Somerby pointed out how three witnesses to the Vietnam events in question who had stepped up for the first time and strongly rejected the mudslinging at Kerry were ignored by the television cable networks. Using Lexis-Nexis, Somerby indicated how the names of three vets who supported Kerry's story, Wayne Langhofer, Jim Russell, and Robert Lambert, were rarely mentioned in the cable news network discussion of the controversy that dominated the airwaves for weeks, except for Lambert, whose statement was mentioned once on the NBC cable network. As for CNN and Fox, the other two major cable networks, Langhofer's name was never mentioned, Russell's name was mentioned once on CNN, and Lambert's statement was never mentioned by either. Major newspapers like the *New York Times* and *Washington Post* also neglected the testimony, as did most of the country's other newspapers, leading Somerby to conclude that key members of the corporate media are unprepared, lazy, incompetent, or simply complicit with Republicans.[31]

The Republican Convention and Spectacle of Protest

> Security is the essential roadblock to achieving the road map to peace.
> —*George W. Bush, July 25, 2003*

You're free. And freedom is beautiful. And, you know, it'll take time to restore chaos and order—order out of chaos. But we will.
—*George W. Bush, April 13, 2003*

My views are one that speaks to freedom.
—*George W. Bush, January 29, 2004*

On the economic front, the Kerry campaign got a boost when U.S. Census Bureau figures indicated that things are getting worse for more and more people: "the number of Americans living in poverty rose by 1.3 million last year, to 35.9 million, while those without health insurance climbed by 1.4 million, to 45 million."[32] The report indicated that the fraction of the nation's total income going to the poorest 20 percent of U.S. households fell from 3.5 percent to 3.4 percent, but the fraction going to the richest 20 percent of households rose to nearly 50 percent in 2003. The figures gave Kerry impetus to criticize the Bush administration for "a sluggish economy and failing to protect consumers from the 'debt trap' set by predatory lenders, as the Democratic nominee prepared to retreat to Nantucket late Saturday and cede center stage to the Republican Convention for much of the next week."[33]

The buzz on protests against the Republicans in New York during their convention began in earnest with reports in the alternative media presenting detailed descriptions of what to expect from marches, art projects, bicyclists, anarchists, and mass demonstrations.[34] The Bush administration had been making clear for weeks that it was going to blame any excessive disruption or violence on the Democrats, leading to a rash of speculation that violence might help Bush.[35] There were also reports about FBI intimidation and harassment of would-be protestors, infiltration of protest groups, and the danger of police provocateurs who would urge violence to trigger arrests of demonstrators. Hence the spectacle of protest at the convention could be a dramatic one.

Despite intimidation and negative media presentation of demonstrators, a coalition of environmental groups began holding daily vigils at the World Trade Center site to inform the nation that the area was still contaminated with toxins and to denounce the Bush Environmental Protection Agency, which along with Bush himself, soon after September 11 proclaimed the area "safe to breathe." The Bush administration stuck to the claim despite a U.S. Government Accountability Office report finding that hundreds of thousands of New Yorkers were subjected to air quality so dangerous that chronic disease and death is expected for many in the future. Studies documented serious illness among workers in the area from contamination still on-site, and demonstrators wished to dramatize the dangers.[36] Greg Sargent wrote:

To make matters yet worse in New York City, the Bush administration pressed the Environmental Protection Agency to "omit cautionary language about the possible hazard from air pollutants such as asbestos, cadmium, and lead after the World Trade Center towers fell." This was according to the EPA's Inspector General, who also noted that the EPA's early statements failed to include proper guidance for cleaning indoor spaces, leading lower Manhattanites to return to their homes before they were completely safe. Large numbers of emergency and construction workers spent weeks at the center of destruction, most without respirators, falsely encouraged by the EPA's September 18th declaration that the air was "safe." Thousands who worked in lower Manhattan during and after the terror attacks saw "their lives turned upside down by illness without access to care." This was according to Dr. Stephen Levin, who headed a program at Mt. Sinai Hospital that screens people with Ground-Zero-related illnesses. Last year Levin told New York Magazine writer Greg Sargent that the Bush administration's failure to approach his 9/11 patients with a comprehensive and serious response is "an intolerable outrage," from "a public-health standpoint. Many of the people who spent months in the pit at ground zero," Sargent learned, "have respiratory ailments. And no health insurance. And no help from the government. There is a patchwork, at best," Levin reported, "of treatment" for those who have breathed in the "hydrochloric-acid mist released by plastics smoldering in the wreckage" and/or the "huge amounts of concrete" that was "ground into powder so fine that it could be inhaled deep into the lungs" (one wonders if Bush's heralded 7-minute mile running times have fallen since his own visit to the site of destruction).[37]

On the eve of the convention, warning New Yorkers of the invasion of Republicans about to take place, protesters staged a Paul Revere–like ride on horseback down Lexington Avenue, shouting out to all: "The Republicans are coming!" A variety of protests unfolded, including a highly publicized "nude-in" by ACTUP to protest Bush's AIDS policies. A group of more than 100 women in an "Axis of Eve" coalition planned to "expose and depose" President Bush panties containing slogans "Lick Bush," "Give Bush the Finger," and "Drill Bush Not Oil."

On Friday, August 27, a Brooklyn group called "Mothers Opposing Bush" assembled their "Kids for Kerry" and marched across the Brooklyn Bridge with their strollers. An abortion rights protest organized by NARAL Pro-Choice America had an estimated 25,000 turn out to protest Bush administration policies.[38] As reported by *AlterNet:* "People who dismiss abortion as a second-wave old feminist issue should see the young women in the crowd, many of whose t-shirts and signs have a girl power aesthetic. 'My Bush would make a better president' is a popular sign. A gorgeous young woman with long dreads wears a t-shirt that says 'I [heart] pro-choice boys.' The even younger children carry signs, some of them made with parents' help, that say, 'Everyone poops but Bush stinks' and 'Bush needs a time out.'"[39]

A protest in New York sponsored by the anticar/urban reclamation organization Critical Mass on Saturday yielded 5,000 cyclists against Bush; blocked streets caused "massive disruptions" to traffic according to New York police. In Central Park, Quakers and the families of soldiers killed in the Iraq war laid out 972 pairs of combat boots to symbolize those who had lost their lives. On the Long Island beaches, antiwar activists flew an airplane trailed by a large banner reading "Give Bush a Pink Slip." At Ground Zero, another group opposed to Bush administration policies sounded 2,749 bells—one for each victim of the September 11, 2001, attacks. In a daring piece of agit-prop, activists unfurled a 40 by 60 foot banner down the side of the Plaza Hotel looking into Central Park with a "Truth" and arrow-up graphic contrasted to a "Bush" and arrow-down image.

On the weekend before the convention, New York was eerily deserted in Times Square and other popular locations, as many New Yorkers fled the city in fear of disruption from terrorism and protesters. But on the eve of the convention Sunday, hundreds of thousands of Bush administration opponents poured into Manhattan's streets, angrily denouncing Bush and the war in Iraq and demanding the United States withdraw its forces. Organized by an ad hoc coalition of groups named, after much debate, United for Peace and Justice, the group's original protest rally plan and request for a demonstration in Central Park had been denied by the city, which waited until the last minute to approve the march route, an obvious attempt to harass the group and make it difficult to organize a coherent demonstration.

There were reports that activists all over the United States who planned to come to New York to protest had been visited by the FBI asking about their intentions, whether they approved of violent protest, and other questions aimed to intimidate potential demonstrators. Moreover, tabloid journalism presented would-be protestors as violent anarchists plotting days of mayhem and destruction. In one lurid account, Rupert Murdoch's *New York Post* in an August 16 article titled "Finest Prep for Anarchy" featured a photo of Jaggi Singh armed with a pistol at a firing range. Singh wrote a widely distributed response indicating that he was not planning to come to New York, that the photo was a fake, and that the whole story was fraudulent, providing a telling indictment of the Murdoch tabloid press.[40]

But despite the harassment and media hysteria, people from all over the country came to protest against the Bush administration in what was described as one of the largest marches in New York's history. Estimates of the Sunday march before the opening of the Republican Convention ranged from 200,000 to 500,000 protestors marching through Manhattan as they decried Bush's tax cuts for the rich, oil favoritism, repressive domestic policies, failed environmental policies, and incompetence as president. Pallbearers marched with a thousand mock coffins draped in black representing the U.S. soldiers killed in Iraq, and a papier-mâché tank moved along the route with Bush's head in a cowboy hat peeking out. "Billionaires for Bush," with men in top hats and women in shawls and pearls throwing fake money, carried signs reading "Leave no billionaires behind" and "Tax wages not wealth." The group defined itself as a "grassroots network of corporate lobbyists, decadent heiresses, Halliburton CEOs, and other winners under George W. Bush's economic policies." They proclaimed: "we'll give whatever it takes to ensure four more years of putting profit over people. After all, we know a good president when we buy one." The billionaires entertained audiences with right-wing twists on typical protest chants: "What do we want? Sweatshop labor! How do we want it? Cheap!" "No justice! No problem!" and "Whose Florida? Our Florida! Whose voting machines? Our voting machines!"

As the marchers passed Madison Square Garden, chants of "Liar! Liar!" filled the air and demonstrators flashed signs reading "Asses of Evil" at the Republicans. When confronted with Republican groups chanting "Four more years!" the crowd responded with "Four more months!" *NBC News* showed marchers streaming by a Republican yelling "Four more years!" A middle-aged Jewish woman stopped, looked him in the eye, and said "For what?" reducing the shouter to silence. Marchers satirized the Republican's favorite mantra, shouting "Four more *wars!*" A group from Greene Dragon, self-defined as "modern-day patriots celebrating the American Revel-ution against Corporate Monarch George II," lit their dragon float on fire and 15 of them were arrested. At 7th Avenue and 34th Street, pro-Bush supporters confronted demonstrators with a sign "Support President Bush—Trust Jesus," and one self-described "right-wing conservative Christian" shouted "Trust Jesus!" The crowd chanted back "Who would Jesus bomb!" When confronted by a "Kerry Is Unfit" sign the group cried out "Shame! Shame!" at the woman parroting right-wing anti-Kerry slogans. Flanked by police in riot gear and led by a line of celebrities including Jesse Jackson, actor Danny Glover, and filmmaker Michael Moore, the protesters moved through the fortified city on a circular route that took them through midtown and past Madison Square Garden, where the convention would open the next day. The marchers filled nearly 20 city blocks. The march took six hours to complete, forming a raucous but peaceful spectacle for television, although few corporate networks covered the protests in any depth.

After the march, some protesters went up to Times Square where they confronted Republicans in midtown hotels and restaurants, leading to the arrest of more than 50 for blocking the entrances to the Marriott Marquis Hotel and the Milford Plaza. A group called Queer Fist tried to disrupt traffic by staging a kiss-in at the theater district where Republicans were planning to go to Broadway shows. As reported in *Salon:* "Jamie Moran, a member of the collective RNCnotwelcome.org, was dressed like a young Republican in khakis and a button-down shirt, so he was able to get somewhat close to the delegates as they left the musical *Aida*. Moran shouted, 'Your presence here is offensive, no one supports you.' The delegates responded, 'Four more years,' and people screamed back, 'Four more days,' meaning, Moran said, the delegates were in for four more days of abuse."[41]

Other protesters wandered to Central Park, where they had been denied a permit, congregating in groups of less than 20 to avoid arrest. The "Billionaires for Bush" strolled into the park and told crowds: "Everything is wonderful. We'll soon be privatizing the lawn" and "Goodbye, middle class. It was nice knowing you." A man in an oversized Dick Cheney mask danced, dangling a tiny puppet of George W. Bush in front of him. A group calling themselves "Raging Grannies" sang songs that parodied familiar melodies to spoof Bush and Cheney, such as one to the tune of "The Battle Hymn of the Republic" that went: "No more lies from Dick and Georgie/We deplore their wartime orgy!"

Meanwhile, the Republicans kicked off their convention festivities with Dick Cheney making a speech on Ellis Island, in a controlled zone far from protesters, where he could celebrate George W. Bush as a great "war president." Campaigning in West Virginia, George W. Bush deemed "Iraq" a "catastrophic success," leading vice-presidential candidate John Edwards to retort that Bush was only half-right, and that "it was catastrophic to rush to war without a plan to win the peace."

On Monday, August 30, as the Republican Convention opened, the first of two "poor people's" marches organized by the Still We Rise coalition wove through Manhattan from Union Square to the convention site. Representing a number of New York–based activist groups, the organizers said that they were working to register 100,000 voters in the upcoming election. Later in the afternoon, another group, "March for Our Lives," convened in a small park near the United Nations building. In Michelle Goldberg's description:

A cadre of mothers with small children and people in wheelchairs was followed by a diverse crowd of the homeless and formerly homeless, social workers, public-housing tenants, clergy, students, and sympathizers. Led by Cheri Honkala, the formerly homeless leader of the group, it was the culmination of six weeks of protest throughout New York and New Jersey. Dozens of people who've slipped off the lowest rung of America's economic ladder had joined her on a grueling pilgrimage meant to dramatize the plight of the poor, pooling their food stamps and sleeping in churches or under the summer skies. Few walked the entire time; people would spend a few days and then rotate out, to be replaced by others.

The event proceeded peacefully and, although they did not have a parade permit, the group was allowed to make its protest.[42]

Preparing for their opening-night activities, the Republicans leaked that former New York Mayor Rudy Giuliani would compare Bush to Churchill, intoning: "Winston Churchill saw the dangers of Hitler, when his opponents and much of the press characterized him as a warmongering gadfly." Although it is easy to see Bush as a warmonger, it is hard to view him as Churchillian. In Giuliani's speech, he constantly evoked 9/11 and defended Bush's Iraq policy as part of the war on terror, generally presenting Bush as a great wartime leader a la Churchill.[43] The theme for the night was "A Nation of Courage" and a large choir sang a medley of Armed Forces theme songs, accompanied by a video of soaring jets, weapons, and U.S. military forces, all exploited for the sake of Bush's reelection. In a mantra-like incantation, Giuliani intoned "9/11" over and over, making for great satirical footage the next day on Jon Stewart's *Daily Show*.

John McCain claimed in his speech that September 11 had created a new world and that Bush had risen to the occasion as a great leader. There were incessant references, film clips, and evocations of Bush and 9/11, as if Bush's mere connection with the moment should qualify him for reelection. As McCain tried to evoke remembrances of American unity after September 11 and Bush's role in the (temporary) unification of the country, the protesters outside and the large segment of the country that opposed Bush and his administration belied McCain's rhetoric. McCain also made reference to a "disingenuous filmmaker" who tried "to make Saddam's Iraq look like an oasis." Michael Moore was in the audience with a *USA Today* press pass and stood up smiling and waving as the crowd turned to him chanting "Four more years!" Moore held up two fingers to signal that they only had two more months, and then held up his index finger and thumb in an "L" (a sign for loser by which Moore meant Bush), but it is doubtful that the Republican crowd got it.

Machismo served as an undercurrent of the Republican Convention, with attempts by the party to evoke the image that Republicans are more manly than Democrats, as tough-guy Rudy Giuliani and war hero John McCain took

Loan Receipt
Liverpool John Moores University
Learning and Information Services

Borrower ID: 21111146963111

Loan Date: 23/07/2009

Loan Time: 4:23 pm

Media spectacle and the crisis of democracy

1111011564430

Due Date: 27/07/2009 23:59

Please keep your receipt
in case of dispute

center stage during the first day of the convention and action-hero-turned-California-governor Arnold Schwarzenegger swaggered into the keynote position the following night. Not by accident, these men are also among the few moderate Republicans—the party deliberately kept its hard-right cadre out of sight.

As Bush campaigned around the country and hit the top media venues in preparation for his triumphant entrance into the Republican Convention, NBC interviewer Matt Lauer caught Bush admitting "I don't think you can win the war on terror." This statement led Democrats to criticize Bush for flip-flopping from previous predictions of victory. But after realistically conceding that the war on terror does not have an endpoint and is not a conventional war, Bush flip-flopped again the next day in a speech to veterans, thumping his chest and saying "We Will Win!" to get back on the macho track that the Republican Convention was promoting. It is interesting that Bush often says impolitic things off the cuff, admitting, for example, that Iraq is a "catastrophic success" and that "miscalculations" were made in his Iraq policy.

The motif for the second night of the Republican Convention was "People of Compassion" with Karen Hughes and Karl Rove trying to orchestrate a spectacle that would resell "compassionate conservatism," a product that had perhaps produced some votes in 2000, but that had been roundly undercut by the Bush administration hard-right extremism and militarism. Speakers included Secretary of Education Rod Paige, whose Houston School District had been revealed to have fudged numbers of students taking tests to illicitly boost its scores; and Senators Bill Frist of Tennessee and Elizabeth Dole of North Carolina to defend severely limiting stem-cell research, opposing gay marriage, and other aspects of the Republican platform that had been approved earlier in the evening (and would help mobilize an army of right-wing Christians).

Just as during the first night speakers such as Giuliani and McCain stressed Bush's determination, resolve, and leadership after 9/11, on the second night Arnold Schwarzenegger reprised the manly Republican image of the previous night, and Bush's daughters and wife tried to project a more compassionate side of him. Many praised Arnold Schwarzenegger's speech as the best of the convention so far, but, like the other speakers, Arnold did not have one positive thing to say about anything specific that Bush had accomplished or anything specific that he would do, except keep fighting terrorists. After Arnold extolled the virtues of America and zapped Democrats for a convention he said should have been called "True Lies," he gushed about "Bush's vision, will, courage, perseverance, steadfastness, and capacity for action." Arnold claimed: "He's a man of inner strength. He is a leader who doesn't flinch, doesn't waver, and does not back down," characteristics that constitute an ideal fascist.

After Arnold, the Republicans turned to soft-selling Bush with the highly anticipated convention debut of his twins Jenna and Barbara. The twins joked about how they had been working hard to stay out of the headlines and then put on a stand-up comic routine, telling jokes about popular culture, sex, and Barbara Bush, how their parents call each other Bushie, and other silly irrelevancies. A *Los Angeles Times* commentator wrote:

> The Bush daughters, fresh from their booing this week at the MTV Video Music Awards in Miami, came onstage at the Republican National Convention on Tuesday night and introduced a new strategy in the war on terrorism: giggling. The strategy Tuesday, apparently, was to have sisters Jenna and Barbara humanize and soften the grim-faced Politburo image that dogs the Bush-Cheney campaign, which hasn't made much of an effort to court those young Americans who call it a good day if they've remembered to TiVo *The Simple Life*. So here they were, girlie and giggly and glammed-up (Jenna in some kind of Juicy couture-looking track suit top over white pants, Barbara in a black cocktail dress).[44]

The twins then introduced their father, who was attending a local softball game in Pennsylvania, and as the game proceeded behind him, George introduced his wife Laura and the crowd went wild. Laura Bush is believed to be one of his strongest campaign assets and she took center stage to tell the world how wonderful her husband was, to defend the war in Iraq for liberating women, and to advocate a "compassionate stem-cell research" that maintained "respect for life."[45]

While the "compassionate conservative" Republicans occupied Madison Square Garden, the mean streets of New York were occupied by police who had arrested hundreds in order to keep mobs of young protesters from harassing Republicans on the way to the convention, invading hotels where Republican delegates were in residence, or attacking right-wing Bush-Cheney-connected corporations like Halliburton, the Carlyle Group, and Fox TV.

One group, the pacifist War Resisters League, planned for a "day of action" against Bush's war policies, including a march from Ground Zero to Madison Square Garden and then a planned "die-in" to demonstrate the effects of Bush's wars. Accompanied by the newly formed Iraq Veterans against the War, antiwar protesters were a prime target for the police, and 200 were arrested before the march even started. When another protest group was ordered away from Union Square, its members were threatened with arrest by a policeman in front of a phalanx of shield-bearing officers. The crowd chanted "Go Arrest Bush" and then switched to "the police deserve a raise!" The group then marched 1,000 strong toward Madison Square Garden; police swarmed in and arrested 200 who refused to move when police surrounded them and blocked their entry. As Republicans entered the convention site, a surveillance blimp and police helicopters flew overhead, cadres of cops with helmets and sticks stood ready for action, troopers on horseback paraded around the Garden, and New York looked like a police state.

In addition to phalanxes of storm-troopers, formations on horseback, and squads of cars, buses, motorcycles, and bicycles, there were plainclothes officers within the protest groups, some of whom had the groups targeted for arrest. Pundits speculated that the tens of thousands of armed police constituted the fourth-largest police force in the world. Police deployed hi-tech surveillance cameras that provided panoptic views of every street in the protest area and had swept down upon the demonstrators when they deemed it appropriate, providing a show of overwhelming force as if New York were Baghdad. Using giant nets to literally scoop up protesters, they also captured many seniors who were just out on the streets observing the spectacle, as well as catching reporters and tourists, whom the police released if they chose to do so, or hauled them away at their discretion.

A loose coalition of groups calling themselves A31 had promised a day of activism and nonviolent protests on August 31. The coalition had spontaneous demonstrations throughout the day against symbolic sites that represented aspects of Republican power, such as Fox TV. Several hundred gathered around the Fox News building near Times Square, and in Michelle Goldberg's description: "A bus, decorated with posters for Robert Greenwald's documentary *Outfoxed,* drove by, while a monitor on the bus's side showed clips from the movie. As a few bemused Fox employees stood outside and gawked, the crowd chanted 'Shut Up! Shut Up!' à la Bill O'Reilly. A group of male cheerleaders wearing skirts and O'Reilly and Sean Hannity masks danced around."[46] Demonstrators shouted slogans like "Shut the Fox Up!" and "The less you know, the more you watch." Groups of protesters also attacked Chris Matthews' outdoor studio in Herald Square, heckling MSNBC employees and Republicans heading for Madison Square Garden. Two protesters broke through security and pounded on Matthews' *Hardball* set's table before being arrested. In the words of *Washington Post* reporters Michelle Garcia and Mary Fitzgerald:

"It's propaganda," said Deborah Ben-Elizer, 34, a New Yorker wearing glasses with swirled lenses to represent what she called a zombie public that has fallen under the spell of Fox. "They're in bed with [the Bush administration]. They're sleeping together," she said.

Police built a double barricade four blocks from Madison Square Garden in all directions, and at one point, Fox reporter John Deutzman was interviewing protesters there when several realized he was from Fox and surrounded him, yelling, "Liar! Liar!" About 50 protesters joined in until police opened the barricade and gave Deutzman a haven inside.[47]

Around noon, Fox News played the latest television ad put together by the ironically named Swift Boat Veterans for Truth. The ad depicted Kerry's anti–Vietnam War protests, including discarding his combat ribbons, with a narrator intoning: "How can the man who renounced his country's symbols now be trusted?" Liberal *Newsweek* columnist Eleanor Clift admitted it was a powerful ad, but claimed one needed the context of the antiwar protest of the day to understand it. She was cut off by archconservative Charles Krauthammer, who said that Kerry had "betrayed the comrades he left behind" and added that the senator should be asked: "Have you no shame?" The Fox host Rick Folbaum joined in, sneering at Kerry, "Is he going to have to go on the *Daily Show* and talk to Jon Stewart about it?"

There were other actions throughout the city, including a brawl with the police at the New York Public Library, marauding crowds cursing at delegates in midtown, and creative groups engaging in diverse protest. A group of seniors wearing T-shirts emblazoned with slogans like "Ferme le Bush" and "Fire the Liar" stayed away from midtown and marched locally with walkers, wheelchairs, and canes since they explained that "we are just not able" to march to demonstration sites.[48] One group was allowed to wear masks (technically a violation of the law) to symbolically protest the abuse of U.S. prisoners in Abu Ghraib in Iraq and elsewhere. Another group presented itself as employees of "Halli-bacon." Outfitted in pig snouts and wallowing in stacks of fake money, they passed out fake $100 notes featuring a sneering face of Dick Cheney and chanted: "We love money. We love war. We love Cheney even more." Groups of protestors wearing masks in a Harlem subway station were arrested, and as police arrested demonstrators throughout the city, there were chants of "Oink, Oink, Oink," while a "skinny girl danced around singing, 'We all live in a military state' to the tune of 'Yellow Submarine.'"[49]

By the end of the day, more than 1,000 people had been arrested, bringing the total arrests to over 1,600. Hundreds of protestors were hauled off to a makeshift detention center on a pier on the Hudson River. According to *New York Times* reporter Christine Hauser:

> Protesters have complained about being held for as long as 30 hours in miserable conditions before being arraigned or receiving a desk appearance ticket. Several said they had contracted rashes from sleeping on the pier's floor, had

gone hours without food, and were given a Dixie cup to use to drink water. Some complain they have no access to their lawyers.

Detective Eric Crisafi said today that the police have no estimates for the number of people in the holding center at any one time. "We process everyone in a timely manner," he said. "Obviously, the system is overloaded."

Many fear that the intensity and frequency of the clashes could escalate, and have questioned police tactics.

"It's an example of the police suckering the protesters," said Donna Lieberman, executive director of the New York Civil Liberties Union, referring to the arrest of some 200 protesters who said they thought they were abiding by an agreement they had negotiated with the police as they marched from Ground Zero on Fulton Street on Tuesday.

"It was a bait-and-switch tactic," she added, "where they approved a demonstration and the protesters kept up their end of the bargain. They undermined people's confidence in the police, and that's a serious problem as we go forward."

The police, in cars and vans or on bikes and scooters, have said their aggressive actions and arrests have pre-empted more widespread disruptions.

"Today a number of anti-R.N.C. activities failed to materialize, including a takeover of the lobby of the Warwick Hotel, perhaps because of the police presence there," Police Commissioner Raymond W. Kelly told reporters at a news conference on Tuesday evening.[50]

Although many protesters were now in detention, creative events continued on Wednesday as thousands of demonstrators formed a symbolic unemployment line that stretched for miles to protest the high rate of joblessness under the Bush administration. In Christine Hauser's description:

Holding up pink slips of paper symbolizing the notices employees sometimes receive when their jobs have been terminated, the demonstrators held a line from Wall Street in Manhattan's downtown and stretched north about three miles to the midtown area where the Republican National Convention is in its third day today at Madison Square Garden.

"The Next Pink Slip Might Be Yours!" the fliers read.

"I've been unemployed before," Gary Goff, 57, a data processor, said to the Associated Press. "I'm concerned that unemployment is going up so drastically under the Bush administration. I think Bush is a disaster for working people."

The demonstration was organized by People for the American Way, a nonprofit group based in Washington that advocates for institutions that sustain a diverse and democratic society.

The group said in a statement today that 5,000 people participated in what it called "The World's Longest Unemployment Line" representing "the 1.2 million jobs lost overall since March 2001 and the more than 8 million Americans who are currently unemployed" (ibid.).

New York's labor unions rescheduled their annual Labor Day rally to march against Bush administration loss of more than 1 million jobs, weakening overtime protection and health benefits, and the Republicans' general hostility toward unions. Thousands of protesters chanted "No More Bush!" and marched with signs reading, "Mr. President, Where Are the Jobs?" and "More Layoffs on November 2."

AIDS demonstrators disrupted a Republican youth gathering on the floor of the party convention Wednesday, shortly after President Bush's twin daughters left the stage. As Bush's chief of staff Andrew Card began speaking, a group of about 10 protesters sitting in the crowd jumped up, blew whistles, and began to chant, "Bush kills" and "Bush lies." Young Republicans attacked the demonstrators, a fight broke out, and the police moved in to remove the demonstrators. The AIDS activist group ACTUP later claimed responsibility. At least one Republican was injured and police said there was at least one arrest.[51] But the Wednesday night Republican festivities proceeded without major disruption, although during Cheney's speech a demonstrator in the activist group Code Pink was hauled off by security after she stripped off a jacket and revealed a pink slip with the words: "Cheney's in bed with Halliburton and we got screwed." Another Code Pink demonstrator raised a banner saying, "Cheney and Halliburton are making a killing in Iraq."

After the mushy multiculturalism of compassionate conservativism night, the third night of the Republican convention featured Mean Old White Men who would cut John Kerry down to size and puff up George W. Bush. The first angry and cantankerous Old White Man, "ZigZag" Zell Miller, who delivered the Republican keynote address of the evening. In this speech, which was supposed to embody the spirit of the convention, Miller claimed that Kerry would arm the military with "spitballs" and "outsource our national security to Paris," as Republicans roared with laughter. Miller accused Kerry of voting against the "very weapons system that won the Cold War and that is now winning the war on terror," and repeated a litany of weapons against which Kerry had voted. Although Miller claimed that Kerry would give France and the United Nations veto power over U.S. policy—an argument phrased more abstractly by Cheney and Bush—in fact Kerry had made it clear that "I will never give any nation or international institution a veto over our national security." Playing the masculinist card, Miller described Kerry as "more wrong, more weak and wobbly than any national figure," and praised Bush's faith-based leadership. As the Republican crowd ate up his conversion to conservative Republicanism and attacks on Kerry, Miller appeared to many as rather offensive and off-putting. Indeed, Senator John McCain was furious with Miller's performance and publicly criticized it, as did most nonpartisan commentators. When CNN and MSNBC commentators confronted him, pointing out that his claims about Kerry's voting record and positions on defense were counterfactual, Miller lost it. He challenged Chris Matthews to a duel when Matthews persisted to question him concerning his false allegations on stage.[52]

The highlight of the night was the Meanest Old White Man of all, Dick Cheney, who pledged "I will give this campaign all that I have, and together we will make George W. Bush president for another four years." Launching into his attack, Cheney claimed: "Even in this post–9/11 period, Senator Kerry doesn't appear to understand how the world has changed. He talks about leading a 'more sensitive war on terror,' as though Al Qaeda will be impressed with our softer side. He declared at the Democratic Convention that he will forcefully defend America—after we have been attacked. My fellow Americans, we have already been attacked, and faced with an enemy who seeks the deadliest of weapons to use against us; we cannot wait for the next attack. We must do everything we can to prevent it—and that includes the use of military force." Cheney completely twisted Kerry's remarks on the need for a "sensitive" approach that develops coalitions with allies rather than just striking out with one's own military power as the United States largely did in Afghanistan and Iraq, with the result that bin Laden and the Al Qaeda and Taliban leadership escaped and the U.S. invasion of Iraq fractured a potentially potent coalition against terrorism.

Cheney's reference to Kerry's "sensitive" war on terrorism was pure demagoguery, as Kerry had countered with the proper context of his comments; moreover, the television networks themselves had shown clips of Bush and Cheney frequently using the term "sensitive" as they explained that it was out of context. Attacking Kerry's multilateralism and defending the Bush administration unilateralist approach, Cheney intoned: "Senator Kerry denounces American action when other countries don't approve—as if the whole object of our foreign policy were to please a few persistent critics. In fact, in the global war on terror, as in Afghanistan and Iraq, President Bush has brought many allies to our side. But as the President has made very clear, there is a difference between leading a coalition of many, and submitting to the objections of a few. George W. Bush will never seek a permission slip to defend the American people."

Cheney had once again fundamentally distorted Kerry's position that providing real leadership requires bringing allies together to meet common goals. Bush and Cheney, by contrast, failed to convince any but a few countries to support their militarist and unilateralist policies on Iraq and other international issues. As reports circulated the very same evening of violent terrorist attacks in Israel, Russia, Iraq, and elsewhere, the Bush-Cheney approach had obviously isolated the United States in an increasingly dangerous world. Cheney's attack on Kerry was aided by the Republican audience on the floor. One of the most popular artifacts for the delegates to wear was small purple bandages to symbolize that Kerry had not received serious wounds for his Purple Heart decoration, which they held up to the television cameras. With delegates chanting "Flip-flop!" Cheney mocked Kerry for supporting the "No Child Left Behind" legislation and then opposing it; for voting for and then against the Iraq funding bill, and for "flip-flopping" on other key issues. In fact, on the education bill, Kerry had voted for it, but opposed the Bush administration failure to fund it.

On PBS, in a segment just before Bush's official nomination, Karl Rove, when asked about the Bush administration's position on the swift boat veterans' anti-Kerry attack ads, said that although he honored Kerry's service in Vietnam, he thought it was shameful that upon his return Kerry attacked U.S. troops who had served in Vietnam. Earlier in the day, Rove had said to the Associated Press: "I think that was painting with far too broad a brush to tarnish the records and service of people who were defending our country and fighting communism and doing what they thought was right." In fact, Kerry was criticizing Nixon administration Vietnam policy and not the vets with whom he identified. He was defending the vets by fighting to end the war. Former Air Force General Merrill McPeak responded by asking "Who in the hell is Karl Rove, talking about John Kerry's war record?" noting that Rove got a student deferment in 1969. Two prominent Vietnam veterans and Kerry supporters, former Senators Bob Kerrey and Max Cleland, shot back and demanded that Rove resign. Kerry declared that, "If the question is whether or not there is any independence left between the campaign and those swift boat ads, the question has now been answered."

The second set of swift boat veterans' ads cited a series of allegations Kerry made in congressional hearings as an antiwar vet; the ads cited the most inflammatory statements and the Republican spin was that these comments were a traitorous attack on U.S. troops in Vietnam. In fact, Kerry was reporting what he had heard about U.S. troops in Vietnam from testimony of troops in various hearings, and was not reporting what he himself saw, nor was he giving his own opinion or version of Vietnam. Kerry had clearly criticized Nixon administration Vietnam policy, but at the same time wanted to help the troops get home alive. Thus the Republican spin blatantly distorted Kerry's testimony by making citations of other vets' words appear as if they were direct quotes from Kerry himself. Kerry had repeatedly made it clear that his testimony was in support of the troops and against U.S. government policies, but Rove continually spun out a distortion that seemed to be eroding Kerry's support. None of the PBS commentators questioned Rove's version of Kerry's Vietnam service and subsequent antiwar statements. In a revealing image, Rove leaned menacingly toward Mark Shields, the liberal on the panel, as he spoke, threatening Shields with aggressive body language. Neither Shields nor other PBS commentators said anything to contradict the bullying Rove, who was able to smear Kerry without contradiction.

The other Republican campaign line was that it was inconsistent for Kerry to attack the swift boat veterans' ads and not be against the anti-Bush ads from the 527s, supposedly independent groups not connected to the campaigns. In a *Fox News* appearance on Sunday, Republican House Speaker Dennis Hastert insinuated that billionaire liberal George Soros, who had been contributing to moveon.org and other 527 groups dedicated to defeating Bush, may have gotten some of his money from "drug groups." The Fox interviewer was taken aback and said "Excuse me?" and asked if Hastert thought that Soros "may be getting money from the drug cartel." Hastert blurted, "I'm saying we don't know. The fact is we don't know where his money comes from." Soros later responded to Hastert: "Your recent comments implying that I am receiving funds from drug cartels are not only untrue, but also deeply offensive. You do a discredit to yourself and to the dignity of your office by engaging in these dishonest smear tactics. You should be ashamed. I must respectfully insist that you either substantiate these claims—which you cannot do because they are false—or publicly apologize for attempting to defame my character and damage my reputation." Hastert's attacks fall into a pattern of assaulting anti-Bush figures with vicious innuendo, as Republicans did when books by insiders Paul O'Neil and Richard Clarke revealed Bush administration failures on the economy and terrorism. Hastert, Bill Frist, and other Republican leaders were sent out by the Bush administration to smear insider establishment critics, sending out a message that anyone who criticizes the Bush administration can expect immediate retaliation to besmirch their reputations.[53]

On the second night of the convention, a group of Republicans sitting next to the CNN box had suddenly started chanting "Watch Fox News! Watch Fox News!" That night, Fox outdrew the three big networks for the first time, and had almost four times as many viewers as CNN. In the prime-time convention hour when Arnold Schwarzenegger and Laura Bush were giving speeches, Fox drew an average of 5.2 million viewers, compared with 5.1 million for NBC, 4.4 million for CBS, and 4.3 million for ABC, according to figures from Nielsen Media Research. This marked the first time that a cable news network had beaten all three major broadcasting networks in prime-time coverage of a political convention.[54] According to the same *Los Angeles Times* article, the first two nights of ratings showed that the Republican Convention drew about the same number of viewers as the Democratic Convention in August, and polls showed the race as too close to call. George W. Bush's speech would obviously be one of the key determinants of whether the Republican Convention would be marked a failure or success. Coming up to Bush's finale, the Republican Convention record was mixed at best. There was almost universal condemnation of Zell Miller's vitriolic speech, and the one-two punch of him and Dick Cheney showed the meaner and nastier side of the Republicans. Both systematically distorted Kerry's record, engaged in below-the-belt attacks on him, and provided reams of material for critics who could rightly label them as liars.

Big Lies, Bold Lies, and Brazen Lies: Welcome to Bushspeak

I'm the master of low expectations.

—*George W. Bush, June 4, 2003*

There's an old saying in Tennessee—I know it's in Texas, probably in Tennessee—that says, fool me once, shame on—shame on you. Fool me—you can't get fooled again.

—*George W. Bush, September 17, 2002*

It was obvious that the Bush-Cheney Gang was exploiting the 9/11 tragedy to advance its campaign, just as it was used to push through a right-wing agenda. But the Bush administration failure to address Al Qaeda and terrorism before 9/11, their unilateral military action in Afghanistan that renounced offers of help from U.S. allies, and invasion of Iraq did more to destabilize the Middle East, win recruits for terrorism, and make the world more dangerous and less safe than any policy in recent history. Having no positive record to run upon, the Republicans attempted to present themselves as the party of national security and George W. Bush as the leader to fight the war against terrorism. Obviously, such a strategy requires completely neglecting facts and history and substituting words for reality. The overall Republican strategy since the stolen election of 2000 and in the 2004 election campaign had been to engage in Big Lies about the actual achievements and policies of the Bush administration. Adolph Hitler's Big Lies involved repeating a falsehood over and over until people thought it was true. During his 2000 campaign and throughout his four years in office, Bush had regularly deployed lies concerning who his tax cuts would benefit, how much his Medicare package would cost and add to the federal deficit, why he went into Iraq, and how his administration represented forces of freedom, democracy, and small government (Corn 2003; Waldman 2004). But the Big Lies had played out and Bold Lies were needed where falsehoods about John Kerry's policies, character, and history could be told and repeated day after day, even after they had been refuted and countered.

Bold Lies involve knowing that you are lying and doing it anyway, boldly proclaiming whoppers that informed people know are lies, and in the face of facts, counterevidence, and arguments, continuing to intrepidly and resolutely repeat the untruth. Karl Rove and Karen Hughes have long been producers and purveyors of Big Lies, and with George W. Bush and Dick Cheney as reliable performers, the Big Lies could be morphed into Bold Lies. For Bold Lies to work, the media must be complicit and not contradict what is obviously and demonstrably a falsehood. The standard media format of presenting both sides of an issue and remaining neutral between opposing parties helped the Republicans purvey their Big and Bold Lies with minimal mainstream media criticism. Such was the chutzpah of Republican liars that they could boldly lie to media reporters and pundits knowing that the media knew they were lying. Once Tucker Carlson of CNN recounted a surreal experience with Karen Hughes where she lied boldly to him, knowing that he knew she was lying.

It is a Brazen Lie when media figures know that the speaker is lying and he or she does it anyway, hoping to get away with it. Karen Hughes and Karl Rove have made a career of Brazen Lies, where they tell things to the media and public that they and informed members of their audience know to be untrue. To enforce Bold and Brazen Lies requires intimidation and retaliation against anyone who catches you in your lie and confronts you with the untruth that is spoken. Conservative pundits are complicit in reproducing Bold and Brazen Lies because they are part of a Republican attack group that is willing to do and say anything to maintain power. Liberals and media types who see themselves as fair and objective are put in a troubling position when confronted with Bold and Brazen Lies. The night of PBS's presentation of George W. Bush's presidential nomination speech was especially revealing because both Karl Rove and Karen Hughes used intimidating body language when they confronted PBS commentators before Bush's speech. Karen Hughes leaned over liberal Mark

Shields when she spoke and glared at him in the same intimidating fashion as Rove, in effect, daring him to call her a liar and face the consequences. Hughes had long lied for Bush, browbeaten reporters who dared to question her, and retaliated against those who published stories critical of Bush, who lost access, were bad-mouthed, or worse.

There are a number of reasons why lying comes so easily to the Bush-Cheney Gang. On one hand, there is a raw lust for power evident in Cheney, Rove, Bush, and others in the Bush administration by which the ends justify the means, and anything can be done or said to get elected and maintain power. Karl Rove and Dick Cheney perhaps best represent the raw, brutal power politics of the Bush administration in which telling lies constantly and systematically is justified by economic gain for the administration's beneficiaries. Karl Rove, deemed by some a "Mayberry Machiavellian" to denote the combination of his provincialism and utter ruthlessness, seems to be driven by a fanatic love of power and money for himself and his Republican allies. Rove lies constantly, shamelessly, and aggressively because he knows that lies help gain his political ends. For Rove, winning is all and anything that helps him win is justified.

Dick Cheney also probably fits into the utterly amoral power politics camp, believing that the ends justify the means. Cheney's audacious mendacity was clear the night of the debate with John Edwards when Cheney first denied that he had ever linked Al Qaeda and Iraq, and then falsely declared that he'd never seen John Edwards before that night. The former claim was, as everyone knew, a Brazen Lie, as Cheney had countless times insinuated and even asserted direct connections between Al Qaeda and the Iraqi regime, as an impressive array of news images and print clippings documented the next day. The episode revealed Cheney's proclivity to simply say whatever he felt was politically expedient at the moment and to have zero respect for truth or even concern that he would get caught up in his lies, since truth and lying were of no interest to the power- and money-mad Cheney.[55]

There are also more elaborate theological and philosophical justifications for lying evident among certain sectors of the Bush cabal. The influence of the German philosopher Leo Strauss, who legitimated Plato's "Noble Lie" as an important tool for ruling the ignorant masses, has been often cited. Strauss was also a devotee of Machiavelli, and his philosophy provided justification for the raw power politics and economic graft of the Bush administration. In a moment of candor, leading neocon Paul Wolfowitz admitted that the Bush administration pushed the issue of "weapons of mass destruction" to justify their Iraq war largely because manipulation of fear of Iraqi weapons was the best way to sell the Iraq policy to the public, suggesting that among Bush's neocons a neo-Straussian proclivity to lie to justify policies that the ignorant masses cannot understand is perfectly kosher.

The religious right, which makes up a significant segment of Bush administration core support, has an elaborate theological justification to legitimate lying. As Mark Miller suggests (2004, 279ff.), certain Christian fundamentalist groups that fervently support Bush take the biblical story of Rabab (Joshua 2, 1–24) to legitimate the principle of deception in a state of war. For the Christian right, Bush represents the godly side in the war on terror as well as the multiple cultural wars at home; hence anything that he says or that is said on his behalf is justifiable as advancing the cause of good versus evil. Likewise, cult leader Reverend Sun Myung Moon, who owns the right-wing *Washington Times* and strongly supports the Bush family, preaches a doctrine "called Heavenly Deception. Religious recruits are told that the 'non-Moon world' is evil. It must be lied to so it can help Moon take over" (Brock 2004, p. 179).

The political genius of George W. Bush is that it is not certain that he is lying because he seems to believe many of the things that Cheney, Rove, Hughes, Rice, and his other handlers tell him. Often when he lies daily on the campaign trail, he is just repeating what he's been told to say and may not even know it's a lie. Seymour Hersh ends his book *Chain of Command* (2004) with reflections on Bush's relation to truth and falsity: "There are many who believe George W. Bush is a liar, a President who knowingly and deliberately twists facts for political gain. But lying would indicate an understanding of what is desired, what is possible, and how best to get there. A more plausible explication is that words have no meaning for this President beyond the immediate moment, and so he believes that his mere utterances of the phrases make them real. It is a terrifying possibility" (367). The charitable interpretation of Bush's campaign spinning is that Bush will say anything that he is programmed to say and is blissfully unaware of the mendacity in his daily assault on Kerry. A less charitable interpretation would be that he is a complete cynic who doesn't really care about the truth or falsity, or that he is a cool, calculated, skilled, and highly accomplished liar who will willingly deceive to promote his agendas.

Thus, whereas at one time conservatives were defenders of truth, and from the 1960s into the 1980s battled "relativists" in the academy and polity, curiously, conservatives are now systematic practitioners of the Big Lie and of Bushspeak. Certainly, there had never been such shameless, systematic, and daily lying as in the 2004 political campaign, in which Bush, Cheney, and their operatives systematically misrepresented and lied about the positions of John Kerry, following four years of lying about their tax breaks for the rich, their Iraq policy, their energy policy, Medicare, and just about everything else of import. In any case, Big, Bold, and Brazen Lies were the dominant discourse of the Bush campaign. Republicans would therefore not need to be bothered with mere facts, with evidence, or counterarguments, because all they had to do was to repeat the Bold Lie and project hostility and the possibility of retaliation against anyone foolish enough to stand up to the Bold Lies of the moment (which can be easily replaced when they are deemed "inoperative").[56] The Republicans got away with the lies because their own right-wing attack media provided an echo chamber so that even the most outrageous smears and falsehoods could assume the façade of legitimacy if repeated enough times and if attempts to counter the lies were aggressively attacked and labeled "partisan." The mainstream media was hesitant to accuse the Bush-Cheney campaign of lying because they would be accused of partisanship and savaged by the right-wing attack apparatus. They were hesitant to apply the label of "loser" to the president.[57]

Although the Big Bold Bush Lies are audacious, even some of the smaller Orwellian lies are breathtaking. In George Orwell's dystopic novel *1984*, a future state is at permanent war and uses language to describe the opposite. In Orwell's universe, war is peace, freedom is slavery, and ignorance is strength. In Orwellian language, the Bush administration called its Iraq occupation a "liberation" and its imposition of a government on Iraq "democracy."[58] On the domestic front, it calls its cutbacks on pollution control and environmental regulation a "Clear Skies Initiative" and its initiative to eliminate regulations for logging and mining forests a "Healthy Forest Act." As Marilyn Young describes it, the Bush administration systematically uses Orwellian language:

> In order to "better harmonize the environmental, social, and economic benefits of America's greatest natural resources, our forests and grasslands," the administration gave the Forest Service the power to skip environmental reviews before approving lumber company requests to log national forest land. In order to move "toward more effective prevention of black-lung disease," the federal Mine Safety and Health Administration raised the limit on the amount of coal dust allowed in mines. In order to "save hundreds of lives," the Department of Transportation increased the number of hours long distance truckers could drive before a mandated rest period. Through budget cuts, the Occupational Safety and Health Administration has lost seventy-seven enforcement agents; it created two new jobs for staff who would "help industry comply with agency rules." Rules on mercury, the efficiency of air conditioners, food labeling, training of health care workers, restoration of wetlands, and media concentration have all been weakened. As "regulatory initiatives," these achievements on behalf of business require no new legislation and can be halted only through costly legal action. According to the president's spokesman, the new rules are the expression of the

"President's common-sense policies [that] reflect the values of America, whether it is cracking down on corporate wrong-doing or eliminating burdensome regulations to create jobs." This is a sentence of genuine Orwellian grandeur.[59]

Leading up to Bush's Republican Convention speech there was almost no defense of his domestic record; what few references there were to domestic policies were perfunctory at best and often misleading. Secretary of Education Ron Paige praised Bush's "No Child Left Behind" program, as did Dick Cheney. But critics have long argued that the Bush administration did not adequately fund the program and educators all over the country have deemed it a resounding failure. There were likewise a few feeble attempts to present Bush's tax cuts as helping the economy get out of the "Clinton recession" (another Bold Lie). The vicious attacks on Kerry made it clear that Bush was a divider and not a uniter and, astonishingly, Bush reprised the discredited and laughable phrase in his speech by praising his "coalition of the willing" and presenting himself as leader of something like a united front against terror. In fact, partly because of his divisive Iraq policy, Bush has deeply alienated the key U.S. allies as well as creating new enemies throughout the world with his administration's arrogance, aggression, and brutality.

The emptiness of the Republican case for Bush and lack of reasons to reelect him were made abundantly clear in the short film introducing Bush at the Republican Convention. With a corny narration by Senator Fred Thompson, the motif of the film was that Bush proved his greatness with a bullhorn after 9/11. Next, a video was played of Bush marching to the mound of Yankee Stadium and tossing out the first pitch of the World Series with the crowd roaring and chanting "USA! USA!" As Bob Woodward (2002) wrote:

> The president emerged wearing a New York Fire Department windbreaker. He raised his arm and gave a thumbs-up to the crowd on the third base side of the field. Probably 15,000 fans threw their arms in the air imitating the motion.
>
> He then threw a strike from the rubber, and the stadium erupted.
>
> Watching from owner George Steinbrenner's box, Karl Rove thought, "It's like being at a Nazi rally." (277)

The entire convention had been orchestrated to present Bush as the grand leader, and finally the big moment arrived. Walking between two gigantic U.S. flags down a runway to a specially constructed platform that put Bush on top of what looked like a pitcher's mound emblazoned with the seal of the presidency, Bush triumphantly swaggered up to the teleprompter to read his speech and the crowd went wild. After genuflecting to the Republican audience, his wife, daughters, and parents, Bush took up the 9/11 theme immediately, as this was obviously what he considered his strongest reelection card.

Cocky and confident during the opening segment, Bush intoned: "Since 2001, Americans have been given hills to climb and found the strength to climb them. Now, because we have made the hard journey, we can see the valley below. Now, because we have faced challenges with resolve, we have historic goals within our reach and greatness in our future." For Christians in the audience, the imagery evoked Moses going to the mountaintop or Jesus preaching the sermon from the mount, although the speech also reprised Ronald Reagan's "City on the Hill." In any case, Bush's rhetoric falsely suggested that the United States had emerged triumphant from its trials and tribulations and faced a great future. In fact, no president had lost more jobs, immersed the United States in such disastrous wars, piled up such an enormous deficit, so divided the U.S. public, and alienated the country from the rest of the world.

In the most frightening refrain in his speech, Bush intoned that he would "build a safer world and a more hopeful America *and nothing will hold us back!*" He claimed that he had "passed the most important federal education reform in history," strengthened Medicare, and strengthened the economy. Bush likes simple incantations to push home a point, and when "we've turned the corner in Iraq" failed as a slogan because of setbacks there, Bush's handlers came up with the phrase "*and nothing will hold us back!*" The veiled threat accurately characterized Bush's tax cuts to pay back rich corporate supporters, to unleash the military when Bush and his coterie see fit, to cut back on civil liberties and environmental legislation, to disregard all international law, and in general to promote a right-wing agenda. The phrase also highlighted the bullying tone of Bush's campaign and its threats to democracy itself in the macho assertion that Bush would triumph, he would do what he pleased, and he would destroy all opponents. Indeed the Republican Convention appeared like a fascist rally when the Republican crowd roared on cue during Bush's punch lines, held up signs to highlight his points, and like trained seals chanted "flip-flop" when signaled during Bush and Cheney's speeches to make fun of Kerry. It was a highly disciplined and disturbing spectacle.

Bush's proposals on the economy were not new and, since he had done little to promote a "compassionate conservative" agenda and present positive public policy programs, he could only engage in empty rhetoric punctuated with a laundry list of proposals. It was remarked that the phrase "I will..." was the most common of the night, offering empty promises rather than big ideas or concrete proposals. He advanced his "ownership society" concept whereby more people would own homes, manage their retirement funds, and choose their own medical coverage. Critics began to see that this notion was basically a proposal to undo New Deal programs by privatizing federal programs, a boondoggle for private insurance and investment companies, but hardly a sound program for the majority, as it means cutting taxes on capital investments, providing tax credits for saving, and privatizing Social Security, all of which benefit the wealthy and do not help the less well-off.[60]

Bush's audience perked up when he began ridiculing John Kerry, something that he genuinely loved to do and that invariably worked with his audience, although since his attacks on Kerry regularly distorted his opponent's record, Bush set himself up as a liar. Bush's mocking of Kerry received the first strong response to his speech all night:

> Bush: Senator Kerry opposed Medicare reform and health savings accounts. After supporting my education reforms, he now wants to dilute them. He opposes legal and medical liability reform. He opposed reducing the marriage penalty, opposed doubling the child credit, opposed lowering income taxes for all who pay them.
>
> Audience: Boo.
>
> Bush: Wait a minute, wait a minute. To be fair, there are some things my opponent is for.
>
> (laughter)
>
> He's proposed more than $2 trillion in new federal spending so far, and that's a lot, even for a senator from Massachusetts.
>
> (applause)
>
> And to pay for that spending, he is running on a platform of increasing taxes. And that's the kind of promise a politician usually keeps.
>
> His policies of tax and spend, of expanding government rather than expanding opportunity, are the politics of the past. We are on the path to the future, and we're not turning back.
>
> (applause)
>
> Audience: Four more years. Four more years. Four more years.

Once again, Bush blatantly misrepresented and distorted Kerry's proposals. Kerry did oppose Bush's Medicare program because according to him it gave too much to drug companies, did not allow importing cheaper drugs from Canada, and did not provide enough help for the poor and middle class. Bush raised questions concerning how Kerry could pay for his programs (in fact, Kerry had proposed that ending tax breaks for the very rich would pay for many of his programs); the same question might be put to Bush. Indeed, Bush's proposals would cost trillions, and with raising military spending and cutting taxes for the rich, only a Reaganesque "voodoo economics" would fund Bush's programs.

After promises for new programs, Bush then threw some red meat to his conservative supporters, promising further welfare reform, protecting the "unborn child," strengthening religious charities, protecting marriage against "activist judges," appointing federal judges "who know the difference between personal opinion and the strict interpretation of the law," and defending conservative values. After more mocking of Kerry, Bush turned serious and claimed that his strategy in the Middle East was succeeding as "more than three-quarters of Al Qaida's key members and associates have been detained or killed," and that "We have led, many have joined, and America and the world are safer."

In fact, the Middle East is much more chaotic and dangerous since Bush assumed office, with the Palestine-Israel conflict getting nastier every day, and with Afghanistan, Pakistan, Iraq, and Saudi Arabia hotbeds of Islamic fundamentalism rendering the United States less safe than ever before. Bush also tried to portray Iraq as part of the war on terror and claimed that its "liberation" is part of a democratization of the Middle East. In fact, Bush chose to invade Iraq, lied about its alleged "weapons of mass destruction" and its imminent threat to the United States, and lied about Iraqi compliance with UN mandates for weapons inspection. He said "we gave Saddam Hussein another chance, a final chance, to meet his responsibilities to the civilized world. He again refused, and I faced the kind of decision that comes only to the Oval Office, a decision no president would ask for, but must be prepared to make. Do I forget the lessons of September 11 and take the word of a madman, or do I take action to defend our country? Faced with that choice, I will defend America every time." But it is simply false to claim that Iraq refused to let in weapons inspectors; Iraq allowed full inspections, turned over 12,000 pages of documents, and the United Nations was satisfied with the progress and withdrew inspectors only when Bush claimed that attack was imminent. It was an utterly specious dichotomy to accept the word of Saddam Hussein or go to war, as clearly Bush chose war when there was no threat to U.S. national security. As Robert Parry puts it:

> The reality, of course, was different. Starting in fall 2002, Hussein did grant the U.N. weapons inspectors free rein to search any suspect WMD site of their choosing. U.N. chief inspector Hans Blix wrote that he was encouraged by the Iraqi cooperation in letting his inspectors check out sites identified by Washington as possible WMD hiding places. Though finding no WMD at those sites, Blix's in-

spections team was expanding its operations in early 2003. But Bush wanted to go to war. So he forced the U.N. inspectors to leave in mid-March 2003. "Although the inspection organization was now operating at full strength and Iraq seemed determined to give it prompt access everywhere, the United States appeared as determined to replace our inspection force with an invasion army," Blix wrote in his book, *Disarming Iraq*.[61]

As Bush tried to defend his record in the "war on terrorism" and equate Iraq with it, he was twice interrupted by hecklers and lost his focus and momentum. Indeed, on the whole Bush's speech was extremely uneven, lacking in cogent arguments to vote for him, poorly defending his mediocre record, and failing to outline an appealing agenda for the future. Bush spoke in a patronizingly simplistic tone and kept his nose buried in his text to make sure he didn't misspeak. When Bush was interrupted by protesters from the floor, he continued dutifully to read the speech, but began losing the attention of the audience. One camera caught Lynne Cheney angrily looking around and shaking her head as her husband Dick grimaced and the Cheney daughters nervously looked behind them wondering if a protester would attack the family (on Monday night, a 21-year-old Yale student and antiwar protester, Thomas Frampton, had penetrated the security in Madison Square Garden to shout slogans within 10 feet of Vice President Dick Cheney before he was hauled away). Bush was obviously rattled. In the words of *Washington Post* TV critic Tom Shales:

> It's doubtful that four more years in office would turn George W. Bush into a great speechmaker.... Bush still has problems maintaining poise. Twice, when cheers from the crowd were interrupted by jeers from protesters—who were quickly hustled out of the hall by security guards and police—Bush looked flustered, even frightened, though he did keep reading from the prompting devices encircling him. Ronald Reagan in the same situation would have responded with a quip and dismissed the protesters with a tolerant smile. Bush clung carefully to his text, his eyes darting anxiously around the hall.[62]

Bush's darting eyes revealed a deep nervousness and unsureness if people would believe what he was saying. After his specious arguments that "the world is more just and will be more peaceful," Bush emitted another set of bold lies:

> Bush: Again, my opponent and I have different approaches. I proposed, and the Congress overwhelmingly passed, $87 billion in funding needed by our troops doing battle in Afghanistan and Iraq. My opponent and his running mate voted against this money for bullets and fuel and vehicles and body armor.
> Audience: Boo.

Bush: When asked to explain his vote, the senator said, "I actually did vote for the $87 billion, before I voted against it."

Audience: Flip-flop. Flip-flop. Flip-flop.

Bush: Then he said he was "proud" of his vote. Then, when pressed, he said it was a "complicated" matter.

There's nothing complicated about supporting our troops in combat.

Kerry had explained that he strongly supported U.S. troops in combat and was in favor of the $66 billion in the bill for direct military expenses, but did not support the $18.2 billion provisions for reconstruction of Iraq and therefore had voted against the $87 billion allocation. Kerry wanted to finance the Iraq reconstruction aid by rescinding Bush's tax cut for the rich so as not to add to the deficit. Moreover, Bush's "nothing complicated" glosses over the fact that he was ready to veto the $87 billion Iraq package if the reconstruction money was presented as a loan. Many in Congress, including members of his own party, wanted it that way, rather than as an outright grant, as Bush and Cheney wanted it (knowing that the grant would go into Halliburton and corporate coffers of others who supported the Bush-Cheney Gang). Thus, the issue of Iraqi aid *was* highly complicated, including the issue of who the contracts went to (Bush-Cheney supporters and allies), the lack of bidding for and control over the contracts, and the corruption that had already occurred, leading the Pentagon to threaten not to pay Halliburton, which was obviously overcharging (see the discussion in Chapter 6).

John Dean has pointed out in *Worse Than Watergate* (2004) the Nixonian dimension of the Bush administration, including smearing political opponents and misusing arms of the federal government to promote a partisan agenda (as the Bush Gang misused intelligence agencies to shape public sentiment on Iraq to support their intervention). But one needs to return to the McCarthy era to capture the depth of Bush administration corruption. The smears on John Kerry by not only the swift boat veterans but also Bob Dole, George H. W. Bush, Laura Bush, and many of the speakers at the Republican Convention involved the most blatant mudslinging, innuendo, and lies seen since the days of Joe McCarthy's red-baiting. Of course, Karl Rove's campaigns for Bush had always involved smear campaigns of opponents, but never before had an entire convention reeked so of McCarthyism, with speaker after speaker impugning Kerry's patriotism and brazenly lying about his record as convention delegates displayed their purple Band-aids to belittle Kerry's war injuries.

The reception to Bush's speech was predictable, with Republicans and their media support groups gushing about it, Democrats attacking it, and "neutral" pundits balancing pros and cons. Summing up editorial commentary in the major newspapers, Dan Froomkin concluded:

"Tonight," President Bush said at the top of his hour-long convention speech last night, "I will tell you where I stand, what I believe, and where I will lead this country in the next four years."

Not much luck on that last part.

Bush's speech stirringly made the argument that he is resolute. . . . But in substance, there was essentially nothing new last night, no detailed agenda— and nothing remotely unscripted. Many lines were refugees from previous speeches and Bush meticulously stuck to his prepared text, even when interrupted by hecklers.

Laying out his domestic policy, Bush was vague on the big stuff and otherwise small-bore. He didn't address the job losses that have plagued his tenure.

Mired in an increasingly unpopular war in Iraq, Bush defended his actions, but didn't describe a way out.

Standing accused of having fudged the connection between the war on terror and the war on Iraq, he continued his attempt to conflate the two, without substantiation, leaving unclear where we go from here.

In the long run, in fact, Bush's speech may be more newsworthy for what he didn't say than what he did.[63]

Kerry went on the offensive forty minutes after Bush concluded his speech, "denouncing the GOP convention for its 'anger and distortions' and belittling Vice President Cheney for avoiding the military draft during the Vietnam War era."[64] Kerry claimed that Bush was "unfit" to lead, saying he misled the country on the Iraq war and had a failed record on jobs, health care, and energy costs. Ratcheting up the attack, Kerry thundered: "I'm not going to have my commitment to defend this country questioned by those who refused to serve when they could have and by those who have misled the nation into Iraq."

Kerry also went after the vice president: "I'm going to leave it up to the voters whether five deferments makes someone more qualified than two tours of duty." Fiercely assailing Bush and Cheney, Kerry stated: "Let me tell you what I think makes someone unfit for duty. Misleading our nation into war in Iraq makes you unfit to lead this nation. Doing nothing while this nation loses millions of jobs makes you unfit to lead this nation. Letting 45 million Americans go without health care makes you unfit to lead this nation. Letting the Saudi royal family control our energy costs makes you unfit to lead this nation. Handing out billions [in] government contracts without a bid to Halliburton while you're still on their payroll makes you unfit." Kerry was offended by Cheney's use of the word "unfit" since it echoed the title of the book by John O'Neil and Jerry Corsi, *Unfit for Command* (2004). The fact that Cheney was using the term showed once again the connection between the Republicans and the swift boat gang. The Bush-Cheney-Rove strategy was to associate Kerry with words like "flip-flop" and "unfit" to alienate voters from him. It was one of the most vicious character assassination campaigns in U.S. political history, and it remained to be seen whether it would work or not.

On the Republican Convention protest front, according to a *Washington Post* report by Michael Powell and Dale Russakoff:

> A criminal court judge ordered the release of hundreds of Bush protesters Thursday, ruling that police held them illegally without charges for more than 40 hours. As the protesters began trickling out of jail, they spoke of being held without access to lawyers, initially in a holding cell that had oil and grease spread across the floor. ...
>
> Several dozen of those detained said that they had not taken part in protests. Police apparently swept up the CEO of a puppet theater as he and a friend walked out of the subway to celebrate his birthday. Two middle-age women who had been shopping at the Gap were handcuffed, and a young woman was arrested as she returned from her job at a New York publishing house....
>
> Hours before President Bush made his speech to the Republican National Convention, Manhattan Criminal Court Judge John Cataldo held city officials in contempt of court for failing to release more than 500 detained demonstrators by 5 P.M. The judge said that the detentions violated state law, and he threatened to impose a fine of $1,000 per day for each person kept in custody longer than 24 hours without being arraigned.[65]

As the protesters were released, there were more anti-Bush activities during the last day of the convention. In the words of a *New York Times* reporter:

> A crowd stretching five blocks chanted and roared outside Madison Square Garden in an area designated for protests that was out of view of the delegates, while thousands of others gathered a few miles south in Union Square Park, holding candles, singing protest songs, and voicing rage against the Iraq war and the president.
>
> In the middle of Mr. Bush's speech, more than a thousand people marched out of the park down 15th Street and north on 8th Avenue toward the Garden, chanting "No more Bush!" and other slogans. The police reached an agreement with the group shortly before allowing the procession to proceed, escorted by scores of officers.[66]

New York Mayor Michael Bloomberg was not pleased with the protest activity and likened the demonstrators to "terrorists," an inflammatory term to be used in a city that had suffered so grievously from the September 11 attacks. Although Bloomberg and Police Commissioner Raymond Kelly praised police restraint and claimed that "every NYPD officer did a great job," the Michael Powell and Michelle Garcia story was different:

> interviews with state court officials, City Council representatives, prosecutors, protesters, and civil libertarians—and a review of videos of demonstrations— point to many problems with the police performance. Officers often sealed off streets with orange netting and used motor scooters and horses to sweep up hundreds of protesters at a time, including many who appear to have broken no laws. In two cases, police commanders appeared to allow marches to proceed, only to order many arrests minutes later. Most of those arrested were held for more than two days without being arraigned, which a state Supreme Court judge ruled was a violation of legal guidelines. Defense attorneys predict a flood of civil lawsuits once protesters have settled the misdemeanor charges lodged against them.[67]

Civil libertarians criticized the New York police and insisted that many of the arrests were unjustified. There were complaints that the Secret Service was active in infiltrating protest groups, targeting certain leaders and demonstrators, and carrying out arrests, leading to charges by the ACLU of discriminating against Bush administration critics.[68] When protesters used websites and text messaging to help assemble anti-Bush groups, the police monitored these sources and were often at demonstration sites before the protesters, using bikes, scooters, motorcycles, and fleets of cars to get around.[69] Donna Lieberman, executive director of the New York Civil Liberties Union, indicated that the "overriding problem during the convention was the indiscriminate arrests . . . of people who did nothing wrong. They were arrested because they were . . . participating in a lawful demonstration." At a City Council hearing in September on police action at the demonstrations, people testified that they were arrested simply for walking in an area where a demonstration was underway, others talked of how their children were held in "legal limbo" for over 50 hours without charges, and videos depicted how New York police arrested demonstrators who were following agreed-upon rules. The nation got a preview of a U.S. police state and it was not a pretty picture.

Perhaps never before had such widespread and continuous demonstrations been seen at a U.S. political convention. Still, there had been no major violence, and the protesters had their say and got some publicity, although the cable networks and television news gave perfunctory coverage considering the massive numbers and unprecedented impact of the protesters upon the life of a major metropolitan city. Independent media sites provided coverage and groups and individuals around the country were able to circulate the protest material, inspiring others to develop creative protest activities in the final two months of the campaign.

The first Gallup poll out after the Republican Convention was not as alarming for Democrats as the *Time* and *Newsweek* polls, which showed Bush pulling ahead of Kerry by double-digit figures. In a sharp analysis, Ruy Teixeira claimed the small bounce that the Gallup Poll showed indicated Bush had a poor response to his Republican Convention performance:

> Bush's acceptance speech, which the media fawned over so ostentatiously, was not rated any better by the public than was Kerry's—in fact, it received slightly worse ratings. Kerry's acceptance speech was rated excellent by 25 percent and good by 27 percent; Bush's was rated excellent by 22 percent and good by 27 percent.
>
> In terms of whether the Republican convention made voters more or less likely to vote for Bush—the real point of the convention after all—there were almost as many saying the convention made them less likely to vote for Bush (38 percent) as said it made them more likely (41 percent).
>
> This is actually quite a poor performance. The Democratic convention this year had a substantially better 44 percent more likely/30 percent less likely split. In fact, looking back to 1984, which is as far back as Gallup supplies data, no candidate has ever had a more likely to vote for/less likely to vote for split even close to as bad as Bush's this year.[70]

Yet Democrats were seriously worried over whether John Kerry could regain his momentum and retake his lead over George W. Bush. It was clear that Kerry had an extremely difficult month of August with an unprecedented barrage of mudslinging ads and a carefully orchestrated attack on him by the Republican Party at their convention. Meanwhile, word that Bill Clinton had chest pains, had been admitted to a hospital, and would undergo quadruple bypass surgery led both campaigns to take pause and present good wishes to Clinton (although when Bush first mentioned Clinton's name to the Republican audience, they started booing before Bush could tell them to "pray" for Clinton's recovery). There were widely publicized accounts of Bill Clinton's 90-minute phone conversation with Kerry before undergoing his surgery, urging Kerry to be more aggressive against Bush and stress domestic issues more, and several Clinton aides joined the Kerry campaign.

Promising a tougher campaign, the Kerry camp announced an $8 million advertising blitz that would air in swing states after Bush visited them in a postconvention tour. His communication director Stephanie Cutter announced: "We're going to be very aggressive throughout the fall in painting the real picture of George Bush....We are going to remind voters of what George Bush said in 2000 and what he did. It is a much more aggressive stance," presaging a down and dirty final two months leading up to the November election. Over the weekend of September 4–5, both parties campaigned in the swing states and the Kerry camp released video ads on "Bush's Broken Promises" in the television markets of each city in which Bush appeared. Kerry seemed newly energized and in an account of Kerry's holiday weekend campaigning, Tim Grieve writes:

> During the two-day tour through Ohio, Kerry criticized Bush for misleading the country about the reasons for war, for rushing into war, for going to war because he "wanted to," for ignoring the advice of military leaders about the war, for failing to build a bigger coalition for the war, for forcing out Army Gen. Eric Shinseki after he raised questions about troop levels that would be required for the war, for failing to provide body armor for the troops he sent to war, for misrepresenting the costs of the war, for spending $200 billion on the war when people are suffering back home, and for "opening firehouses in Baghdad" when budget cuts are forcing firehouses to close back in the United States.
>
> "I would not have done just one thing differently than the president on Iraq," Kerry said at a campaign stop Monday in Pennsylvania. "I would have done everything differently than the president on Iraq."[71]

In the final months of the campaign, Iraq would emerge as a central issue and new issues would come to the fore in the increasingly hard-fought battle for the White House.

Notes

1. For compiling the George W. Bush epigraphs upon which I draw in this and the next chapter, I am grateful to Jacob Weisberg's "Bushisms" available at http://slate.msn.com/id/76886.

2. By August 2004, a record $1 billion had been raised by both candidates, double the amount for the previous cycle. See Thomas B. Edsall, "Fundraising Doubles the Pace of 2000," *Washington Post*, August 21, 2004, p. A01.

3. For details, see Kellner (2001).

4. Many media pundits were cool toward Dean from the beginning, although the long-shot contender got good press when he became a surprise frontrunner. On the very negative coverage of the Dean campaign by the media pundits and corporate networks, see Peter Hart, "Target Dean: Reestablishing the Establishment," *Extra!* March–April, 2004, pp. 13–18.

5. Matt Drudge immediately posted an amped-up version of Dean's "scream" on his website and framed Dean as going out of control. It circulated rapidly through the mainstream and right-wing media and was played by the major television networks more than 700 times in the days immediately following the Iowa caucuses, according to a January 29, 2004, *Good Morning America* report. Belatedly, ABC and Diane Sawyer provided context for the image, pointing out that Dean was forced to raise his voice over the din of his supporters and that listening to how it sounded in the room "the so-called scream couldn't really be heard at all."

6. See the former intern's account, "The Education of Alexandra Polier," *New York Magazine*, June 7, 2004.

7. For a debunking of the story see Michael Janofsky, "McCain Fights Old Foe Who Now Fights Kerry," *New York Times*, February 14, 2004. The story was also debunked by many bloggers, who contrasted the faked photo with originals; see, for example, http://www.snopes.com/photos/politics/kerry2.asp. The Bush administration itself was using simulated video, circulating video news releases (VNRs) featuring Karen Ryan "reporting" on Medicare; it later came out that Ryan was a U.S. government employee simulating a television reporter. The U.S. General Accounting Office ruled that the VNRs violated bans on government-funded "publicity and propaganda." See Laura Miller, "The 2004 Falsies Awards," *AlterNet*, December 30, 2004.

8. See Howard Kurtz, "Media Notes," *Washington Post*, July 28, 2004.

9. See "Quick Takes," *Los Angeles Times*, July 23, 2004, p. E23.

10. For documentation of Bush family support for key businesses involved with financing German fascism, see Loftus and Aarons (1994), pp. 356–360, and Philips (2004).

11. See Richard Clarke, *Against All Enemies* (2004).

12. See Peter Hart in *Extra!* August 2004.

13. Bob Somerby, who documented Cheney's Big Lie, claimed that the mainstream media pundits allowed Cheney to get away with it; see "Cheney Conquers the Rubes! Cheney Lied in the Voters' Faces—Your "Press Corps" Knows Not to Tell You" at http://www.dailyhowler.com/dh080904.shtml.

14. Zachary Roth, "The Boys and Girls on the Bus," *Columbia Journalism Review*, August 27, 2004, at http://www.campaigndesk.org/archives/000858.asp.

15. See Charles Tiefer, "And You Thought His First Term Was a Nightmare," *Salon*, August 25, 2004.

16. Mark Miller provides a hilarious description of how Watergate burglar and right-wing macho man Gordon Liddy, in a gushy celebration of Bush with Chris Matthews, enthused over the hypermasculinity of Bush and the phallic bulge his flight suit produced (2004, pp. 153ff.). Other media pundits also celebrated the event that would later come back to haunt Bush's premature declaration of victory in Iraq.

17. Ann Gerhart, "Roadshow: The America-Can Tour Revs Up as Multitude and Platitude Noisily Collide," *Washington Post*, May 6, 2004.

18. David Tarrant, "What's That You Say? What's Riskier to a Democracy—Letting Dissent Ring Out or Stifling It?" *Dallas Morning News*, October 24, 2004.

19. Leo Brauchili, "Protecting the President from Dissent," *Daily Camera*, August 28, 2004, at http://www.dailycamera.com/bdc/opinion_columnists/article/0,1713,BDC_2490_3142885,00.html.

20. Hanna Rosin, "Bush Q&A's Are All on the Same Side: Pep Sessions Keep Protesters Out of Sight," *Washington Post*, August 19, 2004, p. C01.

21. See "Unwilling Participants: Iraqi Soccer Players Angered by Bush Campaign Ads" at http://sportsillustrated.cnn.com/2004/olympics/2004/writers/08/19/iraq/index.html.

22. Hanna Rosin, "Unfriendly Fire: A Vietnam Vet Saw His Honor under Attack, and Took the Fight to the Kerry Camp," *Washington Post*, October 3, 2004, p. D01. This article documents the role of another one of the organizers of the swift boat campaign, Roy Hoffman. The story indicates that Hoffman was angered at the negative presentation of himself in David Brinkley's book on Kerry's Vietnam activity and struck back hard at Kerry; there are indications in Rosin's account that Hoffman may have been involved in war crimes in Vietnam.

23. Kate Aernike and Jim Rutenberg, "See Friendly Fire: The Birth of an Anti-Kerry Ad," *New York Times*, August 20, 2004.

24. William B. Rood, "Swift Boat Skipper: Anti-Kerry Vets Not There That Day—I Was," *Chicago Tribune*, August 22, 2004.

25. Ben Wasserstein, "You Can Report, But We Will Decide," *Los Angeles Times*, August 24, 2004, p. B11. Wasserstein criticizes cable television commentators and interviewers for allowing the swift boat veterans to propagate their lies on television, even after newspaper articles in the *Washington Post, New York Times, Los Angeles Times*, and other major sources had clearly refuted them. Tracking conservative print and Internet sources and cable television news, Wasserstein describes how program after program on Fox and other cable networks reported the swift boat vets' false allegations against Kerry and failed to counter them, despite the fact that the major charges had been strongly rebutted.

26. Lois Romano and David Naramura, "Kerry Unveils Ad Countering Attacks over Vietnam," *Washington Post*, August 23, 2004, p. A02.

27. Ellen Terich, "The Election Is Not about Vietnam," August 23, 2004, at http://www.smirkingchimp.com/print.php?sid=17528.

28. For a detailed overview of the connections to the Bush administration of the swift boat veterans, see Robert Sam Anson, "Kerry-Loathing Swift Boaters Sinking Facts," *New York Observer*, August 26, 2004.

29. Julian Borger, "Bush Hails Kerry's 'Admirable' War Record: Democrats Say It Is Not Enough as He Fails to Denounce Adverts," *Guardian*, August 24, 2004. The revealing documentary by George Butler, *Going Upriver: The Long War of John Kerry* (2004), vividly demonstrated the danger of the swift boat voyages, Kerry's heroism, and his principled critique of the Vietnam War, a theme distorted by the second round of swift boat ads.

30. See Alessandra Stanley, "On Cable, a Fog of Words about Kerry's War Record," *New York Times*, August 24, 2004.

31. See "Profiles in Cowardice (Part 1)! Three Swift Vets Defended Kerry, but the 'Press' Didn't Dare Let You Know," at http://www.dailyhowler.com/dh083004.shtml.

32. Brian Knowlton, "More Americans Are Living in Poverty, Census Bureau Says," *International Herald Tribune,* August 26, 2004.

33. Jim VandeHei, "Kerry Attacks Bush on 'Debt Trap,'" *Washington Post,* August 28, 2004, p. A08.

34. See Michelle Goldberg, "New York Lockdown," *Salon,* August 11, 2004; and Don Hazen, "Taking It to the Streets," *AlterNet,* August 25, 2004. For a view from abroad, see Gary Younge, "The Protesters Are Coming. . . . It Seemed Like the Perfect Location for Next Week's Republican Convention. But With Widespread Anti-War Feeling, Hordes of Protesters Descending on the City and Alleged FBI Intimidation Fueling the Fear of Violence, New York Is Preparing a Noisy Reception for President Bush," *Guardian,* August 24, 2004.

35. Rick Perlstein, "Protesters Risk Playing into GOP Hands: Get Mad. Act Out. Re-Elect George Bush," *Village Voice,* August 24, 2004. Tom Hayden defended the protestors, suggesting "that loud protests at the convention will damage Bush's already-tarnished claim to be a uniter, not a divider. Voters are likely to reject a president who, having needlessly brought death and disorder to the U.S. standing in the world, would needlessly provoke disorders at home in a second term." Tom Hayden, "Scapegoating the Protests," *AlterNet,* August 27, 2004.

36. See Paul Street, "Insult to Injury," *Z-Net,* September 1, 2004, at http://www.zmag.org/content/showarticle.cfm?SectionID=87&ItemID=6145.

37. Greg Sargent, "Zero for Heroes," *New York Magazine,* October 27, 2003, at www.newyorkmetro.com/nymetro/ news/politics/columns/citypolitic/n_9384. For detailed criticism of Bush's deceptive environmental politics, see Dean (2004), pp. 160–170.

38. Randal C. Archibold, "100 Cyclists Are Arrested as Thousands Ride in Protest," *New York Times,* August 28, 2004. See also Michelle Garcia and Michael Powell, "Protesters Gird to Send a Message: Groups' Objectives Differ, But GOP Target Is the Same," *Washington Post,* August 29, 2004, p. A29.

39. Rachel Neumann, "Reproduce This March," *AlterNet,* August 29, 2004.

40. See the posting on *Z-net* and http://newstandardnews.net/alivewires/elections2004.

41. Michelle Goldberg, "We the People Say No to Bush: Hundreds of Thousands of Protesters Filled the New York Streets Sunday. Clash Songs Blasted, Anarchists Taunted 'Aida'-Goers, and Moms, Queers, and Wall Street Bankers Told the Bush Administration It Must Go," *Salon,* August 30, 2004.

42. Michelle Goldberg, "Poor and Proud: Cheri Honkala's Diverse Group of Anti-Bush Marchers Arrives in New York, Declaring That Homelessness Is a Societal, Not a Personal, Failing," *Salon,* August 31, 2004.

43. Adam Nagourney, "Giuliani Lauds Bush's Leadership on Terror as Convention Opens," *New York Times,* August 31, 2004.

44. Paul Brownfield, "No Joke, Twins' Act Needs Work," *Los Angeles Times*, September 1, 2004, p. A24.

45. A brilliant play by Tony Kushner, *Only We Who Guard the Mystery Shall Be Unhappy*, featuring Laura Bush reading to dead Iraqi children from Dostoyevsky, had been circulating, and Kushner added an act to the play for a moveon.org fundraiser in New York and a Progressive Majority fundraiser in Los Angeles; on the former, see Rebecca Traister, "Laura Bush Hits Broadway: A Fight Breaks Out at a New Tony Kushner Play as Celebrity, Political Activism, and the First Lady Collide at an Antiwar Benefit," *Salon*, August 3, 2004.

46. Michelle Goldberg, "Gotham Rebels: While Platitudes Ring Out at the GOP Garden Party, Protesters—From Iraq Veterans against the War to Activists in Bill O'Reilly Masks—Fan Out across the City. Police Crack Down with Handcuffs, Nets, and Mass Arrests," *Salon*, September 1, 2004.

47. Michelle Garcia and Mary Fitzgerald, "Police Stifle Protests across N.Y.: Officers Fend Off Demonstrators, Arresting about 1,000," *Washington Post*, September 1, 2004.

48. Christine Hauser, "Protestors Heed Calls for Widespread Civil Disobedience," *New York Times*, August 31, 2004.

49. Michelle Goldberg, "Gotham Rebels," op. cit.

50. Christine Hauser, "Thousands Form Symbolic Unemployment Line in N.Y.," *New York Times*, September 1, 2004.

51. "AIDS Activists Disrupt Convention Event," Associated Press, September 1, 2004.

52. The *Columbia Journalism Review* "Fact Check" pointed out that it was really the roasting Miller received on CNN, informing him that the weapons systems that he excoriated Kerry for voting against were also opposed by the former President Bush and Defense Secretary Dick Cheney, that exhibited real journalistic work and that Matthews did not confront Miller with any original criticisms, questions, or follow up his questions; see "Wednesday Night Report Card," September 2, 2004, at http://www.campaigndesk.org/archives/000884.asp. The "Fact Check" also pointed out that Matthews "had characterized Cheney's speech as 'a powerful indictment of John Kerry's record' containing 'no rhetoric'—a ludicrous statement, given that for long periods Cheney simply strung together campaign slogans."

53. Jonathan E. Kaplan, "Soros Blasts Hastert Over 'Drug Money' Allegation,'" *The Hill*, September 6, 2004.

54. Elizabeth Jensen, "Fox News Overtakes Broadcast Rivals," *Los Angeles Times*, September 2, 2004, p. A28. The last two nights of the Republican Convention, *Fox News* also had more viewers than the other cable networks and the big three networks.

55. There is also the possibility that Cheney is so caught up in his ideological world that he can no longer tell the difference between truth and falsehood, fantasy and reality, and thus believes many of the lies that he articulates; I discuss this possibility concerning Bush below.

56. In the home stretch of the campaign, Ron Suskind (2004) published a widely discussed article indicating that Bush and Co. scorned "reality-based" journalists who reported "facts," since the Bush administration was constantly changing the world and creating new realities. Such hubris and arrogance were dumbfounding and widely discussed, as I indicate in the introduction to this book.

57. See David Corn (2003, pp. 311ff.), who documents how the mainstream media, with the exception of Paul Krugman in his *New York Times* op-ed column, were afraid to use the word "lie" to apply to Bush, which in my view best sums up George W. Bush's epistemology and relationship to truth. Corn argues that Bush has systematically engaged in "strategic lying ... about the fundamental elements of his presidency" (p. 2), that "Bush has not been held responsible for his lies" (p. 309), and that lies have been a defining theme of Bush's presidency (p. 316). Chapters 5 and 6 of this book demonstrate that systematic lying was the strategic discourse of the Bush-Cheney campaign and a defining feature of Bushspeak.

58. For a systematic discussion of Bush administration use of Orwellian language in its "war on terror," see Kellner (2003a).

59. Marilyn Young, "How the Bush Administration Used 9–11 to Advance Its Agenda," September 6, 2004, at http://hnn.us/articles/6824.html. See Mark Fiore's brilliant animation ridiculing Bush's "Clear Skies" initiative at http://www.geocities.com/CapeCanaveral/7639/atmosphere/clnskies.htm.

60. See Jonathan Chait, "Up and Away: Bush's Schemes to Fleece the Poor," *New Republic,* September 3, 2004, at www.tnr.com; and Robert Reich, "A Society of Owers," September 7, 2004, at www.TomPaine.com.

61. Robert Parry, "Bush Trims a Tale," at http://www.consortiumnews.com/2004/092304.html:

62. Tom Shales, "George Bush, No Fastball from the Mound," *Washington Post,* September 3, 2004.

63. Dan Froomkin, "Where's the Agenda?" *Washington Post,* September 3, 2004.

64. Lois Romano and Howard Kurtz, "Kerry Takes Off Gloves," *Washington Post,* September 3, 2004, p. A26.

65. Michael Powell and Dale Russakoff, "Judge Orders Demonstrators Freed: Jurist Holds City in Contempt of Court, Saying Dozens of People Were Held Without Charges," *Washington Post,* September 3, 2004, p. A21.

66. Randal C. Archibold, "Protesters Try to Get in Last Word before Curtain Falls," *New York Times,* September 3, 2004.

67. Michael Powell and Michelle Garcia, "Arrests at GOP Convention Are Criticized: Many in N.Y. Released without Facing Charges," *Washington Post,* September 20, 2004, p. A01.

68. Rachel Newmann, "First They Came for the Protesters," *AlterNet,* September 3, 2004.

69. David Zucchino, "Protests Meet a Nimble NYPD," *Los Angeles Times,* September 4, 2004, p. A21.

70. Ruy Teixeira, "Gallup Poll Gives Bush Only a 2 Point Bounce," September 7, 2004, at http://www.emergingdemocraticmajorityweblog.com/donkeyrising/archives/000641.php.

71. As this article indicates, the corporate media continued to buy into the Bush-Cheney mantra that Kerry was a "flip-flopper." The Bush-Cheney campaign sought to manage public perception by sticking negative labels on Kerry, and the media generally obliged. Hence, what Bush or Cheney said about Kerry did not have to be true if it fit into a dominant frame, such as the portrayal of Kerry as a flip-flopper. In an article by John F. Harris, "Despite Bush Flip-Flops, Kerry Gets Label," convincing examples were presented that Bush flip-flopped on more major issues than Kerry, although the label stuck to the latter (*Washington Post,* September 23, 2004, p. A01). According to Harris: "The flip-flopper, Democrats say, is President Bush. Over the past four years, he abandoned positions on issues such as how to regulate air pollution or whether states should be allowed to deal with the same-sex marriage issue. He changed his mind about the merits of creating the Homeland Security Department, and made a major exception to his stance on free trade by agreeing to tariffs on steel. After resisting, the president yielded to pressure in supporting an independent commission to study policy failures preceding the September 11, 2001, attacks. Bush did the same with questions about whether he would allow his national security adviser to testify, or whether he would answer commissioners' questions for only an hour, or for as long they needed."

But Harris points out: "Once such a popular perception becomes fixed, public opinion experts and strategists say, virtually every episode in the campaign is viewed through that prism, while facts that do not fit with existing assumptions—such as Bush's history of policy shifts—do not have much impact in the political debate." Evidently, the Kerry people eventually gave up on trying to affix the "flip-flop" label to Bush and were content simply to label him a "flop."

Chapter 6

Decision 2004: The War for the White House

> For nothing can seem foul to those that win.
> —*Shakespeare*, Henry IV, Part I

So FAR THE CAMPAIGN HAD BEEN AS DOWN AND DIRTY AS EXPECTED. The swift boat veterans' campaign against Kerry had probably been the sleaziest presidential election campaign ploy in recent history. As we saw in the last chapter, there were significant refutations of the specific claims made against Kerry's Vietnam record, and by the end of August the swift boat veterans were thoroughly discredited. Yet they had had months to circulate their scurrilous charges and despite some serious investigative reporting, on the whole the corporate media posed the controversy in the mold of two opposing partisan sides, rather than denouncing the campaign as unconscionable outright lies by the Republican attack apparatus.

The corporate media had not taken on the systematic Republican lying about Kerry's record throughout the month of August, culminating in their failure to criticize the Republican Convention, which exhibited unparalleled vicious attacks on Kerry. Never before in modern history had there been such an utterly untruthful and demagogic presidential campaign as the Bush team was running against Kerry, but, for the most part, the mainstream corporate media presented the events as "business as usual" in a vigorously fought campaign in a divided country. When harsh charges were leveled against George W. Bush, by contrast, the corporate media would air the charges in the now standard "he said, he said" format, as if the substantial revelations of George W. Bush's shady past and failed record as president were mere partisan mudslinging. Then, the media turned on one of their own when questions were raised concerning a CBS program that attempted for the first time to tell the intriguing story of Bush's missing years.

Bush's Lost Years

I was a prisoner too, but for bad reasons.
—*George W. Bush, to Argentine President Nestor Kirchner, on being
told that all but one of the Argentine delegates to a summit meeting
were imprisoned during the military dictatorship, Monterrey, Mexico.*
January 13, 2004

The debate over Kerry's Vietnam years brought back focus on Bush's inability to find any evidence that he served his last year of National Guard service in 1972–1973. No one made credible claims to have seen Bush on duty either in Alabama or Texas during this period, leading Dave Moniz and Jim Drinkard of *USA Today* to query:

At a time when Democratic presidential candidate John Kerry has come under
fire from a group of retired naval officers who say he lied about his combat record
in Vietnam, questions about President Bush's 1968–73 stint in the Texas Air National Guard remain unresolved:
　Why did Bush, described by some of his fellow officers as a talented and enthusiastic pilot, stop flying fighter jets in the spring of 1972 and fail to take an
annual physical exam required of all pilots?
　What explains the apparent gap in the president's Guard service in 1972–73,
a period when commanders in Texas and Alabama say they never saw him report for duty and records show no pay to Bush when he was supposed to be on
duty in Alabama?
　Did Bush receive preferential treatment in getting into the Guard and secur-
ing a coveted pilot slot despite poor qualifying scores and arrests, but no convic-
tions, for stealing a Christmas wreath and rowdiness at a football game during
his college years?[1]

David Corn documented how for years Bush repeatedly claimed he was in the Air Force when in fact he was in the Texas Air National Guard, and raised the question of whether Air Force Veterans for Truth would emerge to go after Bush concerning his alleged service.[2] Ben Barnes, former lieutenant governor of Texas, said that he was ashamed of having been involved in getting George W. Bush and other rich sons of the Texas elite deferment from military service.[3] Bush's controversial military service record would soon emerge as a major is-sue in the election, although the CBS segment that purported to document the extent to which Bush shirked his military obligations would itself be one of the most controversial stories in Election 2004.

　An Associated Press story on Labor Day of 2004 signaled new evidence con-cerning Bush's lost year in the Texas Air National Guard that suggested he was indeed absent without leave and had not completed his military obligations. AP had put in requests under the Freedom of Information Act for five sets of documents that should have been filed during Bush's last year of National Guard service, none of which had surfaced, leading to suspicion that his record may have been purged and cleaned up as many had charged. According to Matt Kelley's report: "Documents that should have been written to explain gaps in President Bush's Texas Air National Guard service are missing from the military records released about his service in 1972 and 1973, according to regulations and outside experts." The five missing files included:

A report from the Texas Air National Guard to Bush's local draft board certifying that Bush remained in good standing. The government has released copies of those DD Form 44 documents for Bush for 1971 and earlier years but not for 1972 or 1973. Records from Bush's draft board in Houston do not show his draft status changed after he joined the guard in 1968. The AP obtained the draft board records Aug. 27 under the Freedom of Information Act.

Records of a required investigation into why Bush lost flight status. When Bush skipped his 1972 physical, regulations required his Texas commanders to "direct an investigation as to why the individual failed to accomplish the medical examination," according to the Air Force manual at the time. An investigative report was supposed to be forwarded "with the command recommendation" to Air Force officials "for final determination."

Bush's spokesmen have said he skipped the exam because he knew he would be doing desk duty in Alabama. But Bush was required to take the physical by the end of July 1972, more than a month before he won final approval to train in Alabama.

A written acknowledgment from Bush that he had received the orders grounding him. His Texas commanders were ordered to have Bush sign such a document; but none has been released.

Reports of formal counseling sessions Bush was required to have after missing more than three training sessions. Bush missed at least five months' worth of National Guard training in 1972. No documents have surfaced indicating Bush was counseled or had written authorization to skip that training or make it up later. Commanders did have broad discretion to allow guardsmen to make up for missed training sessions, said Weaver and Lawrence Korb, Pentagon personnel chief during the Reagan administration from 1981 to 1985.

"If you missed it, you could make it up," said Korb, who now works for the Center for American Progress, which supports Kerry.

A signed statement from Bush acknowledging he could be called to active duty if he did not promptly transfer to another guard unit after leaving Texas. The statement was required as part of a Vietnam-era crackdown on no-show guardsmen. Bush was approved in September 1972 to train with the Alabama unit, more than four months after he left Texas.[4]

An interview with Ben Barnes, who had arranged for Bush's National Guard service, was planned for CBS' *60 Minutes* and Bush's missing year would receive some of the scrutiny that Kerry's Vietnam service had received. So far it had been mostly the alternative press that had investigated Bush's military "service." An article in *Salon*, for instance, provided new documentation of Bush's missing year. Mary Jacoby tracked down Bush family friend Linda Allison, who, contradicting Bush campaign positions over the years, told Jacoby how her husband had received a plea from George H. W. Bush to put young George to work in the campaign of family friend Red Blount because Bush Junior was becoming an embarrassment and political liability to the family in Texas. This story "contradicts the Bush campaign's assertion that George W. Bush transferred from the Texas Air National Guard to the Alabama National Guard in 1972 because he received an irresistible offer to gain high-level experience on the campaign of Bush family friend Winton 'Red' Blount." Moreover, when asked whether anyone saw him do any National Guard service in Alabama, she answered: 'Good lord, no.'"[5]

Allison said that Bush did little work on the campaign and recollected Bush Junior in his late 20s just after Blount lost his U.S. Senate bid:

Leaving the election-night "celebration," Allison remembers encountering George W. Bush in the parking lot, urinating on a car, and hearing later about how he'd yelled obscenities at police officers that night. Bush left a house he'd rented in Montgomery trashed—the furniture broken, walls damaged, and a chandelier destroyed, the *Birmingham News* reported in February. "He was just a rich kid who had no respect for other people's possessions," Mary Smith, a member of the family who rented the house, told the newspaper, adding that a bill sent to Bush for repairs was never paid. And a month later, in December, during a visit to his parents' home in Washington, Bush drunkenly challenged his father to go "mano-a-mano," as has often been reported. (ibid.)

Allison's story was consistent with an account on National Public Radio (NPR) by Murph Archibald, Blount's nephew. Archibald tells how young Bush had worked on the campaign, but was replaced due to poor performance because of excessive drinking. Speaking to NPR's *All Things Considered* in March 2004, Archibald commented, "in a campaign full of dedicated workers, Mr. Bush was not one of them. . . . Ordinarily, George would come in around noon; he would ordinarily leave around 5:30 or 6:00 in the evening." Evidently, Bush would brag of his drinking exploits of the previous night, leading Archibald to conclude: "I thought it was really unusual that someone in their mid-20s would initiate conversations, particularly in the context of something as serious as a

U.S. senatorial campaign, by talking about their drinking the night before. I thought it unusual and, frankly, inappropriate." Moreover, Archibald revealed that Bush bragged that his family connections protected him from the law: "He told us [campaign staffers] whenever he was stopped [for erratic driving while at Yale], as soon as the law enforcement found out that he was the grandson of Prescott Bush, they would let him go. And he would always laugh about that" (ibid.).

On September 8, 2004, two significant articles chastised Bush for his failures to meet his National Guard obligation. *New York Times* columnist Nicholas Kristof provocatively titled his article "Missing in Action." Kristof talked to former Alabama National Guardsmen Robert Mintz, who recounted how he had been looking forward to getting to know George W. Bush and had been looking out for him the entire year, but he never showed up. Mintz recalled

> he had heard that Mr. Bush—described as a young Texas pilot with political influence—had transferred to the base. He heard that Mr. Bush was also a bachelor, so he was looking forward to partying together. He's confident that he'd remember if Mr. Bush had shown up.
>
> "I'm sure I would have seen him," Mr. Mintz said yesterday. "It's a small unit, and you couldn't go in or out without being seen. It was too close a space." There were only 25 to 30 pilots there, and Mr. Bush—a U.N. ambassador's son who had dated Tricia Nixon—would have been particularly memorable.

Kristof cited another "particularly credible witness," Leonard Walls, "a retired Air Force colonel who was then a full-time pilot instructor at the base. 'I was there pretty much every day,' he said, adding: 'I never saw him, and I was there continually from July 1972 to July 1974.' Mr. Walls, who describes himself as nonpolitical, added, 'If he had been there more than once, I would have seen him.'" Kristof concludes that the "sheer volume of missing documents, and missing recollections, strongly suggests to me that Mr. Bush blew off his Guard obligations." Kristof also cited Gerald Lechliter, a retired Army colonel who posted a 32-page analysis on the Internet, which Kristof believes constituted "the most meticulous examination I've seen of Mr. Bush's records." Lechliter concluded: "The record clearly and convincingly proves he did not fulfill the obligations he incurred when he enlisted in the Air National Guard." Further, Lechliter notes "that Mr. Bush received unauthorized or fraudulent payments that breached National Guard rules, according to the documents that the White House itself released."[6]

Salon's Eric Boehlert complained that ABC and CNN, as well as Fox, were using a completely discredited Republican, Lieutenant Colonel John "Bill"

Calhoun to testify that he'd seen Bush "five or six times" with the 187 Tactical Reconnaisance Group in Montgomery, Alabama, where he claimed the two men occasionally ate lunch together. But the initial dates given by Calhoun for his Bush-sighting preceded Bush's supposed request for a change of Guard venue and his arrival in Alabama. In Boehlert's summary:

> When Calhoun first emerged in February, he announced he'd seen Bush "eight or 10 times" on the base performing drills between May and October of 1972. But within 24 hours of his statement, the White House released Bush's military pay records—which aides touted as definitive proof of Bush's service—definitively proving that Bush was not credited for any training in Alabama for the months of May, June, July, August, and September 1972, and that Bush showed up only in late October. So how could Calhoun have seen Bush several times in one summer if Bush's own records indicate he was never there?
>
> Calhoun's story is even less believable in light of the fact that Bush in 1972 originally tried to transfer from his Texas Air National Guard unit in Houston to a National Guard unit at Maxwell Air Force Base in Alabama. That request was eventually denied, so Bush ended up at the Montgomery unit where Calhoun served. But again, according to Bush's records, he didn't even *apply* for the transfer to Montgomery until September and didn't show up until late October. How did Calhoun see Bush performing drills throughout the summer of 1972 when Bush didn't even request an assignment there until the fall?[7]

Although it was not surprising that Bush handlers would haul out the only person to claim he saw Bush do Alabama Guard service, it is incredible, Boehlert argues, that ABC and CNN would bring out a completely discredited witness. No doubt the Bush campaign strategy was to reduce the argument about Bush's Guard service to a "he said/he said" debate, where the Bush campaign could discuss critiques of his character and service as "partisan."

Indeed, the White House had released some documents in February 2004 that showed Bush had received payment for at least some of the missing months of guard duty, and had received dental treatment under the medical plan. The Bush administration claimed that these records constituted the full dossier of Bush's military service and proved that he had fulfilled his duty. Closer examination showed that the documents did not answer the questions raised by the AP concerning where and when Bush served, how he met his obligations, and why he stopped flying and refused to take a physical exam. In response to the AP request for some specific documents concerning Bush's service, the Pentagon released on September 7, 2004, "what it called newly found records on Tuesday night showing that Mr. Bush flew 336 hours in a fighter jet and ranked in the middle of his flight training class." Yet the AP indicated that the documents in fact raised more questions concerning why certain parts of Bush's records were suddenly discovered and released and why key documents remained missing.

One researcher published analysis on his website that suggested the released Pentagon documents themselves indicted Bush's military service and refuted White House positions. In Eric Boehlert's words, "researcher Paul Lukasiak ... has spent time closely examining the paperwork, and more important, analyzing U.S. Statutory Law, Department of Defense regulations, and Air Force policies and procedures of the 1960s and 1970s. As a result, Lukasiak arrived at the overwhelming conclusion that not only did Bush walk away from his final two years of military obligation, coming dangerously close to desertion, but that he attempted to cover up his absenteeism through swindle and fraud." Boehlert summarizes:

> Bush's request to transfer to an Alabama Guard unit in 1972, in order to work on the Senate campaign of a family friend, Lukasiak found, was not designed to be temporary, but rather was Bush's attempt to sever ties completely with the Texas Air National Guard and find a new, permanent unit in Alabama for which he was ineligible, where he wouldn't have to do any training during his final two years. His superiors in Texas essentially covered for Bush's getaway. However, the Air Reserve Personnel Center (ARPC) in Denver, Colo., which had final say, uncovered the attempted scam, put an end to it, and admonished Bush's superiors for endorsing Bush's bogus request. ... Soon afterward, large gaps began appearing in Bush's paper trail. Lukasiak concludes that only last-minute intervention, likely from Bush's local Houston draft board, saved him from active duty, as well as finally securing his honorable discharge, removing his "Inactive Status." Ironically, that means strings were pulled to get Bush out of the Guard in 1973, just as they were pulled to get him enrolled in 1968 (ibid.).

A *Boston Globe* "Spotlight" report opened: "In February, when the White House made public hundreds of pages of President Bush's military records, White House officials repeatedly insisted that the records prove that Bush fulfilled his military commitment in the Texas Air National Guard during the Vietnam War." But "Bush fell well short of meeting his military obligation. ... Twice during his Guard service—first when he joined in May 1968, and again before he transferred out of his unit in mid-1973 to attend Harvard Business School—Bush signed documents pledging to meet training commitments or face a punitive call-up to active duty."[8]

The documents later signed when Bush went to Harvard Business School constitute another example of the privileged son whom Jeffrey St. Clair calls the "High Plains Grifter."[9] Although Bush had signed papers upon entering Harvard committing himself to find a local Guard unit and sign up for drilling and "mobilization augmentation," he evidently failed to do so, leading Colonel Lechliter to conclude: "He broke his contract with the U.S. government—without any adverse consequences."

A *U.S. News and World Report* study indicated that the documents released by the White House regarding Bush's Guard service suggest that he was indeed absent without leave for a year and clearly did not meet his required obligations.

Last February, White House spokesman Scott McClellan held aloft sections of President Bush's military record, declaring to the waiting press that the files "clearly document the president fulfilling his duties in the National Guard." Case closed, he said.

But last week the controversy reared up once again, as several news outlets, including *U.S. News,* disclosed new information casting doubt on White House claims.

A review of the regulations governing Bush's Guard service during the Vietnam War shows that the White House used an inappropriate—and less stringent—Air Force standard in determining that he had fulfilled his duty. Because Bush signed a six-year "military service obligation," he was required to attend at least 44 inactive-duty training drills each fiscal year beginning July 1. But Bush's own records show that he fell short of that requirement, attending only 36 drills in the 1972–73 period, and only 12 in the 1973–74 period. The White House has said that Bush's service should be calculated using 12-month periods beginning on his induction date in May 1968. Using this time frame, however, Bush still fails the Air Force obligation standard.

Moreover, White House officials say, Bush should be judged on whether he attended enough drills to count toward retirement. They say he accumulated sufficient points under this grading system. Yet, even using their method, which some military experts say is incorrect, *U.S. News*'s analysis shows that Bush once again fell short. His military records reveal that he failed to attend enough active-duty training and weekend drills to gain the 50 points necessary to count his final year toward retirement.

The *U.S. News* analysis also showed that during the final two years of his obligation, Bush did not comply with Air Force regulations that impose a time limit on making up missed drills. What's more, he apparently never made up five months of drills he missed in 1972, contrary to assertions by the administration. White House officials did not respond to the analysis last week but emphasized that Bush had "served honorably."

Some experts say they remain mystified as to how Bush obtained an honorable discharge. Lawrence Korb, a former top Defense Department official in the Reagan administration, says the military records clearly show that Bush "had not fulfilled his obligation" and "should have been called to active duty."[10]

There had been recurrent reports, always denied by the White House, that Lieutenant Colonel Bill Burkett of the Texas Air National Guard had seen Bush aides going through military files in 1997 to remove any embarrassing documents, which they threw away. Burkett had told *Salon* in February 2004 that: "in the spring of 1997, on the eve of Bush's reelection campaign for governor, and with his spokeswoman Karen Hughes planning to write Bush's biography, a call was placed to Maj. Gen. Daniel James, head of the Texas National Guard. According to the conversation Burkett says he overheard, Bush's chief of staff, Joe Allbaugh, asked James to assemble Bush's military files, so his aides, including Dan Bartlett, could go over them, and to make sure there was nothing there that would embarrass the governor. Burkett says days later he also saw pages from Bush's military file in a garbage can." He concluded: "Activities occurred in order to, in my opinion, inappropriately build a false image of the governor's military service."[11]

There were also stories that Bush was engaged in heavy alcohol and drug abuse in 1972–1973, that he had been arrested, and that his father cut a deal with a Texas judge to allow Bush to engage in community service—in which he engaged with a Houston group called Operation PULL in 1973. On February 13, 2004, when Helen Thomas tried repeatedly at a White House press conference to get Bush spokesman Scott McClellan to answer the question of whether or not Bush had been sentenced to do community service work, McClellan refused to comment.[12]

Texans for Truth, a group funded by a veteran Democratic operative, unveiled a series of ads attacking Bush's failure to fulfill his Guard service and offering $50,000 to anyone who could prove that Bush fulfilled his required duties in the Alabama Air National Guard in 1972. Robert Mintz stated in the ad that he and his friends never saw Bush in Alabama. Mintz further declared: "I heard George W. Bush get up there and say, 'I served in the 187th Air National Guard in Montgomery, Alabama.' I said, 'Really? That was my unit. And I don't remember seeing you there.' So I called my friends and said, 'Did you know that George W. Bush served in our unit?' and everyone said, 'No I never saw him there. It would be impossible to be unseen in a unit of that size.'" The Democratic National Committee also launched Operation Fortunate Son, and released a video criticizing Bush's actions during Vietnam.

The CBS Memo Wars

> Washington is a town where there's all kinds of allegations. You've heard much of the allegations. And if people have got solid information, please come forward with it. And that would be people inside the information who are the so-called anonymous sources, or people outside the information—outside the administration.
>
> —*George W. Bush, Chicago, September 30, 2003*

It was just a matter of time until Bush's shady past and record of lying about it would break into public view. Just as the attacks on Kerry's military record and character had been fast and furious in August, in September, the revelations of the moral failures, lies, and cover-ups concerning Bush's military service and lost years became a major focus of the media and blogosphere. On September 8, *60 Minutes* aired its long-anticipated interview with former Texas Lieutenant Governor Ben Barnes on how he'd pulled strings to get Bush into the Texas National Air Guard and felt guilty about it. Although the story had been circulating for some time, the *60 Minutes* segment put the issue on the map. As Dan Rather reported:

> A few months before Mr. Bush would become eligible for the draft, Barnes says he had a meeting with the late oilman Sid Adger, a friend to both Barnes and then-Congressman George Bush.
>
> "It's been a long time ago, but he said basically would I help young George Bush get in the Air National Guard," says Barnes, who then contacted his longtime friend Gen. James Rose, the head of Texas' Air National Guard.
>
> "I was a young, ambitious politician doing what I thought was acceptable," says Barnes. "It was important to make friends. And I recommended a lot of people for the National Guard during the Vietnam era—as speaker of the house and as lt. governor."
>
> George W. Bush was among those he recommended for the National Guard. Was this a case of preferential treatment?
>
> "I would describe it as preferential treatment. There were hundreds of names on the list of people wanting to get into the Air National Guard or the Army National Guard," says Barnes. "I think that would have been a preference to anybody that didn't want to go to Vietnam or didn't want to leave. We had a lot of young men that left and went to Canada in the '60s and fled this country. But those that could get in the Reserves, or those that could get in the National Guard—chances are they would not have to go to Vietnam."[13]

In addition, *CBS News* and *60 Minutes* exposed documents that indicated Bush's squadron commander Lieutenant Colonel Jerry B. Killian refused to write a positive report about Bush and in fact grounded him. Another document, dated May 1972, referred to a conversation between Killian and Bush where they "discussed options of how Bush can get out of coming to drill from now through November," because young Bush "may not have time." The memo indicated that there was pressure on Killian to grant Bush special privileges because "I think he's also talking to someone upstairs." Most damaging to Bush's reputation, Killian allegedly wrote in a report dated August 1, 1972, that he had ordered Bush "suspended from flight status" because he had failed to perform to standards of the Air Force and Texas Air National Guard as well as failed to take an annual physical examination "as ordered." Another memo suggested that Killian's superiors were forcing him to give Bush a favorable review, but that he was refusing, complaining "I'm having trouble running interference and doing my job." Major newspapers carried this story on their front pages, and finally there seemed to be a focus on how certain parts of George W. Bush's life history had been erased. Although other books had documented Bush Junior's scandalous past, which contradicted statements he and his handlers had made over the years, these embarrassing stories had been kept out of the mainstream media.[14]

Within hours of the initial CBS reports, bloggers questioned the authenticity of the memos, claiming that they were computer-generated, and that they contained superscripts after the numbers not available to typewriters of the era, that the font was a recent computer font also not available on typewriters at the time, that the spacing was proportional in a way characteristic of computers and not typewriters, and that the signature was forged. Television reports on both ABC and NBC raised the question of whether the documents were forgeries, and Fred Barnes on Fox called them "fake." Right-wingers like Sean Hannity on Fox claimed that "the hoax" was evidence of how far CBS and the "liberal media" would go to destroy the president. There was thus tremendous anticipation concerning how Dan Rather and CBS would respond to the fierce criticism. On *CBS News,* after a story about the latest hurricane in the Caribbean, Rather took on the critics and defended his show:

> There were attacks today on the CBS News *60 Minutes* report this week raising new questions about President Bush's Vietnam-era time in the Texas Air National Guard. ... Today, on the Internet and elsewhere, some people—including many who are partisan political operatives—concentrated not on the key questions the overall story raised but on the documents that were part of the support of the story. They alleged the documents are fake.

Rather continued that the typeface of the memos was compatible with typewriters of the period, that Killian's signature was judged authentic, and that

CBS News stood by its story: "This report was not based solely on recovered documents, but rather on a preponderance of evidence, including documents that were provided by unimpeachable sources, interviews with former Texas National Guard officials, and individuals who worked closely back in the early 1970s with Killian and were well acquainted with his procedures, his character, and his thinking," his statement on the CBS website read. "In addition, the documents are backed up not only by independent handwriting and forensic document experts but by sources familiar with their content," Rather said.[15]

Senator Tom Harkin (D-Iowa) claimed that Bush had been constantly lying to the American people and in a news conference with Richard Klass, a retired U.S. Air Force colonel, repeatedly questioned Bush's character and honesty. Democratic National Committee Chair Terry McAuliffe admitted that he was not certain the CBS documents were authentic, noting that perhaps Karl Rove was responsible.[16] On the other hand, in a fierce race, a Democratic operative could have forged the documents as well. The debate over the authenticity of the memos, however, deflected attention from their content, which was highly damning to Bush.

On CBS, Dan Rather continued defending the network's Bush National Guard documents, reaffirmed their authenticity, and cited some documents received by *USA Today* that seemed to confirm the CBS story. The next day, however, the *Washington Post* published a story questioning the authenticity of the documents, arguing again that they appeared to be computer-generated and citing document expert Laura Bush, who "became the first person from the White House to say the documents are likely forgeries. 'You know they are probably altered,' she told Radio Iowa in Des Moines yesterday. 'And they probably are forgeries, and I think that's terrible, really.'"[17]

In a media war against CBS, rival network ABC and its Disney Corporation–affiliated *Washington Post* bolstered the case that the CBS memos were fake by interviewing two "experts" who said that they had been interviewed by CBS to authenticate the memos and that they had refused to do so because CBS had not addressed their concerns.[18] But the *New York Times* interviewed the 86-year-old Texan woman, Marian Carr Knox, who was the typist for Lieutenant Colonel Killian.[19] Knox said that the memos accurately reflect the thoughts of Killian, but "I doubt it's anything that I wrote because there are terms in there that are not used by Guards, the format wasn't the way we did it. It looks like someone may have read the originals and put that together." Knox said that Killian often discussed Bush's conduct and that "it was a problem Killian was concerned about....I think he was writing the memos so there would be some record that he was aware of what was going on and what he had done."

But, she said, words like "billets," which appear in the memorandums, were not standard Guard terms.

For the right wing, the allegedly faked memos were evidence that Dan Rather and the liberal media were attempting to destroy the president, and its attacks on CBS intensified ferociously. About 40 House Republicans demanded that CBS retract its report. Stories circulated feverishly in the blogosphere that CBS News was going to make a retraction and admit that the memos were fake, but instead on the *CBS News* Rather reported that he was going to interview Killian's 86-year-old ex-secretary, who would maintain that the substance of the memos was correct even if she did not type them. Ms. Knox recounted in detail in a *60 Minutes* interview how Bush had received preferential treatment, how other reservists resented it, and how Killian was angry that Bush was going off to a political campaign in Alabama and was not fulfilling his service in the Texas Air National Guard. She told Rather that her boss wrote a "cover-your-back file" to keep a record of his dealings with the politically connected Bush.

Rather announced that CBS was further investigating the authenticity of the memos and would continue reporting on the story. Many Kerry supporters, however, believed that the story was harming him because it was sucking up major television airtime; CNN opened its news with a five-minute report on the CBS memo controversy and then had only seconds on Iraq and on Kerry's campaign of the day.[20] The CBS memo story continued to receive a lot of play, and a *Los Angeles Times* story detailed how a *60 Minutes* team had spent months on the story.[21] The story and an accompanying one, "GOP Activist Made Allegations on CBS Memos," indicated how on the morning of the September 8 broadcast, CBS had sent the memos to the White House, CBS reporter John Roberts interviewed Bush campaign spokesman Dan Bartlett, and then when the Bush White House did not attack the authenticity of the memos, CBS decided to run with them.

But only an hour after the broadcast, an extremely sophisticated and well-written critique circulated on a right-wing Internet site by a blogger called "Buckwheat," who made the now-famous accusations concerning the authenticity of the documents. Within hours, the right-wing blogosphere circulated them, they were linked by Matt Drudge, and the next day the discussion broke out in the mainstream media. The *Los Angeles Times* article tracked down the now infamous blogger "Buckwheat," who had bragged that "Freepers [i.e., contributors to the right-wing extremist Free Republic website] collectively possess more analytical horsepower than the entire news division at CBS." It appears that the Bush campaign may have provided some of the analytical power, as well as their copies of the documents, as it turned out that "Buckwheat" was Harry W. MacDougald, an Atlanta attorney and conservative Republican activist, who among other causes, had helped draft the petition urging the Arkansas Supreme Court to disbar President Clinton during the Monica Lewinsky scandal. Thus it was something of a myth that the conservative blogosphere had detected the potential forging of the CBS memos, as the White House had prior access to them and the first blog critique appeared only hours after the initial CBS broadcast.

There were several articles that suggested Bill Burkett, the former Texas National Guardsman who had earlier sworn he had witnessed the cleansing of Bush's records in Guard offices by Bush's operatives, was the source of the memos. On Sunday, September 19, Dan Rather interviewed him; the next day CBS admitted that it no longer had confidence that the memos were authentic and apologized for airing them. Hence, it appears that Dan Rather and CBS were conned on the Killian memos, raising the question of who was behind the hoax. Was it, as some suggested, Karl Rove and the Republicans who wanted to sting CBS and discredit media investigation of Bush's failure to fulfill his Guard service? Did the Republicans provide the forged memos to Bill Burnett who then provided them to CBS, or did Burnett and some Texas friends concoct the memos, convinced that Bush had indeed failed to meet his service requirements? These questions have not been answered as of late 2004, nor have there been studies of what effect, if any, the CBS memos war had on the election.

Discussion of the facts of Bush's Guard years and whether he actually fulfilled his obligations were largely erased, however, from the media agenda when CBS and Dan Rather admitted that they could no longer authenticate the memos that suggested Bush had not fulfilled his duties. The CBS memo wars had become a terrible distraction for the Kerry campaign and the media, and seemed to have shut down the story of Bush's Guard service as well as investigative reporting of his past. Ironically, CBS broadcast at the last minute the story of the Killian memos instead of an investigation of how the Bush administration had doctored evidence concerning the alleged "weapons of mass destruction" that were used as the justification for invading Iraq. Iraq and other issues, however, would soon be fiercely debated again as the intense discussion of the CBS report petered out.

The Debates

They've seen me make decisions, they've seen me under trying times, they've seen me weep, they've seen me laugh, they've seen me hug. And they know who I am, and I believe they're comfortable with the fact that they know I'm not going to shift principles or shift positions based upon polls and focus groups.

—*George W. Bush*, USA Today, *August 27, 2004*

In a U.S. presidential election, the debates are often the crucial determinant of the outcome. Although both parties work to forge messages during the primaries, present their candidate and program in a convention spectacle, deluge the airwaves with ads, organize daily media events, and mobilize support groups who telephone, write, e-mail, text-message, and knock on doors to try to win voters, the debates have focused national attention more than any other element in recent U.S. presidential elections.

The long-awaited moment of the 2004 presidential debates finally came on October 1 in Coral Gables, Florida. Jim Lehrer moderated the debate, sketching some of the ground rules, and introducing the candidates. Lehrer indicated: "The umbrella topic is foreign policy and homeland security, but the specific subjects were chosen by me, the questions were composed by me, the candidates have not been told what they are, nor has anyone else. For each question there can only be a two-minute response, a 90-second rebuttal and, at my discretion, a discussion extension of one minute." Bush strode out first, walking so fast that he met Kerry beyond the midpoint of the stage, in front of Mr. Kerry's lectern. Kerry leaned over to chitchat with Bush, with his 6' 4" frame overwhelming the 5' 10" Bush. Kerry managed to grab Bush's hand and hold on and continue bantering, as a flustered smaller president tried to break away and return to his lectern.

John Kerry proved that he is one of the best debaters in the world, scoring point after point against the underprepared George W. Bush. Kerry was forceful, articulate, and presidential; Bush was defensive, confused, and petulant. As Kerry criticized Bush's "colossal mistake" on Iraq and other blunders, the split screen revealed the president to be frowning, shaking his head, squirming, and nervously quaffing water. He appeared confused, obviously knocked off stride by hearing criticisms from which his handlers appeared to have previously protected him. A couple of times Bush interrupted, as if he was going to make a point, and then blanked out with his characteristic "deer in the headlights" look, and after painful silences sputtered out his "message" of the night, "I'm firm, resolute, and I'll stay on course" and "Kerry changes his position, shouldn't send mixed messages" (Bush used this phrase about ten times), and so on. Also more than ten times, Bush emphasized how much "work" the war on Iraq was, and by extension the presidency. It was clear from his debate performance that Bush does not articulate arguments or even sentences, but sputters code words to his base. Often, he hunched up his shoulders, leaned over the lectern, and tried to speak directly into the camera, but usually repeated his set lines and didn't really communicate anything of particular interest or substance.

Hence, on the issue of style versus substance that is often the focus of pundit discussion, Bush was dreadful on style and weak on substance, whereas Kerry scored big on both. Although the pundits worried that the rigid debate format and 32 pages of rules would inhibit spontaneous exchange and lead both candidates to simply regurgitate their standard stump speeches, in fact the exchanges were often dramatic, the differences in position and style were striking, and both candidates clearly revealed their opposed positions and personalities. Many observers found the debates to be engrossing affairs (although for Bush fans the first debate must have been rather painful as the magisterial Kerry dominated the scene and Bush appeared not at all ready for prime time, much less the presidency).

Iraq was a major focus of the debate and from the beginning, Kerry put Bush on the defensive. Asked to respond to Republican criticism that the United States would be more vulnerable to terrorist attack with Kerry in the White House, the senator responded:

> I believe in being strong and resolute and determined. And I will hunt down and kill the terrorists, wherever they are.
>
> But we also have to be smart, Jim. And smart means not diverting your attention from the real war on terror in Afghanistan against Osama bin Laden and taking off to Iraq where the 9/11 Commission confirms there was no connection to 9/11 itself and Saddam Hussein, and where the reason for going to war was weapons of mass destruction, not the removal of Saddam Hussein.
>
> This president has made, I regret to say, a colossal error of judgment. And judgment is what we look for in the president of the United States of America.

Kerry rattled off all the high-level military officers who supported him, and soon after was asked by the moderator to indicate what "colossal error of judgment" President Bush made. Kerry criticized Bush's failure to get significant allies involved in the Iraq venture, only going to the United Nations after his father's top advisers insisted on it, promising to go to war only as a "last resort," and rushing to battle without a plan to win. Then in perhaps the key statement of the night Kerry noted:

> And so, today, we are 90 percent of the casualties and 90 percent of the cost: $200 billion—$200 billion that could have been used for health care, for schools, for construction, for prescription drugs for seniors, and it's in Iraq.

And Iraq is not even the center of the focus of the war on terror. The center is Afghanistan, where, incidentally, there were more Americans killed last year than the year before; where the opium production is 75 percent of the world's opium production; where 40 to 60 percent of the economy of Afghanistan is based on opium; where the elections have been postponed three times.

The president moved the troops, so he's got 10 times the number of troops in Iraq than he has in Afghanistan, where Osama bin Laden is. Does that mean that Saddam Hussein was 10 times more important than Osama bin Laden—than, excuse me, Saddam Hussein more important than Osama bin Laden? I don't think so.

An obviously rattled and defensive president confused Saddam Hussein and Osama bin Laden, a Freudian slip that indicated his difficulty in naming the one that got away: "Of course we're after Saddam Hussein—I mean bin Laden. He's isolated. Seventy-five percent of his people have been brought to justice. The killer—the mastermind of the September 11th attacks, Khalid Sheik Mohammed, is in prison." In fact, no one knows what percentage of Al Qaeda leadership has been captured or neutralized, and most salient reports indicate that Al Qaeda has expanded, has increased recruits as a response to Bush's Iraq disaster, and is more dangerous than ever.

Perhaps Kerry's strongest argument was that Bush's invasion of Iraq was a diversion in the war on terror and that it was a mistake to go after Saddam Hussein before Osama bin Laden was dealt with and Afghanistan was pacified. Kerry caught Bush's major gaffe of the evening after Bush summed up his reason for invading Iraq with the phrase "because the enemy attacked us." Kerry quickly responded by pointing out that Saddam Hussein had not attacked the United States, but, under Osama bin Laden's direction, Al Qaeda had. Kerry also trumped Bush when he talked about the failure to get bin Laden at Tora Bora because Bush had "outsourced" the job of closing down Al Qaeda, even when their leaders were cornered, hiring Afghan warlords to do the fighting instead of U.S. ground troops.

A flustered Bush responded by noting that of course bin Laden was behind the attacks and nervously added, "I knew that." He blustered on, "to think that another round of resolutions would have caused Saddam Hussein to disarm, disclose, is ludicrous, in my judgment. It just shows a significant difference of opinion." Indeed there was a significant difference. On Iraq, Kerry insisted that he had the credibility, ability, and plan to deal with the Iraq crisis and that Bush had no plan to get out, no credibility to organize alliances, and nothing but "more of the same" to offer. Bush insisted that his "plan" was to train Iraqi troops and let them create their own security forces, but he greatly exaggerated the number of troops already trained; most reports from the ground indicated that the Iraqi military forces often refused to fight, in some cases sided with the insurgents, and were utterly incompetent to guarantee security in the country. Kerry repeatedly argued that allies needed to be brought in to share the responsibilities and rewards. Scoring a big point, he noted that Bush had given all the major contracts to Halliburton and other U.S. corporations who financed his campaign and had told countries who had not supported the invasion to forget about bidding for contracts.

Kerry also made much stronger arguments on Iran and North Korea than Bush, accusing the president of letting both countries develop nuclear capabilities. Kerry's general motif was that by focusing all the country's energy on Iraq, more dangerous problems such as nuclear proliferation were not addressed. Bush insisted that it was not feasible to carry out bilateral discussions on North Korea, that it was better to have a multilateral force negotiating, and that China would be marginalized and lose its leverage if the United States began bilateral talks. Kerry insisted that both could be done and in fact China and other countries in the multilateral North Korea talks had been urging the United States to get involved in dealing with North Korea directly.

After the debate, the candidates' wives came on stage, both dressed in white, and Bush's daughters also appeared. Teresa Kerry engaged Laura Bush in conversation as Kerry tried to talk to the Bush daughters who giggled and scurried away. Their father, eager to get off the stage where he had performed so miserably, quickly left the auditorium with them, as the wives continued talking and Kerry eagerly plunged into the audience knowing that he had scored big.

Although none of the network television pundits claimed that either candidate had scored a knockout, most agreed that Kerry had easily won the debate and that Bush had performed poorly. As commentary on the debates began rapidly circulating in the media, most pundits admitted that Bush had an extremely bad night and Kerry a very good one, although some Republican spinners just couldn't admit the truth. Fox News host Sean Hannity, for instance, said of Bush "I've never seen him more passionate, more on message, more articulate." Chris Sullentrop's *Slate* summary noted "Karl Rove must have known things didn't go well when the *New York Post* asked him whether this was the worst debate of President Bush's life. No, Rove insisted. 'This was one of the president's best debates, and one of John Kerry's worst.' 'Really?' asked the reporter, Vince Morris. 'You can say that with a straight face?'"[22]

In fact, Rove to the contrary, it was probably Bush's worse major televised debate ever. Although many had thought that Gore had beaten Bush on debating points and substance in the first presidential debate in Election 2000, others claimed that Bush had won on style and likeability, but it would be hard to make this claim in the opening 2004 debate. The Democratic National Committee released a tape the next day showing Bush's reactions to Kerry's charges, and rarely had a presidential candidate looked so unpresidential.

Of course, the Republican spin machine was working overtime to marshal arguments against Kerry and to insist that Bush had made the stronger case. Yet the extent of Bush's poor performance was noted in the media the next day, even by Bush supporters. Sidney Blumenthal claimed that Kerry effectively deconstructed Bush's epistemology of certainty. As Kerry hammered Bush, the hapless president stammered and said "I am certain that...," "I know that...," and other phrases of absolutism, and then Kerry zinged him by saying "It's one thing to be certain, but you can be certain and be wrong." In Blumenthal's words, "For Bush, certainty equals strength. Kerry responded with a devastating deconstruction of Bush's epistemology. Nothing like this critique of pure reason has ever been heard in a presidential debate."

In a widely circulated article, "Father Kerry versus Boy George," Steven Rosenfeld and Jan Frel made the argument that "John Kerry came across as a mature candidate during the debate, while George Bush squirmed repeatedly at challenges to his record."[23] The authors asserted that Bush came off as an immature fraternity boy, unprepared for his assignment and mean-spirited. It seemed that Bush was losing the battle of machismo; Kerry appeared much more likely to be seen as a father and leader. Gone was the cocky, relaxed, and bantering Bush and instead he appeared without the gravitas to do the job. Richard Reeves claimed that Bush suffered from "ovalitis," a malady produced by staying too long in the Oval Office of the White House surrounded by "yes men," not getting alternative information. Bush's presidential bubble is rarely punctured by anyone giving him bad news, letting him in on the negative effects of his policies, or exposing him to different sides of an issue upon which he has already decided.[24]

It was apparent from the debates that Bush is thin-skinned when he is exposed to criticism of a type he rarely confronts in his ideological fantasy world. Bush was also highly defective on the facts. *Time* magazine filled pages with misstatements Bush and Kerry had made, although the president's errors were much more damning. Kerry had exaggerated the $200 billion bill for Iraq (supposedly "only" $120 billion had been spent, although more than $200 billion was budgeted). Bush had claimed, however, that the majority of insurgents fighting in Iraq were "foreign terrorists," whereas the U.S. military and others on the ground claimed that the majority fighting the U.S. occupation were Iraqis and not foreigners. Interrupting Kerry, Bush insisted that he had forgotten

Poland as one of the initial countries involved in the Iraq invasion, but in fact Poland had come in later and was planning to pull out.

Bush had repeated his Big Lie that Saddam Hussein "had no intention of disarming and was systematically deceiving inspectors," but the fact was that no weapons of mass destruction had been found and the U.S. inspection team had concluded that Iraq had indeed disarmed. Bush claimed that he had tried diplomacy in Iraq and only went to war when it had failed, whereas in the *Time* summary, "Numerous accounts from within the U.S. and allied governments suggest the Bush administration had decided to invade Iraq even before it went to the UN in the fall of 2002, and had gone back to the international body only under pressure from moderates in its own ranks and from Britain's Prime Minister Tony Blair. The termination of the UN inspection process had nothing to do with its progress; it was based primarily on the window of opportunity for an invasion presented by the seasonal calendar."[25]

On many other issues as well, Bush had misspoken. He claimed: "The A.Q. Khan network has been brought to justice." (Khan is the Pakistani nuclear scientist who shipped nuclear weapons technology to North Korea, Iran, Libya, and possibly other states.) But according to *Time:* "Observers generally concur that there's no way Khan could have acted without the authorization and support of Pakistan's military leadership, yet the U.S. accepted an outcome in which Khan received a slap on the wrist and wasn't even made available for questioning by U.S. officials, nor was any obvious attempt made to hold his superiors accountable—perhaps because of Pakistan's crucial role in hunting al-Qaeda." Bush claimed "Bilateral talks with North Korea would be a fatal mistake that would precipitate the collapse of the six-party talks on Pyongyang's nuclear program." But, *Time* stated, "Some of the key parties to those talks, including China, Russia, and South Korea are in favor of the U.S. talking directly to North Korea in order to provide Pyongyang with security guarantees that would improve the prospects for success in the six-party process." Bush continued to claim that his "coalition of the willing is a strong and vigorous force," but, according to *Time,* "There isn't a single Arab country in the coalition, in contrast to the wide Arab participation in the Gulf War. And the U.S. and Britain between them provided more than 90 percent of the troops. Moreover, eight of the countries that initially joined the U.S. have since pulled out their soldiers, and more are expected to follow. Efforts to persuade Muslim countries to send troops have foundered."

A national television audience of 62.5 million people watched the first debate, 34 percent more than those who saw Gore and Bush in the first 2000 debate. Although the Bush spin machine in 2000 provided video frames of

Gore sighing and claimed that Gore exhibited a tendency to exaggerate and lie after Gore's impressive debate performance in 2000, there wasn't much the Bush spinners could do to counter Kerry's obviously superior performance. But Bush gamely went back on the campaign trail doing what he likes best: reading pre-packaged sound bytes that mock Kerry to a prepicked audience that cheers his every smirk and does not require that he clarify or defend his positions. Strictly speaking, Bush did not make campaign speeches, but read prepackaged applause lines that his carefully picked audiences cheered on cue. These talking points were tested in focus groups, and if they evoked the strongest responses, Bush would put them in his speech even if they were lies.

Bush's campaign strategy thus involved systematic misrepresentation of Kerry's positions, as when Bush told a rally of party faithful at Allentown, Pennsylvania: "The cornerstone of Senator Kerry's plan for Iraq is that he would convene a summit. I've been to lots of summits. I've never seen a meeting that would depose a tyrant or bring a terrorist to justice." Continuing to mock Kerry, Bush took out of context Kerry's insistence that preemptive strikes or military action had to pass a "global test" as well as be acceptable to the American people. The anti-intellectual Bush brayed that "He wants our national security decisions subject to the approval of a foreign government." Of course, Kerry had said nothing of the kind.

Since the Republicans did not have a good record on which to campaign, they covertly played their secret trump card—God. Columnist Arianna Huffington documented how the Republicans were sending out "an incendiary mass mailing warning that, if elected, 'liberals' (and I'll give you one guess which presidential candidate that includes) will try to—I kid you not—ban the Bible. The full-color flyer features a picture of the Bible with the word 'Banned' stamped across it, and a photo of a man, on bended knee, placing a wedding band on the hand of another man, accompanied by the word 'Allowed.'" The "God is on our side" attack, Huffington claimed, came directly from the Bush-run Republican National Committee, which was also using, she pointed out, "the official Georgewbush.com campaign website to attack Kerry, a Catholic, as being 'Wrong for Catholics,' while an RNC website, KerryWrong ForCatholics.com, slams him for not being loyal enough to the Pope." Huffington concluded "The idea that Kerry and the Democrats are anti-Bible and that Bush has a hot line to The Man Upstairs is both offensive and patently absurd. One look at the latest statistics showing the rise in the number of Americans living in poverty proves that Republicans—who, contrary to their claims, do not hold a copyright on the Bible—have grotesquely perverted its core teachings."

With about a month to go before the election, Bush and Kerry were back on the campaign trail. Kerry, buoyant after what many saw as his debate triumph over an incompetent Bush, hit the trail energized and for the first time got a rock star reception with crowds chanting his name, eating up attacks on Bush, and intently listening to his serious proposals. Repeating the "Strong America" motif that the Democrats had set out at their summer convention, Kerry insisted that under his presidency the United States would continue to hunt down and kill terrorists, that no country would veto the U.S. right to defend itself, and that he would strengthen both the military and intelligence forces as well as forge robust alliances with key U.S. allies, whom Bush administration unilateralism had alienated.

Bush continued to ridicule Kerry about his "global test" for using U.S. military force, even though Kerry repeatedly indicated he had never remotely implied what Bush was claiming. On the day of the much-anticipated vice-presidential debates, however, two major bombshells hit the Bush campaign. The *Washington Post* published a story revealing that Paul Bremer, who had been in charge of the Iraq reconstruction that had so disastrously failed, turned on his former bosses and said that he had requested more troops immediately after the collapse of the Saddam Hussein government and that the Bush administration had turned him down repeatedly.[26] Bremer had claimed at DePauw University on September 17 that he had often raised the problem of more troops with the Bush administration and "should have been even more insistent." He also spoke on October 4 at an insurance conference in West Virginia, where he apparently thought his comments were off the record, declaring "we never had enough troops on the ground."

In addition, Donald Rumsfeld said in response to a question after a talk at the Council of Foreign Relations meeting in New York that he had never seen "strong, hard evidence" linking Al Qaeda and Iraq, undermining a position that Bush, Cheney, Rice, and Rumsfeld himself had repeatedly used as a justification for the Iraq intervention. There had also been an investigative article by Michael Gordon in the *New York Times* indicating that during the 2002–2003 debate over the Iraq intervention, there were many conflicting intelligence reports and analyses concerning whether Iraq did or did not have nuclear and other deadly weapons, and the Bush administration systematically suppressed evidence that put their claims concerning Iraqi WMD in question.[27] The Bush-Cheney Gang now faced new accusations of both mendacity and incompetence.

Scrambling to deal with the fallout over Bremer's explosive remarks, the Bush administration, after first denying that Bremer had ever requested more troops, then claimed that the U.S. troop levels had been set by military commanders on the ground in Iraq and that the commanders had not indicated that they needed more troops. Kerry seized on the rapidly proliferating reports questioning Bush administration justifications for a war in Iraq and told an audience in Iowa that President Bush "may be constitutionally unable to level with" the public and called on Bush to own up to his mistakes in Iraq. Bush retorted on October 5 in a speech before supporters in Wilkes-Barre, Pennsylvania, that Kerry had a "20-year record of weakness" in the U.S. Senate and would "paralyze America" in the war against terrorism if elected. Bush was escalating his rhetoric against Kerry, using harsher language than previously as he attempted to rebound from what was widely considered a lackluster debate performance.

The vice-presidential debate took place in Coral Cables, Florida, on October 5, and, once again, it was a major spectacle with a nasty and aggressive Dick Cheney attacking the vigorous and feisty Democratic candidate John Edwards. Cheney referred constantly to Edwards' lack of experience and allegedly mediocre record as a senator, as well as fiercely assaulting the qualifications and record of John Kerry. Edwards retorted with a passionate defense of Kerry, sharp attacks on Bush administration policy in Iraq and the war on terror, and advocacy of a Kerry-Edwards administration solution to the domestic and foreign policy problems generated by the Bush-Cheney administration. There had not been in recent times in a vice-presidential debate such acrid personal attacks and sharp articulations of policy differences. Both candidates fought so hard, however, that they seemed out of energy and arguments in the last thirty minutes or so of the debate. Hence, it was not a decisive victory for one side or the other.

Cheney refused to answer many questions and played fast and loose with facts, as when he made the astonishing statement: "I have not suggested there's a connection between Iraq and 9/11." Of course, Cheney had made the claim constantly and after the debate the media replayed or cited many instances when Cheney connected Al Qaeda and Iraq, such as on National Public Radio's *Morning Edition* in January 2004 where he stated: "I think there's overwhelming evidence that there was a connection between Al Qaeda and the Iraqi government." Cheney also lectured John Edwards about his poor attendance record in the U.S. Senate (notoriously, campaigners for higher office miss Senate meetings and votes), claiming that Edwards' presence in the Senate was so scarce that he had met him on stage for the first time the night of the debate. This too was quickly revealed to be a lie as footage soon surfaced of Edwards next to Cheney at a prayer breakfast and of Cheney and Edwards together at Senate events. Moreover, it came out that Cheney himself had a dismal attendance record in the Senate, only showing up twice to vote to break a tie.

Although Cheney appeared somewhat sinister as he sat hunched over looking down at his hands throughout most of the debate, the commentators on NBC and CNBC claimed that he won the debate hands-down. Chris Matthews of *Hardball* gushed:

> I am stunned! I wish everybody would show an equal exclamation point after their thoughts here tonight! Dick Cheney was prepared! He was loaded for bear tonight! He was out on a hunting trip looking for squirrel!
> (laughter)
> Matthews: And he found squirrel! Does anybody share that? Because I think the newspapers are going to share that tomorrow.[28]

Matthews' CNBC and NBC colleagues made similar judgments, leading Bob Somerby to reflect upon whether they were following a corporate script. The next morning as reports critical of Cheney's performance and positive about Edwards' performance circulated, it was clear that Matthews and his fellow NBC ideologues were wrong (ibid.).

The day after the vice-presidential debate, another devastating moment came for the Bush administration rationale for the Iraq war. A report by chief U.S. Iraqi arms inspector Charles A. Duelfer was circulated indicating that Iraq appeared to have destroyed its stockpiles of illicit weapons within months of the Persian Gulf War of 1991, and that by the time of the U.S. invasion in spring 2003, its capacity to produce such weapons had been severely eroded. Duelfer claimed that the last Iraqi factory capable of producing militarily significant quantities of unconventional weapons was destroyed in 1996. The finding amounted to the starkest portrayal yet of a vast gap between the Bush administration's prewar assertions about Iraqi weapons and the facts found by a 15-month postinvasion inquiry by U.S. investigators.[29]

Meanwhile, John Edwards, campaigning in Florida, claimed that Bush and Cheney "are in a complete state of denial" about deteriorating conditions in Iraq. "This president is completely out of touch with reality," Edwards insisted, and "won't acknowledge the mess in Iraq." Edwards added, "[Bush and Cheney] still don't recognize that there's any problem with jobs and the economy. ... You can't fix these problems until you recognize there is a problem. ...They're in denial. They're in denial about everything."

Dick Cheney, also in Florida, echoed Bush's latest criticisms of the Democratic opposition. "John Kerry and John Edwards cannot with tough talk obscure a record that goes back 30 years that had him on the wrong side of virtually every issue that dealt with national security," Cheney said at a rally in Tallahassee. Kerry spent the day in Colorado, and called Edwards to congratulate him on his debate performance. "These guys could only resort to fear and distortion," Kerry said on the phone as television news cameras rolled. "You held them accountable." In a speech in Pennsylvania, Bush accused Kerry once again of waffling in his position on the war on terrorism, pushing for higher taxes, and sending "mixed messages" to allies and enemies. "In the war on terror, Senator Kerry is proposing policies and doctrines that would weaken America and make the world more dangerous," Bush said. On the economy, he added, "My opponent is a tax-and-spend liberal; I'm a compassionate conservative."

The second presidential debate took place at Washington University in Saint Louis, Missouri, and had a town hall format with ABC commentator Charles Gibson fielding questions from the audience. The give-and-take between the candidates was as fierce as in the first debate, clearly etching the differences in policy and personality between the two candidates. The opening thirty minutes rehashed the contest over Iraq in the first debate. Bush interpreted the Duelfer report as "evidence" that Saddam Hussein was a threat who was planning to reconstitute his arms programs after the UN sanctions were ended. Kerry let this fantastical claim go by, choosing instead to hammer home the points he'd made in the first debate that Bush had made a "catastrophic error" in going into Iraq, that it was a diversion from Osama bin Laden and Al Qaeda in the war on terror, that Bush had no plan to win the war, and that he had basically made a big mess in Iraq.

Knowing that he had been harshly criticized after the first debate for making weird faces when Kerry was speaking, Bush tried his best to keep a blank face while appearing to listen intently to Kerry, but occasionally his eyes would blink, in rapid reaction, signaling intense psychological turmoil. As the debate proceeded, Bush appeared to be more tightly wound and at one point he jumped up after Kerry's criticism of his largely unilateral Iraq policy and failure to build broader alliances. Although moderator Charles Gibson, according to the rules of the debate, was beginning to pose another question, Bush interrupted in a remarkable exchange that put on display his inability to take criticism and his explosive temper:

> Kerry: We're going to build alliances. We're not going to go unilaterally. We're not going to go alone like this president did.
> Gibson: Mr. President, let's extend for a minute …
> Bush: Let me just—I've got to answer this.
> Gibson: Exactly. And with Reservists being held on duty …
> (crosstalk with Bush interrupting, breaking the rules of the debate)

Bush: Let me answer what he just said, about around the world.

Gibson: Well, I want to get into the issue of the back-door draft ...

Bush [shouting]: You tell Tony Blair we're going alone. Tell Tony Blair we're going alone. Tell Silvio Berlusconi we're going alone. Tell Aleksander Kwasniewski of Poland we're going alone.

Bush's shouting perhaps has Oedipal roots as it was in response to Kerry's constant comparisons of Bush Senior's construction of a multilateral coalition to throw Saddam Hussein out of Kuwait in Gulf War I with Bush Junior's failure to construct such a coalition in Gulf War II. Kerry had also quoted Bush's father's memoirs about why he did not send the U.S. military into Iraq to overthrow the Saddam Hussein regime, and sharply criticized Bush's failure to have a plan to win the peace in Iraq. Bush's competitive relationship with his father was made the subject of a Sunday, October 10, "Doonesbury" cartoon that shows the Empty Helmet, signifying the Mindless Warrior George W. Bush, talking on the phone to his father about the Iraq debacle, as the father reads from his book warning against the impossibility of occupying Iraq, an argument also made by Kerry that obviously unnerved Bush Junior.

Bush insistently pandered to his base, defending his positions on Iraq, stem-cell research, restricting abortion, the Patriot Act, and tax breaks for the rich. He tried to argue that Kerry would raise taxes on the middle class to pay for his programs, although Kerry insisted he would only raise taxes on those who made over $200,000. In response to a question from the audience, Kerry looked into the camera and promised he would not raise taxes for the middle class and working people.

Bush's worst moment came in response to a question asking him to recall the three worst mistakes he'd made in office, a question similar to one in his last live press conference where he hemmed and hawed and just couldn't think of any mistakes. This time Bush went on the offensive, saying that he had not made any mistakes on Iraq, taxes, or major issues, but conceding he was disappointed in some of the appointments he had made. Revealingly, Bush seemed incapable of self-reflection and self-critique as well as unforgiving of all those who had crossed him, such as his former Secretary of the Treasury Paul O'Neill, who wrote a memoir after Bush removed him from office indicating that Bush would not discuss economic policy, was planning an Iraq invasion from the beginning of his presidency, and refused to compromise on his massive tax break for the rich even after 9/11 and competing priorities (Suskind 2004).

Kerry continued to sharply criticize Bush administration policy and insisted that he had better plans for Iraq, domestic security, jobs and the economy, health care, and the environment. Although Kerry scored many debate blows, he did not throw any knockout punches and was not as sharp in deconstructing

Bush's debate points as he had been in the first debate. Most network television commentators called it a draw, although early polls showed that viewers tended to see Kerry as the winner and that he had done better with undecided voters.

The third and final presidential debate was held at Arizona State University in Tempe, Arizona, with CBS's Bob Schieffer as moderator. With the debate focusing on domestic issues, Kerry attacked Bush's record and argued that the Democrats had better plans on health care, jobs and the economy, Social Security and Medicare, and education. Although some conservatives before the debate complained that Bob Schieffer should be removed as moderator because CBS was allegedly anti-Bush, in fact, Schieffer's brother was a business partner and close friend of Bush who had been appointed ambassador to Australia by the president. Schieffer's questions were largely softballs, especially the last two, which concerned faith and the women in their lives, giving Bush a chance to wax nostalgic and play to his conservative base without having to defend his record. Schieffer failed to raise any questions about the environment, education, stem-cell research, or reproductive rights.[30] Hence, the third debate was the most unmemorable of the three and basically allowed Bush to jump through the hoops to avoid the self-destruction evident in the first two debates.

Bush's goal for the night was to paint Kerry as a "liberal" and he repeated the Bold Lie that Kerry was the most liberal senator in Congress, more liberal than Ted Kennedy. In fact, the *National Journal* rating to which Bush referred only scored Kerry the highest-ranking liberal of the previous year, in which he missed votes while on the campaign trail. Overall, however, his record was not in the top ten liberals ranked by the journal, whereas Ted Kennedy was ranked at number five, ahead of Kerry. Astonishingly, on the campaign trail the next day, Bush once again called Kerry "the most liberal member of the Senate," crowing "he can run but he can't hide." This empty demagoguery showed the desperation of the Bush campaign, which depended on lies and insults to demean Kerry. Meanwhile, the Kerry campaign brought up Bush's unbalanced second debate performance and issued a three-page document describing the president as "Nixon-like" and "hot under the collar." Kerry criticized Bush's "refusing to show the maturity" to build a bigger alliance in Iraq and argued that it was time to put "adults" in charge of foreign policy.

Wired Bush?

> God loves you, and I love you. And you can count on both of us as a powerful message that people who wonder about their future can hear.
> —*George W. Bush, March 3, 2004*

One of the most intriguing stories of the debates concerned images that suggested George W. Bush seemed to have a wire running up his back during the first debate. There was speculation over whether Karl Rove was feeding Bush answers, or if the wire malfunctioned, causing Bush evident grief. John Reynolds in a commentary "Bush Blows Debate: Talks to Rove in Earpiece!" suggested that in the middle of an answer while the green light was still flashing Bush impatiently blurted out, "Now let me finish," even though no one was seemingly interrupting him. Reynolds noted:

> The "let me finish" quip was clearly Bush talking to someone (probably Rove) in his earpiece—saying "let me finish" (before you give me the next answer).
>
> He blows it 60 seconds into his 90-second reply—so no warning lights had gone off and the moderator had not motioned for him to end as there was plenty of time left.
>
> There is really no other plausible explanation for this huge blunder—who was he telling to "let him finish"? The voices in his head?
>
> Is he talking to God again? Shouldn't this be enough to warrant a major investigation of some sort—Bush is so incompetent he needs an earpiece to speak in public![31]

Indymedia and other Internet sites circulated the images of the bulge and a website quickly appeared to collect all the key stories on the phenomenon at http://www.isbushwired.com. After *Salon* broke the story, all of the major newspapers had a story with lower-level Bush spokespeople saying it was "preposterous." Yet the story persisted, and ABC's Sunday-morning show featured the images of Bush with the bulging coat, which by then had been blamed on his tailor. Yet the television footage of the debate clearly showed what appeared to be a wire running along his back with a noticeable bulge around it.[32]

Hence, when the third debate began many were looking closely to see if there were any signs of a telltale wire in the back of Bush's coat. Although his shoulders and rump revealed rather strange tailoring, there was no evidence of a wire as there was throughout the first debate, until the end of the debate when he crossed the stage to meet with his and Kerry's families. A picture in *Salon* suggested that a wire appeared to have popped out, as an astonished Kerry daughter looked at the strange lump in the back of Bush's jacket.[33]

Speculations continued to fly over the Internet concerning whether Bush was wired, whether he had diabetes and the bulge was an insulin device, whether he had a heart attack (he had allegedly postponed his yearly physical this year), or whether the bulge was a flak jacket. Tailors weighed in and most said that the telltale bulges could not be explained by poor tailoring. The *New York Times* did an op-ed feature that showed pictures of New Yorkers walking down the street with big bulges in their clothes, but in these cases one could discern money-belts, shoulder pistols, flak jackets, and other devices. Critic Dave Lindorff began looking at other tapes of the Bush presidency and finding evidence of a wired Bush:

> I just got a look at the full Fox tape of President Bush's May '04 joint news conference with French President Jaques Chirac. In that tape, as in several other tapes I've seen, Bush can be heard seemingly getting prompting from another voice. About 12 seconds into the piece, the leading voice says, "And I look forward to working to" Bush comes in with "And I look workin'... And I look forward to workin' to." The verbal slip-up makes it clear that this is no electronic echo or sound synchronization problem.
>
> At another point, about one minute and sixteen seconds into the tape, the leading voice lets out a loud exhale of breath. Bush does not follow suit. There is no preceding voice when a reporter is heard asking a question. Also, at one minute and 28 seconds into this tape, Bush reaches up and manipulates something in his ear, at which point there is a static noise and the sound of a speaker acting up, until he removes his fingers from his ear.
>
> There is no wire going up to his ear, indicating that the earpiece in his right ear is wireless.[34]

My own contribution to the controversy emerged from a viewing of the extras on Michael Moore's DVD *Fahrenheit 9/11,* where one link features Bush's press conference right after the meeting between the president, Cheney, and the 9/11 Commission. A subdued Bush went out to the White House lawn to make a press statement; after fumbling and mumbling, he found the words to describe the meeting ("good!") and generally provided brief answers to reporters' questions, often after a concentrated pause. Afterward, as Bush turned around to return to the White House, one can clearly observe a bulge in his jacket similar to the bulge observed during the presidential television debates.

A wired Bush might explain his tendency to give answers in brief code words rather than sentences, although it is also possible that he is simply linguistically challenged. Although Jon Stewart, Jay Leno, Dave Letterman, and other comedians continued to make wired Bush jokes, the controversy was ignored by the mainstream media until Charles Gibson confronted Bush in an October 26 *Good Morning America* interview. In the summary of *Washington Post* columnist Dan Froomkin:

> As you recall, the bulge, most clearly photographed during Bush's first debate, raised conspiracy theories that Bush was possibly getting audio cues over some sort of wireless device.

This morning, in part two of his interview with Bush on ABC's *Good Morning America*, Charlie Gibson spit it out. Brandishing a copy of the photo, he asked: "Final question. What the hell was that on your back, in the first debate?"

Bush chuckled.

Bush: "Well, you know, Karen Hughes and Dan Bartlett have rigged up a sound system."

Gibson: "You're getting in trouble."

Bush: "I don't know what that is. I mean, it is, uh, it is, it's a—I'm embarrassed to say it's a poorly tailored shirt."

Gibson: "It was the shirt?"

Bush: "Yeah, absolutely."

Gibson: "There was no sound system, there was no electrical signal? There was …"

Bush: "How does an electrical—please explain to me how it works so maybe if I were ever to debate again I could figure it out. I guess the assumption was that if I was straying off course they would, kind of like a hunting dog, they would punch a buzzer and I would jerk back into place. I—it's just absurd."

Gibson: "So it's the shirt? Sure doesn't look like a shirt."[35]

Salon weighed in with another story on the mysterious bulge as a NASA and Caltech scientist did an electronic enhancement of the images. In Kevin Berger's summary:

George W. Bush tried to laugh off the bulge. "I don't know what that is," he said on *Good Morning America* on Wednesday, referring to the infamous protrusion beneath his jacket during the presidential debates. "I'm embarrassed to say it's a poorly tailored shirt."

Dr. Robert M. Nelson, however, was not laughing. He knew the president was not telling the truth. And Nelson is neither conspiracy theorist nor midnight blogger. He's a senior research scientist for NASA and for Caltech's Jet Propulsion Laboratory, and an international authority on image analysis. Currently he's engrossed in analyzing digital photos of Saturn's moon Titan, determining its shape, whether it contains craters or canyons.

For the past week, while at home, using his own computers, and off the clock at Caltech and NASA, Nelson has been analyzing images of the president's back during the debates. A professional physicist and photo analyst for more than 30 years, he speaks earnestly and thoughtfully about his subject. "I am willing to stake my scientific reputation to the statement that Bush was wearing something under his jacket during the debate," he says. "This is not about a bad suit. And there's no way the bulge can be described as a wrinkled shirt."[36]

The wired Bush controversy did not make significant inroads into the mainstream media, so it is doubtful that it had any effect on the election. Right after the election, the Internet publication *The Hill* posted a spin from Bush administration insiders that "the mysterious bulge on President Bush's back during the first presidential debate was not an electronic device feeding him answers, but a strap holding his bulletproof vest in place." Secret Service agents told *The Hill* that Bush frequently wears such a vest in public and that the "conspiracy" can be laid to rest.[37]

Yet suspicions remain. Why didn't the Bush administration immediately indicate that the bulge was produced by a bulletproof vest? Why did his tailor not mention this? When Bush was confronted with the picture by Charles Gibson of ABC, why didn't he just say, "You know, the Secret Service makes me wear a bullet-proof vest when I'm in public," rather than saying it was just bad tailoring? Curiously, when *The Hill*'s bulletproof vest story seemed to put the issue to rest, Karl Rove kicked in and blamed it on the tailor. A November 7, 2004, Associated Press story reported that: "On one sideline row during the campaign, Rove said the president's tailor was devastated about a controversy over a box-shaped bulge in Bush's back that television cameras captured during the first debate. . . . 'Nothing was under his jacket,' Rove said. 'The poor tailor . . . he's an awfully nice fellow, he's a rather flamboyant dude,' Rove said. 'I'm not going to use his name, but he's just—he's horrified. And, you know, it's—there was nothing there.'" Commenting on the failure of the mainstream media to investigate the story, the website http://www.isbushwired.com noted:

> Oddly, though, the president never seemed to have his bulgy protective strap on when he spoke at huge campaign rallies in his shirtsleeves—though he's donned it for assassin-free zones, such as the East Room of the White House. Perhaps the Secret Service was speaking figuratively. It seems unlikely, though, that the Secret Service would ask that Bush lie about the device on television, as he did when he told ABC's Charles Gibson that he was "embarrassed" to say that it was just a wrinkle in his shirt.
>
> The *New York Times* reports in tomorrow's paper (Nov. 8) that the Secret Service won't comment on the question. The *Times* story doesn't point out that *The Hill*'s attempt at Bush-buffing doesn't even make sense: Presidential body armor is hardly a secret, and how exactly would keeping it quiet help deflect attempts on the president's life? Wouldn't it have the reverse effect? Not to mention that people who know what bulletproof vests look like, i.e., actual soldiers, say there's no body armor in the world with that Rube Goldberg configuration.
>
> I apologize for repeating myself, but what's a blogger to do when respectable journalists at the *Times* are more intent on writing entertainingly than on providing readers with all the relevant facts? It used to be that *Times* reporters, even those based in Washington, tried to do both.

So, here we are, a month and two days after we first broached the question of Bush's wire (Oct. 5). Nothing has changed except that a few more people know about the fraud. But most major news media seem to prefer that the people be protected from this knowledge. They wish they didn't know it themselves. Soviet-style, newspapers around the country ran Doonesbury's strips on the Bush prompter without investigating their premise. How did they expect their readers to know what the strips were about, and whether or not they amounted to fair criticism or dishonest slurs?

More details on the failure to report the story by two major papers: According to Dave Lindorff, the *Washington Post*'s Bob Woodward advised the NASA scientist who analyzed the video images of Bush's box to take the story to *Salon*, since he wouldn't be able to get it past his own editors before Nov. 2. And the *New York Times* killed a story scheduled for October 28 by reporters William Broad and John Schwarz because, Lindorff says, the *Times* feared that printing the news might influence the election. Of course, failing to inform the public *also* influenced the election, as the voters pathetically quoted in the *Times* as having chosen Bush because they felt he was "honest," demonstrate.[38]

No doubt Bush's bulges will continue to be scrutinized and there will continue to be suspicions that Bush is wired. The entire spectacle reveals how television can capture minute details of behavior and personality tics, and focus attention on issues—or ignore them. The debates provided unparalleled scrutiny of Bush's behavior, reaction to issues, and odd repertoire of facial expressions. The wired Bush controversy was initially an Internet story that snuck into the margins of the mainstream media, but did not penetrate far into the center. Failure of the mainstream corporate media to investigate the phenomenon shows the pack journalism conformity of the mainstream corporate media. When the mainstream picks up on an issue, it can be devastating, as the Dean Scream spectacle proved for Howard Dean and the Watergate saga for Richard Nixon. Watergate was initially a highly marginal story, which briefly appeared before the 1972 election, and then returned to haunt Nixon and drive him from office after the election. Marginal images and stories can proliferate and can generate unforeseen consequences and effects—or they can disappear into obscurity. In an age in which politics is mediated by media spectacle, those who live by the media can also die by it.

The Sprint to the End

After standing on the stage, after the debates, made it very plain, we will not have an all-volunteer army. And yet, this week—we will have an all-volunteer army. Let me restate that.
—*George W. Bush, Daytona Beach, Fla., October 16, 2004*

After the debates, once again the campaigns got into photo-op mode, used television ads to attack their opponents and promote their candidates, attempted to mobilize their respective bases, and prepared to respond to an "October Surprise"—or a November one if there were voting irregularities or another "too close to call" election. Following the strategy of Bush Senior's successful 1988 campaign against Massachusetts governor Michael Dukakis, Bush Junior set out to paint Kerry as a "Massachusetts liberal." Bush and Cheney were enacting the politics of division that marked their administration. Often, Bush would contrast liberal "Hollywood" or "Massachusetts" values to the traditional "American" values, which he supposedly represented. The Bush administration promotion of a constitutional anti–gay marriage amendment divided the country, and after Bush had done so poorly in the debates, the Republicans continued day after day to use Kerry's reference to Cheney's lesbian daughter as evidence "he would say or do anything to get elected."

The final stage of the Bush campaign involved creating fear about the dire effects of a Kerry presidency. Cheney continued to argue that a Kerry presidency would make the nation more vulnerable to a terrorist attack. In one of the Republican advertisements, a clock ticked menacingly as a young mother pulled a quart of milk out of a refrigerator in slow motion, a young father loaded toddlers into a minivan, and an announcer intoned ominously, "Weakness invites those who would do us harm." Another attack ad claimed that Kerry was proposing a "government-run" health care program that would bring "rationing, less access, fewer choices, and long waits." Another Bush ad showed packs of wolves gathering in the woods, symbolizing dangers to the polity, and was being used to scare voters into "staying the course" and voting for Bush.

The Democrats countered with their own ads suggesting that Bush would bring back a military draft, privatize Social Security, and not be able to resolve the mess in Iraq. Not surprisingly, during the final sprint to the presidency, negative ads proliferated from both campaigns and from the 527 groups who supported the respective candidates. But both campaigns used their "top guns" to savage their opponents, believing that in such an information-cluttered environment, only the voices of the best known could break through the noise. In a prescient article, Ryan Lizza dissected the Bush-Cheney closing strategy and how they targeted for attack specific media that strongly criticized them:

> the White House has always relied on the press to convey Bush's message to readers and viewers in a relatively unmediated fashion. That has proved more difficult this year due to a surge in coverage that fact-checks what the candidates are saying. This development has hurt Bush more than Kerry because the president's strategy is to destroy his opponent's credibility, a tactic that, ironically enough,

has relied disproportionately on false statements. The Bushies have become so frustrated by the fact-checking of the president's statements that a spokesman told the *Washington Post*'s Howard Kurtz, "The Bush campaign should be able to make an argument without having it reflexively dismissed as distorted or inaccurate by the biggest papers in the country."

In response to the media's new obsession with truth-squading the candidates, the Republican National Committee's opposition research department has started to do something remarkable: going negative on the press. "RNC Research Briefings," e-mailed to hundreds of reporters, now regularly target members of the media. On October 6, the RNC put *Hardball* host Chris Matthews, a former staffer for House Speaker Tip O'Neill, in its sights. "Democrat Chris Matthews' Selective 'Analysis,'" read the headline on a three-page press release that accused Matthews of erroneously claiming Cheney had contradicted himself during the debate when he denied tying September 11 to Saddam Hussein. Accompanying the release, the RNC posted a video online attacking Matthews. A few days later, Republicans took issue with the *New York Times*' Elisabeth Bumiller's accurate statement that, despite Bush's claims, Kerry "essentially voted for one large tax increase, the Clinton tax bill of 1993." "The *New York Times* Shades the Truth," read the headline of a press release the RNC quickly put out. Next up was Ron Suskind, who wrote a critical piece in the *New York Times Magazine*. "Liberal Democrat Suskind Has Creativity but Not Facts," the RNC noted. A few days later Paul Krugman became the RNC's target. In Suskind's and Krugman's cases, the oppo was unusually personal and included unflattering pictures of the men, the kind that candidates dig up of their opponents, not of journalists.

The fact that the RNC is now devoting a good deal of its time to attacking reporters speaks volumes about how much Bush is relying on negative, unchecked distortions to secure a second term. And that means that, in its own way, the Ashley Faulkner ad—with its warm and fuzzy image of Bush—ultimately leaves voters with as false an impression as the Willie Horton ad did in 1988.[39]

The Bush administration had indeed been ruthless throughout their reign against media voices who had spoken out against them. Karen Hughes and Karl Rove, especially, had relentlessly browbeat any reporter who dared criticize the Bush administration. Few critics noticed that the Bush administration had carried through a paradigm shift in presidential and media politics. Previously, the media and the administration in power had engaged in a complex courtship ritual with both sides trying to seduce and manipulate the other. The mainstream media needed sources and material, and the administration needed the media to get across its messages. All this had changed with the Bush administration, which viciously attacked any reporters who contested its statements or positions. If a media institution broadcast or published material deemed hostile by the Bush team, their shock troops bombarded the offending institution with e-mails, phones call, and letters, attacking them for exhibiting "bias" against Bush. This helps explain why the mainstream corporate media were so reluctant to contradict Bush campaign distortions and lies and why they did not do more serious investigative reporting into the scandalous backgrounds of Bush and Cheney and the striking failures of their administration. The cowardly mainstream media, for the most part concerned with reputation and profits, mainly submitted to the Bush-Cheney-Rove Gang coercion, and sacrificed their journalistic integrity by rarely refuting their lies except in the mildest possible terms. As a result, few administrations had ever so successfully controlled the media.

The Bush-Cheney campaign unleashed an unparalleled barrage of advertising during the last two weeks of the campaign, especially in the swing states. Although the Democrats appeared to have the most 527 groups supporting them, in the last weeks of the election, Republicans outspent Democrats 3 to 1 on television ads, resulting in a barrage of manipulative ads presenting George W. Bush as the protector of the nation against terrorism and John Kerry as weak on national security.[40] One ad, "Road to Victory," had a confident George W. Bush intoning: "I know what I need to do to run this country," suggesting that Bush could best protect the country. Showing Bush as an ordinary guy with his sleeves rolled up campaigning with his wife Laura, the video evokes Bush's religious faith and ends with the statement: "God bless you all, and may God bless our country." Despite its attempts to stay relentlessly on message and beguile the masses with staged events and television ads, nonetheless, the Bush campaign had to contend with a lot of breaking news stories.

News of current events tended to break in the last two weeks of the election for Kerry. For example, there was a flu vaccine shortage and during the last debate Bush was asked what he would do about the shortage. He answered that he and other healthy people should not get a flu shot. Television showed long lines of seniors day after day waiting for the dwindling numbers of available flu shots, and the Kerry campaign exploited the crisis as emblematic of Bush's failed health program. The Bush bureaucrats provided neither a coherent explanation for the flu shot crisis or any solution.

The *New York Times* broke on October 25 a frightening story indicating that more than 350 tons of deadly explosives had been missing from an Iraqi weapons site that the International Atomic Energy Agency (IAEA) had secured. The IAEA had told the Bush administration that the dangerous explosives were missing but nothing was done to secure them during or after the Iraq invasion.

Senator Kerry immediately began interpreting the fiasco as evidence of another devastating national security failure, since the explosives could be used to attack the United States and its allies anywhere, as well as against U.S. troops in Iraq.[41]

Another disturbing news report had come out two weeks earlier indicating that the IAEA had told the United Nations that nuclear material in Iraq they had secured was now missing because the U.S. occupation authorities had allowed the dangerous material to be stolen and perhaps sold on the nuclear black market.[42] Although Bush claimed to go into Iraq to protect the United States against a WMD attack, his failure to protect the weapons stockpiles in the country only made it more likely that terrorists would get their hands on nuclear material or other dangerous weapons, so Bush's reckless intervention had actually made the world more dangerous and not safer.

A dramatic media spectacle on October 25 focused attention on the Democrats as Bill Clinton triumphantly returned to the campaign trail with John Kerry after recent major heart surgery. More than 100,000 enthusiastic supporters crowded Philadelphia to hear Clinton endorse Kerry and both speak against Bush.[43] Watching Clinton perform on stage before an adoring crowd reminded the country of the relative peace and prosperity of the Clinton years compared with the nightmares of the Bush regime.

The same day of Clinton's triumphant return, there were reports that U.S. Supreme Court Chief Justice William Rehnquist had just been hospitalized for cancer surgery, calling attention to his age and frailty and the fact that perhaps as many as four Supreme Court justices would be replaced during the next presidency. Suddenly, the media began speculating on the effects of a Kerry or Bush presidency on the Supreme Court. Bush had often mentioned that Clarence Thomas was his favorite Supreme Court justice, and there were rumors that he might actually nominate Thomas to replace the ailing Rehnquist and would certainly nominate a string of right-wing activist justices when current members of the Court retired.

A revealing study by the University of Maryland's respected Program on International Policy Attitudes (PIPA) indicated that Bush supporters were ill informed about almost every major issue, including Bush's own positions, and Kerry supporters were relatively well informed. In Molly Ivins' summary:

> In further unhappy evidence of how ill-informed the American people are (blame the media), the Program on International Policy Attitudes found Bush supporters consistently ill-informed about Bush's stands on the issues (Kerry-ans, by contrast, are overwhelmingly right about his positions). Eighty-seven percent of Bush supporters think he favors putting labor and environmental standards into

international trade agreements. Eighty percent of Bush supporters believe Bush wants to participate in the treaty banning landmines. Seventy-six percent of Bush supporters believe Bush wants to participate in the treaty banning nuclear weapons testing. Sixty-two percent believe Bush would participate in the International Criminal Court. Sixty-one percent believe Bush wants to participate in the Kyoto Treaty on global warming. Fifty-three percent do not believe Bush is building a missile defense system, a.k.a. "Star Wars."

The only two Bush stands the majority of his supporters got right were on increasing defense spending and who should write the new Iraqi constitution.

Kerry supporters, by contrast, know their man on seven out of eight issues, with only 43 percent understanding he wants to keep defense spending the same but change how the money is spent, and 57 percent believing he wants to up it.[44]

Obviously, decades of right-wing media from the Fox television network, Rush Limbaugh and a bevy of other conservative talk radio hosts, a strong right-wing Internet presence, and extensive print media had produced a conservative propaganda machine that had influenced scores of people to continue to support George W. Bush (see Brock 2004).

Would "reality" intrude and wake up a majority of U.S. voters? Economic indicators were not going well for Bush as oil prices rose, stock prices fell, and anxiety about jobs, health care, and Social Security accordingly increased, focusing attention on the domestic issues in the campaign. Television news showed nightly pictures of people desperately trying to find the flu vaccine, with scores of elders traveling to Mexico or Canada to get an inoculation. In addition, Iraq looked increasingly out of control as discussions of the missing explosives intensified, Iraqi Prime Minister Allawi accused the U.S.-led forces of "gross negligence" in allowing the massacre of 49 Iraqi National Guardsmen by insurgents, and the highly respected leader of CARE in Iraq was kidnapped, threatened with beheading, and eventually executed.

There were also serious concerns over Republican attempts to suppress Democratic votes in key battleground states. The Democrats had gone all out on a voter registration campaign, and Republicans were claiming that there were many fraudulent registration forms and that they would challenge these votes and any provisional ballots on election day, creating the specter of another hung and perhaps stolen election. Reports surfaced that thousands of Republican operatives would challenge newly registered voters (mostly people of color) in Ohio. On October 27, *BBC Newsnight* reporter Greg Palast released an insider document from Bush campaign headquarters in Florida "suggesting a plan—possibly in violation of U.S. law—to disrupt voting in the state's African-American voting districts."[45]

There were deep concerns about whether computer voting machines would function reliably and whether they would be vulnerable to hacking.[46] The first time that the new touch-screen voting machines were tested, many manufactured by Diebold, whose president had promised he'd help deliver Ohio to Bush, the machines had malfunctioned and there were serious worries of computer fraud.[47] Citizens who had voted early worried about whether their vote would be counted. There was a report that a Republican-connected voter registration company called Voter Outreach of America, run by former chair of the Arizona Republican Party Nathan Sproul, had signed up new voters but thrown away Democratic registration cards. Several employees reported that it was clear that the company largely wanted to recruit Republican voters; one former worker showed the media torn-up Democratic registration cards that he claimed he had seen fellow staff throw away.[48] Obviously, large numbers of voters were intensely interested in the election, both sides were becoming increasing impassioned, and both sides had teams of lawyers ready. Hence, in a close election there might be litigation on a scale perhaps never before seen. The United States was deeply divided and it appeared that neither side would be likely to give up without a fight.

Kerry continued to hammer Bush on the missing explosives in Iraq and when Bush finally addressed the issue after two days of silence, he accused Kerry of making "wild charges" and "denigrating the actions" of troops in the field. Kerry said in response that U.S. troops were performing admirably and that it was the commander in chief who was not up to his job. In a real zinger, Kerry stated: "I'm going to apply the Bush standard to this. Yesterday, George Bush said, and I quote him: 'A political candidate who jumps to conclusions without knowing the facts is not a person you want as your commander in chief when it comes to your security.' Well, Mr. President, I agree with you!" Revealing disarray in the Bush camp, former New York City Mayor Rudolph W. Giuliani stated in an NBC debate with John Edwards: "No matter how you try to blame it on the president, the actual responsibility for it really would be for the troops that were there. Did they search carefully enough or didn't they search carefully enough? We don't know." Edwards quickly responded: "Let me say this very carefully on behalf of John Kerry and myself. Our men and women in uniform did their job. George Bush didn't do his job." This exchange happened at the same time Bush was attacking Kerry for blaming the troops and Kerry quickly responded that he was blaming the Bush administration, not the troops, for failing to protect the explosives, while an off-message Giuliani put the blame on the troops.

Bush, Cheney, and the right-wing spin apparatus continued to take the offensive against Kerry's speaking out on the missing Iraq explosives, insisting that they may have been stolen before the U.S. invasion. Dick Cheney insisted that Kerry was just "dead wrong" and didn't know the "facts," claiming: "Before our guys even arrived on the scene … upwards of 125 tons had been removed." Shortly afterward, ABC video footage showed U.S. troops arriving on the scene days after the invasion with the weapons intact—therefore it was Cheney who was dead wrong. The ABC video showed a huge supply of explosives still at the contested site nine days after the fall of Saddam Hussein, apparently including some sealed earlier by the IAEA. The Pentagon tried to defend the president with a satellite photo of trucks supposedly parked in the site from which the explosives had disappeared, but, in an error that echoed those in Colin Powell's war brief to the United Nations, the picture showed the wrong bunkers.[49]

In more embarrassing mishaps, the Bush-Cheney campaign released a television ad titled "Whatever It Takes," showing Bush surrounded by adoring troops. But a blogger quickly recognized digital manipulation of an image of soldiers surrounding the commander in chief and compared the Bush ad images with the original photo, and the Bush campaign had to admit to enhancing the image with Photoshop. The Republicans tried to counter any momentum Kerry got out of Boston's World Series victory by announcing that Red Sox pitcher Curt Schilling would campaign with Bush. Schilling backed out at the last moment, allegedly on "doctor's orders." When songwriter and performer John Hall complained about the Bush campaign's exploitation of his song "Still the One" because of his opposition to Bush, the Bush team was forced to apologize and promise not to play it anymore.

On October 26, Bush headed to Columbus, Ohio, to appear with actor-politician Arnold Schwarzenegger. But the Arnold event was overshadowed by the appearance of a video from Osama bin Laden, who had not been heard from for months and who was rumored to be badly injured or even dead. A calm bin Laden slowly read a long speech in an 18-minute video attacking both Kerry and Bush, demonstrating that it was a recent tape, and mocking Bush for reading a goat story on September 11 after the first plane attacked the Twin Towers, suggesting bin Laden may have seen Michael Moore's *Fahrenheit 9/11* film. Insulting Bush, who had repeatedly contrasted terrorism versus freedom in his claims that Al Qaeda was attacking U.S. freedom, bin Laden countered: "I say to you that security is an important pillar of human life, and that free persons do not neglect their own security, contrary to the allegations of Bush that we despise liberty. He should let us know why we did not strike at Sweden, for instance (if that were true). . . . We only waged battle with you because we are free persons, and we cannot sleep knowing that injustice is being done. We want to regain freedom for our nation. As you damage our security, we will damage yours."

Bin Laden continued:

We found no difficulties in dealing with the Bush administration, because of the similarities of that administration and the regimes in our countries, half of which are run by the military and half of which are run by monarchs. And our experience is vast with them.

And those two kinds are full of arrogance and taking money illegally.

The resemblance started when Bush, the father, visited the area, when some of our own were impressed by America and were hoping that the visits would affect and influence our countries.

Then, what happened was that he was impressed by the monarchies and the military regimes, and he was jealous of them staying in power for tens of years, embezzling the public money without any accountability. And he moved the tyranny and suppression of freedom to his own country, and they called it the Patriot Act, under the disguise of fighting terrorism. And Bush, the father, found it good to install his children as governors and leaders.[50]

Admitting for the first time his complicity in the 9/11 attacks, bin Laden claimed that they were first inspired by the 1982 Israeli invasion of Lebanon in which towers and buildings in Beirut were destroyed in the siege of the capital. "While I was looking at these destroyed towers in Lebanon, it sparked in my mind that the tyrant should be punished with the same and that we should destroy towers in America, so that it tastes what we taste and would be deterred from killing our children and women." Obviously, bin Laden timed the release of his video to get maximum coverage before the U.S. election; it was not clear which candidate his video would help or hurt, but both sides were unnerved by the release and the possibility of an attack that could disrupt the election.

Both Bush and Kerry strongly denounced bin Laden, stressed that Americans were united against him, and resolved to destroy Al Qaeda. The next day, Kerry went on the attack again, condemning Bush for missing an opportunity to let bin Laden get away at Tora Bora. Bush responded by lambasting Kerry's remarks as "shameful." The bin Laden spectacle overshadowed other stories, such as news that the FBI was investigating possible violations of military procurement rules by the Pentagon when it awarded Halliburton the five-year no-bid contracts to repair oil fields in Iraq. John Edwards quickly seized on the news and told a cheering crowd in Iowa: "You cannot stand with Halliburton, big oil companies, and the Saudi royal family and still stand up for the American people." But with the specter of bin Laden again haunting the mediascape, complex issues were generally avoided in the mainstream media during the last days of the election campaign.

One of the peculiar features of the election was the growing cult of Bush among the faithful. "Ashley's Story," one of the most widely circulated Bush ads, featured an Ohio teenager whose mother was killed in the World Trade Center attacks. Produced by the right-wing group Progress for America Voter Fund, the young girl in the ad says of Bush, "He's the most powerful man in the world, and all he wants to do is make sure I'm safe, that I'm OK." The frame slides to a shot of Bush hugging the girl and then to a close-up of Bush. According to Eric Boehlert, the ad tested well, bringing some audiences to tears, and "was backed by the most expensive TV ad buy of the campaign, which blanketed nine states—Ohio, Florida, Pennsylvania, Iowa, New Mexico, Nevada, Minnesota, Wisconsin, and Missouri—and both network and cable channels at a cost of $14.2 million."[51]

Ryan Lizza provided a frightening description of the Bush cult:

Inside Columbus's Nationwide Arena, Bush's 20,000-strong crowd seemed re-energized. They roared with approval at all the cult-of-personality stimuli that mark a Bush campaign event in these final days. A four-person African-American a cappella group warmed up the crowd with a song in which the word "love" was replaced with the word "George":

George!
So many people use your name in vain
George!
Those who have faith in you sometimes go astray
George!
Through all the ups and downs, the joys and hurts
George!
For better or worse I still will choose you first
At first you didn't mean that much to me
But now I know that you're all I need
The world looks so brand new to me
Now that I found George
Everyday I live for you
And everything that I do
I do it for you

As they sang, a group of clean-cut white kids marched into the stands. They wore black athletic shorts and red shirts emblazoned with the letter W and sat down in a pattern that formed a giant scarlet W in the stands. Up on the Jumbotron, a rock-video-style short film opened with quick cuts of various GOP all-stars shouting Bush's name. "George W. Bush!" said Jeb Bush. "George W. Bush!" said Laura Bush. "Viva Bush!" said George P. Bush. After the film, one side of the arena shouted "B-U" and the other side returned "S-H." When Arnold Schwarzenegger and Bush arrived, the crowd cheered for seven minutes straight.[52]

The Cult of Bush had arrived. There were masses of people who simply adored Bush. He had achieved rock star status among the faithful, although he was held in contempt by those who opposed him. Bush's religious and conservative code words in his speeches resonated deeply with the Republican faithful who had bonded deeply with him. Perhaps these crowds also identified with Bush's plain folks aura and loved him because he was one of them, a conservative Christian, plain spoken and not articulate, and for his audiences simple and direct. Impervious to criticisms of his lies and defects, his band of followers wrote off these criticisms as stemming from the liberal media, intellectual elite, or Hollywood types, whom they held in contempt. True Bush believers thus constituted a Body of the Faithful who responded to Bush with Groupthink, unwavering devotion, and total submission.

For months preceding the election, Fox News had helped produce the Cult of Bush by adoringly presenting him day by day as a great national leader. His every appearance was welcomed with excitement. The documentary *Outfoxed* examined how Fox executives passed memos to their news teams about how to hype Bush and attack Kerry, a propaganda campaign coordinated with the Republicans. In the same film, Vermont Congressman Bernie Sanders explained how since the Reagan years, the Republicans' political operatives would send a "message of the day" to friendly media so that on any given day the Republican message would get out via print, broadcasting, and word of mouth.[53] The Republican echo chamber had been finely tuned for the election and their attack machine savaged Kerry and deified Bush.

As the election neared, the question would be whether the Bush Faithful would outnumber Kerry voters and, in particular, how new voters, younger ones, and minorities would vote. Voting participation for 18–24 year olds had precipitously declined in recent years and many groups had attempted to mobilize youth. Bruce Springsteen had organized a well-publicized tour, caught in the documentary *National Anthem*, to get out the youth vote and had campaigned for Kerry. Springsteen, who had never previously ventured into partisan politics, wrote in an opinion piece for the *New York Times* that the war was his paramount reason for joining "Vote for Change," stating "the Bush administration dived headlong into an unnecessary war in Iraq ... offering up the lives of our young men and women under circumstances that are now discredited."[54] On October 30, Springsteen campaigned with Kerry in Madison, Wisconsin, and Columbus, Ohio, drawing enormous crowds and getting saturation media coverage. Kerry quipped that Bush supporters had heard that "The Boss" was campaigning for him and they thought it referred to Dick Cheney. To an adoring crowd, Springsteen quietly strummed his guitar and spoke from his heart: "As a songwriter, I've written about America for 30 years. I've tried to write about who we are, what we stand for, what we pray for, and I believe that these essential ideas of American identity are what's at stake on November 2."

Republicans countered Springsteen's "Vote for Change" tour by sending an 18-wheeler called "Reggie the Registration Rig" to NASCAR races and state fairs, claiming that such efforts helped register more than 3 million new voters. MTV continued its "Rock the Vote" project to get out the youth vote. P. Diddy's "Vote or Die" project, "Music for America," and other groups went on music tours aimed at increasing young voters and in some cases supporting Kerry. "Music for America" bypassed big names and venues in favor of trying to reach potential voters who attend smaller club shows. "Redeem the Vote" used Christian musicians to get out the evangelical vote for Bush. The nonpartisan "Your Country, Your Vote" enlisted musicians such as Ricky Skaggs to get country music fans registered. "PunkVoter," an anti-Bush group, organized concerts nationwide, and "Smackdown Your Vote!" a nonpartisan project of World Wrestling Entertainment, attempted to reach wrestling fans under age 30. Another nonpartisan voter registration outfit, "HeadCount," was tailored to the tastes of those who follow jam bands such as Phish and The Dead.[55] Jim Hightower, Harold Meyerson, and others were optimistic that Kerry was going to win because of all the progressive groups mobilizing against Bush.[56] But there were also major get-out-the-vote efforts by the Republicans and the Christian right, so going into election day, it appeared to be a toss-up.

By the end of the election campaign, the decision depended on the outcome in some 12 battleground states. The last two days of the election "ground war" unfolded with an unprecedented blitz of advertising, armies walking neighborhoods knocking on doors, telephone banks ringing out messages, including a barrage of Bill Clinton messages for John Kerry and Boston Red Sox pitcher Curt Schilling for Bush (although the owners and many of the Red Sox stars appeared in New Hampshire at a Kerry rally), and both candidates made a final trip through key swing states like Ohio and Florida.

Endgame: Internet Euphoria and Television Debacle

> As democracy is perfected, the office of president represents, more and more closely, the inner soul of the people. On some great and glorious day the plain folks of the land will reach their heart's desire at last and the White House will be adorned by a downright moron.
>
> —*H. L. Mencken*

The evening of Election 2004 was déjà vu all over again. In 2000, it looked like it was a Gore win from early election results after Florida and Pennsylvania were called for Gore. In 2004, it looked like a Kerry victory was in the making after exit polls showed Kerry ahead in every swing state. Respected pollster John Zogby called it for Kerry early in the evening, and the respected website http://www.electoral-vote.com, put Kerry ahead 262 to 261. The Bush camp looked dispirited, and Bush himself looked resigned and ready to accept defeat, whereas the Kerry camp was ebullient and the Internet rang with victory predictions for Kerry. On election night 2000 as the television spectacle unfolded, state after state's votes went for Bush and when Florida was switched over to Bush late in the night, it appeared Bush had won the election as several channels declared him the winner. Likewise, in 2004 it looked like Bush was on an election night victory roll as he took state after state, went ahead by 3 million votes in the popular vote, and when NBC called Ohio for Bush it looked like he had the election sown up.

Despite network television flip-flops on election night 2000, both NBC and Fox called the election for Bush. But as in Election 2000, things then appeared to have entered the twilight zone of uncertainty. In 2000, suddenly Florida was deemed too close to call and the election was hung up, taking 36 days of fierce postelection war to resolve. As the Bush team in 2004 prepared its motorcade for a victory celebration and Karl Rove told the networks that Bush had won, John Edwards came out from Kerry headquarters in Boston and in a brief speech declared that they would wait until the next day for a decision, which meant potentially a delay of days since provisional ballots in Ohio cannot be counted for eleven days before they are verified.

Once again it appeared to be a hung election, with both sides gearing up for legal and recount battles and the inevitable surprises. In 2000, there were many statistical anomalies in Florida that suggested there was foul play in the election count, but the Democrats never really pushed this issue and there were no investigations that ever pinned down any major fraud (but see Kellner 2001 for the details). In 2004, however, although Internet sources began discussing the possibility of computer voting fraud and other irregularities in Ohio, Florida, and elsewhere, the issue did not make it into the mainstream media to a significant extent on election night or in the days following.

By the early morning of November 3, it appeared that the Ohio vote was stacked against Kerry, and his camp concluded that he had little chance of prevailing in a count of the provisional ballots. He called Bush to concede and then made a painful concession speech, calling for unity and healing painful wounds. There were reports that John Edwards did not want Kerry to concede and in the aftermath of the election, many believed that Kerry conceded prematurely, eliminating the possibility of at least calling attention to problems with voting machines, voting suppression, potential voter fraud and corruption, and other problems that would need to be addressed if U.S. democracy was to survive.

Notes

1. Dave Moniz and Jim Drinkard, "Questions about Bush's Guard Service Unanswered, *USA Today*, August 25, 2004.

2. David Corn: "Liar: Bush Overstated His Military Record," *Nation*, August 25, 2004.

3. Jeff Horwitz, "'I'm Very Ashamed,'" *Salon*, August 27, 2004.

4. Matt Kelley, "Bush's National Guard File Missing Records That Would Explain Gaps in Service," Associated Press, September 6, 2004.

5. Mary Jacoby, "George W. Bush's Missing Year: The Widow of a Bush Family Confidant Says Her Husband Gave the Future President an Alabama Senate Campaign Job as a Favor to His Worried Father? Did They See Him Do Any National Guard Service? 'Good Lord, No.'" *Salon*, September 2, 2004. Allison had earlier been interviewed by Russ Baker; see his "Why Bush Left Texas," *Nation*, September 28, 2004.

6. For Lechliter's summary, see http://www.nytimes.com/packages/pdf/opinion/lechliter.pdf.

7. Eric Boehlert, "Stung! A Swarm of New Media Stories on Young George W. Bush's Dereliction of Duty Pops His Heroic-Leadership Bubble," *Salon*, September 9, 2004.

8. "Bush Fell Short on Duty at Guard: Records Show Pledges Unmet," *Boston Globe*, September 8, 2004.

9. See Jeffrey St. Clair's multipart series on George W. Bush, "High Plains Grifter," at http://www.counterpunch.org.

10. Kit R. Roane, "The Service Question: A Review of President Bush's Guard Years Raises Issues about the Time He Served," *U.S. News and World Report*, September 20, 2004.

11. Eric Boehlert, "Bad News Doesn't Get Better with Age: The Retired Officer Who Saw Bush National Guard Files in a Trash Can Talks Back as the White House Tries to Discredit Him, and Urges the President to Finally Come Clean," *Salon*, February 14, 2004, at http://www.salon.com/news/feature/2004/02/14/burkett.

12. See Ian Williams, "Kerry Fights Back," *AlterNet*, September 7, 2004. McCellan's father had published a book holding LBJ responsible for the Kennedy assassination. For earlier accounts of Bush's lost years and allegations of heavy drug and alcohol use, see Hatfield (2000); Moore and Slater (2004).

13. *60 Minutes* text at http://www.CBSnews.com/stories/2004/09/08/60II/main641984.shtml.

14. See Duboise and Ivins (2000); Hatfield (2000); Kelley (2004); Phillips (2004); and St. Clair (2004).

15. "CBS Stands By Bush Guard Memos," September 22, 2004, at CBSNews.com.

16. McAuliffe is cited in "Amid Skepticism, CBS Sticks to Bush Guard Story," *Los Angeles Times*, September 11, 2004, pp. A1 and A18.

17. Michael Dobbs and Howard Kurtz, "Expert Cited by CBS Says He Didn't Authenticate Papers," *Washington Post*, September 14, 2004, p. A08.

18. Howard Kurtz, "Document Experts Say CBS Ignored Memo 'Red Flags,'" *Washington Post*, September 15, 2004, p. A10. Kurtz's hatchet job on CBS ignores the evidence that affirmed the content of the CBS story, if not the authenticity of the memos. Kurtz did not, in fact, cite the *New York Times* or *Los Angeles Times* stories that interviewed Killian's secretary in his news summary of the major stories of the day, either a sign of his incompetence or part of an ABC/*Washington Post*/Disney campaign to discredit their media rival.

19. "Memos on Bush Are Fake but Accurate, Typist Says," *New York Times*, September 15, 2004.

20. Maureen Dowd, "Pre-emptive Paranoia," *New York Times*, September 16, 2004.

21. "In the Rush for a Scoop, CBS Found Trouble Fast," *Los Angeles Times*, September 17, 2004.

22. Chris Sullentrop, "Scenes from Spin Alley: Karl Rove, Mike McCurry, and Other Surrogates Score the Debate," *Slate*, September 30, 2004, at http://slate.msn.com/id/2107516.

23. Steven Rosenfeld and Jan Frel, "Father Kerry versus Boy George," *AlterNet*, October 1, 2004.

24. Richard Reeves, "The President Has 'Ovalitis,'" October 2, 2004, at http://story.news.yahoo.com/news?tmpl=storyandu=/ucrr/20041002/cm_ucrr/thepresidenthasovalitisande=4.

25. Tony Karon, "Reality Check: George Bush," *Time*, October 1, 2004, at http://www.time.com/time/election2004/article/0,18471,703924,00.html.

26. See Mike Allen and Dana Priest, "Report Discounts Iraq Arms Threat," *Washington Post*, October 6, 2004, p. A01.

27. Michael Gordon, "Catastrophic Success: Poor Intelligence Misled Troops about Risk of Drawn-Out War," *New York Times*, October 20, 2004.

28. See Bob Somerby, "Did Welch Make a Call? We Wondered If NBC's Coverage Was Fixed—Watching CNN, Shafter Asked the Same Thing," http://www.dailyhowler.com/index.shtml. *Slate*'s media critic Jack Shafter raised similar criticism of CNN's calling the debate for Cheney.

29. Douglas Jehl, "U.S. Report Finds Iraq Was Minimal Weapons Threat in '03," *New York Times*, October 6, 2004.

30. See the running commentary and critique of Schieffer's debate questions on the October 13, 2004, *American Prospect* weblog "Tapped," at www.prospect.org/weblog. See also Bob Somerby's systematic critique of Schieffer, "The Bias Bob Schieffer Chokes Down Tonight May Not be the Liberal Variety," October 13, 2004, and "Is a Vote for

Kerry a Sin? And Did Schieffer Show What Friends Are For?" October 14, 2004, at http://www.dailyhowler.com/archives-2004.shtml.

31. John Reynolds, "Bush Blows Debate: Talks to Rove in Earpiece!" at http://bellaciao.org/en/article.php3?id_article=3562.

32. See Mike Allen, "Bulge under President's Coat in First Debate Stirs Speculation," *Washington Post,* October 9, 2004, p. A16.

33. Farhad Manjoo, "The Bulge Returns: As This Screen Shot from the Wednesday Night Debate Indicates, the Bush Mystery Will Not Disappear," *Salon,* October 13, 2004, at http://www.salon.com/news/feature/2004/10/13/bulgefoto/print.html. Tongue partly in cheek, Manjoo noted: "*Salon* looked hard for evidence of the president's mystery bulge this evening, but for much of the debate, on the ABC feed we screened, Bush's back remained out of view. At the end, though, as the president crossed the stage to thank his opponent, we caught this glimpse of something strange pushing out of the commander in chief's tailored coat. Is it part of an in-ear prompting device? Is it a back brace? Body armor? Confirmation that Bush is an alien? The mystery deepens." (Earlier in the day, trying to make light of the whole affair, a Bush spokesman had said jokingly that the pictures of Bush's humped back and mysterious bulge reveals that Bush is an alien.)

34. Dave Lindoff, "At Each Ear a Hearer: Bulletin on the Bush Bulge," *Counterpunch,* October 18, 2004, at http://www.counterpunch.org/lindorff10182004.html.

35. Dan Froomkin, "Bush Tackles the 'Bulge,'" *Washington Post,* October 26, 2004.

36. Kevin Berger, "NASA Photo Analyst: Bush Wore a Device during Debate—Physicist Says Imaging Techniques Prove the President's Bulge Was Not Caused by Wrinkled Clothing," *Salon,* October 29, 2004. In "Battle of the Bulge," Dennis Romero interviewed the physicist, in which Nelson reiterated his conviction that Bush wore a radio transmission device during the debates and told how both the *Los Angeles Times* and *New York Times* refused to take the story (*CityBeat,* November 4–10, 2004, p. 8). Romero speculates that both politicians and media personnel use radio devices themselves and did not want to call attention to the phenomenon.

37. "The Last Word on Bush's Bulge," *The Hill,* November 4, 2004, at http://www.hillnews.com/under_dome/110404.aspx. Dave Lindorff points out that the Secret Service rarely comments on security issues and, in any case, there is no bulletproof armor on the market that exhibits the peculiar bulge in Bush's back. See "*The Hill:* Taking a Leak on Bush's Bulge," November 10, 2004, at www.counterpunch.com.

38. See also a whole gallery of "wired Bush" photos with commentary at http://www.visualfuturist.com/bushiswired.

39. Ryan Lizza, "Backward," *New Republic,* November 1, 2004.

40. David M. Halbfinger and Jim Rutenberg, "Frantic Presidential Race Ends with a Flood of Ads," *New York Times,* November 1, 2004. According to a study by the Center for Public Integrity, the Republicans' huge television spending spree during the last three weeks of the election totaled $6.5 million, more than the spending of all the Democratic independent groups during that period put together.

41. See James Glanz, William J. Broad, and David E. Sanger, "Huge Cache of Explosives Vanished from Site in Iraq," *New York Times,* October 25, 2004; and Terence Neilan,

"Kerry Says Missing Explosives in Iraq Illustrate Bush's Failures," *New York Times*, October 25, 2004.

42. See Ian Traynor, "Nuclear Materials from Iraq 'Missing,'" *Guardian*, October 13, 2004.

43. Maria Newman, "Clinton Gets Rock Star's Welcome at Rally in Philadelphia," *New York Times*, October 25, 2004.

44. Molly Ivins, "Clueless People Love Bush," October 27, 2004, at http://www.smirkingchimp.com/print.php?sid=18432.

45. See Greg Palast's home page for information on computer voting fraud at http://www.gregpalast.com.

46. See, for example, the material assembled at http://www.ejfi.org/Voting/Voting-1.htm.

47. On Diebold voting machines and the possibility of computer voting fraud, see Bev Harris' site at http://www.blackboxvoting.org and another project at http://www.blackboxvoting.com.

48. Richard Serrano and Ralph Vartabedian, "Signs of Voter Fraud Appear," *Los Angeles Times*, October 27, 2004, p. A01.

49. Mark Mazzetti, "Soldiers Describe Looting of Explosives," *Los Angeles Times*, November 4, 2004. This story documented how U.S. soldiers observed Iraqi looters loading powerful explosives from the Al Qaqaa site into pick-up trucks and driving them away.

50. Transcript of Osama bin Laden speech at http://www2.cnn.com/2004/WORLD/meast/10/29/bin.laden.transcript.

51. Eric Boehlert, "The TV Ad That Put Bush over the Top," *Salon*, November 5, 2004.

52. Ryan Lizza, *New Republic Online*, October 30, 2004, at http://www.tnr.com/docprint.mhtml?i=express&s=lizza103004.

53. The strategy of framing a "message of the day" and then sending it out to the party apparatus, friendly media, and targeted spokespeople began in the Reagan administration and is described in Hertsgaard (1988), and Kellner (1990); it has been followed by every administration since then.

54. "Chords for Change," *New York Times*, August 5, 2004.

55. Thanks to Linda Furto for providing the information and references of popular culture groups and campaign projects. See also HeadCount at http://www.headcount.org; Music for America at http://www.musicforamerica.org; PunkVoter at http://www.punkvoter.com; "Redeem the Vote" at www.redeemthevote.com; "Smackdown Your Vote!" at http://vote.wwe.com; and "Your Country, Your Vote" at http://www.yourcountryyourvote.org.

56. See Harold Meyerson, "The Tsunami," *LA Weekly*, October 29–November 4, 2004; and Jim Hightower, "Happy Days Are Here Again!" *Salon*, October 29, 2004.

Conclusion

Salvaging Democracy after Election 2004

> Morality, thou deadly bane, thy tens o' thousands thou has slain.
>
> —*Robert Burns*

> I feel—I feel it is necessary to move an agenda that I told the American people I would move. Something refreshing about coming off an election, even more refreshing since we all got some sleep last night, but there's—you go out and you make your case, and you tell the people this is what I intend to do… Let me put it to you this way: I earned capital in the campaign, political capital, and now I intend to spend it. It is my style.
>
> —*George W. Bush November 4, 2004*

SHORTLY AFTER KERRY'S CONCESSION ON NOVEMBER 3, Bush and Cheney assembled their faithful for a victory celebration. Cheney predictably crowed about a "mandate," making it clear the Republicans would continue and intensify the extreme right-wing politics of the past four years. Bush smirked about a "historic victory" and then made conciliatory comments about unity and reaching "out to the whole nation," but it was clear that this was empty rhetoric. Bush had voiced similar sentiments after the election theft of 2000 and quickly went on to push a hard-right agenda and end up as the most divisive U.S. president in recent memory.

The disunion of the country has become increasingly intense because the Bush administration governs in part through a politics of division and never before has there been such polarizing media, ranging from Fox Television and right-wing talk radio stations on the right to Pacifica Radio, Air America, and a

213

resurgence of progressive documentary films on the left, and the Internet blazing with many different constituencies. Bush governs by dividing and conquering, bringing over conservative members of the other party to go along with his right-wing politics, so there is little possibility of healing and the likelihood of ever greater and deeper wounds in the body politic as the inevitable conflicts of the second Bush administration , some of which I signal below, unfold.

On March 10, 2004, when speaking to AFL-CIO union workers in Chicago, John Kerry said in what he thought was an off-mike comment: "Let me tell you—we're just beginning to fight here. These guys are the most crooked, lying group of people I've ever seen." Although Kerry was savaged by the Republican attack apparatus for this comment, in retrospect, he was quite correct. It is well documented that the Bush-Cheney administration has governed with lies and deception (Conason 2003; Corn 2003; Dean 2004; Waldman 2004). As Chapters 5 and 6 indicated, Big, Bold, and Brazen Lies characterized the distinctive discourse and strategy of the Bush-Cheney 2004 campaign.

In a *New York Times* op-ed piece, "The Dishonesty Thing," Paul Krugman wrote that the key election issue was a "pattern of lies... on policy issues, from global warming to the war in Iraq." Krugman recounts how years ago when he began questioning Bush administration figures on tax cuts, the deficit, and other economic issues, he and other critics were denounced as "shrill." Citing a variety of establishment economic figures and reports, Krugman says that these documents reveal that he and other Bush critics were right and that the Bush administration was lying about their economic policies, using "fuzzy math" and fake figures to clothe the dubious results of their policies. Worrying that Bush's economic policies might create a disaster and that so far the Bush administration has not begun to indicate solutions for economic problems they've created, such as the skyrocketing deficit, Krugman concluded: "Some not usually shrill people think that Mr. Bush will simply refuse to face reality until it comes crashing in: Paul Volcker, the former Federal Reserve chairman, says there's a 75 percent chance of a financial crisis in the next five years. Nobody knows what Mr. Bush would really do about taxes and spending in a second term. What we do know is that on this, as on many matters, he won't tell the truth."[1]

For Bob Herbert of the *New York Times*, Bush's Big Lie was the war on Iraq, a disastrous policy that had now killed more than 1,000 young Americans and placed the United States in a Vietnamesque quagmire. Seething with anger, Herbert cited the previous day's *Times*, which published photos of the first 1,000 who died: "They were sent off by a president who ran and hid when he was a young man and his country was at war. They fought bravely and died honorably. But as in Vietnam, no amount of valor or heroism can conceal the fact that they were sent off under false pretenses to fight a war that is unwinnable. How many thousands more will have to die before we acknowledge that President Bush's obsession with Iraq and Saddam Hussein has been a catastrophe for the United States?"[2]

In retrospect, the smears on Kerry by the Republican attack apparatus and Bush-Cheney's systematic lying throughout the campaign represent a low point in U.S. electoral politics. The studies in this book suggest that the conjuncture of media spectacle, which has colonized U.S. culture with a politics of lying, has produced a crisis of democracy in the United States. I suggest that three convergent trends have seriously undermined U.S. democracy: the corporate control of mainstream media, which biases dominant media toward conservativism and profit; an implosion of information and entertainment and rise of a culture of media spectacle, which makes politics a form of entertainment and spectacle; and the rise of a right-wing Republican media propaganda and attack apparatus, which systematically deploys lies and deception to advance the agenda of conservative groups and interests. In conclusion, I want to suggest the depth of the current crisis and offer some proposals for solutions.

Divided Country

> In your re-election, God has graciously granted America—though she doesn't deserve it—a reprieve from the agenda of paganism. You have been given a mandate. We the people expect your voice to be like the clear and certain sound of a trumpet. Because you seek the Lord daily, we who know the Lord will follow that kind of voice eagerly. Don't equivocate. Put your agenda on the front burner *and let it boil.* You owe the liberals nothing. They despise you because they despise your Christ. Honor the Lord, and He will honor you.
>
> —Bob Jones III, president of Bob Jones University

Once again in the 2004 elections, the country was deeply divided according to gender, race, region, ideology, religion, and age. According to the first round of election exit polls, turnout vastly increased among African Americans, with almost 90 percent of them voting for Kerry as they did for Gore. Latinos also increased their turnout, with 54 percent of the Hispanic votes going for Kerry, down about 10 percent from Gore's total. As 55 percent of Asian American voters chose Kerry, 75 percent of Jewish voters went for the Democrat. Women voted for Kerry approximately 53 to 47 percent, a loss from Gore's 10 percent advantage, although 62 percent of unmarried women voted for Kerry. More than 60 percent of the newly registered voters chose Kerry, who won 54 percent of the youth vote in the 18–24 age range. Those concerned about the economy voted overwhelmingly for Kerry, as did those citing the war in Iraq as a key issue. And 60 percent of urban voters opted for Kerry, down from the 71 percent who voted for Gore.[3]

Bush won a large percentage of white male votes, with 61 percent of them voting for him. He also won rural voters, Protestant voters, and 54 percent of Catholic voters, when for the first time a majority of Catholics voted Republican. Of the 45 percent of voters who earn less than $50,000 a year, Kerry won 56 percent to 43 percent, but of the 18 percent who earn above $100,000 a year, 57 percent voted for Bush. Gays and lesbians went for Kerry 77 percent to 23 percent. Gun owners voted for Bush 61 percent to 37 percent. Perhaps the major surprise of the election was how many voters surveyed said that values were more important to them than terrorism, Iraq, the economy, health care, or the other issues focused on largely by the Democrats. One survey indicated that one out of five voters interviewed in exit polls claimed that morality was their major issue, and more than 80 percent of these voters chose Bush.

It appears that issues of reproductive rights, gay marriage, and stem-cell research so incensed conservatives that they voted for Bush even against their own economic interests. The spectacles of gay marriage, so-called partial-birth abortion, and Bush's "sanctity of life" orientation obviously motivated Republican voters. Anti–gay marriage initiatives were put on 11 state ballots and this issue helped to mobilize large numbers of pro-Bush voters. There were reports that evangelical churches prepared voting literature for churchgoers, that pastors came out strongly for Bush in sermons, and that entire congregations went en masse to vote for Bush. Likewise, conservative "pro-life" Catholic bishops wrote letters to their parishioners articulating anti-Kerry and pro-Bush positions. Thus, below the media radar, there was something like religious revivalism that turned out the Christian right for Bush.

It also seems that Bush's anti-intellectualism was extremely potent with many people, who identified with his "plain folks" aura and saw Kerry as an aristocratic intellectual. So, once again, people's perceived image of the president influenced their voting behavior. It also appears that 9/11 was a powerful bonding experience between Bush and his supporters, who at one time constituted much more than half of the population after 9/11. It seems that many of these supporters stuck with him through problems of the economy, exposures of Bush's blunders on 9/11, Iraq, poor debate performances, and other issues that mobilized about half of the voters strongly against Bush.

Later polls and analyses indicated that the so-called values issue was exaggerated in initial election retrospectives and that fear of terrorism was the most

potent electoral issue.[4] The Bush-Cheney campaign successfully played on voters' fears of terrorism and liberal social change, at the same time appealing to
conservative and religious values. The right-wing media apparatus, which presented powerfully positive images of Bush and negative images of Kerry, was of
decisive importance in winning what appeared to be a Bush-Cheney popular
vote majority and narrow Electoral College victory. It's no real mystery how
large numbers of voters went for the Republicans with right-wing propaganda
going 24/7 on Fox TV (and its NBC soft-core versions), ubiquitous talk radio,
a global Murdoch media apparatus, and a powerful right-wing Internet sector
supported by conservative think tanks, book publishers, and periodicals.

Hard-core Bush supporters were impervious to reason and argumentation.
They believed in Bush and had deep faith in him, and reviled Democrats and
the "liberal media." When the 9/11 Commission report came out questioning
ties between Al Qaeda and Iraq in the 9/11 attack, the Republican spin machine and their followers read it as confirming that Iraq was involved in 9/11
and that Iraq and Al Qaeda were interconnected. When the Duelfer report was
released indicating that there really were no "weapons of mass destruction" in
Iraq, Bush and his followers came out and said that the report indicated there
were weapons of mass destruction. When Dick Cheney was asked if he still
believed that there were connections between Iraq and Al Qaeda in 9/11, he
claimed that he'd never made such an allegation, whereas there were sound
bytes and print sources indicating he had many times (see Chapter 6).

No matter, truth and reason had little purchase on true Bush believers. They
had decided in advance that whatever Kerry and the Democrats said was a
personal attack on the president. Many of the faithful were also immune to
critical media reports, which they took as "liberal media" attacks against Bush
and accordingly disregarded them, getting their opinions and information instead from Fox TV, talk radio, or "politically correct" right-wing sources.

Bush believers had all the traits of the "authoritarian personality" dissected
by T. W. Adorno and his colleagues (1950): deeply dualistic thought patterns
that divided the world into good and evil, and us and them. Such personality
types project "evil" onto their opponents and believe themselves to be "good."
Like classic authoritarian personality types, many on the right are consumed
with rage and scapegoat targets like liberals, feminists, gays, or other objects of
their anger rather than seeing sociopolitical causes and solutions. Like Bush,
his followers wanted simple explanations and solutions to complex situations
and eschewed nuance. Bush's true believers were highly conformist, following
the words and deeds of their leader, flip-flopping thongs at the Republican
Convention or Bush events and chanting the slogans of the moment en masse.

Immersed in crowd behavior, these followers were incapable of critical thought or seeing the flaws of their beloved leader.

A shocking survey that I mentioned in Chapter 6 indicated that Bush supporters were deeply uninformed, even on Bush's record, whereas Kerry supporters generally knew what issues he stood for. A CBS demographic map shown the day after the election revealed that almost every major urban area in the country voted for Kerry, as did university and college towns like Austin, Texas; Raleigh, North Carolina; and Iowa City, Iowa, but many rural areas went for Bush, providing fuel for those who like to distinguish between "metro" and "retro" America. The retro folks evidently dislike intellectuals and "elitists," voting for a man whom they perceived embodied their "down-home values."

The left-liberal cultural initiative to turn out young voters seemed to have mixed results. A massive turnout among young voters was supposed to favor Kerry. Exit polls showed that young voters, aged 18–29, favored Kerry by 12 points, a margin of 8 more points than Al Gore over Bush four years ago. In the final analysis, youth voters chose Kerry 54 percent over 46 percent for Bush. In a misleading election night story suggesting that the get-out-the-youth-vote efforts had failed, the Associated Press reported that "fewer than one in 10 voters Tuesday were 18 to 24, about the same proportion of the electorate as in 2000, exit polls indicated." In fact, many more young voters turned out, but so did other sectors of the population.

Later surveys showed that more than 20 million Americans younger than 30 voted, resulting in a 51.6 percent turnout for the group, a 9-point increase and significantly higher turnout than previous elections. In some battleground states, youth turnout was as high as 65 percent, and television showed pictures of young people waiting in line for hours to vote.[5] Thus the 527 organizations such as moveon.org, all the anti-Bush documentary films, the Bruce Springsteen Vote for Change concert, P. Diddy's Vote or Die campaign, Rock the Vote, Choose or Lose, and the other campaigns definitely had an impact, although not the one desired by some who organized them. There were also cadres of young Republicans and conservatives, and church groups also took their young voters en masse to vote for Bush.

Perhaps the most overblown division, however, concerned the alleged rift between red and blue states. The entire southern region of the country appeared to be firmly Republican and conservative, and the Northeast and West Coast seemed to be strongly liberal and democratic. But the so-called swing states are themselves deeply divided, as are some of the "red" and "blue" states. Hence, although there are significant regional divides between conservativism and liberalism, it is misleading to simply characterize the deep divisions in U.S.

culture as those between "red" and "blue" states, as many media commentators are wont to do.

Another myth of the election was that Bush and the Republicans had received a "mandate" to govern, a myth pushed by the corporate media as well as the Republicans. Although Bush had won more votes than any presidential candidate in U.S. history, Kerry won the second-highest number of votes and never before had so many people voted against a presidential candidate as voted against Bush. The Republicans mobilized their troops, but so did the Democrats and the results were a record turnout from a highly divided country.

Indeed, well-respected surveys by the Chicago Council on Foreign Relations (CCFR) confirmed what many surveys had shown over the years, documenting the extent to which overwhelming majorities of U.S. citizens favored strengthening health care, education, and Social Security. Many surveys also showed that strong majorities favored women's right to choose and gay and lesbian rights (if not gay marriage). The CCFR surveys also revealed that a large majority of the U.S. public believes that the United States should join the International Criminal Court and World Court, sign the Kyoto Protocols, allow the United Nations to take the lead in world crises, and rely more on diplomatic and economic measures than military ones in the "war on terror." Majorities also believe that the United States should resort to force only when "there is strong evidence that the country is in imminent danger of being attacked," thus rejecting the Bush doctrine of "preemptive war."

On Iraq, the University of Maryland Program on International Policy Attitudes (PIPA) survey indicated on the eve of Election 2004 that "three quarters of Americans say that the United States should not have gone to war if Iraq did not have WMD or was not proving support to Al Qaeda," although nearly half said that the war was the "right decision." The PIPA survey indicated that large numbers of Americans, especially Bush voters, believed that Iraq did have WMD and ties to Al Qaeda. Other PIPA surveys confirmed the CCFR studies in that a large majority believes that the United Nations, not the United States, should take the lead in matters of security, reconstruction, and political transition to democracy in Iraq.

There is thus an underlying basis for progressive change in the United States that was not adequately mobilized in the 2004 presidential election. There were, however, many local successes. As Tim McFeeley notes, Democrats gained control of at least seven legislative chambers (the Colorado House and Senate; the Oregon and Washington Senates; and the Montana, North Carolina, and Vermont Houses of Representatives. In contrast, the Republicans only gained control of four chambers: the Tennessee Senate and the Georgia, Indiana, and Oklahoma Houses of

Representatives).⁶ Moreover, "Progressives also won many crucial ballot measures: increasing the minimum wage in Florida and Nevada, approving stem-cell research in California, legalizing medical marijuana in Montana, promoting renewable energy in Colorado, and banning nuclear waste dumping in Washington." In addition, as McFeeley points out, during the past two years:

- While the federal government increased racial profiling in the name of fighting terrorism, Arkansas, Connecticut, Illinois, Montana, and New Jersey all banned racial profiling.
- While the Bush administration increased its power to prosecute and imprison through the USA Patriot Act, Alabama, Connecticut, Indiana, Kansas, Missouri, Nebraska, Tennessee, and Washington all enacted sentencing reforms that decrease jail sentences and sanction drug treatment instead of incarceration.
- While the Justice Department pushed federal prosecutors to demand the death penalty, South Dakota and Wyoming banned the juvenile death penalty, Illinois implemented substantial death penalty reforms, and seven states (Colo., Conn., Ga., Ohio, Mont., Nev., and N. Mex.) guaranteed death row inmates the right to DNA testing to prove their innocence.
- While the administration opposed an increase in the federal minimum wage, legislatures in Illinois, Rhode Island, and Vermont (as well as voters in Florida and Nevada) approved higher state minimum wages.
- While Bush sided with the prescription drug manufacturers on a host of policies to maintain high drug prices, nearly every state has taken some action to lower drug prices, led especially by Maine, Hawaii, Illinois, Michigan, and Vermont.
- While the federal Food and Drug Administration refused to make emergency contraceptive pills (ECPs) more accessible, Hawaii and Maine enacted laws to make ECPs available from pharmacists without a prescription, and New York and New Mexico required hospital emergency rooms to provide ECPs to rape victims.
- And while the administration encouraged companies to plunder our natural resources, states have enacted dozens of pro-environment laws: lowering fuel emissions, cleaning up power plants, banning mercury, requiring energy efficiency, mandating recycling, and restricting greenhouse gasses.

Progressives have even won victories in "red" states: Georgia cracked down on payday lending; Idaho allowed some juvenile offenders to get criminal records expunged; Kansas and Oklahoma sanctioned in-state tuition at state colleges for undocumented immigrants; Tennessee became the first state to enact an anti-offshoring statute; and Utah repealed term limits (ibid.).

Obviously, building on these victories will take significant energy and focus on state and local issues, but several organizations like Democracy for America, the Center for Policy Alternative Strategy, the Progressive Democratic Majority coalition, ACORN, and other groups are keenly focused on local issues as they work toward coalitions on national ones. In addition, there were other positive features for progressives in the 2004 election. As Evan Derkacz points out in "Bright Spots":

> The seven Democratic senators who voted against the Iraq war all won re-election—and they did it by an average margin of nearly 30 percent.
> Anti-war Democrat senators who won:
>
> > Barbara Boxer—California—58 percent–38 percent
> > Daniel Inouye—Hawaii—76 percent–21 percent
> > Barbara Mikulski—Maryland—65 percent–34 percent
> > Patty Murray—Washington—55 percent–43 percent
> > Russ Feingold—Wisconsin—55 percent–44 percent
> > Ron Wyden—Oregon—63 percent–32 percent
> > Pat Leahy—Vermont—71 percent–25 percent
>
> Zoom in and the point becomes even clearer. In Oregon, where Kerry, who voted for the war, won by a mere 4 percent, Oregon Sen. Ron Wyden won by over 30 percent "despite" his vote against it. Wisconsin, which was too close to call on election night, didn't take very long to declare Russ Feingold, who voted against the war (ignoring warnings from his staff), the winner. He won by 11 percent. Writer John Stauber concludes, "The lesson is this: Russ Feingold proves that an anti-war, populist Democrat, a maverick campaigning to get big money out of politics, can win and win big."
> These statistics should strike fear *out* of the Democrats the next time issues of war and peace are on the table. Maybe, just maybe, if they can persuade the Democratic establishment to disabuse itself of the mistaken belief that reelection comes to those who adopt the safest position, rather than to those who make a strong case for the values they hold most dear, it has a shot at being relevant in the 21st century.[7]

Derkacz also points out that Howard Dean's "Democracy for America" picked progressive candidates in state and local campaigns all over the country and 31 of the 102 Dean Dozen candidates won, including:

- The mayor of Republican-dominated Salt Lake City, Utah, is now a Democrat.

- Openly gay candidate, Nicole LeFeveur, won a seat in the Idaho state legislature.
- In heavily Republican Alabama, progressive Anita Kelly was elected as Circuit Court Judge.
- In Florida, a first time, Dean-inspired candidate, Susan Clary, won as Soil and Water Conservation District Supervisor.
- Montana's governor is now a Democrat, Brian Schweitzer.
- Heavily Republican New Hampshire elected Democrat John Lynch, kicking the incumbent and ethically challenged Governor Benson out of office.
- Arthur Anderson won the race for supervisor of elections in electorally challenged Palm Beach County, Florida.
- Suzanne Williams won a state senate seat in Colorado, giving the upper house a Democratic majority.
- In North Carolina, openly gay Julia Boseman was one of several Democrats to defeat Republican incumbents to take back control of the State House. (ibid.)

As noted, there were progressive measures passed in so-called red and blue states on raising the minimum wage, increasing funding for education, expanding health care programs, funding stem-cell research, and opposing a cap on property taxes. On the environment, of the League of Conservation Voters (LCV) 18 "Environmental Champions," all 18 won. In the eight congressional races that LCV focused on, seven environmentally "dirty" candidates went down to defeat. Hence, although there were dispiriting conservative trends in the national elections, there were many local examples that demonstrated a progressive base exists in the United States. But perhaps the underlying story of the election is that once again, as in Election 2000, the United States suffered from a dysfunctional electoral system, open to fraud, corruption, and confusion. Until there is radical change of the U.S. election system, democracy in the United States will continue to be in severe crisis.

A Dysfunctional Electoral System

The essence of democracy is the confidence of the electorate in the accuracy of voting methods and the fairness of voting procedures. In 2000, that confidence suffered terribly, and we fear that such a blow to our democracy may have occurred in 2004.

—*John Conyers, Jr., Jerrold Nadler, Robert Wexler,
members of the U.S. House Judiciary Committee*

In retrospect, it is tragic that John Kerry conceded so quickly because challenging the voting system, insisting that all votes be counted, pointing to well-documented examples of voter suppression, demonstrating problems with machines that do not provide accurate counts, and dramatizing the dangers of computer hacking to fix elections could have produced impetus to reform the system. As critics have pointed out, Elections 2000 and 2004 produced more than 3 million spoiled ballots that could not be read by voting machines, generally because old machines often malfunction; 75 percent of the machines in Ohio were of this vintage. A hand-count of these votes could have made a difference. There were also thousands of provisional ballots to be counted in Ohio, many absentee ballots, and many irregularities to check out. It would have been important to carry out close examinations of the computer voting machines in Ohio and Florida to see if they provided accurate results.

Examining voting machines could lead to voting reforms, such as those in California and Nevada, which required more transparency in the process, a paper trail to scrutinize in the case of a disputed election, and attempts to block voter fraud. There should be increased efforts to enable voter access and prevent voter suppression. Voting and counting procedures should be transparent, uniform, safe, and efficient. There should be agreed-upon recount procedures, criteria to count contested votes, and scrutiny of the process by members of both parties and professional election officials.

The problems with the U.S. election system, however, go far beyond the machines. The dysfunctionality evident in Election 2000 and 2004 reveal problems with the arguably outmoded Electoral College system and the problematical nature of the U.S. system of proportional voting. Many citizens were surprised to learn in the disputed Election 2000 that the Electoral College involved a system whereby those chosen to vote in the ritual in which the president was chosen did not necessarily have to follow the mandate of the voters in their district. In practice, state legislatures began binding electors to the popular vote, although as was abundantly clear in Election 2000, "faithless electors"— electors who vote for whomever they please—were theoretically possible. (Half of the states attempt to legally bind electors to the popular vote in their state, but it would still be possible for an elector to shift his or her vote, a dangerous outcome for a genuinely democratic society and a possibility much discussed after Election 2000.) "Electors" are rather mysteriously chosen in any case and this process should be examined and fixed.

Initially, the Electoral College was part of a compromise between state and local government. Allowing electors to choose the president provided guarantees to conservatives who wanted the Electoral College to serve as a buffer between what they perceived as an unruly and potentially dangerous public and the more educated and civic-minded legislators who could, if they wished, overturn votes by the people. Originally, the U.S. Congress was also elected in this manner. But in 1913 a constitutional amendment led to direct election of senators. Many argue this should also be the model for presidential elections. The current Electoral College system, as critics have maintained, is based on eighteenth-century concerns and is arguably obsolete and in need of systematic reconstruction in the twenty-first century.

Moreover, the proportional representation system in the Electoral College has serious problems that surfaced in the heated debates over Election 2000. Smaller states are disproportionately awarded with Electoral College votes, so that voters in less populated states such as Idaho or Wyoming have more proportionate influence in choosing the president than in states such as California or New York. As Jim Hightower notes, Wyoming's electors and proportionate vote represent 71,000 voters each, while Florida's electors each represent 238,000.[8] In New York, 18 million people now get 33 electoral votes for the presidency, but fewer than 14 million people in a collection of small states also get 33. As Duke University's Alex Keyssar argued in a November 20, 2000, *New York Times* op-ed piece, disproportionate weighting of the votes of smaller states violates the principle of one person, one vote, which according to a series of Supreme Court decisions in the 1960s, lies at the heart of U.S. democracy. "To say that a vote is worth more in one district than in another would ... run counter of our fundamental ideas of democratic government," the Court announced in 1964. "Legislators," wrote Chief Justice Earl Warren, "represent people, not trees or acres." Thus, the current system of proportionate state votes where all states get two votes and then the rest are divided according to population is unfair. A more reasonable system would simply allot states proportionate votes according to their populations, so that each vote throughout the nation would be equal in choosing a president.

Further problems with the U.S. Electoral College and system of proportional representation involve the winner-take-all rule operative in most states. As the Election 2000 Florida battle illustrates, in a winner-take-all system, 100 percent of the state's electoral votes goes to a 50.1 percent majority in presidential elections (or less if there were more than two candidates, as is increasingly the case in presidential elections). Maine and Nebraska are exceptions, and it would be possible to follow their example and to split presidential state votes proportionately according to the actual percentage of votes candidates get in each separate state, rather than following the winner-take-all rule, where a handful of votes in a state such as Florida, or Ohio, gives the entire state, and even the election, to one candidate.

Hence, the Electoral College and U.S. system of proportional representation should be seriously debated and reforms should be undertaken if U.S. democracy is to revitalize itself in the coming years after the debacle of 2000 and persistent questions concerning 2004. As many have argued, there are strong reasons for proportionate representation in U.S. presidential elections.[9] However, separation of election officials from political operatives and the training of professional, nonpartisan election workers should also be on the reform agenda. In Election 2000, Florida Secretary of State Katherine Harris, also head of the Bush-Cheney ticket in Florida, did everything possible to steal the election from Al Gore, and in 2004, Ohio Secretary of State Kenneth Blackwell played a similar role. To deal with all of these problems, a high-level commission could be appointed to study how to modernize and update the system of electing the president in the United States. Since the political establishment cannot be counted upon to undertake these reforms, it will be necessary for constituencies—academic, local, and national—to devise reforms for the seriously challenged system of "democracy" in the United States.

Furthermore, it is clear that money has corrupted the current electoral system and that campaign finance reform is necessary to avoid overwhelming influence by lobbies, corporations, and the corruption that a campaign system fueled by megabucks produces. The current election system, in which millions of dollars are needed for a federal election, ensures that only candidates from the two major parties have a chance of winning, that only candidates who are able to raise millions of dollars can run, and that those who do run and win are beholden to those who have financed their campaigns—guaranteeing control of the political system by corporations and the wealthy.

In Elections 2000 and 2004, the excessive amount of money pumped into the $3-billion-plus electoral campaigns guaranteed that neither candidate would say anything to offend the moneyed interests funding the election, and would thus avoid key issues of importance and concern. The debts accrued by the two major parties to their contributors were obvious in the initial appointments made by the Bush-Cheney Election 2000 transition team, which rewarded precisely those corporations and supporters who financed the Bush presidency. The Bush administration provided legislative awards for its major contributors, allowing the big corporations that supported them to write Bush administration energy and communication policy and to help draft legislation for deregulation that served their interests, in effect allowing big contributors to make public policy (see Kellner [2001], 187ff.).

In 2001, a McCain-Feingold finance reform bill was passed, but it has been continually watered down and is unlikely to reform U.S. political funding.

Indeed, a record amount of money was raised for the 2004 election as loopholes were exploited to create new types of fundraising and political action groups. Thus, there is a definite need for public financing of elections. Four states currently allow full public financing for candidates who agree to campaign with fundraising and spending limits (Arizona, Maine, Massachusetts, and Vermont), and this would be a splendid model for the entire nation.[10] Public financing for elections at local, state, and national levels would only be viable in a media era with free national television, free access to local media, and Internet sites offered to the candidates. Hence, the television networks should be required to provide free national airtime to presidential candidates to make their pitches, and television-paid political advertising should be eliminated (see the elaboration of this argument in Kellner 1990). The broadcasting networks were given a tremendous bonanza when the Federal Communications Commission provided a wealth of spectrum to use for digital broadcasting, doubling the amount of space it licensed to television broadcasters with estimates of the value of the space costing up to $70 billion. Congress failed to reestablish public service requirements that used to be in place before the Reagan-Bush-Clinton deregulation of telecommunications. As fair payback for the broadcast spectrum giveaway, broadcast media should provide free airtime for political discourse that strengthens democracy.

Efforts were made to get the television networks to enable the public to get free messages from the candidates, but they were defeated. President Clinton appointed an advisory panel to assess how to update public service requirements of television broadcasts in the wake of the spectrum giveaway. The panel recommended that television broadcasters voluntarily offer five minutes of candidate-centered airtime in the 30 days before the election. Clinton proposed this recommendation in his 1998 State of the Union address, but broadcasters fiercely rejected the proposal. In the Senate, John McCain and Conrad Burns announced that they would legislatively block the FCC's free airtime initiative. In fact, political advertising is a major cash cow for the television networks who regularly charge political candidates excessively high rates, although they are supposed to allow "lowest unit charge" (LUC) for political advertising. Such LUC rates, however, mean that the ads could be preempted, and desperate campaigns want to make sure that they get their advertising message out at a crucial time and thus are forced to pay higher rates.[11]

Voter rights initiatives also need to be carried forth to prevent voter suppression and provide adequate voting machines to all precincts, independent of their wealth or political connections. Once again in 2004, the Republicans practiced systematic voter suppression, challenging voters at the polls and intimidating potential voters in a myriad of ways. In addition, once again there were a shocking lack of voting machines and personnel, especially in swing minority and student precincts that typically vote Democratic. There should be strong penalties for voting suppression, fraud, too few voting machines, and inadequate poll staffing.[12]

There also should be a National Voting Day holiday, as many countries have, so that working people can vote without economic penalty. One of the scandals of Election 2004 was the terribly long lines in minority and working-class neighborhoods in Ohio and elsewhere, due to inadequate numbers of voting machines and not enough polling staff. There were reports in Ohio of lines lasting hours (especially in heavily Democratic neighborhoods), forcing many to leave the lines to return to work. This is an intolerable situation in a democracy and efforts should be made to maximize voting access; to simplify voting procedures; and to provide adequate, trained, and nonpartisan election staff as well as reliable and trustworthy machines.

In addition, schools should provide, as Dewey argued (1917), citizenship education as well voter literacy. Ballots are often highly complex and intimidating and there should be efforts to begin educating people of all ages and walks of life on how to vote. Better designed ballots and more reliable voting systems are obviously a prerequisite for voting reform, but individuals need to be better informed on how to vote and what the specific issues are on ballots, ranging from local to state and national issues.

There is little doubt that U.S. democracy is in serious crisis, and unless there are reforms, its decline will accelerate. Although voter participation increased from an all-time low in 1996 of 49 percent of the eligible electorate to 51 percent in Election 2000 and 60 percent in Election 2004, this percentage is still fairly low. The United States is on the low end of democratic participation in presidential elections among democracies throughout the world. Obviously, much of the country remains alienated from electoral politics despite hotly contested elections in 2000 and 2004.

The Media and Democracy

> A popular government without popular information, or the means of acquiring it, is but a prologue to a farce or a tragedy, or perhaps both.
> —James Madison

What is the role of a free and independent press in a democratic society? Is it to be a passive conduit responsible only for the delivery of information between a government and its people? Is it to aggressively print allegation and rumor independent of accuracy or fairness? Is it to show boobies? No. The role of a free press is to be the people's eyes and ears, providing not just information but access, insight and, most importantly, context.

—The Daily Show *with Jon Stewart, and* America (The Book)

A democratic society requires a separation of powers in which the media can serve as a check and balance against excessive power or corruption of the state and other major institutions as well as help to create informed citizens who can intelligently participate in public affairs. Sovereignty, in this framework, thus rests both in the constitutional order and with the will of the people.[13] A free press was deemed vitally necessary to maintain a democratic society and it is often claimed by champions of democracy that freedom of the press is one of the features that defines the superiority of democratic societies over competing social systems.

This concept of a free press was extended in the twentieth century to the broadcast media, which were assigned a series of democratic responsibilities. In countries like Britain, which developed a public service model of broadcasting, radio and then television were considered part of the public sector, with important duties to reproduce the national culture and provide forums of information and debate for citizens (Tracey 1998). Even in the United States, where a private industry model of broadcasting came to dominate, in the Federal Communications Act of 1934 and subsequent legislation and court decisions, broadcasting was to serve the "public interest, convenience, and necessity, ascribing certain democratic functions to the media," until the setting aside of these strictures in the 1980s and 1990s.[14]

In the era of intensifying globalization in the 1990s and into the new millennium, market models of broadcasting generally emerged as dominant, and a series of global mergers took place that consolidated media ownership into ever fewer hands. The result has been that a shrinking number of giant corporations have controlled a widening range of media in corporate conglomerates that control the press, broadcasting, film, music, and other forms of popular entertainment as well as the most accessed Internet sites. Media have been increasingly organized on a business model, and competition between proliferating commercialized media have provided an impetus to replace news with entertainment, to generate a tabloidization of news, and to pursue profits and sensationalism rather than public enlightenment and democracy.[15]

Since the 1960s, the decline of television documentaries and public affairs programming helped produce a less informed electorate, more susceptible to political manipulation. Democracy requires vigorous public debate of key issues of importance and an informed electorate, able to make intelligent decisions and to participate in politics. Corporate control of the media meant that corporations could use the media to aggressively promote their own interests and to cut back on the criticism of corporate abuses that were expanding from the 1970s to the present. The tabloidization of news and intense competition between various media meant that the corporate media ignored social problems and focused on scandal and tabloid entertainment rather than issues of serious public concern.

During the Clinton era, for instance, the media focused intensely on the O.J. Simpson scandals in the mid-1990s and then turned toward the Clinton sex scandals (Kellner 2003c). Although previously, corporate media tended to support presidents in office, and had been especially uncritical of the ruling administration in the Reagan and Bush Senior years, during the Clinton era the media became fierce watch dogs, pouncing on every potential scandal involving the Clintons and feasting on the sex scandals, which eventually became dominant in the media in the 1990s. This was an era of right-wing talk radio, the rise of conservative television networks like Fox, and the proliferation of the Internet, which had many anti-Clinton activists and gossips like Matt Drudge, whose website first broke the Clinton sex scandals.

The 1990s were an era of escalating social problems caused by globalization and the abuses of corporate capitalism, ecological crisis, decline in public health, growing inequality between rich and poor, and dangerous corporate practices that would eventually explode in 2002 in the Enron, WorldCom, and other corporate scandals. It was an era of neoliberalism in which not only were the media deregulated, but so too were corporate practices, financial markets, corporate accounting, and the global economy. The media tended to celebrate the "new economy" and the period of economic boom and growing affluence, but overlooked the dangers of an overinflated stock market, an unregulated economy, and the growing divisions between haves and have nots. During this era, the corporate media thus neglected social problems in favor of celebrating the capitalist economy and technological revolution. The media also overlooked the growth of terrorism, dangerous consequences of the growing division between the haves and the have-nots throughout the world, and escalating ecological problems (Kellner 2003a).

Although the mainstream media in the United States tended to be largely uncritical of Reagan and Bush, they were *attack dogs* against Clinton and his administration in the 1990s (Alterman, 2003; Kellner 1990, 1992, 2001, and 2003a; Miller 2004). Thus, it was not surprising that during the 2000 election key sectors of the media would be highly critical of Democratic Party candidate

Al Gore and give George W. Bush, son of the former president, an easy time (see Kellner 2001 and Chapter 1 of this book). During the Bush-Cheney administration, the corporate media tended to be *lap dogs,* failing to investigate in any depth the scandals of Bush and Cheney, their bogus claims about weapons of mass destruction in Iraq, and the destructive consequences of their domestic and foreign policies. Thus, the corporate media have largely abandoned their role as a "fourth estate" or *watch dogs,* investigating economic and political scandal and corruption in the public interest.

Over the past decade or more, the investigative function of traditional journalism has largely fallen to alternative media and the Internet. The only way that a democratic social order can be maintained is for the mainstream media to assume their democratic function of critically discussing all issues of public concern and social problems from a variety of viewpoints and fostering spirited public debate, accompanied by the development of vigorous and competent investigative and alternative media. The democratic imperative that the mainstream corporate press and broadcasting provide a variety of views on issues of public interest and controversy has been increasingly sacrificed, as has their responsibility to serve as a check against excessive government or corporate power and corruption. As I have documented, there is a crisis of democracy in the United States in part because the mainstream corporate media have been biased toward Republicans and conservatives over the past two decades. Mainstream corporate media tend to promote the interests of the corporations that own them, which tend to be promarket and antiregulation and have largely advanced the interests of corporate institutions and conservative politics.

To remedy this situation, first of all there must be a strengthening of the media reform movement and recognition of the importance of media politics in the struggle for democratization and the creation of a just society, and support and development of alternative media.[16] Democratizing the media system will require development of a dynamic reform movement and recognition for all progressive social movements of the importance of invigorating the media system for forward-looking social change and addressing urgent social problems and issues. This process will involve sustained critique of the corporate media; calls for reregulation; and the revitalization of public television, cultivation of community and public radio, improved public access television, an expansion of investigative and public service journalism, and full democratic utilization of the Internet. Since corporations control the mainstream press, broadcasting, and other major institutions of culture and communication, there is little hope that the corporate media will be democratized without major pressure or increased government regulation of a sort that is not on the horizon in the present moment in most parts of the world.

The Internet, by contrast, provides potential for a democratic revitalization of the public sphere. The Internet makes more information accessible to a greater number of people, more easily, and from a wider array of sources than any instrument of information and communication in history. It is constantly astonishing to discover the extensive array of material available, articulating every conceivable point of view and providing news, opinion, and sources of a striking variety and diversity. Moreover, the Internet allows two-way communication and democratic participation in public dialogue, activity that is essential to producing a vital democracy.

One of the major contradictions of the current era is that for the wired world at least, and increasingly the public at large, a rich and diverse information environment is expanding, consisting of a broad spectrum of radio and television broadcasting networks; print media and publications; and the global village of the Internet, which itself contains the most varied and extensive sources of information and entertainment ever assembled in a single medium. The Internet can send disparate types and sources of information and images instantly throughout the world and is increasingly being used by a variety of progressive and oppositional groups (see Best and Kellner 2001; Kellner 1999; and Kahn and Kellner 2003).

Still, the majority of people get their news and information from a highly ideological and limited corporate media, creating a major division between the informed and uninformed in the contemporary era. Of course, right-wing and reactionary forces can and have used the Internet to promote their political agendas as well. In a short time, one can easily access an exotic witch's brew of websites maintained by the Ku Klux Klan and myriad neo-Nazi assemblages, including the Aryan Nation, various militia groups, and the right-wing Republican attack apparatus. Hence, the Internet is a contested terrain with progressive, reactionary, and corporate forces using the technology for their conflicting agendas. To be sure, much of the world is not yet wired, many people do not even read, and different inhabitants in various parts of the globe receive their information and culture in very dissimilar ways through varying sources, media, and forms. Thus, the type and quality of information vary tremendously, depending on an individual's access and ability to properly interpret and contextualize it.

Democracy, however, requires informed citizens and access to information and thus the viability of democracy is dependent on citizens seeking out crucial information, having the ability to access and appraise it, and to engage in public conversations about issues of importance. Democratic media reform and alternative media are thus crucial to revitalizing and even preserving the democratic project in the face of powerful corporate and political forces. How media can be democratized and what alternative media can be developed will of course be different in various parts of the world, but without a democratic media politics and alternative media, democracy itself cannot survive in a vigorous form, nor will a wide range of social problems be engaged or even addressed.

Reinvigorating democracy also requires a reconstruction of education with expanded literacies, democratized pedagogies, and education for citizenship. As John Dewey long ago argued (1917), education is an essential prerequisite for democracy and public education should strive to produce more democratic citizens. A reconstruction of education also requires cultivating media, computer, and multiple literacies for a computer-based economy and information-dependent society.[17] In an increasingly technological society, media education should become an important part of the curriculum, with instruction focused on critical media and computer literacy as well as on how to use media for expression, communication, and social transformation.

Alternative media need to be connected with progressive movements to revitalize democracy and bring an end to the current conservative hegemony. After the defeat of Barry Goldwater in 1964 when conservatives were routed and appeared to be down for the count, they built up a movement of alternative media and political organizations; liberals and progressives now face the same challenge. In the current situation, we cannot expect much help from the corporate media and need to develop ever more vigorous alternative media. The past several years have seen many important steps in the fields of documentary film, digital video and photography, community radio, public access television, an always expanding progressive print media, and an ever-growing liberal and progressive Internet and blogosphere. While the right has more resources to dedicate to these projects, the growth of progressive democratic public spheres has been impressive. Likewise, the energy, political organization, and finances mobilized to attempt to defeat the Bush-Cheney Gang were impressive, but more needs to be done to defeat the conservatives, building on the achievements of the past years.

One result of the 2004 election has been the decentering and marginalizing of the importance of the corporate media punditocracy by Internet and blogosphere sources. A number of websites and blogs have been dedicated to deconstructing mainstream corporate journalism, taking apart everyone from the right-wing spinners on Fox to reporters for the *New York Times*. An ever-proliferating number of websites have been attacking mainstream pundits, media institutions, and misreporting; with the possible exception of the *New York Times*'s Paul Krugman, Internet and blog sources were often much more interesting, insightful, and perhaps even influential than the overpaid, underinformed, and often incompetent mainstream corporate media figures. For example, every day the incomparable Bob Somerby on www.daily howler.com, savages mainstream media figures, disclosing their ignorance, bias, and incompetence.[18]

As a response there have been fierce critiques of the blogosphere by mainstream media pundits and sources, although many in the corporate mainstream are developing blogs, appropriating the genre for themselves. Yet mainstream corporate broadcasting media, and especially television, continue to exert major political influence, and constant critique of corporate media should be linked with efforts at reform, as activists continue to create ever better alternative media linked to ever-expanding progressive movements. Producing alternative media and a progressive movement also requires the production of emancipatory political ideas and vision to animate alternative political organizations.

Cosmopolitan Globalization

> In the absence of governmental checks and balances present in other areas of our national life, the only effective restraint upon executive policy and power in the areas of national defense and international affairs may lie in an enlightened citizenry— in an informed and critical public opinion which alone can here protect the values of democratic government.
> —*Supreme Court Justice Potter Stewart on the* Pentagon Papers *case*

In addition to creating alternative media projects and alliances and solidarities with progressive organizations, it is necessary to have a democratic and emancipatory vision for the future. Democracy needs to be rethought and radicalized with more effective and just voting systems, alternative media and public spheres, participation in social movements, and a globalized vision of solidarity with democratic forces and struggles throughout the world. An antiwar movement could be combined with strong antiterrorism positions, declaring both terrorism and militarism assaults on a sane and peaceful world. Terrorism would thus be criminalized; dealt with by global police, judicial, financial, and, if necessary, military institutions; and would not be an excuse for constantly escalating militarism. In addition, progressives need a vision of cosmopolitan globalization to counter the antiglobalization sentiments that linger, as well as Bush administration fantasies of empire and corporate versions of neoliberal globalization.

On a global level, the largely unilateralist and militarist Iraq intervention clearly shows the dangers and destructive effects of the Bush administration preemptive strike doctrine, and the need for strong multilateralism and genuinely global solutions to problems like terrorism, dangerous weapons, and rogue regimes. For many, the Bush administration doctrine of preventive wars and preemptive strikes embedded in the Iraq invasion contravenes international law. In particular, the Bush administration invasion of Iraq and use of military force to overthrow the Iraqi regime violated sections three and four of Article 2 of the UN Charter, which stipulates that: "All members shall settle their international disputes by peaceful means in such a manner that international peace and security, and justice, are not endangered [and shall] refrain in their international relations from the threat or use of force against the territorial integrity or political independence of any state."[19]

John Dean argues in *Worse Than Watergate* (2004, 155) that Bush administration lies to Congress concerning the need to take military action against Iraq constitutes an "impeachable offense." Dean argues that congressional support for Bush to take military action against the Iraqi regime required a "determination" that all diplomacy had failed and that there was an imminent threat from Iraq that would require immediate military action. Bush's determination was utterly specious. Dean describes Bush's "extraordinary document" as "accurately analogized to male bovine droppings" (2004, 148). Against the backdrop of his intimate knowledge of congressional impeachment actions against Nixon, when he was the former president's lawyer, Dean argues that there are constitutional grounds for impeachment.

In addition, the so-called Bush doctrine has alienated the United States from its key allies and large segments of the world who increasingly oppose U.S. policy.[20] Bush administration and Pentagon ideologues believed that with the collapse of the Soviet Union, the United States was all powerful and should use U.S. military might to enforce its will and interests. The Bush-Cheney Gang's Iraq fiasco clearly demonstrates the limitations of this position, making evident the follies of preventive wars, preemptive strikes, and unilateralism.[21]

The Iraq case suggests that multilateral solutions are needed for global problems and that as with Bosnia, Kosovo, Haiti, and other recent political crises, global and multilateral alliances and forces were necessary. With Immanuel Wallerstein (2004), I would agree that this should not be taken as an endorsement of "weak multilateralism," defined as a U.S.-dominated system of alliances whereby the United States dictates to allies, controls the United Nations and global institutions, and imposes its will on the world. Such a form of "weak multilateralism" is top-down and not really multilateral, but conceals U.S. hegemony and global corporate domination. Bill Clinton pursued such a multilateral strategy and it is likely that John Kerry might have pursued a similar type of multilateralism. This form of what I would call "neoliberal globalization" is opposed to a strong or genuine multilateralism that is multipolar, involves autonomous partners and alliances, and is radically democratic. A true democratic and global multilateralism would include NGOs, social movements, and popular institutions as well as global institutions like the United Nations. A democratic and multipolar globalization would be grounded philosophically in enlightenment cosmopolitanism, democracy, human rights, and ecology, drawing on notions of a cosmos, global citizenship, and genuine democracy.[22]

The need for cosmopolitan multilateralism and globalization shows the limitations of one-sided antiglobalization positions that dismiss globalization out of hand as a form of capitalist or U.S. domination. Taking this position is admitting defeat before you've started, conceding globalization to corporate capitalism and not articulating contradictions, forms of resistance, and possibilities of democracy grounded in globalization itself. Rather, a U.S.-dominated or corporate globalization represents a form of neoliberal globalization that, interestingly, Wallerstein claims is "just about passé" (2004, 18). The Bush administration unilateralism has united the world against U.S. policies, so that the United States can no longer push through whatever trade, economic, or military policies that they wish without serious opposition. Wallerstein points to the widely perceived failures of IMF and WTO policies, the collapse of recent Cancun and Miami trade meetings that ended with no agreement as strongly united so-called southern countries opposed U.S. trade policy, and, finally, global opposition to the Bush administration Iraq intervention. He also points to the rise of the World Social Forum as a highly influential counterpoint to the Davos World Economic Forum, which has stood as an organizing site for a worldwide anti-neoliberal globalization movement.

Cosmopolitan globalization thus overcomes the one-sidedness of a nation-state and national interest dominant politics and recognizes that in a global world the nation is part of a multilateral, multipolar, multicultural, and transnational system. A cosmopolitan globalization driven by issues of multipolar multilateralism, democratization, and globalization from below would embrace women's, workers', and minority rights as well as strong ecological perspectives. Such cosmopolitan globalization thus provides a worthy way to confront challenges of the contemporary era ranging from terrorism to global warming.

The Bush administration intervention in Iraq showed the limitations of militarist unilateralism and that in a complex world it is impossible, despite awesome military power, for one country to rule in a multipolar globe. The failures of Bush administration policy in Iraq suggest that unilateralist militarism is not the way to fight international terrorism, or to deal with issues such as "weapons of mass destruction," but is rather the road to an Orwellian nightmare and era of perpetual war in which democracy and freedom will be in dire peril and the future of the human species will be in question.

At this moment in history, the United States is confronted with the question of whether it wants to preserve its democratic republic or attempt to expand its empire, a project likely to create new enemies and alienate old allies.[23] Global problems require global solutions, and Bush administration unilateralism and its quest for empire has arguably created new enemies, overextended U.S. military power, and weakened international alliances. These are frightening times and it is essential that all citizens become informed about the fateful conflicts of the present, gain clear understanding of what is at stake, and realize that they must oppose at once international terrorism, Bushian militarism, and an Orwellian police-state in order to preserve democracy and make possible a life worthy of human beings.

Bushgate/Cheneygate: The Coming Conflicts

> The accumulation of all powers, legislative, executive, and judiciary, in the same hands, whether of one, a few, or many, and whether hereditary, self-appointed, or elective, may justly be pronounced the very definition of tyranny.
>
> —*James Madison*, Federalist Paper 47

There is little doubt but that economic, social, cultural, and other crises will intensify significantly in the years to come, which will be an epoch of enormous struggle against the disasters that the second Bush administration is certain to unleash. Bush now has to deal with and suffer the consequences of the messes he made in his first term: Iraq, increasing Islamic radicalism, growing isolation of the United States and intensifying anti-Americanism, an out-of-control deficit, a dramatically declining dollar, a deteriorating environment, a health care system in crisis, and a Social Security system that Bush is perfectly willing to destroy to help undo the "welfare state."

Although one of the Big Lies of the Bush-Cheney campaign was that Kerry's election would make the United States more susceptible to a terrorist attack, the continuation of Bush administration policies may make the United States more likely to be hated by many and attacked by terrorists for years to come. As Mark Follman writes:

> One well-known conservative thinks that President Bush's reelection will lead to a horrific al-Qaida attack. According to the *Jerusalem Post,* Yossef Bodansky, the Israeli-born former director of the U.S. Congressional Task Force on Terrorism and Unconventional Warfare and author of *Bin Laden: The Man Who Declared War on America,* says that an al-Qaida attack on the U.S. with nonconventional weapons is virtually "inevitable," and that the organization is likely "tying up the knots" for such an attack. "All of the warnings we have today indicate that a major strike—something more horrible than anything we've seen before—is all but inevitable," he told the *Post* on Sunday.
>
> After 9/11 and the launch of the U.S. global war on terrorism, a theological debate began within the operational arm of al-Qaida, Bodansky says, over whether the mass killing of innocents using weapons of mass destruction was permissible. Former CIA analyst and bin Laden expert Michael Scheuer asserted in his book *Imperial Hubris* that bin Laden has had the Islamic world's approval to use nuclear weapons against U.S. civilians since May 2003, when a Saudi cleric condoned it in a "lucidly written" treatise citing Islamic law and rebuking U.S. transgressions against Muslims.
>
> Bodansky argues that Bush's reelection has poured fuel on that fire.
>
> "While bin Laden and his associates argued that by virtue of their participation in U.S. democracy, U.S. citizens were enabling their rulers to fight, other Islamic luminaries contended that this does not permit such massive attacks," Bodansky said. "The reelection of Bush in November," he said, "was viewed by bin Laden and his cohorts as a decisive answer to this deliberation, with Americans now 'choosing' to be the enemies of Islam." "In bin Laden's mind-set," he said, "the stage was set for a non-conventional attack." While there may still be some vestiges of debate and doubt within Islamic circles, he believes that planning for such an attack is finished. "They got the kosher stamp from the Islamic world to use nuclear weapons," he said.[24]

Moreover, the Bush-Cheney economic policies make economic crisis more likely. As Randolph T. Holhut writes:

> Economists are starting to use words like "meltdown," "Armageddon" and "banana republic" to describe what may be ahead for the United States.
>
> How bad are things? Stephen Roach, the chief economist for Morgan Stanley,

recently gave a closed-door briefing to New England mutual fund managers in Boston. The *Boston Herald* received a copy of Roach's talk and what he had to say is bloodcurdling.

Roach said the United States has about a one in 10 chance of avoiding a complete financial collapse, a three in 10 chance that another recession will hit and a six in 10 chance that "we'll muddle through for a while and delay the eventual Armageddon."

America has a record trade deficit (according to the Commerce Department, it was $549 billion in 2003—$124 billion with China alone). We're importing far more goods than we're exporting and once they're tallied, the 2004 numbers will be even worse. To fund this deficit, the United States borrows more than $550 billion a year from foreign sources.

The federal government is running up record deficits, closing in on $500 billion in the current federal budget. The dollar is going down, down, down against the world's other currencies, making the imported goods that this nation has come to rely on that much more expensive.

As the trade deficit keeps rising, Roach said the dollar's value will keep falling and foreign investors will be less interested in lending us money. As the federal deficit keeps rising, the government will have to borrow more money, which will fuel inflation. Federal Reserve Chairman Alan Greenspan will end up having to raise interest rates higher and quicker than he'd like. Once interest rates go up, over-mortgaged and over-indebted households will hit the financial wall. Foreclosures will increase. Consumer spending will decrease. Unemployment will rise, as will the federal deficit.

Roach said the total debt of U.S. households 20 years ago was equal to half the size of the total domestic economy. Today, it's 85 percent. With Americans spending a record share of their disposable income to service their debt, a wave of bankruptcies seems inevitable if interest rates rise.

Paul Krugman, the Princeton economist and columnist for the *New York Times,* said in a recent interview with the Reuters news service that the U.S. economy now resembles Argentina in the 1990s.[25]

Viewed from a historical perspective, second-term presidencies have been fraught with disaster, such as Lyndon B. Johnson's Vietnam quagmire, which forced him to renounce reelection in 1968; Nixon's Watergate; Reagan's Iran-Contra scandal, which checkmated his aggressive foreign policy; or the Clinton sex scandals, which blocked his ability to deal more strongly with foreign policy issues such as terrorism and to push through his domestic agenda. Karl Rove likes to make comparisons between George W. Bush's presidency and the William McKinley presidency in which the conservative Republican narrowly won the election in 1896 over William Jennings Bryan, but defeated the populist decisively in 1900, producing a strong Republican majority. McKinley's chief advisor Mark Hanna, with whom Rove identifies, saw this victory as a Republican realignment that would provide conservative rule for the foreseeable future. McKinley was assassinated in 1901, however; the Republicans splintered and Theodore Roosevelt pursued progressivist policies at home, laying the foundation for the New Deal, and imperial policies abroad. He then ran against his conservative Republican successor William H. Taft in 1912 on the Progressive Party ticket, splitting the Republican vote and providing a win for Woodrow Wilson and the Democrats.

The case of Newt Gingrich and the Republican right's "Contract with America" is also instructive. Gingrich led a right-wing congressional initiative that won Republicans a strong House majority in the 1994 midterm elections and promised a "political sea change" and Republican "revolution" with a 10-point program for change. There was a strong backlash against the Republican right; Gingrich became "the most hated man in America" and resigned in disgrace.[26]

History is, of course, without guarantees, but it is likely that scandals, mistakes, or unforeseen events could undo the Bush administration. The Bush-Cheney regime is the most scandal-ridden in modern history, far out-shadowing the Tea Pot Dome scandals that undid the Harding administration in the 1920s. Dick Cheney is under investigation for activities undertaken when he was CEO of Halliburton, and there are now FBI and Justice Department investigations of Cheney's connection to the no-bid contracts secured by Halliburton in Iraq. On September 17, in the heat of the election, John Kerry charged that the Bush administration had ignored overcharging in defense contracts awarded to Halliburton, the company once headed by Vice President Dick Cheney, calling it evidence of the president's mismanagement of the war in Iraq. Kerry stated: "Dick Cheney's old company, Halliburton, has profited from the mess in Iraq at the expense of American troops and taxpayers. While Halliburton has been engaging in massive overcharging and wasteful practices under this no-bid contract, Dick Cheney has continued to receive compensation from his former company."

The Cheney-Halliburton connections were indeed tight and controversial. Cheney had been CEO of the energy supply and construction company in the mid-1990s and after a duck-hunting trip merged with military supplier and construction megacorporation Kellog, Brown, and Root (KBR), a Texas-based company with longtime connections to the Bush family (see Nichols 2004). Unfortunately for Cheney and Halliburton, KBR was facing mega-asbestos suits that threatened to bankrupt the company. Cheney desperately sought government contracts and engaged in creative accounting that would make Ken Lay proud, setting up dummy subsidiaries, faking profits on selling one asset in the company to another, using Arthur Anderson company to cook the books, setting up offshore bank accounts, bribing foreign countries to get contracts, selling illegally to Iraq and Iran when they were on an embargo list, and on and on, worse than Enron.

It was astonishing that Cheney got away with his Halliburton mismanagement, but when George W. Bush asked him to vet a list of potential vice presidents, Cheney got his opportunity. Halliburton stock was plunging, there was a stockholders suit, and Cheney faced potential jail time. Knowing that he would be less likely to be perp-walked and put in the slammer from the vice president's office (although it had happened to Spiro Agnew), Cheney told Bush Junior that he himself was the choice to serve as vice president, and Bush quickly made Cheney his veep and, in the view of many, his copresident. As copresident Cheney fought tooth and nail to get the United States to invade and occupy Iraq and to get no-bid contracts for Halliburton that would improve the floundering colossus. And lo and behold! Halliburton got a no-bid contract for a cool $7 billion, its stock price stabilized, and Cheney had avoided disaster for his old company.

During the last phase of the campaign, there were many criticisms of the Cheney-Halliburton connection and it remained to be seen if his controversial past as Halliburton CEO and the role Cheney played in getting them Iraq contracts would come back to haunt him.[27] In addition, many of the Bush neoconservatives are involved in national security scandals, including the felonious exposure of a CIA agent married to Bush administration critic Joseph Wilson, for which Dick Cheney's chief of staff Scooter Libbey and Karl Rove are under investigation. Other Bush neocons are under investigation for giving secret state information to Israel and to Taiwan. As Seymour Hersh argues (2004), the Abu Ghraib prison abuse and torture scandals go to the top of the Bush administration "chain of command." A U.S. judge recently declared the entire policy of detaining "enemy combatants" at Guantanamo Bay, Cuba, illegal and there are sure to be intense legal battles over these and other issues. Moreover, recent documents released show that U.S. prisoner abuse was far more extensive than previous noted, taking place in Afghanistan, Iraq, and at the U.S. base in Cuba.[28] Most shockingly, in Ari Berman's summary:

> redacted email sent to FBI officials and signed by an "On Scene Commander—Baghdad" on May 22, 2004, states that "an Executive Order signed by President Bush authorized the following interrogation techniques, among others: sleep

'management,' use of MWDs (military working dogs), 'stress positions' such as half squats, 'environmental manipulation' such as the use of loud music, sensory deprivation through the use of hoods, etc." The letter alleges that after the abuses at Abu Ghraib—which incorporated many aspects of the Executive Order—Bush revised the command so that "certain techniques can only be used if very high-level authority is granted."

All of these treatments violate the Geneva Conventions, and, if done in the extreme, cross the line into torture, says Dinah PoKempner, general counsel for Human Rights Watch. They also contradict the U.S. Army's own prior policy on intelligence and interrogations.

The FBI refused to follow Bush's orders. "We have instructed our personnel not to participate in interrogations by military personnel which might include techniques by the Executive Order but beyond the bounds of standard FBI practice," the email said.[29]

Bush's extremist right-wing Attorney General John Ashcroft resigned on November 9, leaving a letter claiming that he had solved U.S. terrorist and national security problems, when in actuality his failure to focus on terrorism before 9/11, illegal rounding up of Arab and Muslim suspects, putting forth a USA Patriot Act that seriously undermined basic liberties, and failure to prosecute a major case of domestic terrorism makes him one of the worst attorney generals in U.S. history. Bush chose to replace Ashcroft with his close Texas friend and attorney Alberto Gonzalez, infamous for drafting a document allowing torture and contravention of the Geneva Conventions, leading the way to Abu Ghraib (Hersh 2004). Gonzalez was also involved in some of Bush's generally overlooked Texas scandals, including the execution of more than 150 prisoners, often without adequate scrutiny of their cases.

Dramatizing the even more extreme right turn to come, Colin Powell announced his resignation as secretary of state, and close Bush crony Condoleezza Rice, who had once inadvertently referred to Bush as "my husband," was named to replace him. As noted in Chapter 5, Rice was one of the worst national security advisors in recent history, failing to put terrorism on her agenda pre–9/11 and afterward making the astonishing claim that "none of us ever envisaged planes flying into buildings" when there were a series of reports that had predicted the danger. Rice was also caught up in a slew of lies concerning Iraq's alleged "weapons of mass destruction" and was one of the most discredited and disgraced figures in an administration that had repeatedly failed at national security and foreign policy.

On November 25, the Bush administration made it clear that they were going to pay off the religious right, which had supported them with new antiabortion measures, as Congress passed a bill that permits health providers rang-ing from doctors and nurses to HMOs and hospitals to deny abortion services to women. This meant that any employer could deny workers abortion cover-age and presaged a Child Custody Protection Act that would make it illegal for anyone but a parent or guardian to take an underage girl across state lines for an abortion. During the campaign, the Bush-Cheney Gang organized "Focus on Women's Issues" forums, filled with hundreds of "W Stands for Women" signs. But in fact, the Bush administration had been one of the most anti-women administrations in history, so it was highly hypocritical to claim that "W" stood for women. The Bush administration began by closing down women's rape crisis centers that critics claimed were recruiting grounds for feminism. The Bush administration mandated that family planning agencies not give out birth control information advice on abortion and sided with the most rabid antiabortion forces in the party.[30] The Bush administration did not adequately fund the No Child Left Behind Act, cut back on after-school programs and day care, and closed the White House Office on Women's Issues, thus having disas-trously bad policies on issues that meant the most to women. On April 25, 2004, more than 1 million women marched on the Washington Mall against Bush, in the largest march in U.S. history, the "March for Women's Lives."

Likewise, the Bush administration had an unparalleled bad record on the environment. On December 22, it issued broad new rules overhauling the guide-lines for managing the nation's 155 national forests and making it easier for regional forest managers to decide whether to allow logging, drilling, and off-road vehicles, thus opening previously protected forest area to exploitation. Felicity Barringer documented how the Bush administration had "accelerated resource development on public lands" and "pushed to eliminate regulatory hurdles for military and industrial projects." Her article cited an e-mail by Sena-tor Jim Jeffords of Vermont, who had shifted from Republican to independent during the first months of the Bush administration when it took a hard-right turn. Jeffords wrote: "I expect the Bush administration to continue their as-sault on regulations designed to protect public health and the environment. I expect the Bush administration to continue underfunding compliance and enforcement activities." He concluded, "I expect the Bush administration will go down in history as the greatest disaster for public health and the environ-ment in the history of the United States."[31]

Barringer recounted how during the first months of the Bush administra-tion, federal regulations governing carbon dioxide, arsenic, and other poisons were cut back; how the 1997 Kyoto Protocol on the environment was aban-doned; how the Bush administration was pushing to allow oil drilling in the

Arctic National Wildlife Refuge and had scrapped the phase-out of snowmo-
biles in Yellowstone; how the Environmental Protection Agency under Bush
abandoned environmental regulatory projects; and how the "Clear Skies Act"
provided a phony retreat from the Clean Air Act (see Chapter 5). The Bush
administration had indeed been a disaster for the environment and it was surprising that the Kerry campaign had not pushed the issue harder.

The Bush-Cheney administration made it perfectly clear that they would
accelerate the extreme hard-right policies of its first administration. Like many
second-term presidencies, George W. Bush and his cronies will likely overreach
and might self-destruct. The presidential debates showed that Bush is utterly
incompetent, incapable of thought and argumentation, and only able to reproduce sound-bytes—perhaps with the aid of a wire (see Chapter 6). As far as
one can see on the public record, Bush has never had a policy idea in his life
and has little interest in the ideas, debate, and dialogue necessary for democracy. The debates also showed Bush's hot temper and proclivity to explode in
anger, as he did when Kerry attacked his unilateralism (see Chapter 6). Bush
put on display his explosive temper again when on a November trip to Chile he
went thrashing into a crowd when Chilean security would not let his Secret
Service entourage into a government building, prompting the Chilean president to cancel a state dinner for Bush because his security detail was too demanding and insulting.

George W. Bush already is a national and world historical disgrace, and it is
highly probable that things will only get worse under his rule. Sidney Blumenthal
detailed Bush's petty behavior at the inauguration of the Clinton Memorial
Library shortly after the election:

> Offstage, beforehand, Rove and Bush had had their library tours. According to
> two eyewitnesses, Rove had shown keen interest in everything he saw, and asked
> questions, including about costs, obviously thinking about a future Bush library
> and legacy. "You're not such a scary guy," joked his tour guide. "Yes, I am," Rove
> replied. Walking away, he muttered deliberately and loudly, "I change Constitu-
> tions, I put churches in schools . . . " Thus he identified himself as more than the
> ruthless campaign tactician—as the invisible hand of power, pervasive and ex-
> pansive, designing to alter the fundamental American compact.
>
> On his tour Bush appeared distracted and glanced repeatedly at his watch.
> When he stopped to gaze at the river, where Secret Service agents were stationed
> in boats, the guide said, "Usually, you might see some bass fishermen out there."
> Bush replied: "A submarine could take this place out."
>
> Was the president warning of an al-Qaida submarine, sneaking undetected
> up the Mississippi, through the locks and dams of the Arkansas River, surfacing

suddenly under the bridge to the 21st century to dispatch the Clinton library with a torpedo that could travel on water and land? Is that where Osama bin Laden is hiding?

Or was this a wishful, paranoid fantasy of ubiquitous terrorism destroying Clinton's legacy with one blow? Or was it a projection of menace and messianism, with only Bush grasping the true danger, standing between submerged threat and civilization? Was his apparent non sequitur a reflection of his inner logic about American politics in a fog of war, where little is discernible in the miasma but fear? Or was this simply his way of saying he wouldn't build his library near water?

Clinton concluded his remarks with a challenge to Bush couched in terms of his own failure: "Where we fell short . . . the biggest disappointment in the world to me . . . peace in the Middle East . . . I did all I could." He turned to face Bush seated behind him: "But when we had seven years of progress toward peace, there was one whole year when, for the first time in the history of the state of Israel, not one person died of a terrorist attack, when the Palestinians began to believe they could have a shared future. And so, Mr. President, again, I say: I hope you get to cross over into the promised land of Middle East peace. We have a good opportunity, and we are all praying for you."

At the private luncheon of distinguished guests afterward, in a heated tent pitched behind the library, Shimon Peres delivered a heartfelt toast to Clinton's perseverance in pursuing the Middle East peace process. Upon entering the tent, Bush, according to an eyewitness, told an aide, "One gulp and we're out of here." He had informed the Clintons he would stay through the lunch, but by the time Peres arose with wine glass in hand the president was gone.[32]

After Bush demonstrated his lack of interest in political dialogue and promoting the Middle East peace process during his rude appearance at the Clinton library, he made one of the most significant appointments of his new administration, choosing Bernard Kerik as head of Homeland Security. Democrats were upset with the choice because during Election 2004 Kerik appeared as a brutish Republican hit man, repeating Dick Cheney's Big Lie that a Kerry victory would make the United States more vulnerable to terrorist attack. Kerik's perceived loyalty to Bush and tough-guy façade made him appear to be a strong enforcer for Bush's aggressive national security policy. However, immediately after the announcement, stories proliferated concerning Kerik's colorful past: as a security chief in Saudi Arabia, Kerik allegedly spied on his superior's lovers and was thrown out of the country; as head of prisons in New York, Kerik had allegedly taken gifts and associated with mob figures, connections that intensified when he became head of the New York police force. After 9/11 Kerik used an apartment overlooking Ground Zero for carrying on affairs with two different women, one an associate and the other a well-known publisher. A third wife not mentioned in his biography came to the fore, as did other juicy tabloid stories long known to the New York press corps.[33]

In addition, Kerik had obviously failed when appointed to train an Iraqi police force, leaving months before his appointed term was over and leaving the Iraqi police in a shambles. Watching the stories accumulate day-by-day, Kerik withdrew from the post, claiming he had overlooked an illegal immigrant nanny for which he had not paid taxes (although there were soon questions whether this nanny existed or was just a convenient cover story to resign).[34] The Kerik affair raised questions concerning the competency of Alberto Gonzalez, the White House lawyer in charge of the vetting process, himself Bush's choice for attorney general. It also pointed to gross incompetence and corruption in the Bush administration, which was willing to entrust one of the most important national security jobs to an individual with a record of scandal and job failures.

In a stunningly Orwellian ceremony on December 14, Bush awarded medals of freedom to three men who were perhaps most responsible for the Iraq debacle: CIA Director George Tenet, who had not responded adequately to pre–September 11 warnings concerning an imminent terrorist attack on the United States and told Bush in a crucial meeting that it was a "slam dunk" that Iraq, possessed weapons of mass discussion, legitimating an invasion; Paul Bremer, who had led the failed Iraq reconstruction, illegally turned Iraqi businesses over to American owners, and left the country in complete chaos (see Chapter 4); and Tommy Franks, the general who had allowed Osama bin Laden and other Al Qaeda and Taliban leaders to get away in Afghanistan by failing to put U.S. troops on the ground, and who also failed to produce a "Phase Four" plan to deal with an Iraqi insurgency after the invasion.

Bush boldly rewarded three of the most egregious failures of his administration, trying to redefine their debacles as triumphs, in typical Orwellian "doublespeak" fashion (e.g., war is peace, freedom is slavery). When his failed Secretary of Defense Donald Rumsfeld came under attack in mid-December for a callous remark about why U.S. troops in Iraq did not have sufficient body armor and for using a machine to sign letters home telling families that one of their members had been killed in action, Bush responded by saying what an excellent defense secretary and "good man" Rumsfeld was.

Bushspeak involves systematic distortion of the truth and using lies to advance public policy. This defining feature of the Bush administration was put on display December 17–18, 2004, at an "economic summit" where Bush reprised one of the Big Lies of his administration—Social Security was in crisis and needed a privatization plan to save it.[35] Bush thus signaled that his second administration would be governed by the same mendacity, incompetence, and favoritism toward the rich as his first administration. On December 23, Bush signaled that he would renominate the 20 extremist and highly controversial federal judges the Democrats had filibustered in previous years. This showed that Bush would continue a hard-right partisan agenda and would fight for a reactionary judiciary. There were rumors that Bush might even deploy the "nuclear option" and get his majority Republican U.S. senators to end the filibuster tradition, thus allowing him a free hand to ram through the Senate whatever extreme right-wing policies he saw fit to advance.

In this situation, there can be no "national unity" but only sustained struggle against Bush administration policies to help to bring his regime to an end, and to fight for a revitalization of democracy and a progressive agenda. To conclude, I'd like to quote a passage from Tony Kushner's recent play *Caroline, or Change*. The play is set in the 1960s at the time of the Kennedy assassination when much of the world looked to the United States as a beacon of hope and to the Kennedy administration as an instrument of progress. Coming out of the civil rights struggles, there was new hope that democracy and freedom really were on the march and that reactionary forces were being defeated, making one proud to be an American. In the play's epilogue, Caroline's teenage daughter talks of how she and some friends had just torn down a Civil War statue, signifying the legacy of racism, and she declared

> You can't hold on, you nightmare men,
> Your time is past now on your way
> Get gone and never come again!
> For change come fast and change come slow but
> Everything changes!
> And you got to go!

Notes

1. Paul Krugman, "The Dishonesty Thing," *New York Times*, September 10, 2004.

2. Bob Herbert, "How Many Deaths Will It Take?" *New York Times*, September 10, 2004.

3. See the analysis of the polls in the *New York Times* special Election 2004 section on November 4, 2004, and the CNN Election Results analysis of voting patterns at http://www.cnn.com/ELECTION/2004/. As I indicate below, there was later questioning of some of the initial exit polling results.

4. See the analysis by Ira Chernus, "Voting Their Fears," at http://progressive trail.org/articles/041214Chernus.shtml. Chernus notes:

The news told us ad nauseam that 22 percent of the voters chose "moral values" as their number one issue. But the real news is that this is a historically low number. It was 35 percent in 2000 and 40 percent in 1996. In the exit polls, when asked what one quality they wanted most in a president, only 8 percent chose "religious faith." Among those who called themselves "heavy churchgoers," Bush did no better in '04 than in '00. What about the states that passed gay-marriage bans, often cited as crucial for the Bush win? They gave Bush 57.9 percent of their votes; the other states, totaled, gave him only 50.9 percent—a 7-point margin for Bush. But four years ago, Bush's share in these same states was 7.3 points higher than in the other states.

In a Pew poll taken just a few days after the election, voters were asked to choose from a list of factors that influenced their votes. Twenty-seven percent chose moral values; 22 percent chose Iraq. But when they were asked to name their most urgent issue (with no list to choose from), 27 percent named Iraq and only 9 percent moral values.

When a post-election *New York Times-CBS News* poll asked: "What do you think is the most important problem facing this country?"—only 5 percent chose either moral values or abortion. Only 8 percent said yes to: "Should government officials try to use the political system to turn their religious beliefs into law?" Eighty-five percent said no. (Ten years ago, 23 percent had answered yes to the same question.) "Which worries you more, public officials who don't pay enough attention to religion and religious leaders, or public officials who are too close to religion and religious leaders?" Thirty-five percent worried about not enough attention to religion; 51 percent worried about leaders paying too much attention.

And here's another little anomaly to take into consideration: Bush voters are more liberal than the media would have us believe. Nearly half of them worry most about public officials who are too close to religion. In the exit polls, about 22 percent of them favor gay marriage and 52 percent would legalize gay or lesbian civil unions. Twenty-five percent of Bush voters want no restriction on a woman's right to choose; another 38 percent think abortion should be legal in most cases.

The often-quoted statistic about "moral values" begs the question of how voters interpreted those key words in post-election polls. In a Zogby poll, 68 percent of self-identified "liberals" said that "faith and/or morals" were important in deciding their vote (14 points higher than "moderates"). When voters were asked to identify the single greatest moral crisis facing America, one-third selected "materialism and greed" and 31 percent chose poverty, while the combined total for abortion and same-sex marriage was only 28 percent. In the Pew poll, only about 40 percent of those who said "moral values" influenced their vote named gay marriage or abortion as their highest concern. Pew pollster Andrew Kohut summed it up: "We did not see any indication that social conservative issues like abortion, gay rights, and stem cell research were anywhere near as important as the economy and Iraq." In addition, voters for Bush chose their pocketbook and not necessarily religion in many cases, since in the 2004 election, 58 percent of those making more than $100,000 a year voted for Bush, compared to 54 percent in 2000. This income group made up 18 percent of the electorate in 2004, up from 15 percent in 2000.

5. See the sources in Note 3.

6. Tim McFeeley, "Progressive Incubators," November 5, 2004, at http://www.tompaine.com/articles/progressive_incubators.php.

7. Evan Derkacz, "Bright Spots," *Alternet*, November 10, 2004.

8. See Jim Hightower's proposals for Electoral College reform at www.alternet.org. In his December 4 online interview, Howard Kurtz noted that Gore would have won the Electoral College if every state received electoral votes in proportion to population: "Bush won 30 states for 271 and Gore won 21 for 267. But if you take away the two electors for each senator, and just apportion electors by number of Representatives (i.e., in proportion to population), Gore wins 225 to 211" (http://www.washington post.com/wpsrv/liveonline/00/politics/media backtalk120400.htm).

9. In a chapter on "Electoral Reform" after Election 2000, Ceaser and Busch lay out the case for a proportional representation system, as opposed to a direct popular majority vote electoral system, but do not consider the strong arguments that I cite above to eliminate the "unfaithful elector" problem by mandating direct presidential voting, nor do they take seriously arguments against the current U.S. system of proportional voting with its winner-take-all electoral vote system. In any case, in the current political climate, there is little pressure for major electoral reform, although on the local level there have been attempts to require updating of voting machines, streamlining of voting processes, stipulation of recount procedures, and other technical changes to avoid a recurrence of the debacle of the 2000 election in Florida; unfortunately, efforts to replace punch-card and optical-scan ballots with computerized voting machines may have made matters worse, necessitating another cycle of reform.

10. On the need for public financing of elections, see Nick Nyhart and Joan Claybrook, "The Dash for Cash: Public Financing Is the Only Way to End the Unfair Tilt of the 'Wealth Primary,'" *Los Angeles Times*, April 27, 2003. The authors' groups Public Campaign and Public Citizen have been working for public financing of elections.

11. On the history of efforts to reform television advertising, see Charles Lewis, "You Get What You Pay For: How Corporate Spending Blocked Political Ad Reform and Other Stories of Influence," in Schechter (2001), pp. 62–73; and the Alliance for Better Campaigns, "Gouging Democracy: How the Television Industry Profiteered on Campaign 2000," in Schechter (2001), pp. 77–92. In another important article in Schechter (2001), Lawrence K. Grossman notes that one of broadcasting's "dirty little secrets" is its "sustained and high-priced lobbying against finance reform" (p. 75).

12. For a wide range of materials on voter suppression, machine malfunctions,

potential fraud and corruption, and thousands of voting problems in Election 2004, see the sources at http://www.ejfi.org/Voting/Voting-1.htm; http://www.votersunite.org; http://www.openvotingconsortium.org; http://www.demos-usa.org; and http://www.verified voting.org; and http://www.blackboxvoting.org. The only mainstream media figure following the 2000 voting fraud and corruption controversy was MSNBC's Keith Olbermann on his nightly news show *Countdown* and in his blog Bloggermann at http://www.msnbc.msn.com/id/6210240.

13. The conception of democracy upon which I am drawing here has been developed in Kellner (1990, 2001) and other writings that indicate how corporate media have undermined democracy in the United States during the past few decades.

14. See the discussion of the media and democracy in Kellner (1990), Chapters 2 and 3; on the Federal Communications Act of 1934 and the battle for democratic media in the 1930s, see McChesney (1993). For an excellent history and overview of corporate media and politics in the United States, see Halberstam (1979).

15. On media consolidation and its impact over the past two decades, see Bagdikian (1997); Herman and Chomsky (1988); Kellner (1990); McChesney (2000, 2004); and Schiller (1990).

16. For more detailed proposals for democratizing the media and producing alternative media and politics, see Best and Kellner (2001); Kellner (1990, 1999); and McChesney (1997, 2000, and 2004). See also Jeffrey Chester and Gary O. Larson, "A 12-Step Program for Media Democracy," *Nation*, July 23, 2002.

17. On new literacies and the reconstruction of education, see Kellner (2002, 2004).

18. See my own blogleft at http://www.gseis.ucla.edu/courses/ed253a/blogger.php, which links many good blogs and websites.

19. Cited in Cox (2004), p. 153. Author and former Justice Department prosecutor William J. Cox lays out in detail the ways that the Bush administration Iraq invasion contravenes several articles of the UN Charter and has no legal justification, thus constituting an "illegal use of force" (153ff.). Cox also documents Bush administration "illegal detention of prisoners" (154ff.) and how by violating the norms of international law Bush could be subject to impeachment (157ff.). In Chapter 4, I noted how UN chief Kofi Annan also has stated the illegality of the U.S. invasion and occupation of Iraq.

20. PEW Institute global attitude reports over the last several years document dramatically increasing anti-Americanism and disgust with Bush administration policies; see http://people-press.org/pgap.

21. This argument is made by Ivo H. Daalder and James M. Lindsay, "Shooting First: The Preemptive War Doctrine Has Met an Early Death in Iraq," *Los Angeles Times*, May 30, 2004, pp. M1, M6. The authors also argue that "Bush's conception of preemption far exceeded responding to an imminent danger of attack. He instead advocated preventive wars of regime change. The United States claimed the right to use force to oust leaders it disliked long before they could threaten its security."

22. On cosmopolitanism, see Cheah and Robbins, *Cosmopolitics* (1998); and special issue of *Theory, Culture & Society* 19 (1–2) (February–April 2002).

23. On the dangers of perpetual war and threats to the U.S. democratic republic in the expansion of empire, see Mann (2004); and Vidal (2002, 2003). On the dangers of Bush administration unilateralist militarism and the need for global solutions to global problems, see Barber (2003); Clarke (2003); and Kellner (2003). Clarke warns that the Bush administration has planned a series of wars against the "axis of evil" to promote U.S. hegemony and to use U.S. military power to further a neoconservative agenda of control of the Middle East.

24. Mark Follman, "Terrorism Expert Says Bush's Reelection Gave bin Laden a 'Kosher Stamp from the Islamic World' to Use Nukes on U.S.—and a Major Attack Is 'Inevitable'." *Salon*, December 1, 2004.

25. Randolph T. Holhut: "Economic Armageddon? It May Come Sooner Than You Think," December 3, 2004, at http://www.smirkingchimp.com/print.php?sid=18926.

26. See Alan Maass: "The Rise and Fall of Newt Gingrich: A Parable for Our Times," November 14, 2004, at http://www.counterpunch.org/maass11132004.html.

27. See Robert O'Harrow, Jr., "Halliburton Is a Handy Target for Democrats: Ties to Secret Deals, Cheney Keep Issue Alive," *Washington Post*, September 18, 2004. See also Edward Chen, "Kerry Uses Halliburton to Attack Cheney's Record," *Los Angeles Times*, September 18, 2004.

28. R. Jeffrey Smith and Dan Eggen, "New Papers Suggest Detainee Abuse Was Widespread," *Washington Post*, December 22, 2004, p. A01.

29. Ari Berman, "Torture at the Top," *Nation*, December 22, 2004.

30. On the Bush administration attack on women and feminism, see Flanders (2004) and Hammer (2002).

31. Felicity Barringer, "New Priorities in Environment," *New York Times*, September 14, 2004.

32. Sidney Blumenthal, "Counterinaugural at the Clinton Library: At the Dedication of the Clinton Library, the Former President Calls for Transcending Divisions, while Bush Strangely Muses That 'A Submarine Could Take This Place Out'," *Salon*, November 25, 2004.

33. For a summary of the Kerik stories circulated through the media in mid-December, see Josh Marshall's "Talking Points," December 17, 2004, at http://www.talkingpointsmemo.com/archives/week_2004_12_12.php#004244; and David Corn, "All the President's Problems," *LA Weekly*, December 16, 2004.

34. Nina Bernstein and Robin Stein, "Mystery Woman in Kerik Case: Nanny," *New York Times*, December 16, 2004.

35. Informed commentators have been insisting that Bush is greatly exaggerating the Social Security "crisis" to push through his privatization plan, which will basically help stockbrokers and the rich; see, for example, Paul Krugman, "Inventing a Crisis," *New York Times*, December 7, 2004; and "Buying into Failure," *New York Times*, December 17, 2004. Media critic Bob Somerby published a series of detailed analysis of the flaws of Bush's Social Security plan and how uninformed mainstream media talking heads reproduced Bush's lies and simplicities without critical distance; see Somerby's Daily Howler columns for December 7–17, at http://www.dailyhowler.com/archives-2004.shtml.

Selected Bibliography

Achcar, Gilbert. 2002. *The Clash of Barbarisms.* New York: Monthly Review Press.

Adorno, et al. 1950. *The Authoritarian Personality.* New York: Norton.

Ali, Tariq. 2002. *The Clash of Fundamentalisms: Crusades, Jihads, and Modernity.* London and New York: Verso.

———. 2003. *Bush in Babylon: The Reconstruction of Iraq.* London and New York: Verso.

Alterman, Eric. 2000. *Sound and Fury: The Making of the Punditocracy.* Ithaca, NY: Cornell University Press.

———. 2003. *What Liberal Media? The Truth about Bias and the News.* New York: BasicBooks.

Alterman, et al. 2004. *The Book on Bush: How George W. (Mis)leads America.* New York: Viking.

Artz, Lee, and Yahya R. Kamalipour, eds. 2004. *Bring 'Em On: Media and Politics in the Iraq War.* Lanham, MD: Rowman and Littlefield.

Bagdikian, Ben. 1997. *The Media Monopoly.* 6th ed. Boston: Beacon Press.

Barber, Benjamin R. 2003. *Fear's Empire: War, Terrorism, and Democracy.* New York: Norton.

Begala, Paul. 2000. *Is Our Children Learning? The Case against George W. Bush.* New York: Simon and Schuster.

Best, Steven, and Douglas Kellner. 1997. *The Postmodern Turn.* New York and London: Guilford Press and Routledge.

———. 2001. *The Postmodern Adventure: Science, Technology, and Cultural Studies at the Third Millennium.* New York and London: Guilford and Routledge.

Boggs, Carl, ed. 2003. *Masters of War: Militarism and Blowback in the Era of American Empire.* New York and London: Routledge.

Brewton, Pete. 1992. *The Mafia, CIA, and George Bush.* New York: SPI Books.

Brock, David. 2004. *The Republican Noise Machine: Right-Wing Media and How It Corrupts Democracy.* New York: Crown.

Bruni, Frank. 2002. *Ambling into History.* New York: HarperCollins.

Bugliosi, Vincent. 2001. *The Betrayal of America: How the Supreme Court Undermined the Constitution and Chose Our President.* New York: Thunder's Mouth Press/Nation Books.

Byrd, Robert. 2004. *Losing America: Confronting a Reckless and Arrogant Presidency.* New York: Norton.

251

Ceaser, James W., and Andrew E. Busch. 2001. *The Perfect Tie.* Lanham, MD: Rowman and Littlefield.

Cheah, Pheng, and Bruce Robbins. 1998. *Cosmopolitics.* Minneapolis: University of Minnesota Press.

Chomsky, Noam. 2001. *9-11.* New York: Seven Seals Press.

Clark, Wesley. 2003. *Winning Modern Wars: Iraq, Terrorism, and the American Empire.* Washington: Public Affairs Books.

Clarke, Richard A. 2004. *Against All Enemies: Inside America's War on Terror.* New York: Free Press.

Cole, David. 2003. *Enemy Aliens: Double Standards and Constitutional Freedoms in the War on Terrorism.* New York: New Press.

Collins, John, and Ross Glover, eds. 2002. *Collateral Language.* New York: New York University Press.

Conason, Joe. 2003. *Big Lies: The Right-Wing Propganda Machine and How It Distorts the Truth.* New York: Thomas Dunne Books.

Corn, David. 2003. *The Lies of George W. Bush: Mastering the Politics of Deception.* New York: Crown Publishers.

Cox, William J. 2004. *You're Not Stupid! Get the Truth: A Brief on the Bush Presidency.* Joshua Tree, CA: Progressive Press.

Dean, John. 2004. *Worse Than Watergate: The Secret Presidency of George W. Bush.* Boston: Little, Brown.

Derschowitz, Alan. 2001. *Supreme Injustice: How the High Court Hijacked Election 2000.* New York: Oxford University Press.

Dewey, John. 1997 [1919]. *Democracy and Education.* New York: Simon and Schuster.

Final Report of the National Commission on Terrorist Attacks upon the United States. 2004. The 9/11 Commission Report. New York: Norton.

Flanders, Laura. 2004. *The "W" Effect: Bush's War on Women.* New York: Feminist Press.

Franken, Al. 2003. *Lies and the Lying Liars Who Tell Them.* New York: Dutton.

Friedman, Alan. 1993 *Spider's Web.* New York: Bantam Books.

Gabler, Neil. 1998. *Life the Movie: How Entertainment Conquered Reality.* New York: Knopf.

Graham, Phil, Thomas Keenan, and Anne-Maree Dowd. 2004. "A Call to Arms at the End of History: A Discourse–Historical Analysis of George W. Bush's Declaration of War on Terror." *Discourse and Society* 15(2–3): 199–221.

Gross, Bertram. 1982. *Friendly Fascism.* Boston: South End Press.

Halberstam, David. 1979. *The Powers That Be.* New York: Knopf.

Hammer, Rhonda. 2002. *Anti-Feminism and Family Terrorism.* Lanham, MD: Rowman and Littlefield.

Hatfield, J. H. 2000. *Fortunate Son: George W. Bush and the Making of an American President.* New York: Soft Skull Press.

Herman, Edward S. 1998. *The Real Terror Network: Terrorism in Fact and Propaganda.* Boston: South End Press.

Herman, Edward, and Noam Chomsky. 1988. *Manufacturing Consent: The Political Economy of the Mass Media.* New York: Pantheon.

Hersh, Seymour. 2004. *Chain of Command: The Road from 9/11 to Abu Ghraib.* New York: HarperCollins.

Hertsgaard, Mark. 1988. *On Bended Knee: The Press and the Reagan Presidency.* New York: Farrar, Straus, and Giroux.

Horkheimer, Max, and T. W. Adorno. 1972 [1948]. *Dialectic of Enlightenment.* New York: Herder and Herder.

Huntington, Samuel. 1996. *The Clash of Civilizations and the Remaking of World Order.* New York: Touchstone Books.

Ivins, Molly, and Lou Dubose. 2000. *Shrub: The Short but Happy Political Life of George W. Bush.* New York: Random House.

———. 2004. *Bushwhacked: Life in George W. Bush's America.* New York: Random House.

Jamieson, Kathleen Hall, and Paul Waldman. 2003. *The Press Effect.* Oxford, UK and New York: Oxford University Press.

Johnson, Chalmers. 2000. *Blowback: The Costs and Consequences of American Empire.* New York: Henry Holt.

———. 2004. *The Sorrows of Empire: Militarism, Secrecy, and the End of the Republic.* New York: Henry Holt.

Kahn, Richard, and Douglas Kellner. 2003. "Internet Subcultures and Oppositional Politics." In D. Muggleton, ed., *The Post-Subcultures Reader.* London: Berg.

Kamalipour, Yahya R., and Nancy Snow, eds. 2004. *War, Media, and Propaganda.* Lanham, MD: Rowman and Littlefield.

Kaplan, Esther. 2004. *With God on Their Side.* New York: New Press.

Kelley, Kitty. 2004. *The Family: The Real Story of the Bush Dynasty.* New York: Random House.

Kellner, Douglas. 1989. *Critical Theory, Marxism, and Modernity.* Cambridge, UK and Baltimore, MD: Polity Press and John Hopkins University Press.

———. 1990a. *Television and the Crisis of Democracy.* Boulder: Westview Press.

———. 1990b. "From *1984* to *One-Dimensional Man*: Reflections on Orwell and Marcuse." *Current Perspectives in Social Theory:* 223–252.

———. 1992. *The Persian Gulf TV War.* Boulder, CO: Westview Press.

———. 2000. "New Technologies/New Literacies: Reconstructing Education for the New Millennium." *Teaching Education* 11(3): 245–265.

———. 2001. *Grand Theft 2000.* Lanham, MD: Rowman and Littlefield.

———. 2003a. *From 9/11 to Terror War: Dangers of the Bush Legacy.* Lanham, MD: Rowman and Littlefield.

———. 2003b. "Postmodern Military and Permanent Wars." In Carl Boggs, ed., *Masters of War: Militarism and Blowback in the Era of American Empire.* New York and London: Routledge, pp. 229–244.

———. 2003c. *Media Spectacle.* London and New York: Routledge.

———. 2004. "Technological Transformation, Multiple Literacies, and the Re-vision-ing of Education." *E-Learning* 1(1): 9–37.

Kepel, Gilles. 2002. *Jihad: The Trail of Political Islam*. Cambridge, MA: Harvard University Press.

Loftus, John, and Mark Aarons. 1994. *The Secret War against the Jews*. New York: Saint Martin's Press.

Mann, Michael. 2003. *Incoherent Empire*. London and New York: Verso.

Marcuse, Herbert. 1964. *One-Dimensional Man*. Boston: Beacon Press.

McChesney, Robert. 1993. *Telecommunications, Mass Media, and Democracy: The Battle for the Control of U.S. Broadcasting, 1928–1935*. New York and Oxford: Oxford University Press.

———. 1997. *Corporate Media and the Threat to Democracy*. New York: Seven Stories Press.

———. 2000. *Rich Media, Poor Democracy*. New York: New Press.

———. 2004. *The Problem of the Media: U.S. Communication Politics in the 21st Century*. New York: Monthly Review Press.

Milbank, Dana. 2001. *Smashmouth*. New York: BasicBooks.

Miller, David. 2004. *Tell Me Lies: Propaganda and Media Distortion in the Attack on Iraq*. London: Pluto Press.

Miller, Mark Crispin. 2001. *The Bush Dyslexicon*. New York: Norton.

———. 2004. *Cruel and Unusual: Bush/Cheney's New World Order*. New York: Norton.

Mitchell, Elizabeth. 2000. *Revenge of the Bush Dynasty*. New York: Hyperion.

Moore, James, and Wayne Slater. 2003. *Bush's Brain: How Karl Rove Made George W. Bush Presidential*. New York: John Wiley.

Moore, Michael. 2003. *Dude, Where's My Country?* New York: Warner Books.

Nichols, John. 2004. *Dick: The Man Who Is President (Dick Cheney)*. New York: New Press.

O'Neil, John, and Jerome Corsi. 2004. *Unfit for Command: Swift Boat Veterans Speak Out against John Kerry*. New York: Regnery Publishing.

Orwell, George. 1961 [1948]. *1984*. New York: Signet.

Palast, Greg. 2003. *The Best Democracy Money Can Buy: The Truth about Corporate Cons, Globalization, and High-Finance Fraudsters*. New York: Plume.

Parry, Robert. 1992. *Fooling America: How Washington Insiders Twist the Truth and Manufacture the Conventional Wisdom*. New York: William Morrow.

Parry, Robert. 2004. *Secrecy and Privilege: The Rise of the Bush Dynasty from Watergate to Iraq*. Arlington, VA: Media Consortium.

Phillips, Kevin. 2004. *American Dynasty: Aristocracy, Fortune, and the Politics of Deceit in the House of Bush*. New York: Viking.

Prestowitz, Clyde. 2003. *Rogue Nation: American Unilateralism and the Future of Good Intentions*. New York: BasicBooks.

Rampton, Sheldon, and John Stauber. 2003. *Weapons of Mass Deception: The Uses of Propaganda in Bush's War on Iraq*. New York: Penguin.

Rashid, Ahmed. 2001. *Taliban: Militant Islam, Oil, and Fundamentalism in Central Asia*.

New Haven, CT: Yale University Press.

———. 2002. *Jihad: The Rise of Militant Islam in Central Asia.* New Haven, CT: Yale University Press.

Ritter, Scott. 2003. *Frontier Justice: Weapons of Mass Destruction and the Bushwhacking of America.* New York: Context Books.

Sabato, Larry A., ed. 2002. *Overtime! The Election 2000 Thriller.* New York: Longman.

Sammon, Bill. 2001. *At Any Cost: How Al Gore Tried to Steal the Election.* Washington, DC: Regnery Publishing.

Schechter, Danny. 2001. *Mediocracy 2000—Hail to the Thief: How the Media Stole the U.S. Presidential Election.* Electronic book available at www.mediachannel.org.

Schiller, Herbert. 1990. *Culture, Inc.* New York: Oxford University Press.

Seib, Philip. 1993. *Rush Hour: Talk Radio, Politics, and the Rise of Rush Limbaugh.* Fort Worth, TX: Summit Group.

St. Clair, Jeffrey. 2004. "High Plains Grifter," at http://www.counterpunch.org.

Suskind, Ron. 2004. *The Price of Loyalty: George W. Bush, the White House, and the Education of Paul O'Neill.* New York: Simon and Schuster.

Sussman, Warren. 1984. *Culture as History: The Transformation of American Society in the Twentieth Century.* New York: Pantheon.

Tapper, Jake. 2001. *Down and Dirty: The Plot to Steal the Presidency.* Boston: Little, Brown.

Tarpley, Webster Griffin, and Anton Chaitkin. 1992. *George Bush: The Unauthorized Biography.* Washington, DC: Executive Intelligence Review.

Tracey, Michael. 1998. *Decline and Fall of Public Service Broadcasting.* Oxford, UK: Oxford University Press.

Ungar, Craig. 2004. *House of Bush House of Saud.* New York: Scribner.

Vidal, Gore. 2002. *Perpetual War for Perpetual Peace: How We Got To Be So Hated.* New York: Thunder Mouth Press/Nation Books.

———. 2003. *Dreaming War: Blood for Oil and the Cheney-Bush Junta.* New York: Thunder Mouth Press/Nation Books.

Waldman, Paul. 2004. *Fraud.* Naperville, IL: Sourcebooks.

Wallerstein, Immanuel. 2004. "'Soft Multilateralism.'" *Nation* (February 2): 14–20.

Wilson, Joseph. 2004. *The Politics of Truth.* New York: Carroll and Graff.

Wolcott, James. 2004. *Attack Poodles and Other Media Mutants: The Looting of the News in a Time of Terror.* New York: Miramax Books.

Woodward, Bob. 2002. *Bush at War.* New York: Simon and Schuster.

———. 2004. *Plan of Attack.* New York: Simon and Schuster.

Index

About the Author

Douglas Kellner, George F. Kneller Philosophy of Education Chair at the Graduate School of Education, UCLA, is the author of many books, including *Grand Theft 2000* (Rowman & Littlefield, 2001) about the last presidential election.